HOWARD ADAMS:

OTAPAWY!

The Life of a Métis Leader in His Own Words and in Those of His Contemporaries

Edited by:
Hartmut Lutz
with
Murray Hamilton and Donna Heimbecker

Saskatoon: Gabriel Dumont Institute, 2005

Library and Archives Canada Cataloguing in Publication

Adams, Howard, 1921-2001
    Howard Adams: Otapawy! the life of a Métis leader in his own words and in those of his contemporaries / Howard Adams ; Hartmut Lutz, Murray Hamilton, Donna Heimbecker, editors.

Includes CD-ROM and bibliographical references.
ISBN 0-920915-74-4

    1. Adams, Howard, 1921-2001. 2. Métis activists--Canada--Biography. 3. Educators--Canada--Biography. 4. Métis--Government relations. I. Lutz, Hartmut, 1945- II. Hamilton, Murray, 1953- III. Heimbecker, Donna, 1961- IV. Gabriel Dumont Institute of Native Studies and Applied Research V. Title.

FC109.1.A32A3 2005   971'.00497'0092   C2005-905829-3

Darren R. Préfontaine, Gabriel Dumont Institute Project Leader and Editor
Cheryl Troupe, Gabriel Dumont Institute Project Co-Leader
Karon Shmon, Gabriel Dumont Institute Publishing Coordinator
David Morin, Gabriel Dumont Institute Researcher
Derek Bachman, Art Direction, Graphic Design and Layout
Michael Card, Multimedia CD Design
Ian Jensen, Multimedia CD Design
Printed by Globe Printers, Saskatoon, Saskatchewan
CD Manufacturing, Canada Disc and Tape, Saskatoon, Saskatchewan

The Gabriel Dumont Institute acknowledges the financial support of the Government of Canada, which was used to publish this book.

The Gabriel Dumont Institute of Native Studies and Applied Research
2—604 22nd Street West, Saskatoon, SK S7M 5W1
(T): 306.934.4941 (F): 306.244.0252
(I): www.gdins.org / www.metismuseum.ca

All royalty fees for this book have been donated to "The Marge and Howard Adams Scholarship Fund."

TABLE OF CONTENTS

PART ONE
MEMOIRS: AUTOBIOGRAPHY AND FICTION

1. Going Out

2. Growing Up in St. Louis, Saskatchewan

3. Mountie Years

4. Drifting Between Worlds

5. Mainstreaming in Vancouver

6. Turning Points

7. Métis Leader in Saskatchewan

8. Looking Back and Taking Stock

PART TWO
MEMORIES OF HOWARD ADAMS BY OTHERS

List of Contributors

Dear Reader,

You are about to read a very unusual book. It is based on a series of autobiographical fragments. Howard Adams created them all at different times in his later life, and they were told in different voices that he himself created. They bear witness to how hard he struggled to write a full account of his astounding career from being a poor Métis boy in St. Louis, Saskatchewan, to becoming a political leader and world-renowned scholar. Unfortunately, Howard Adams never finished his autobiographical project, and in order to put this book together, we had to sift through a disarranged pile of almost six hundred pages that he left on his desk. We did not change the author's words, and we decided against rewriting any passages or filling in gaps that he had left open. We also decided against smoothing out contradictions or reducing the voices in which the episodes in Howard Adams life are told, because we did not intend to write a book **about** Howard's life, but were determined to bring out his **own** words. And that is what you will find in this book.

The narrative is often disrupted. Sometimes Howard Adams speaks to us directly in his own voice. At other times you, will suddenly read about Tony or Almighty, fictional characters created by Howard Adams himself, whose lives parallel his own. Unfortunately, there are also large gaps in the narrative. Sometimes the same event is told twice, both by Tony as the narrator and by Howard Adams. To say that this text is sometimes confusing may be putting it mildly, but to edit out contradictions, repetitions or sudden breaks would have meant changing Howard Adams' words.

For readers, who want to know more about how the different fragments were put together, we have provided the following explanation under the title "Two Caveats to the Reader." You may read the "Caveats" now or revert to them later, as questions may occur. In addition, we provided a brief chronology of Howard Adam's life (pp. x-xii), and there is also an "Afterword" (pp. 283 – 302), which explains more about the editing process and the status of this book in its political and literary context. In addition, there are twenty short articles and reminisces of Howard Adams in Part II (pp. 218 – 282) of this book. All together, these texts will provide you with ample material to compose your own picture of the life of that remarkable man, our friend Howard Adams.

The Editors

Two Caveats to the Reader

To our readers, we would like to give two caveats. First, whoever reads the following in the hope of meeting on these pages, Howard Adams the flamboyant revolutionary and frontline political activist, or Dr. Howard Adams the astute scholar and passionate teacher from the ivory tower, will be disappointed. Howard Adams was both. He lived in two worlds, which he tried to bridge and integrate, at times quite desperately. Second, whoever opens this book and starts reading Part I in the hope of being swept away by a captivating success story of a great Métis leader—a voice that rivets the reader's attention from the first page to the last—will also be disappointed. What will be found on the following pages are at least three voices, and at least three types of texts, all written by Howard Adams himself, but collected, disentangled and woven together by the editors.

When Dr. Howard Adams died in his Vancouver home on his 80th birthday, September 8, 2001, he left on his desk a 95-page draft of an unfinished autobiography, and a stack of 476 sheets of handwritten and typed manuscripts, held together by an elastic band under a handwritten title page "WRITINGS, ALL TYPES." Howard Adams had talked about his autobiography project many times. He also explained that at one stage he had tried to fictionalize it, writing about himself in the third person and altering the names of his contemporaries. Unfortunately, he never managed to finish the manuscript on which he had been intermittently working on since his retirement.

While all other materials left by Howard Adams were transferred to Library and Archives Canada in Ottawa, where they are now housed, his wife Margaret retained the autobiographical manuscripts. She handed them over to Hartmut Lutz and asked him to see whether he could prepare them for publication. He said he would try, but that he really had no time to do it. Fortunately, sometimes "things just happen" in wonderful ways. When Hartmut Lutz won the 2003 *John G. Diefenbaker Award*, a twelve-month research grant from the Canada Council for the Arts, editing and publishing the Howard Adams autobiography become a reality. Many of Howard's friends and former comrades, from both the Aboriginal and the non-Aboriginal communities, pledged their support for the project. In the fall of 2003, Maria Campbell brought together Murray Hamilton, Donna Heimbecker and Hartmut Lutz to edit the book. The editors put their minds together in Saskatoon and decided to work together on a book that would contain not only an autobiographical text in Howard's own words (Part I), but also a selection of short essays and memoirs about his remarkable life, shared by those who knew and interacted with him at various stages, and who were willing to contribute in honour of Howard Adams' memory and legacy (Part II).

The three texts written by Howard Adams himself and joined together by the editors are:

(1) **Autobiography (AB):** This is a text of 95-typewritten pages that Howard was working on towards the very end of his life. He wrote this in the first person to describe his life from his childhood until his days as a student at the University of British Columbia, covering the first thirty years of his life (1921–mid 1950s). The book uses this unfinished autobiographical text as its starting point.

(2) **Tony's Biography (TB):** This is a much longer text of 196 pages, written earlier than the **AB** document. In fact, **TB**'s passages constitute the largest part of the book's text. In **TB**, Howard created a fictional character, Tony, whose life history is partly based on his own life, but whose adventures often seem to go into fictional explorations of how things could have, should have, or should not have gone for the author. However, readers are reminded that Tony is not Howard Adams, but a fictional character created by the author. As in all autobiography and all fiction, we are left to wonder how much of Howard's narrative is based on historical reality and how much on its creator's dreams and nightmares. But that is another story…The **TB** manuscript is incomplete, and it was probably never finished. There are handwritten alterations in the typescripts, and sometimes numbered chapter headings. These numbers, however, tell us that there must be entire chapters missing, either lost or destroyed by Howard himself, or perhaps never written. Howard's "alter ego", the main character Tony, appears first under the name of Tony Parker, later under the name of Tony Bruce. Experiences described in the **TB** manuscript often repeat, reflect, complement or contradict parallel experiences in Howard's unfinished autobiography. Wherever the two texts complement one another and serve to comment and explain each other, we left both in this book.

(3) **Miscellaneous (MISC):** Besides containing the **TB** manuscript, the stack of papers left on Howard's desk also comprised various individual sheets of paper, scribbled notes and a few fragmented essays and autobiographical narratives written in the first person. These miscellaneous autobiographical pieces, amounting to 138 pages, were also included wherever they provided information beyond the **AB** and **TB** texts. Again, there is also a fictional text among these miscellaneous manuscripts, written in the first person but using a fictional persona named "Almighty", a young man of Indian (Cree?) background, who is institutionalized in a mental hospital.

In our editing, we have spliced and woven these texts together to form one consecutive "sash." At first, we had to disentangle the whorl of different strands and odd bits and pieces. We then took the **AB** strand as a start and soon began weaving in strings from the **TB** pile. As we went along, we also interwove the lengthening but thinning sash with fillings from Howard's miscellaneous manuscripts.

For readers who may want to be able to identify the individual strands in Howard Adams' life narrative, the origin of each passage is indicated by an appropriate **(AB)**, **(TB)**, or **(MISC)** reference. In addition, the passages taken from Tony's fictional biography, as well as the fictional narrative in the name of the Indian character Almighty, are set in italics, so that readers will be able to know at all times whether they are reading a "factual" autobiographical text or a fictional one. The historical time span covered in the autobiography proper **AB** ends in the 1950s, whereas the **TB** manuscript takes us into the 1970s, while some **MISC** texts reflect Howard's life until his retirement. Because all three types of text were never completed, this book will always remain incomplete and fragmented. There are large gaps, especially in the fictional account of Tony's life, which we did not seek to fill. Passages removed to avoid redundancies are marked by bracketed ellipses ([…]).

People do not constitute their lives and evolve their identities on their own. Forming identities happens in a process of constant dialogue. Howard Adams interacted with hundreds, and many influenced his life. He is remembered, described and historicized by friends, comrades, colleagues and opponents who connected with him. We are grateful to all those who contributed to our book, and who shared their memories. Their essays are contained in Part II, arranged roughly according to the dates when the contributors first came into contact with Howard. While some contributions may be read for the purpose of objectifying our picture of Howard Adams, the aim of this book was never to present the "objective" or "realistic" picture of Howard Adams' life, but rather, as stated before, to bring out his own unfinished life histories in his own words. Taken together, the individual contributions in Part II constitute another multi-stranded sash formed by his life. It only contains the contributions of those who were willing and had the time and ability to write a piece. Thus, the voices in Part II are a selection, constituted by the contributors' willingness to come out and acknowledge Howard Adams' life and struggle.

This book's title, *HOWARD ADAMS: OTAPAWY!*, uses an acronym from the phrase, "Our Thoughts And Prayers Are With You" or "OTAPAWY." This acronym is from a Saskatchewan Métis oral story, which was told to us while we were in the process of compiling this book. We thank Deborah Pelletier and her family for their permission to use it. It expresses our respect for, and fond memories of, Howard Adams.

Murray Hamilton, Donna Heimbecker, and Hartmut Lutz
Saskatoon, Saskatchewan and Bömitz, Germany, March 2005

Publisher's Introduction

The Gabriel Dumont Institute of Native Studies and Applied Research (GDI) and the Métis in general owe a great deal to Howard Adams. His books, essays, lectures and life story have profoundly touched the Institute's students, staff and faculty. Through his role as a professor of Métis History in the Saskatchewan Urban Native Teacher Education Program, the Institute's teacher-training program, Howard Adams instructed dozens of young Métis to be proud of their heritage and history and provided them with the intellectual framework/pedagogy necessary to resist colonization and to decolonize themselves. His many lectures helped to produce a cadre of Métis schoolteachers who are now decolonizing Aboriginal students and informing non-Aboriginal students about the Canadian state's failed attempts to assimilate/integrate Indigenous peoples.

By reading *Prison of Grass* and *A Tortured People*, one is still struck by Howard Adams' visceral and scathing condemnation of Canada's colonial regime vis-à-vis its First Peoples. Howard Adams employed strong polemical language in his academic writing because euphemisms and polite discourse cannot adequately address colonization's decimation of Indigenous cultures and lifeways. For making Canadians and others think more critically about the colonization of Aboriginal peoples, we will always be indebted to Howard Adams.

GDI would like to thank Hartmut Lutz, Donna Heimbecker and Murray Hamilton for their tireless efforts to compile Howard Adams' scattered autobiographical writings into one coherent document and for arranging to include many invaluable contributions about Howard Adams' life, work and academic appeal in this volume. It was a real privilege to work with them to bring you this book. Finally, GDI, an institution born out of Métis activism, is truly honoured to posthumously publish Howard Adams' last book.

The GDI Publishing Department
Saskatoon, Saskatchewan

A Biographical Timeline: Howard Adams, Ph.D.

- 1921 — born September 8 in St. Louis, Saskatchewan
- 1940 — completed high school at St. Louis
- 1940-1946 — Royal Canadian Mounted Police constable; early dismissal granted
- 1944-1955 — school liaison counselor for the Vancouver School Board
- 1950 — completed a Bachelor of Arts degree in Sociology at the University of British Columbia
- 1956-1957 — studied at Ontario College of Education, University of Toronto, and graduated with Secondary Teaching Diploma
- 1957 — February 9, married Margaret (Marge) Belle Baxter, his lifelong wife
- 1957-1962 — taught high school at Coquitlam, British Columbia
- 1958 — first visit to Cuba, to observe a Third World socialist culture
- 1962-1966 — completed a Master of Arts and then a Doctorate of Philosophy degree in the History of Education at the University of California, Berkeley
- 1966-1974 — associate professor at the College of Education, University of Saskatchewan
- 1965-1974 — advocated for and led the Indian and Métis civil rights movement at the local, provincial and national levels
- 1966-1974 — active member in the Métis Society of Saskatchewan (MSS)
- 1967 — second visit to Cuba, to observe the country's progress
- 1968 — first book, *The Education of Canadians 1800-1867: The Roots of Separatism,* published by Harvest House, Montréal
- 1969-1970 — MSS president
- 1970-1972 — Director for the North Battleford region, one of the seven Métis political regions in the province; consultant to MSS, chiefly the Community Development Project (applied for in 1970, funded and begun in 1971, lasted until 1974)
- 1970-1973 — chaired the Red Power League of Saskatchewan
- 1972 — Director of the Education Survey
- 1973 — Director of the Aboriginal Rights Program
- 1973-1974 — pursued and won his suit against MSS president Jim Sinclair and other MSS officials for their personal use of provincial and federal grant funds, money that was supposed to be used for provincial Métis projects
- 1975-1987 — professor, Native American Studies Department, University of California-Davis (UCD), where he developed and taught courses in Native American Studies
- 1975 — second book, *Prison of Grass: Canada from the Native Point of View,* published by General Publishing, Toronto
- 1976 — taught Indian culture courses to Vacaville Prison (near Oakland, California) inmates for UCD
- 1976-1978 — Academic Advisor for UCD Native American students
- 1977-1981 — UCD Master Advisor to the Native American Studies Department
- 1977-1978 — chaired the Administrative Advisory Committee for UCD's Educational Opportunity Program
- 1978 — chaired Native American Studies Department Five-Year Review

Committee
- 1978 — chaired the Human Rights of Native Americans discussion workshop at the Human Rights and US Foreign Policy Conference at Davis
- 1978-1979 — Faculty Advisor to Native American students, UCD
- 1979 — member of several UCD committees, including: Graduate Research Selection Awards; the UCD/California State University Joint Committee; Ethnic Students; Affirmative Action Committee; and others
- 1979-1981 — chaired the Admissions Committee for the Graduate Program in Community Development, UCD
- 1980-1981 — ex-officio member, Native American Studies Major Review Committee, UCD
- 1982-1984 — vice-chaired the UCD Department of Applied Behavioral Sciences, which housed four sub-departments, including the Native American Studies Department
- 1983-1986 — member of UCD Native American Workshop Committee
- 1985-1986 — chaired the UCD Committee to develop courses on Indigenous Cultural Awareness
- 1985-1986 — UCD Master Advisor to the Native American Studies Program
- 1986-1988 — chaired the Behavior & Social Sciences for Minorities Program for the Ford Foundation Doctoral Fellowship, National Research Council, National Academy of Sciences, Washington, DC
- 1987 — retired to Vancouver from UCD with the title of Professor Emeritus
- 1988-1997 — taught summer session Native Studies classes at the University of Saskatchewan, specializing in Indian/Métis historiography and colonization
- 1989 — revised edition of *Prison of Grass: Canada From a Native Point of View*, published by Fifth House Publishers, Saskatoon, Saskatchewan
- 1988-2000 — visited and/or lectured at various national and international academic institutions, most notably, German universities in 1992, Cuba in 1993, Mexico City in 1995 and Toronto in 2000
- 1995 — third book, *A Tortured People: The Politics of Colonization*, published by Theytus Books, Penticton, British Columbia.
- 1996 — retired from his sessional position at the University of Saskatchewan
- 1996 — appointed adjunct faculty to the Education Graduate Program, University of Alberta
- 1996 — helped establish the Métis Nation of British Columbia, the provincial Métis political body
- 1996 — established the Vancouver Métis Association
- 1996-2000 — authored several post-retirement articles and papers dealing with Aboriginal issues
- 1996-2000 — frequently appeared on Vancouver community radio talk shows
- 1999 — revised edition of *Tortured People: The Politics of Colonization*, published by Theytus Books
- 1999 — received a *National Aboriginal Achievement Award* (NAAA) for his advocacy for better treatment of Native peoples in Canada
- 1999 — officially feted by the province of Saskatchewan in recognition of the NAAA, and received a provincial award for outstanding achievement
- 2000 — contributed "The Nature of Eurocentrism" to *Expressions in Canadian*

Native Studies, edited by Ron Laliberte et al, an introductory Native Studies text for Canadian universities and colleges, published by Extension Division, University of Saskatchewan

- 2000 — re-appointed to University of Alberta adjunct faculty position
- 2000 — fourth visit to Cuba, to attend a socialist conference and visit Cuban academic colleagues
- 2001 — worked towards including Métis culture in British Columbia's education curricula, and began writing his memoirs
- 2001 — September 8, died suddenly on his 80th birthday at his home in Vancouver

Part One

MEMOIRES:

AUTOBIOGRAPHY AND FICTION

1. Going Out

Leaving to Become a Mountie

How well I remember the day that a letter from the Mounted Police arrived. It was the most thrilling message I had ever received. All the excitement of being a Mountie raced through my head. I could see myself in a red coat, blue breeches and Stetson hat. How great I would look!

I was now going to leave behind the ugliness of my log shack and the image of bannock eaters. People would no longer look down on me as inferior and stupid. After all, one had to be smart to be a Mountie. I was now moving to a higher and better status, changing my entire image. It would be the end of being the lowest scum that God allows to crawl upon the earth.

In a few days, I would leave on a bus for Regina, two hundred miles away, but in my mind it could be a million miles from St. Louis. I fancied myself a glorious detective, with people admiring and applauding me as I made brilliant criminal arrests. I was going to be somebody, maybe not somebody great; I was tired of being nobody and nothing, of being a despised Métis. I would be leaving home for the first time, but likely for the last time. The letter said the Force supplied all clothes for training; nothing else was needed. Mom said in her usual thoughtful and protective way that I would need a couple pairs of overalls, thick mitts, wool socks and my buckskin jacket. She dug out old cardboard boxes from under the bed, everything that she thought would be useful. She washed and patched things that she felt I should take. **(AB)**

2. Growing Up in St. Louis, Saskatchewan

Mom, A French Métis

Sadly, Mom knew that I was parting for good. I didn't have to tell her. She was naturally wise in the most profound way. She could sense everything about her children and what they were saying without spoken words. She was hurting. When I look back now, I think of how she must have suffered as she helped me prepare my parting, leaving her and her home. It was everything she had worked and sacrificed for—her children and their happiness. I was departing in such an unkind way. In my excitement to get away, I ignored her deep feelings of sorrow. I showed no signs of sadness, no thoughts about being apart from my family, my mother, my father, brother and sisters, and all that they meant to me or what I meant to them, especially Mom. **(AB)**

I have no recollection of my birth. In fact, my mother barely remembers. It was so long ago. But, she claims that Dad can clearly remember. He rushed into the room, took a quick glance and shouted, "It's a boy!" and rushed out in great delight. Obviously, he knew a lot about the importance of boys—or would later say, "the politics of gender." A baby brother had just been born only sixteen months ahead of me. I don't think that Mom was [all too happy] about my arrival. But Dad had been careless in his lovemaking. […]

Mom named me "Joseph." Being a good Catholic, she had no choice. I hated it from that day as I grew up and came to […] despise the name. It took years to stamp it out. I was so angered about it being an offshoot of Catholicism that I abandoned the Catholic Church. The parting was unnoticed and mutual, and I happily became known by my second name, "Howard." Several people questioned Mom about where she got that unusual name. She replied, "from the Bible." […] But we didn't have a bible and, anyway, she couldn't read. Friends tried to support her by claiming that I seemed to be timid, cowardly. **(MISC)**

In my exciting [dreams] of being a Mountie, I slept lightly that night. In the silent darkness, I could hear Mom sobbing quietly. I knew the meaning of those sobs, and they pained me greatly, but I could not go to her and say I would not leave home. No. I had to go to the Mountie Training Depot. It might be my only chance to get out of the ghetto and into a decent position. I was determined that I would not be left stuck as a Métis peasant or labourer for the rest of my life.

Without doubt, Mom was truly an exceptional person who inspired those dear to her, supporting them unconditionally in their search for fulfillment and achievement, a quality she passed on to me. She gave no road map, just motivation and inspiration, without pressure or preaching. In no way did she ever seek greatness for herself through her children. She kept her attitudes and feelings close to her nature and soul in terms of all humanity. As a young child, I had only a slight idea of the stress on my mother. It is to her credit that all four children remember their childhood with affection and pleasure. She made up for our lack of money, food and material things with her cheerful manner and positive attitude. Mom would sit and talk for hours with her children, gossiping about everything within our ghetto. It strengthened the family bond. It was a healthy life, in its limited way, but stunted and distorted in terms of worldview.

One of the greatest things that my mother did was to give me the capacity to understand and the compassion for human relationships, as well the facility to analyze the network of society. My view of life was coloured by my mother's outlook. Her early influences helped me develop an analytical mind. At the same time, she instilled in me a suspicion of White mainstream society and its power structure. This may have been the seed that developed a distrust of liberalism. In most conditions, she had a strong sense of right and wrong, which was clear and far-reaching. For instance, during the 1940s when there was much thundering about the great war in Europe, Mom was bitterly opposed to it in any and all forms. To her, war was totally and absolutely wrong. It could not be justified morally, politically and nationally. There was no way her sons would serve in the military. I knew that I was a conscientious objector even before I approached military age.

In most respects, Mom was an easy person to relate to. During the twenty years in our ethnic community, it was Mom who kept life pleasurable and with the comforts of home. Being the eldest in a family of five brothers and four sisters, Mom was always working like a hired maid and baby-sitter. Living in a big log house that was primitive and crude made work demanding and strenuous. It was still only a log shack and was extremely cold in winters. Unhappy about seeing her mother work so hard, as well as being pregnant much of the time, Mom tried in every way to relieve this misery.

At the age of fourteen, Mom started working for an English farmer, Mr. McKenzie, who lived only a half-mile away. In addition to farming, he operated a crude ferryboat for carrying passengers across the South Saskatchewan River. At the time, there was no ferry or bridge that crossed the river. She was hired to help Mrs. McKenzie with housework, as well as other casual office duties necessary with McKenzie's ferry operations. Although it was hard work, it was interesting. The ferryboat carried mostly English Métis from the north side. Although Mom was shy, she had a charming smile and an attractive manner. It was this delightful manner that made her a popular and valuable employee for Mr. McKenzie. She could speak enough English to explain instructions to the [English-speaking] Protestant Métis. Since Mom was rather jolly, she was a "big-hit" with the men.

His Parents' Romance

It was on this job that she met my Dad, Billie Adams. He was quite a handsome man, with a pleasing personality. Their acquaintance developed into a romance. Likely, Billie was making trips across the river for romance, and less for business reasons. Naturally, Mom would tell her mother about her romance and later about her plans to marry Billie. It was indeed a shocker for Kokom McDougall. An Anglican in the family was unthinkable. That was heresy. But these lovers were determined to be married. It was eventually agreed that they would marry in the rectory of the Catholic Church in St. Louis. Their ceremony took place in June 1917. **(AB)**

Finally, they got married in the Catholic rectory. That was the closest my Dad ever got to the inside of a Catholic Church. In this cubicle, he promised before the priest that he would bring up his children as Catholics. At the time, he knew he was lying, but he was so much in love with Mom that he would have sworn to greater bogus commitments.

Howard Adams' parents' (Billie and Olive) wedding photograph. Photograph Courtesy—Marge Adams.
Howard Adams' parents, Billie and Olive. Photograph Courtesy—Marge Adams.

I was always curious about how my parents met. Dad could not speak or understand a word of French, and Mom could not converse in even the simplest English. Obviously it must have been love at first sight. But there was a greater problem. Dad lived on the north side of the great South Saskatchewan River and Mom lived on the south side. In the early days of the 1920s, there was no bridge across the river. For certain, they never crossed by boat or raft. Both were terrified of water. The mere sight of the riverbank sent my mother racing for the big, high and dry hills. Dad was about ten miles from the nearest ferry, and Mom approximately fifteen miles. Walking was "out" since Dad had no shoes with solid soles. Now it seems understandable why he had many Indian riding ponies. Courting would have been a struggle and a profound involvement.

April in Saskatchewan is a poor month for honeymooning. The roads are half snow and half mud. In a buggy you travel half the time through snowdrifts, and in a cutter you travel half the time on mud. But, I suppose, when in love one doesn't pay attention as to what one is travelling on. The important thing is whom you are travelling with. To arrive at Dad's shack was not a picture of the Taj Mahal. He was a bad housekeeper. But for Mom the cleanup would start the next day. **(MISC)**

Mom quit her job at McKenzie's and became a housewife in an English Métis shack in Red Deer Hill, a distance of ten miles north of St. Louis. Life and work was even harder now. Furthermore, she had very few friends because of the language problem. It was a very lonely life in the long, cold winters. **(AB)**

Childhood in St. Louis

Looking back on my childhood, I recall a fair, loving family; the severe hard times took away what could have been a loving home. In the 1930s and 40s, St. Louis-Batoche was rigidly segregated racially. Although it had been the home of the Métis for over fifty years, they did not have any prestige.

Ottawa's carnage of the Métis in 1885 ended any hope of economic recovery. The red line of racism was now drawn around the Métis population. It was clearly segregated and rigidly racist. The media made a big circus out of the military events around the battle. The issue of the savagery and barbarity of the Métis was extremely exaggerated for the longest time in order to impress on the […] White population that the land of western plains must be taken from the Aboriginal people. Land was the prize for two main reasons: one, the Canadian Pacific Railway had to have it for their railways; and two, the big land corporations [wanted] to seize it to make fortunes by selling it to the incoming settlers from Europe.

Imperialism is a complex and murderous procedure. After invasion and the holocaust, there are a number of succeeding homicidal actions before the Aboriginal people are exterminated or imprisoned. All Indigenous people of the [European] colonies suffered the same fate: Canada, Australia, or Africa. The Indians and Métis of Canada were no different. Canada probably had better public relations affairs than the other colonies. This is why Canada's history suffers from the greatest distortions and falsehoods of imperial nations.

Yet, my memory of a reasonably happy childhood is consistent with most Métis children of St. Louis-Batoche. Since the area included such a large population of Aboriginals, most lived at the same poverty level. It was an understood equality that did not base status or hierarchy on material wealth. I remember […] when the Vizinas, a neighbouring couple, dropped in to visit. Dad suggested to Mom that she make a snack for them, and she had to answer that we [had] nothing, no food to eat. Then he suggested at least a cup of tea, but she claimed that we had no tea. At which point Dad got up and took the water pail and said, "Well, I'll get a pail of water, and we can at least have a drink of fresh water."

We lived and played together as impoverished people and did not look upon the better off Whites as part of our class. To us, there was a kind of divine or natural division for the Métis, and we adjusted our sights within it. That meant less struggle and pretensions and envy. As I realized later, it was not totally accepted, as I had harboured a hostility or bitterness about it. Some families isolated themselves from the so-called upper-class Métis families, such as the Bouchers and Pauls. But since these families' children were my companions at school, it was not a social status issue. Some Métis families desperately tried to isolate themselves from the low-class Métis, and move closer to the edges of White society [...]. This became a serious and harsh issue in the mid-1960s, when [being] Métis became a public identification [issue].

Martin Luther King claims that in this condition the "black community boasted thriving businesses, impressive churches, superior private colleges, a radio station, churches, a daily newspaper and a rich social network of clubs." Our Métis community had none of these, only the sludge left by White society. The one prideful thing was that we had no crime except for minor bootlegging, but it was not a big thing as no one pushed it. No one was deeply rooted in religion, except Alex McLeod. No one argued over religious issues, as we didn't delve deeply into them. Going to church or mass [...] regularly and praying as the others was adequate. No one asked for more.

We could not be shielded from racism. But, having grown up in such atmosphere, we had conditioned ourselves to the elements. I would explain that most Métis did not make an issue of racism because that would have been a full confession of our Indianness, which most were trying so desperately to hide. Any move or expression that committed us to Aboriginality would have angered almost all the Métis population. Each one of us had that understanding. There are so many hidden and torturous subtleties to hidden racism when living on the outer edges of White supremacy. Your vision and your space are never clearly defined for you. You are always in doubt and things are obscure. Conformity to lower social class values was never a concern for us. All our associations and parties were of that nature.

The community in which I grew up had certain peculiarities about it. But they helped to take our focus off hunger and oppression. However, you could not accuse the people of being hypocritical. They knew their level in terms of social status. Métis were inclined to be the trash workers. It was the work of God. He couldn't be challenged. Neither could you fool the community that you were a Director of Public Services if you were a toilet-hole digger. The most troublesome problem was ethnicity and race. I agonized for most of those twenty years in trying to sort out this distressing problem. To most Métis it was just smog in their brains, but they muddled through. We all played head games, which only flummoxed our minds more than ever. The European Whites served to keep us confused and suppressed. They never socialized with us, invited us to their homes, or to their social events. Being intimidated by them, we probably would not have gone. Our clothes and manners were never good enough in comparison [...]. Yet, everything in our communities was open, even the windows and doors, but nothing but mosquitoes and flies came in.

Mrs. J.M.P. McLeod, the storekeeper's wife, explains in *The History of St. Louis* she was involved in drama and wrote plays. She and her husband played tennis and lawn croquet in their backyard. To the Métis, "drama and plays" could have been buffalo chips, as far we knew. The Halfbreeds were into bareback horse racing, playing hardball with a rock, or swimming in our nature suit. Living in shacks in the woods, our backyards were cow yards—hardly suitable for croquet. The bourgeois McLeods were a far cry from the proletarian Métis. We were assigned to the bottom of society in the beginning and pushed downward ever after. My girlfriend Irene worked at the McLeod home. But she was a servant and did not participate in the bourgeois life. It was very much a servant-master relationship. In all the years that we were lovers, she never mentioned tennis, croquet or drama. Her conversation would be about scrubbing, washing and cleaning. Mrs. McLeod was inclined to think that she was a queen.

Being Métis

Growing up in St. Louis was like most mixed colonized countries, where Halfbreeds, Mestizos and Mulattos were treated as sub-humans. The only differences are the languages spoken. I have visited many of those countries in my adult life and saw and felt the similarities. Our struggle for liberation is the same. We will always be the underclass, subjugated and facing racial discrimination.

You don't become a Métis; you are a Métis at birth. This was a subject I discussed with uncle Mederic [McDougall] when he came to our place. Asking Mom and Dad was useless. Either they didn't know or refused to talk about it. Yet, they were only a second generation from their Indigenous ancestors. But in that short time they had become muted about their heritage. Moshom and Kokom knew plenty about their Métis ancestry, but they never spoke about it. It had to be a very disgraceful matter to hide it so rigidly. Obviously, it was sordid and shameful. For twenty years, I lived in a despicable Métis ghetto and suffered the most heinous discrimination. I don't excuse my hostility and bitterness today. It was the deliberate, vicious, spiteful and hateful purpose of the capitalist system. The system and the rulers cannot be excused [or] forgiven.

Yet, Grandpa was so proud when he was dressed in all his Métis finery: buffalo coat, the wide red Métis sash, leather pants, moccasins and fur hat, and speaking only Michif. He seemed to be so proud of his origins […], whatever he thought it was, because he would strut around town like a proud peacock as he spoke loudly to his Michif friends. Yeah, I don't know what the hell he was proud of. Kokom said he was a vain old man. He didn't need anything to be proud of. He would spend hours in front of the mirror combing his hair, shaving and just admiring himself.

"Well, that's a helluva lot better than hanging your head and being ashamed of yourself," J. said. "But, he never gave credit to his background, of being Métis."

Howard Adams' maternal grandparents, Wilbrod and Virgnie McDougall. Photograph Courtesy—Marge Adams.

"Did all the people of St. Louis come from Red River?"

"Yes. Both the French and English Métis."

"But they don't talk about their heritage and their nationality?"

"No. That is not an issue with them. They are just Native people who were born here and grew up here, and they know nothing about their background. And they do not want to know anything about it."

"What a helluva mix-up, DT. Then I'm not Canadian, either."

"Sure as hell not. Canadians killed our Métis ancestors or tortured them. Or put them in prison, like my great-grandfather [Maxime Lépine]. I hate the Canadians—whoever they are."

Racism

What I hated while growing up in St. Louis was the racial discrimination. It was a different kind of racism than the Blacks of the southern USA experienced. The European Whites would never consider themselves as racists. They would have argued that they treat all people in the region the same, and that all were just as good as any other person. It was a concealed, undisclosed or cloaked racism. It was through their attitudes, behaviour or manners by which they discriminated. Of course, the most evident point was the history of European racism. In imperial conquests, such as in Canada, it was the English who stood out as the nationality that [was the most] ugly [and] racist. Being of English descent automatically made you the "deluxe" and exceptional individual. Your status in England had nothing to do with your status in Canada. It was much the same for France. But the French were slightly lower after the Montcalm-Wolfe War in 1754-1763 [the Seven Years War]. Both groups [English and French Canadians] discriminated against the Aboriginal people and especially after the struggles with the Métis in 1869-70 and 1885. This type of racism was vigorously fostered when the English and French robber barons wanted the land, and resources across Canada when they [claimed] land for the immigrant settlers. Propaganda of stereotypes poured out in every form and through every possible media. Indians and Métis were portrayed as vicious and subhuman, and despised as the most barbarous and cruel creatures. It became part of the Canadian atmosphere, and no one attempted to correct these horrendous falsehoods. The bankers and land companies were making fortunes, so what could the Aboriginals do about such savagery? Fight and resist in the only way they knew.

Racial privilege is most [clearly] expressed in the labour market. When I sought jobs as a young man in the St. Louis area from White employers, they were always manual, dirty, hard work. Most of the Métis men worked only those jobs. My Dad worked out most every fall. He was employed only in unskilled, casual dirty jobs. I never saw him work in a clean, secure job where there was [any] promotion. All jobs for the Métis were low status jobs. White English and French immigrants entered the economic system under more favourable conditions than the Métis. For instance, the families Goddard, Lecoq, Dupire, Pannetier—all from France—started work in the St. Louis area at advantaged positions compared to the Métis. Mr. Galloway from Ontario purchased a farm and machinery when he settled in the St. Louis area. In 1918, he bought a section of land and a big tractor. Harry Grimes, who settled on a farm near St. Louis, bought thirty acres of land in the first year and built a house. Sidney Marvin, who came from England, moved to St. Louis and purchased a general store in town. These White immigrants entered the St. Louis community with privilege and a head start in comparison to the Métis.

"What was it like growing up as a Métis in St. Louis?"

"Very much like that of mixed European race, like the mestizo, mulatto."

"Well, I don't know anything about their growing up […]."

"Well, when the Europeans conquered an Indigenous country, there gradually developed a mixed race of people because White women did not come to the colonies right away. The European conquerors couldn't hold back testosterone, so they impregnated the Native women. And after nine months the colonies had a new race of people—mixed White and Indigenous. In Canada, it was the Whites and Indians. First called Mixed-Bloods, then Halfbreeds and now Métis. They were never considered equal to the Whites. We have always been second class, lower social class, and [have] all the stereotypes that go with that class. Canada is a rigidly racial society, so that Métis suffer the humiliation and cruelty of institutional racism. It's hell, cruel, violent, inhuman."

"The majority of the people in St. Louis were Catholic and French. Most had come from Red River Valley—where'n the hell that is."

"Are they all like you?"

"They are not. They're like us—poor."

"Damn," said B., " I have lots of French Catholic relatives that live up west at the Lépine Flats, and they are poor."

"The French Catholic families from Bellevue are not poor like those that live along the river."

"The rich French Catholics, the poor French Catholics, the rich English, the poor Anglicans—well, where do we fit in?"

"Must be the Anglican poor, because I see some of my cousins at church sometimes, but very few others. There are some Anglicans who are rich like Marvin, Miller, Galloway."

"We can't be part of their group because they come from England."

"I—well, the rich French Catholics from Bellevue come from France, and I don't come from France."

"Then where the hell do we come from?"

"That is a very strange thing. I never hear my parents or any of the older people in our families talking about our country we come from."

"I—we come from right here. I—then don't know […].

"Have they always been in St. Louis?"

"Then, why aren't we proud about it, and talk about it, just as these older people do?"

"We'll just have do ask Mom and Dad, and you do the same, B. & I., and ask our grandparents, too. My Grandpa and grandma Adams are dead. But they used to live here in Red Deer Hill."

"We'll meet back here in a few days and tell all we know."

That was a lost cause. My mother could not tell me anything more than about her Mom and Dad. They were both born here in the St. Louis area. Granny says she must be French, but Grandpa says he is part French and Scots because his name is McDougall. None of his relatives are living today.

My mother was Olive McDougall, a granddaughter of the famous Maxime Lépine, Louis Riel's field commander. My mother could not speak English, and Dad could not speak French, but language is obviously no obstacle in the dimension of love. That wasn't the only obstacle—the South Saskatchewan River is a large swift river, and neither my mother nor Dad could swim. **(MISC)**

My mother, a French-Catholic Métis, was a descendent from the close encounters of the Coureur des bois [Voyageurs] with Plains Cree. She is the granddaughter of the distinguished Maxime Lépine, a loyal member of Louis Riel's council and warrior in the Batoche War of 1885. His courageous guerrilla actions cost him seven years in the Manitoba prison. His bravery and great leadership was completely silenced by all relatives and co-warriors. Mom's families, McDougalls and Lépines, were totally silent on our ancestors and their involvement in the Batoche War. It killed our Métis nationalism and left a vacuum [instead of] a proud heritage. Our family

Maxime Lépine's grave at the St. Louis, SK Cemetery. Photograph Courtesy—Marge Adams.

Maxime Lépine—"Friend of Riel". Maxime Lépine was Howard Adams' maternal great-grandfather. Photograph Courtesy— the Archives of Manitoba (N10909).

background had to be hidden. For that, I am deeply saddened. This agonizing silence was deliberate suppression by the Ottawa government. Instead of being proud of our noble Métis ancestry of St. Louis, we lived in shame and disgrace. The federal government and media imposed this monstrous Métis guilt, which became an everlasting oppression. **(AB)**

Dad, An English Halfbreed

My father, an English Anglican Métis, came from the gregarious behaviour of the English fur traders with the Swampy Cree. He was a firm but gentle father, a hard worker of useless tasks. Like many Anglicans, he was a dour, stoic man. I did not hear him laugh or see him smile much throughout my childhood. But in the 1930s and 1940s, how many parents had fun? **(AB)**

George Adams, my great-great-grandfather, was born in England. He was not from the blueblood aristocracy or even an upper-class family. Nothing is known of George's education, except that he was a rope maker. The job could not have been very interesting because he happily gave it up at age seventeen and sailed to Canada. Among the savages there was no flourishing in the rope making business in 1815. Without knowing about Canada or even where it was, he set sail in 1815 with a group of illusory, arrogant, high and mighty English to the Selkirk Settlement. They docked at the bottom end of the Hudson Bay, [at a post] called Norway House. The settlers moved on to the Selkirk Settlement by walking and boating over several hundred miles. Being terrified of Indians, they stuck together.

They soon realized that they were missing one member: George Adams. He was safely in Norway House in the company of a beautiful Métis girl, Ann Heywood, a beauty-contest winner. It was rumoured that Ann was the daughter of a Hudson's Bay Company employee. George was a man of action. He married Ann as soon as the banns were published in the church, then he and Ann made their way to the Selkirk Settlement. He did not want to miss his opportunity of getting his share of free land, so he hurried to the Selkirk Settlement where he was granted fifty acres. George and Ann farmed in the High Bluff area within the Selkirk Settlement. Typical of Adams, they had twelve children, so the Adams descendants grew rapidly. The last child, Marsia, was born in 1860, and George died a few years later. Ann lived to the ripe old age of 83, leaving 149 Adams descendants. Probably, the Adams tribe was one of the largest Halfbreed [clans].

After the violent and terrorist campaign of John A. Macdonald in 1870 against the Red River Halfbreeds, where their homes and household goods were burned to the ground, the people continued to be hassled and tortured by General Wolseley's troops sent out from Ottawa. Families were forced to flee Red River. The cruel Orangemen were particularly vicious against the Catholic Halfbreeds. The Rwanda ethnic cleansing of today is similar to the 1869/70 cleansing of Red River.

I became interested in the [Métis] population and their history. Most of them migrated to this area after the resistance in Red River in 1870. Prime Minister Macdonald, with his huge military force, drove many out of the Red River area with the brutal methods that are usually employed by soldiers—beatings, rape, burning homes, forcefully driving them off their farms, torture and every imaginable vicious behaviour. The Halfbreeds had to scramble for their lives. So they had to move away, and they decided to go somewhere where the soldiers would not torture them. Prime Minister

Macdonald didn't give a damn where our ancestors moved to, as long as he defeated us as an organized and official nation. The colonizer is always ruthless and brutal. The Halfbreeds were nothing. I don't know why they settled in this area, but I guess they felt they were free from police and military cruelty and violence. They were supposed to get some kind of payment for their land in Red River. It was not cash, but a certificate called scrip that was equivalent to cash.

"But," said Med[eric], "I don't think any people got scrip. I know that Dad did not get scrip or free land. The bank held a big mortgage on our place, and in the end we couldn't keep up the payments and he lost the farm. And I think of all the hard work I did in clearing the land from trees and stones, and got nothing for it. That's what happened to most of the Halfbreed families in the Batoche area. And everybody had such hard time living in log shacks and in such primitive conditions."

It was [the same] damn thing for the English Halfbreeds on the north side of the river. Much of the land was sand and stone. That whole area of twenty-five miles from the river to Prince Albert was populated mostly by Halfbreed families—although not one person would mention it. It seemed that they had taken an oath of silence on their heritage. Yet, it was quite obvious that we were different from those arrogant White people. We stuck to ourselves socially. Our houses were different, our way of life was different, we looked different. The Whites wouldn't come near us. They would not come into our houses or visit us—even if we were dying.

They [George and Ann] became farmers at the High Bluff area—a section of the Red River Settlement. They had a family of twelve children. Ann later moved west to Lindsey district, south of old Prince Albert. Most of her 149 descendants were living in the Lindsey district. Her son, Joseph Adams, was my grandfather. He married a woman by the name of Ann Bird. They had three sons. Tragically, Ann [Bird] died a short time later. Joseph did not like bachelorhood, so he married Christina Fanks, an English woman. They made their home at Lindsey district, near Prince Albert, where they raised nine children. After Joseph's death, Christina continued to farm in the Lindsey district. She had sixty-two heads of cattle, six horses and a large log house. Since she signed her documents with an "X," it claims she was illiterate. They had only two sons, George and William. Four daughters married Halfbreed men, and the two sons married Halfbreed women. Since the entire territories south of Prince Albert were [comprised of] Halfbreeds, it was natural that one's spouse would be Halfbreed. This population was largely the English Halfbreeds who had moved to the Prince Albert region after Macdonald's soldiers and mercenaries had driven the English Halfbreeds out of the Red River. They populated the large territory from old Prince Albert to the southern branch of the Saskatchewan River. Immediately across the river was the homeland of the French Catholic Halfbreeds who had fled from Red River at the same time, [to escape] the vicious attack of Colonel Wolseley and his troops. It was an ethnic cleansing similar to those taking place today throughout the world. **(MISC)**

Living Conditions: Shack and Log Cabin

Métis families live in log shacks with crude and meagre furniture. **(AB)**

Houses for this northern area of Saskatchewan were of a weird build because, where the temperatures in winter drop to fifty below, most families had these small two-room

[buildings], finished inside with a thick cardboard, called beaver board. There was absolutely no insulation between [the building's interior and exterior]. The floors were light poplar and were not insulated or protected by anything to prevent the cold and snow [from coming inside] during the long cold winters. Likewise, there was no insulation in the ceiling.

Old Métis log house on the South Saskatchewan River between Batoche and St. Louis, SK, September 1987. Photograph Courtesy—Hartmut Lutz.

These houses were suitable only for summer cottages at the lake or semi-tropical areas in the south. They were undoubtedly the product of some super salesman [who] caught the small ignorant farmers at a weak moment in the fall after a good crop. There was no way that they could be explained [a] sound, rational consideration [for] an appropriate comfortable dwelling. It was not long before Mom seduced Dad into adding a good, solid, sensible log and mud shack.

The Adams' shack was a weird construction for these tribal people. A part of the house was built from local logs, peeled and nicked at the ends for strength. They were no straighter than an old dog's legs. Hence, they had to be chinked as if they were [forming] a cage, then thickly mudded with heavy clay, straw and manure. On top was glued a paste of a layer of white lime. It held like a barnacle. When finished, it was a thick wall of heavy and closely woven wood and mud plaster. This provided an excellent wall against the arctic winter weather and against the tropical hot summer sun. The floor of heavy wooden plank laid flat against the earth was as good as a furnace in winter, and [was like] a cool ice rink in the summer. The door was a two-thickness slab of wood. But it took four hinges the size of a warehouse to hold it on. In addition, in winter, a horse blanket was nailed over it to keep out the frost. In summer, it was replaced by a screen door to keep out the flies, mosquitoes and barnyard flies. One wrought-iron cook stove [from] 1902 kept it warm in winter, besides cooking all the few edibles we had as food. [The] heavy iron cook-stove was enough to keep it warm. But for the frame cottage, it took a heavy, big, steel barrel-shaped stove to keep the place warm. One had to stick around the stove for warmth. And fires had to be kept going much of the night. Keeping warm in the wintertime was a full time job. Cutting, sawing and splitting wood [to heat the home] took most of the day.

It was impossible to open the door without first moving the cupboard, which opened to the bedroom entrance. The table had to be moved to the centre in order for us to eat our meals together. A small room off to the side served as a bedroom for four of the kids. A curtain was hung between the boys' bed and the girls' bed. Pictures of the Pope and other religious figures were nailed to the walls. A picture of Pope Pius VII was the most imposing and threatening. Dad, a strong anti-Catholic, twisted it each time he walked past it. Like most women in the colony, Mom rarely went to confession or took communion. All four of us kids dropped out as soon as possible, and that was soon. At least the house was not too small for our furniture, as we had only a few bare essentials.

There was no running water, toilet or water basin. Every one had to go to the outhouse. Extreme winter temperatures made life an insufferable trip. One had to hurry so as not to freeze. For the fierce cold winter nights, there was a "honey-bucket" kept under the bed. Smell was a tough ordeal. But the house already smelt of rotten fish from the wet moose-hide jackets and moccasins as they dried by the heat from the stove. These smells permeated the house, clothes and hair. It was a horrible companion with food and particularly [as we ate our] meals. **(MISC)**

Subsistence Farming

As labourers and peasant farmers, we struggled for mere subsistence with primitive hand tools. Often, I would cut the crop with a scythe. **(AB)**

We were accustomed to a peasant life; we were indifferent to its sufferings. We rarely complained about it […]. We accepted it, assuming it was part of being the underclass of society. We were resigned to our submission and to the requirements of the wretched work of picking sow thistle. It was just wasted energy as far as I was concerned. There seemed to be more yellow flowered thistle each morning instead of less. We weren't even keeping up, let alone getting ahead. It would be better to sit in the shade of the house during the day than working in the burning sun. But inactivity was not only a horror, but a sin. In a way, the thistle was keeping us from sinfulness, according to Dad.

There was not enough wheat growing to even bother with. The crop would not grow well enough to produce the necessary wheat for the winter's supply of flour. We all worked barefoot. The soles of our feet had toughened like hoofs. Swirling clouds of dust moved towards us. Soon a gust of wind trapped us in horrid dry hot dust. It was the exodus from the drought of the 1930s. It was useless to try to escape it. It was all around us. It mattered little. We were more dead than alive. What would a little more devastation do to us? Life seemed unimportant anyway. Although we were agitated and angered by our horrible economic conditions, we never summoned the notion or strength to create a mass violent movement against the businesses or corporations, which were making money from our slave labour, our meagre crops. We worked steadily and painfully in the patches of sow thistle, bent over, using our hoes, day after day, from morning till evening. It was painful to straighten up the back after a day's work

Howard Adams' parents, Billie and Olive, with plow.
Photograph Courtesy—Marge Adams.

[…]. The little plot of soil did not produce a living for the starving poor. We struggled on in utter passivity, choking in the dust. This was supposed to be the land of our dreams. Yet it killed all visionary promises and dreams.

To complain to Dad was useless; he never even heard our voices. He was determined this would be a good crop. Only a few years ago, he had cut down the trees, cleared out the brush and broke the soil with a "break plough" and hauled away all the roots. Now it was new soil for producing the best crops in the valley. But the damn sow thistle seeds had blown in from Lones' farm next door. They came with the dust and dry hot wind of the fall or early spring. There was never any rain to dampen them down, not even to moisten them and prevent the soil from drifting. In his mind's eye, Dad could see a beautiful stand of wheat. In the evening, he knelt and prayed to thank God. It was pitiful. He spent all his working hours tending the crop, driving his sons to help him, while the rest of the farm work around the house and barn was left to decay.

The exception was the garden. Mom held control over the big garden and its huge patch of potatoes. A team of strong horses had the exclusive job of hauling barrels of water from the river to water the garden every evening. Regardless of how tired we may have been, the garden and the potatoes had to be weeded and hilled. All the garden produce provided subsistence for winter. The one and most horrid thing about this job was picking the small pests off the potato leaves. They came in clouds with the hot dry wind and settled on the underside of the potato leaves. They could clean out the potato patch in a day if not plucked immediately. It was the most wretched job. […]. You had to turn the leaves over and pick these horrid little bastards off with your bare fingers, often squashing them in your hands, and then dropping them in a bucket of water. On your hands and knees you moved up and down the rows of potatoes. Time was of great importance. Pesticides had not yet been invented. The damn potato bugs always came during school holidays, so we were never free to play and have freedom for doing whatever rowdy youngsters do. All day long at school, I was amidst the throng of school kids. [I was] never alone to be face-to-face with myself. Never allowed to be alone with my thoughts and dreams.

In the evening, after a supper of mostly bannock, lard and potatoes, all members of the family gathered around in the grass beside the house, where a heavy smudge of smoke would be made to keep the hordes of blood sucking mosquitoes from sucking your blood. Their stingers seemed as big as darning needles. And the damn wind went down so as not to blow them away. It was a losing game every day [...]. Finally it was off to bed. Those horrid hideous monster bugs had to be cleaned out of the bedclothes and bed frames in early spring before they got a chance to settle in. The beds were taken outside, stripped down and treated with coal oil. The smell was horrid, but better than bedbugs biting [any of us].

Morning came as soon as the hot sun beamed on the house and land. For a short period, the birds sang in the cool hours of the day. After breakfast, it was time to pick up the hoe and shuffle off to the field of sow thistles. It was painful to see that their yellow heads were thicker and bigger than ever. But Dad argued that to leave them would mean they would overtake the [...] wheat, and one would harvest only thistles—[which meant] no wheat—and we would starve. **(MISC)**

Geez, what a hard way to make a living! Others just sat on their asses in the shade under a tree all summer and got plenty of relief. But Dad said the neighbours would claim we were lazy. Being oversensitive to stereotypes, Dad was a continual whirlwind of motion. He had an obsession for work. He was defenceless against idleness. Mom said that Dad was in constant motion ever since they were married. But was his work worthwhile? No. It was like moving a pile of rocks one day to a certain place and then moving them back to the same place the next day. He never organized a work plan. At the end of the day, it was just sweat. **(AB)**

I did my chores—fed pigs and chickens, gathered and milked cows, fixed fence, cleaned the barnyard, and rounded-up horses in the morning [...]. Dad farmed the fifty acres, and worked out in the fall and spring. I worked at odd jobs for other farmers in fall and spring. Our home was a gathering centre for Halfbreeds.

> We hunted deer, moose, trapped some furs.
> We farmed with horses, and walking plough.
> We never hired anybody.
> We were subsistence farmers
> – barely making a living –
> eking it out by various Indigenous ingenious ways.
> We picked berries, nuts.
> We made a lot of our own goods: soap and jam.
> We built our own log shacks, and mudded them
> – with the help of other Halfbreeds.
> We helped each other out when they needed help.
> Nobody ever kept track of who did what
> in terms of hours, pay, or how much they owed.
> We never learned anything about management
> or operations bigger than necessary for existence.

We never planned for tomorrow, set goals for a career.

We lived from day to day.

I hated the life of intermingling with other Halfbreeds at their low level. I knew it was low level because there were White people who lived in town, and they were a higher social class, and so were the big farmers. We, as Halfbreeds, were kept at a distance from the Whites. Our dealings with them were strictly business.

Often I hung around in the house—so I knew what Mom was doing and what women folks were doing.

Freddie was banging on the door—six o'clock on a Sunday morning, early mass. He wanted to borrow a pony to ride to Hoey. Dad told him to take the pinto and let us sleep. Nobody asked when he would bring the horse back, or what he was going to do with the horse. That wasn't an important concern. The horse was doing nothing, and nobody was going to use the pinto today. Henry came that afternoon and asked for one of us to help him dig the grave tomorrow for Ms. D. I agreed, but told him to hustle up two other Breeds since digging six feet was a helluva lot of digging. Boyer came to get his horses that he had left in the barn over Saturday night. He got drunk last night. He was still drunk. I helped him hitch up. Had a couple of drinks with him.

On Tuesday, I fixed the fence around the house. Mom was complaining that the animals were standing around in the shade of the house, shitting there in piles, attracting the flies and smelling up the place. What a helluva job to find enough nails and wire. **(MISC)**

St. Louis, Saskatchewan

St. Louis is a Métis village, which began in 1870 after the ravage of Red River by Prime Minister Macdonald's troops. The French Métis had to make a desperate flight westward seeking freedom from persecution. Shortly after, the English Métis of Red River fled westward. They followed a northward route to Prince Albert and then gradually moved toward the South Saskatchewan River, settling in the districts of Red Deer Hill, MacDowall, Clouston and Lindsey, where they became small farmers. My father's family came by this route to St. Louis. Gradually these two Métis migrations fostered mixed marriages.

Later, the village of St. Louis would grow in size and eventually become a town, populated by two cultures, French and English, and two different ethnic groups, Métis and White. The main population are French-Catholic Métis who live in town and west along the river, namely Boucher, Boyer, Lépine. The English Métis live on the north side—namely, Adams, Beddome, Brown, Paul, Tate—reaching as far as Prince Albert. East [of the river] are the White English Protestant farmers who migrated from Ontario, England and Scotland, i.e. Galloway, Grimes, Miller, Snell. A group of French people who came from France and Québec occupy the southern community around Bellevue, namely Begrand, Bragner, Doderai, Magnin.

These two European White supremacy groups created an ethnic, racially-divided society that subordinated and excluded Métis from their communities and elevated themselves as superior people. As Métis, we felt this discrimination deeply. A small group of White families owned and operated small businesses in town—namely, J.M.P. McLeod, S. Marvin and H. Grimes. This multicultural pool of people lived almost exclusively within their own cultural group. The storekeepers, however, dealt with all groups because of business. As Métis, we were secluded mostly from the White Europeans who came into our community only when they needed our labour and resources. This large segregated community was always a puzzle to me. In my youth, I could not really understand why each ethnic group held to its own area. There was a unique feeling within each group. I could never solve this feeling. I did not understand at that time that I was an English-French Métis at the bottom, and not a person of the superior pecking order.

White people set themselves apart from us, never inviting us to their cultural or even political functions. They were welcome to our social activities, but never came. The French Bellevue people were, and still are, very snobbish. They think they are much nicer, which makes us feel inferior and shameful. Because of the different levels of status, Métis do not have the same benefits and privileges. For example, Europeans have warm houses, adequate food, nice clothes, and medicine when sick.

Many Métis became confused, puzzled, and lived in constant denial of their history and culture. I did not know why. Nobody ever studied those problems and none of us were clever enough to study or analyze the ethnic and social aspects.

Billam questioned, "'Ethnic'? What, the hell, does that mean?"

"Ethnic means notions about culture, nationality, behaviour and mental things."

In an ethnic-racial society like St. Louis, White minority groups elevate themselves to a superior position, and at the same time repress and take advantage of lower ethnic groups, such as the Métis. In St. Louis, the upper French and English classes dominated the Métis. For the most part, we were excluded from equal participation and a fair share of opportunities in the society. This does not mean that individuals or groups practice deliberate racism, but it is a natural part of the system [based on] defeated and colonized Métis. This system, as a matter of course, benefits the White-European population. An example of this privilege were appointments to offices, such as elevator agents, postmaster, telephone operators, who were White persons, i.e. Harry Grimes, Eugene Benoit, Sid Marvin and Maurice Ferland. Also, the two general stores were owned and operated by White persons, J.M.P. McLeod and Sid Marvin. Métis people do not have the opportunity for these positions or businesses. All government offices and businesses [...] were occupied by White people. It was accepted as God-given. The Métis were clearly outsiders of these governing positions. We were subjugated to the outlying primitive wilderness, scattered throughout the territory as semi-civilized people. We were beyond the pale of government opportunities and appointments, but within the long arm of the law and taxes which […] stretched to our rural ghettos. [A social hierarchy is common] in an ethnic-racial society, that is, a chain of command to operate. In St. Louis, favoured White people automatically occupied power positions. Métis people were never at the top or near it.

St. Louis, viewed in the full picture of the Canadian nation as a colonial White supremacist society, has social institutions such as government, school, church, court and police. These organizations administer the society and the Aboriginal people of St. Louis. Such a society has many stereotypes that oppress minority groups. Together with the government, such a community elevates the White population and oppresses the minorities, whether or not they consciously believe or express it. In St. Louis, these cultural beliefs served to discriminate against Métis, [to bar them] from equal participation and from a fair share in the society, i.e. healthcare, civil rights, and employment. White privileges are ingrained in a colonial system and may not be automatically known or obvious to the minorities. Métis do not even know that such advantages exist. This systematic inequality and injustice is "natural" in the ethnic-racial society.

Historically, the federal government seized the North-West Territories, which included St. Louis, after the Métis struggle in 1885. In a sense, Ottawa was now the landlord of this vast real estate. Lieutenant-Governor Dewdney, a colonial commissioner, was appointed to govern the North-West Territories. In the 1880s, Ottawa's officials were surveying the land of the Métis.

Should the Métis not resist invading imperialist troops? It was their homeland. They settled and developed the territory. This included both the English and French Métis who were involved in the struggle of 1885. The new English imperialist system was rigidly imposed upon our people in every dimension. We were subjugated to a hideous stereotype culture. As Métis, we were compelled to hide or camouflage our identity while mainstream people knew and used the stereotypes. It is a wretched situation, and a disintegrating factor on one's mentality. As Métis, we were condemned; there was no forgiveness. It was a most painful and continuous ordeal that stuck like glue. The distortion of the 1885 Métis resistance could not be corrected or challenged, so we had to live with the fictional historical image of the Métis.

Kokom McDougall is not talkative or friendly on this topic. She has a lot of intimate Métis history in her head, but she is secretive about the bloodshed at Batoche. [Moshom] McDougall is not a damn bit better. He is a great talker socially and a great story teller and a braggart, but for true stories of Batoche, forget it. It is the silent story of the grave. Not a word was ever uttered among the hundreds of English and Catholic Métis in the whole population of St. Louis, Batoche and Red Deer Hill. What was the great shame in this honourable Métis struggle?

Without our noble history, from a Métis point of view, we are nothing, and nobody. We are an ugly and disgraced people. Adrift in a White supremacist mainstream society, we are portrayed as people who are stupid and foolish, who do not know enough to come in from the cold, and to find out who we are nationally. It bothers the English and French Métis, but they suffer in silence. It tortured me continuously throughout my life. Looking back on my childhood, it was wretched and needlessly cruel.

Relief and Exploitation

In the 1930s, Government Relief was the only way of staying alive. Just fifteen dollars a month for the whole family! God Above, that was just enough for bannock and lard for most winter months—the typical Métis diet. No damn wonder Mom felt dumped on when she went to the store and shopped with her relief voucher.

"Could you buy anything you wanted like chocolate or tobacco?"

"Oh Geez, Billam, you're crazy! Mom was humiliated in the most hideous way. One Relief Officer, Casey Elliot, made people kiss the Bible three times and swear a pledge to Canada before they'd be given their relief voucher. Casey oppressed and humiliated the local people. Most relief authorities dehumanized individuals, especially the Métis. You would be cursed about wasting your relief on cigarettes and booze, even though you spent only a few cents on them. The "commander" [the person who dispensed relief food consisting] of frozen codfish and cheese at the boxcar parked on the railroad [and] threw that crap at us. That fish stank worse than fresh manure.

"Did you eat that gut-rot," asked Billam.

"Of course, we had to, we were starving. We cooked it in a big iron barrel in a fire outside, far from the house, before it was fit to take inside. It was like shit, but that was what the Liberal government doled out to us. We got solid blocks of mouldy cheese from the same filthy boxcar. The cheese looked like a furry animal lying still. At first, we were scared to touch it, but eventually we got used to it and even ate the mould. What a hell of a price we paid to prevent starvation and to protect our dignity."

J.M.P. McLeod was the rich storekeeper in town. It was rumoured that he tried to fleece some Métis people on their relief vouchers. He and his wife went to mass every Sunday. He gave a lot of money to the church and to the priest, the way to get right with God, or to have some say over the system?

"Dumbheads, that's what we were; [we] never quarrelled with government big shots." "Oh hell," Graham complained, "the problem is we never stuck together, always fighting among ourselves."

"It's those palefaces that get us to fight each other; and we're stupid enough to do it."

One evening, a couple of smart-alecks dared Billam and me into a fist fight— imagine—and we are first cousins! Those maniacs were standing around and shouting, "Pound the crap out of each other!" while laughing crazily. We should've turned on them and kicked their arses.

One afternoon, I was sitting at a table in the St. Louis beer parlour, with real men over twenty-one. "One beer here," I yelled. The bar attendant, Roland Benoit, came over to me in an ugly mood and shouted in my face, "Get the hell out of here. You are only eighteen." I was slowly taking my time when he grabbed my overalls and dragged me to the door and chucked me out. I picked myself up from the gravel and laughed. To hell with him. I'll buy a bottle from the bootlegger.

We worked like hell all fall for twenty-five cents a day. In spite of the terrible bosses, it meant wages to enjoy. Some of us spent it on booze for a good time.

"Are you telling me, Clovis, that story is true? You're such a bullshitter, I don't know when to believe you."

"No bull, Howard. That old bugger, Galloway, was hiding in the bush at the edge of the field and spying on his workers. When we stopped for a drink of water, he walked out from the bush and shouted, 'You're all fired!' We could not believe it, so we asked, 'When?' He shot back, 'Right now! He paid us for the days we worked, but of course he short-changed every one. We felt like beating the hell out of him, but we were on his property. They claim slavery is a thing of the past, but not if you work for old man Galloway."

"And the old fecker," interjected Archie, "spreads word around to other farmers that Métis are lazy and sneaky."

"That's how most of these farmers treat us. It's disgusting! We are a pitiful lot of buffalo chips. Yet, we call ourselves men. Like hell—we are gutless workers!"

"What can we do about it?"

"Nothing," said Clovis. "Anyway, it's great fun leaving that big belly standing in his field, worrying about finding other workers."

Pastimes

Like a bolt from the blue, Midnite raced from the barn, dragging his rope, galloped through the snow and down to the waterhole. "Damn that bronco," shouted Dad, "I'll crucify him!"

"Hitch him to the sleigh; that'll break in that cayuse (an Indian pony)!"

"Geez, boy, he's too wild. He'll smash everything."

"Come on, Dad, you've got twenty more."

Most Métis families kept many ponies on their farms. "Hitch him with old Queen. She's such a drag that she'll hold him to a walk."

"Yeah, hook them to the sleigh with the hayrack, and let them run wild in the open field. The snow's so damn deep he won't be able to race and jump. That'll be fun!"

Heading for the open field of deep snow, the bronco was gaining speed, scaring the bejesus out of Dad. Around the field they raced. They headed for the bush. "Quick, stop those nags," Dad shouted. Pulling with all my weight did nothing; they raced on. We were at the bush; big trees quickly appeared. Crash! The rack hit the trees. The sleigh stopped dead. It was a blast. Everything was smashed. The horses raced ahead with only the harness. We lay stunned at the bottom of the rack. The nags raced to the barn; we trudged back to the house.

I was so excited that I enjoyed a laugh. That was the kind of fun I wanted. That rebellious cayuse broke free from his masters, snapped free from the harness and machinery. Freedom. That was a lesson. Mom was watching from inside the shack. She had a good laugh. During supper, stories about Midnite were told from different views. It was better than bitching about hunger and poverty.

It was card game night. Dad chewed off a chunk of tobacco from his plug and mashed it in his mouth. [My sister] Olive squirmed. She hated dirty tobacco juice; she knew it would soon be flying around the room. She lit a small lamp and went to the other room. She grumbled about the horrible smell of pig feet boiling on the kitchen stove. I was trying to hang my putrid felt socks behind the stove, but one fell in the pan of soup. I picked it up and said nothing.

[My brother] Graham opened the door; violent wind and blowing snow blasted in. Within a second the house was like an iceberg. "In God's name, it's fifty below. It'll take a pile of wood to keep the shack warm tonight."

Mom was at the table shuffling the cards. There was nothing she and Dad loved more than playing cards. I had to fill in as a fourth when no one else was around. I preferred my homework to playing cards. Dad and I played partners, as he and Graham squabbled if [they were] partners. The coal-oil lamp was in the centre of the table, close to the potbelly stove; the light and heat had to be hugged. Card games were all the rage with Métis families, especially "King Twenty-Five". With it went rowdiness, [...] jokes, laughter and cutting wind.

I added up the tricks, "We've won, Dad, damn good playing!"

"Yeah, by cheating," snorted Graham.

"So what's a little cheating in this rotten society?" I laughed. "I won and that's what counts in our society."

Losers are deadbeats, dumb heads. Winners are smart, go-getters, successful. To win, you've got to be superior. Winning is everything, regardless of how it's done. That's the way to make it. Winning made for good daydreaming. Some dreams were wild and bizarre for a peasant Métis. Sometimes I worried that others might be able to read my thoughts.

We stopped cards while Dad fired up the stove. "We'll have to keep the fires on all night." The big pile of wood would be gone by morning.

Ill Health and Poverty

Our board beds [were] thin paillasses of crushed straw and covers of pieced quilts, coats, and maybe a horse blanket. The pig-feed smell filled the shack; it gave a sense of warmth. Wrapping myself in the clutter of covers, I yelled to Dad, from one champion [card player] to another, "Good night!"

We were awakened shortly by Mom's hurried talk "Dad is having an asthma attack again." She got us up, although there wasn't a helluva lot we could do.

Mom was trying to help Dad get his breath, fearing he might choke to death with that dreadful asthma. I helped Dad up and then walked him around the room. "He shouldn't have gone to the straw pile yesterday. It always chokes him up," said Mom in a panic. He seemed to stop breathing. "Oh God in Heaven, don't let Dad die," she cried. Graham started swinging Dad's arms in a pumping motion.

There was no medicine in the house, and no doctor within a hundred miles. Anyway, doctors never came to Métis homes, even in the beautiful summer days when they could drive their big cars, because they knew Métis had no money to pay fees. They gossiped that Métis did so damn much fighting they'd kill each other sooner or later, or die from too much boozing. And there were always new babies on the horizon to take the place of the dying ones. That was the common image most Whites had of us. How did they get those atrocious images? Our suffering went unattended. Oh Lord, for the day of reckoning. But how and when will it ever come?

"God Above, don't let Dad die." He was very precious to all of us. Life would be unbearable without Dad. It would tear the heart from everyone. This pitiful shack would become a coffin. I panicked. I couldn't stand it. I would die, too. Misery could not be greater, I told myself. I loved Dad as much as I hated the political system of old Mackenzie King. "If it kills Dad, I'll kill it or them, but who the Geez is them? To me, there is nothing but misery in this ghastly rural ghetto; the Métis are crushed to the bottom, trapped like rats."

Mom was throwing Holy Water on dear old Dad. Would God know if Dad dies, and would He care? Dad deserves better; he's a good Christian. I felt like I was walking with death as I helped Dad shuffle around the house. Finally, he opened his eyes and whispered, "I think I'm alright now."

"Oh, God bless you," exclaimed everyone with great relief. Mom made some weak tea, enough for all; then she said the rosary.

More wood was piled in the heater. Everyone except me went to bed. I took the first shift keeping the fires going. Daylight came, bitterly cold and stormy. The cold wind and drifting snow was terrifying. It was like the real world, hostile and deadly.

Mom got up and made porridge. "Dad's staying in bed today," she announced to all. Graham and me went out and did the morning chores. In the fifty-degree below we could hear every sound on the frosty snow for ten miles around. Graham complained it was cold enough to freeze the tits off a nun. Smoke from neighbouring stovepipes went straight up. You couldn't stand still for a minute without freezing [like] a snowman.

Mom made soup from yesterday's chicken fricassee. It was nothing as food, but it sure tasted wonderful. Then Graham and me went out. We sawed, split and carried in wood all afternoon for the three stoves that had to keep burning non-stop. No card game tonight, as coal oil had to be saved. We sat around the warm heater and listened to Mom tell her favourite stories.

The problems of her early life were more interesting to me. I disagreed with her claim that "the Métis were born poor. They'll be poor all their lives. God in Heaven made it that way. We have to suffer because sometimes we are sinful." I felt that she was telling us that someday we might have to live without her. That God would call her; that she may have some terminal disease that we don't know about.

"What do you mean by that, Mom?" I always had some hidden fear of losing Mom before she was an Elder. I felt that life without her would be impossible.

"Well, we don't pray enough, [we] miss a lot of mass."

"Does the Lord treat big-shot Whites better than us?" I was thinking of the rich storekeeper in town, J.M.P. McLeod.

Mom complained about me going out with Irene, a Métis girl in town. "You're too young to be serious over any girl."

"Oh, damn it, Mom, Irene's beautiful and she's a real honey. We're not getting married or anything like that!"

"Maybe she'll become a nun," Dad argued. "Her family is strongly Catholic, but that's okay, I won't complain. Irene is smart and a political young woman."

Mom felt that Irene was trying too hard to hold on to me as her lover. "I worry about you, son. I want you to be on your way to the top of the heap."

Mom got uptight when she thought her children got serious about a lover. What a helluva storm she made about Olive possibly marrying Albert. She kept herself in a miserable state for a long time. How the hell could we ever be anything else but scut workers. We can never train for anything else besides peons. A life shovelling shit is our fate. We might just as well be dead now. But who's brave enough for suicide?

Fixing Fence and Cutting Brush

Thank the Lord himself; the weather began to warm up—a signal for spring farming. Without doubt, Graham was a man of the soil, but definitely a second string farmer. He always horsed around, going into town to watch the train come in and go out, week after week. This would always get Dad all steamed up about his son diddling around and not getting the crop in. The weather was perfect for seeding, yet Graham preferred going to town. At times, I thought Dad was going to come unglued. Gradually he'd calm down—until the next train. Most train watchers would go to the post office and check for mail, but nobody ever wrote to us as we never wrote. No envelope and no stamps.

Fixing fence was the most damnable job. I hated it more than anything. The temperature in the summer would hover between eighty and ninety degrees for most days. The climate had changed a hundred and thirty degrees since winter. It was godforsaken hot and fierce work.

When Billam came to the house, I would talk him into helping me, making outrageous promises that I knew I could never keep. "You're off your nut, Howard. Do you know it's ninety degrees out there?"

"So what—it's the same every damn day. If the fence's not fixed, those dumb cattle will get into the wheat field."

"Listen, cousin, that bummed-out crop isn't worth saving. The grasshoppers will come in like a cloud and wipe it out in a few minutes, or it'll be choked out by those terrible sow-thistle seeds."

"Not a chance; we've picked thistle flowers for nearly a month."

"What good is that?" questioned Billam, "They're just as thick today."

"Yeah, like a field of golden daffodils, all sixty acres."

"Why don't you get your big brother to help fix fence?"

"Don't be an idiot; when did he ever fix fence? New posts have to be put in. And you know what that means. Digging holes with a post-hole auger; over two feet deep in that damn rock hard soil."

"Well, is there any other friggin' way to do it?" Billam complained. "Then we've got to string long lines of barbwire. That's like a tortured execution." **(AB)**

It was a great relief when it came time to go and cut brush and grade the road allowance. We had to work several weeks each summer to pay off the relief that we received during the winter. I felt like a real youngster on this job. Partly because I was treated as one. I was allowed the same rate of pay as other workers. No one received any pay or cash. It was credited to our debt against the farm at the municipal office. It was voluntary in the sense that the municipality or government would not send the police or army around to get you out to work. The part [that] I hated about the arrangement was that if residents did not go and do roadwork, they would not be denied relief the coming winter. A neighbouring family, where there was a father and three grown sons, lazed around all summer playing music, going to picnics and dances. Yet, they received full relief all winter. But in our case, Dad would not allow any unnecessary debt against his farm. Also, he had a sort of Protestant ethic about work.

Mostly, my job was cutting brush. My favourite job was setting fire to the big pile of brush that would be built up from the workers for the day. It was hard to get started because of the greenness of the brush. But once it got going, a huge flame would rise and the fire would roar in great gusts. It gave me an unusual pleasure to see this fierce fire roaring under my control. It was almost a personal thing. Each tree or brush represented some White great official who dominated us. I would stand back from the fire and yell, "Burn, burn, you bastard." Or it could be the general society in which we were presently living in. I delighted in burning it down. The horrible part of this job was the extreme heat from the burning sun.

For a workingman's son, nothing in life is laid out in advance; nothing is planned for your future. There is no road map to the future. There is no future; there is only a present and past. The future is ignorance. Dad is stupid about the future. He works in the fields and bushes and [in the] garbage, and always in the present. Son, like father, fights against his ignorance and frustrations about the present. He cannot forge ahead because there is nothing, only a vacuum, only emptiness, a nothingness. Besides, the present overwhelms him. The future is here and now. It will always be this way. Tomorrow is the same routine—ploughing, digging, cutting wood, and fixing fences. For the son, it is a long and torturous road, an unknown and unplanned one. It can only be planned within his own ignorance. There are no aims or goals. They have been poor and possessed nothing for too many generations […]. **(MISC)**

Politics and Identity

We were fixing fence by the river road, when Joe Slater came driving down the road in his Bennett buggy. He liked to show off his team of slick pacers. Dad and old Joe were rarely friends, although they lived only a mile apart.

Politics. That was the problem. Joe was a strong Liberal—a great supporter of Mackenzie King. Dad was just as passionate in politics, but he was a staunch champion of John Diefenbaker, [when he became] the Conservative leader [in the 1950s]. They could enjoy a short talk about the weather. But most topics drifted into politics, and shortly sparks would be flying.

"Why don't you fix your fence in cool weather," said Joe, smiling to himself. He was an arrogant English colonizer. Dad snapped back, "When have we had cool weather in summer?"

"Well, you should build a decent fence in the spring and not a pitiable fence that a chipmunk can knock down," said Joe pompously.

Outraged, Dad replied, "We don't have that much time. This hideous Liberal government forces us to cut and haul wood to town for payment of winter's relief. King's a dictator who puts the screws to the poor people."

"You're talking nonsense, Bill. The King government is the very best that Canada has ever had. It's the stupid people who make it terrible for themselves. It's your own fault if you're poor and having a hard time."

Dad was about to jump into the buggy and punch Joe in his Anglo mouth. "The government should never have allowed you puffed-up English immigrants into Canada," Dad snapped. Joe promptly pushed towards his crusade for himself.

"See what I mean, Billam? That old Geezer sees himself as superior to us, just like all the rest of those damn Europeans. They dump us into the toilet hole of humanity."

"I think you're making a mountain out of a mole hill," said Billam. "Settle down."

"Hold it, that is the most important and powerful point."

"Are you saying to me, Howard, that this European class causes a racial separation?"

"This is the real critical issue, because each ethnic-racial group hang-out among themselves. How many times have you been invited to the Begrand's, Tessier's, or Snell's?"

"I sure as hell wouldn't want to be invited to those hoity-toity places. I know where I'm not wanted."

"We are the workers who sell our arms and legs to those profit-hungry farmers because we've got no skills and no education. They look at us in ethnic images such as peasoups, welfare bums, and boozers. They gossip about us all the time in that language. Is it little wonder they never visit us on a social basis? They keep their distance."

"Do you really think these people see themselves as English, French, Scots, Belgians, and as superior to us?" asked Billam.

"Of course they do, because it serves their interests!"

Billam went on to say, "But we don't think of ourselves as Métis because nobody ever talks about us as Métis."

"But they sure gossip about us as dumb, lazy Halfbreeds. That is the biggest mistake and the worst thing against us and our heritage. We don't know who in the hell we are! We're just a bunch of ignorant peasants roaming about in our territory. I don't think that you understand the extreme importance of 'The nothingness of ancestry and heritage.' Our Métis history is so well hidden that we don't know anything about it besides our immediate relatives, and they don't know a helluva lot. Do you know if your grandparents are English, French or Scottish?"

"Of course not," says Billam. "But what does it matter?"

"Does this have any psychological effect on your growing up, and how you see and feel about our people? "

"I never think about things like that. I have only enough time to think about trying to get enough bannock for the day."

"Well, I know it sure as hell affects me. I feel stupefied and hopeless in trying to understand my own identity as a Métis."

"What in the hell is the matter with you, Howard? You are going nuts. You're so damn obsessed over this issue for nothing."

"Well, it puzzles me and I worry about it. I'm not satisfied without knowing the full history of my family and heritage. It's too much like a conspiracy, too quiet and hidden, and too many little ugly incidents that arouse my suspicions and curiosity. [There is always] the gossip of [being a] Halfbreed, [or] hearing my grandfather talk Michif. But, immediately, these things are weirdly silenced and hidden, followed by a cloud of shame, and we are left in a quandary."

"Oh to hell with all that heavy thinking," complained Billam. "Can't we go for a drink?"

I never imagined that thirty years later I would be passionately committed to my Métis nationalism, leading critical confrontations against the establishment in the cause for Aboriginal equality and justice.

There was no indication that I would later fight my Métis relatives in St. Louis who absolutely denied that I was Métis, and badmouthed me […].

Elementary School

I started school when I was eight years old. That was common for kids in our community because of the long distance to travel and the battles with [the] weather […]. Mom took me on my first day of school by horse and buggy. She dropped me off in front of the school. I was terrified. There were so many funny kids running around. I didn't want to stay. I wanted to go home with Mom. My cousin Tommy came to comfort me because he could see that I was terrified. That first day was long and scary. I was happy when it was time to go home. However, I soon came to enjoy school.

We lived four miles from school, which was usual in the 1930s. By the time I had finished grade eight I had travelled approximately 12,000 miles. In summer, we often walked. Sometimes we drove in a crude two-wheeled gig pulled by a pony.

In the nice summer days we took shortcuts through the woods and over the sand hills. Time seemed unimportant. We played and wandered the four miles each way. In spring, the hills were covered with crocuses and gophers. I tried to snare gophers at the edge of the hole as they popped their heads out. I rarely caught any. The municipality paid one cent per gopher tail. But I wasn't disappointed when I got none, as I figured gophers needed them more than I did. I preferred to pick a handful of beautiful crocuses and take them to the teacher, but by the time I arrived at his desk, it was covered with flowers.

In the 1930s, every day was rainless and hot, like a burning desert. The world for school kids was wide open and free to explore. There wasn't a house between our home and the school. As I walked, I let my imagination play games of all kinds. I strolled over the sandy hills with much pleasant daydreaming. I stretched my imagination to extreme fantasy. I would lose myself in a world of visions every morning and evening in hours of blissful wandering. Those were wonderful, fickle days. I hated the moment I reached school or home to wake from my flights of fantasy. Only the birds and little animals broke the silence. Not a house. Only an occasional human entered during those eight miles. In summer it was a heavenly walk through the woods and the rolling sand hills. Spring was best with its sudden burst of flowers, streams and birds. The mass of crows with their cawing joined the beautiful meadowlarks, blackbirds and swallows. It was a real song festival. Many birds and animals fought each other for front stage. Redwing blackbirds shot into the sky, showing their bright wings. Gophers scurried across the sandy mounds. The warm bright sun flushed everything into action.

Winter was a very different matter. There were drifts of four feet of snow and forty-below temperatures. Dad would take us to school in a homemade cutter. Stones that had been warmed in the stove oven were placed in the bottom of the cutter to keep us from freezing. The road had been filled in during the night by strong north winds. It was tough for the horses to break through drifts and pull the sleigh at the same time. Often, Dad stayed at the school for the whole day rather than go back home and return for us a couple of hours later. Thinking back on those days, Dad showed tremendous dedication and concern to give up much of his wintertime for the education of his kids. He had no way of knowing that we might not be retarded or that we might turn out to become cattle rustlers.

The Christmas concert was a big event in my school life. Often I played leading parts because of my boldness in [the] performance in Christmas plays. I knew Mr. Lovell had high expectations of me, and I wouldn't let him down; he depended on me. I liked being in the limelight and enjoyed applause from the audience. Usually I was chairperson, announcing program events with my booming voice. These things started me off for doing better. They created expectations that persisted throughout my life. It was during the years of elementary school that I created the driving force to move upwards. I was embarrassed at some of the local Métis' level of performance, education and menial life. **(AB)**

Psychopathology of Colonialism

At grade school, from my permanent seat, I prepared myself for a panic attack. I had to bring in the sense of, and the feeling for, reality. I stood up, reached for the window and opened it. The students or teacher asked, "Why open the window?" and immediately I would be forced to relate to reality. It worked every time for years. Or, I would pinch a student sitting next, and get an immediate sharp reaction. Preparing situations like that, and being on continuous guard, was a serious problem of my daily life. I thought and thought about this problem. I analyzed it to death but I never really solved it. Did it relate to our social economic situation? Of course it did!

We were not only peasants, but the poorest and lowest peons in the whole damn country, and the most snubbed family. Why were we, the Adams, scorned and despised by the White-cultured people of St. Louis? You recognized them by their appearance, manners, snobbishness, [and by their] discrimination against the low class. How stupid were the Métis! We pretended this, and pretended that, but we were only fooling ourselves. We pretended that everybody was in the same class. We did not make a distinction on the basis of race. Yet it was part of the social atmosphere. No one ever talked about different racial groups, which we were. In many [aspects] of our physical appearance, [it] showed [that] we were [part] of the Aboriginal race. We did not talk about different ethnic, social or cultural groups. Yet, as Métis we lived and associated as a tight extended family group, visiting only among our extended family relations. Never did the merchants, Marvin, or J.M.P. McLeod ever visit a Métis home, nor did Lefebvre, the garage owner, or Harry Grimes, the elevator agent, or the nuns or priests.

"Are you looking for the Adams?"

"Yes," said Hazel Boucher in her very official voice.

"Well, bang on the door, someone's in. Maybe sleeping."

"I only want to know if I need to vaccinate some who didn't have smallpox."

The door was opened. "Which ones need to be vaccinated?" she asked.

"I don't know," said Mom. "Why vaccinate?"

"So the disease won't spread." She looked into the house and showed contempt.

"Step in," suggested Mom.

"Oh, I can vaccinate them from here," as she stepped cautiously in the doorway.

Dad and I walked to the door and were vaccinated. As quickly as Hazel pulled the needle out of my arm, she packed up and quickly stepped outside. There was scorn on her face. I hated being looked down on. What the hell was so high and mighty about her?

"What the hell kind of person do you become?"

"A sort of zombie. If you don't act as [as a stereotype of the colonized], you'll suffer my fate. You may hold off until you feel you are mocked. To fight it any longer only puts you into this fantasy, this unreal world, and you lose not only your reality, but also your mind."

"Christ, is that the misery of colonization?"

"You bet. And only a helluva lot worse. But most of us submit to subordination."

"What does that mean?"

"Getting drunk. And that gives you a colonized Aboriginal without any further pretensions. But, if you stay sober, then you've got a lot of stupid acting to do, being silent and dumb. Just being real stupid, being shy and dumb."

"Otherwise, what?"

"Well, you take the road where you act as good or better than the colonizer. You don't subordinate yourself. You believe that you are equal to Whitey, or maybe even better. You give yourself confidence, you almost become cocky."

"Is that what you call 'ego'?"

"Exactly. Boy you're getting smart."

[…]

"What's non-reality, or what the hell you call it? It's nothingness. It's got no reality. A vacuum. Empty space. I can't find myself. My reality keeps escaping me. Only a misty nothingness exists. I'm nobody. Nothing. Only an image."

"How did you get this damn far with such an idiot mind?"

"Guessing and fooling, make-believe, bluffing. But mostly suffering, worrying frantically about the asylum.

I panic frequently, worried that I'll never be able to find reality. Then what would I do? Go totally insane and [then go] to the loony bin?"

"How often does this happen?"

"Frequently. And it can happen very suddenly and I have no control over it. That's what terrorizes me."

"How do you handle these crazy situations?"

"Desperately—whatever way is handy and possible. If nothing is nearby, I bite my arms or fingers until they bleed. I'll cut myself until I feel extreme pain [...]."

"How about drawing somebody else's blood? Or punching him in the gut, or wherever you feel?"

"That's useless, unless he punches me damn good."

"God, what a weird animal you are!"

"No damn different than most of the colonized fools in this ghetto. Only they don't admit it, or can cover it up. Mostly by drinking."

"Why do the Aboriginals drink so much?"

"It's obvious, for Christ's sake. This is what colonization does. More precisely, what suppression and superiority does [to the colonized]. We are forced into a semi-reality in the ghetto. We have to go into this psychological shit if we want to stay sane."

"But, hell, that's not sanity, that's a hideous existence."

"But if we don't sink ourselves into numbness or semi-craziness, we can't suffer it."

"Like what?"

"Drunkenness, being stupid, acting inferior, subordinating ourselves to the boss. Always being silent."

"Just a name, without a family history. Beyond grandparents and St. Louis it was [a] complete vacuum. You were totally lost."

"At times it was an obsession. I suffered from not knowing 'who I am' or 'where I was.' It was a helluva struggle to keep control of reality; it kept leaving me. I was suspended into a misty state of quasi-existence, of horror, where I am never to return. I seemed to be always on the verge of panic. Maybe I would never be able to connect with reality again."

"My panic would ease up somewhat for the moment, but I knew that it [would] not [be] gone for long. My brain and my visible surroundings were the battleground. It not only panicked me until I was able to get hold of reality in some form or another. Such terror exacted a never-ending toll from my sanity, [...as I tried] to stabilize myself in the shack. "

"I hated the silence and order in the room after supper. I was frantic that I would say something, or act foolish, that would be seen or heard as crazy. Insanity had overtaken me. I set up situations that demanded attention and movement by someone. Quietness terrorized me. Outside was the deep, deep snow and cold, cold weather—a winter that forced you to stay inside. The hellhole of a queer mind! How could I say it was anything else! I prayed silently for a quick death."

"The horror of existence! The dreadful pain of living! It has been agony since birth. It is that abominable despair, that half belief. Half the time it is the hazy unreal, a world of unreality, the non-conscious. A world without senses, a world of nothingness! The other half is still there—the world of reality. But such agony! Such despair! And for what? "

"The desperate struggle to keep in the reality of society. The mind wanders uncontrollably into the unreal world. My life is continuously in doubt and hopelessness. Am I in the concrete reality or [in] the unreal? Oh God, it is so agonizing and anxious! It is hell in the hazy unreal world, the continuous oscillation from real to unreal. Do you follow me? Oh, I know that you don't. No one has yet. They don't even pretend. It's so subtle, so hidden, so inward, so intimate, so existential."

"It's impossible to analyze. I have been to the best psychiatrists. They only take my money and mumble something about the libido. Like hell! I'm not creating a fantasy or a dream. Next, you will say that I have been drinking too much, and for too long. How can I explain it? I'm afraid that's impossible. Unless you have experienced that end of hell you cannot possibly know. And what good does it do to tell you? You cannot help. The concrete reality of my world fades into imagery. The concreteness has gone. It is now only a figment. Now I'm only a phantom. Gone with the reality of my environment is my body. My hands and feet are gone. Go ahead and pinch them, and, see […my] pain […]. But I don't give a damn about my body and senses; it's my consciousness [that] I'm concerned about. Oh my God, how desperate I become when this happens."

"How often does it happen?"

"There is no set time or period. It is always on the threshold of happening. And how do I bring myself back to reality? Hit my head; chew my fingers; cut my legs; blood must flow; sometimes I run, run and run until I collapse from exhaustion. My mind is never at rest. I know you do not understand.

"No, it is not a dream. It is not a fantasy. It is not imagination. It's nothing of that kind! That is your knowledge and your concepts! This is totally different."

How I hated those talks when I was a kid. Mostly they laughed at me, mocked me. An idiot. "It's nerves," they would say, "a nervous breakdown." And now, thirty years later, I know the cause of the problem, and I know that they could not understand. But now, I'm spiteful. I'm filled with revenge, hostility and disgust, the psychopathology of colonialism.

As an Indian, I was despised by the White community. But how was I to know then? And the other bitter half was [that] I accepted the stereotyped image of an Indian and integrated it into my consciousness. And I despised myself. I was forced to pretend that I was not Indian, pretend that I was White, and [adapted] all the manners of his style. Of course, I was anxious and desperate because I didn't know what the hell was Indian and what was White. From where I stood in those days: [I was] half on each side.

"Listen carefully. I was in a constant desperate experience."

"Why?"

"Because, because, oh my God, I was afraid of revealing my innate inferiority—my Indianness. I was terrified that my mind would lose control of my behaviour and allow my body to reveal my true self. Then I would be exposed, naked, an Indian, a despised and hideous Indian.

"Oh God, let my mind keep control," I would cry. I struggled so desperately with my mind to keep control.

What could be worse than being a colonized Aboriginal? What a horrid disease!""Of course, you can't see it; there are no open veins, no running sores, no twisted bones or ugly scars. No, it's not visible, it's not leprosy, it's not arthritis, it's not a hunchback, or a deformation. It's malnutrition, it's tuberculosis, it's smallpox, it's rickets, it's depression. Look at those black stubs of teeth, those sunken black eyes, those protruding ribs. It's not genetic. It's environment—political, [and] economic. But I was born into it. I internalized it. I grew into it; or rather, it grew onto me. It's like a barnacle—I've had it since day one. Yet it's unexplainable, it's beyond […] words […]. I can only tell you the pain is excruciating, it's a horror of existence. The agony is unbearable—but I cannot die—I am suspended in the agony of existence. Oh, the comfort of death—the ease of my mind—the quietness of my soul. But death defies me. Life it must be! The totality of agony, the completeness of horror! Life is so grinding, so crushing, so hopeless.

Yes, I helped lower the lucky ones in their shabby pine box six feet under […].

[It's] a world of shadows, of unreality, of non-consciousness, a world without direction, of nothingness. Yet the physical contours of my body were there. I felt them—squeezed them—cut them—opened them for the blood to run. Such despair, such struggle, such anxiety. It's the hell from reality to the unreal, the fantasy, [to] a phantom existence. [It's] the continuous oscillation between the two—and never knowing which is real. The mind moves from one to the other without notification—without a sense of change. It's so subtle, so inward, so hidden, so intimate, so alone.

Yet, in the beauty of the meadows, hunting for the cows—suddenly I would disappear in mind and consciousness—no feeling—no mind. I wandered—knowing not where—or how, without reality, without sense.

How I fought to hold onto my concrete reality—even the trees, the grass, the mud. I [was] terrified when I lost my concrete reality—and it was always threatening to fade and disappear—maybe forever. Where would I go—where would I ever end up—at the bottom of a lake and never [to] be found? Panic was pain [and it was] fully pressuring me. Life was a continuous frantic and terrifying struggle. I could not let the world fade into the imaginary, into shadows, into a pantomime. Is this a deformity? Is it idiocy; is it insanity? No, it's the hellhole of depression! There is no warning—it strikes like lightning, and I am wiped out of reality.

And with this transference to a state of pantomime was violence. Violence was part of the shadow life—the non-consciousness.

"What kind of violence?"

Anything, and everything that meant destruction and injury and pain to others. To rage and create vicious havoc! No one could—or so I imagined. Only death! A horrible death! But not before I left a sordid trail of destruction, blood and death.

But that is not all; there is more.

The loss of reality. Of course you don't know. No one else can know—only you, you alone. Because it is strictly your own private reality [that is] individual to you. It is only [by…] knowing in your mind and connecting it [with] what is around you, […] that it makes sense as to who you are, […where] you are, and why you are. I look, but I see nothing. All this fades into nothingness. There's just a misty cloudiness out there. There are no precise things or figures, only vagueness. It all blends into one hazy grey fuzziness. I cannot locate myself. You can't understand what the hell I'm saying. How can you, you bigoted Anglo colonizer? You know only the colonizer's world. You can never know the colonized. You cannot change. That's why you have to die: You and your system. But the death toll you take, you create. Millions […] die in your oppression. You say God is on your side. But time is on our side.

What the hell is real? Yeah, hell is the only reality. Everything else is unreal. My own body is only a shadow—no, a ghost. I can put my hand right through myself. Don't I have blood and guts? Where are those bones, as rickety and crooked as they are? Everything has disappeared.

A crazy bastard, that's what you say I am. Lock me up in the insane asylum is your answer. I know there are busy and crowded bughouses in the colonizer's society. They are part of the jail system. How do they differ? You can't tell me. Now I'm doubly terrorized. Not only have I lost my reality, but now I'm crazy, and will be hauled away to the nuthouse in chains, and put behind bars to rot in a damp dark cell, to watch the curious oppressors gaze upon me like an idiot. The terror haunts me, of going insane, [of] being an idiot. I cannot prove my sanity. I've dislocated my brain. My brain is not diseased. How in the hell can I prove it? How does anyone prove their sanity? The gangrene of your society has afflicted me. Born as a colonized is to be born with a kind of paralysis. You claim Almighty God blesses us with regressive and withdrawal behaviour. Like hell! You repress and squeeze us into a mould like a turd. Your myths make us into repulsive and repugnant creatures to be mocked and humiliated. And you have the arrogance to ask why we withdraw, retreat? It shows your complete lack of sensitivity. You are incapable of feeling. Why do I even discuss it with you? Because I have an uncontrollable compassion! You wouldn't know what that is.

I cannot stop from withdrawing. The slurs, the shit you throw at me pains me. It aches and aches. I hurt too much. I have no choice. There is no alternative. It is not a possibility. I cannot enter your society. I cannot penetrate it. It is only a hideous pretence. You shut me out absolutely and permanently. Then you pretend something else. What a cruel hoax.

But we are complex people, filled with humanity, desire, ambition and [have] needs for the better things of life. Things you take for granted from our exploitation. But the "larger society"– what a misnomer—invites us in and leads us to believe we are welcome. Just be like you and we will have no trouble entering the pearly gates into the mainstream. What bullshit! Yet that invitation becomes hope in our heads and hearts. So it messes up our heads.

At the same time, you make our society hideous, loathsome, grotesque—the worst sewer of the world. You make it a six-foot septic tank where we have to swim for our lives. I know. I've lived in it. I was imprisoned in it. You've crippled me and glued me to that shit hole. As my absolute commander, oppressor and mythmaker, you screwed into my head all these distortions and myths. You used all your weapons so effectively: your schools, church, court, and parliament.

Uncle Mederic McDougall, Beloved Halfbreed Historian

Mederic was to be such a big part of my life. I took to him very young. He was so lively, smart and full of fun. He was an intriguing young man that any kid would follow. He was my role model for more than fifty years. He appeared often at our place, especially when hunting. At once, the house became [full of] chatter and laughter. I liked his boldness and liveliness. His stories differed very much from the ones I heard from the rest of the family. They were exciting. I learned [a] different family history [...about] Métis heritage and pride [...]. "The Métis are the best hunters in Canada."

"You are always talking Métis.... Who are they?"

"Who, who? For Christ sake, you and everyone in this house, all your relatives!"

"Are Grandpa and Granny Métis?"

"Oh, hell yeah. And their parents, your grandparents. This place we live on is Grandpa Maxime Lépine's."

 None of us had ever heard of those ancestors.

"How do you become Métis?"

"You don't become Métis, you are Métis."

"I don't understand, uncle. When did I become Métis?"

"Geez, boy, you were born Métis. Your parents are Métis."

"Both?! You mean Dad as well as Mom?"

"Of course! He's an English Métis. Most of the people on the north side of the river are English Métis, Protestants."

This was a subject that I would follow up with uncle Mederic every time he came to our place. I would ask Mom and Dad over and over, but they just didn't know, or refused to talk about it. When I went to Grandpa's place, no one would say anything about being Métis. None of the relatives would talk about it. I could not tell if they just flatly refused to say anything about their ancestors, or that they really did not know anything. I was sure that Granny and Grandpa knew… because her grandpa had been a fighter for the Métis.

[…This] feeling […] was so strange. The word Métis seemed to cast a terrible sense of shame. To be Métis was something terribly sinful, sordid or wrong. It took me years to sort this out. I had to live the first twenty years of my life as a Métis in a Métis ghetto. With Mederic's help, I was able to understand the mixture of the different groups of people living in St. Louis, and in the surrounding districts. Since he was the only relative who spoke about the Métis, I could work on this puzzle only when he visited.

"What's wrong with Grandpa? Can't he tell me about Métis? He seems to be proud to be Métis, yet he says little."

"Yeah, he wears typical Métis clothes. When he dresses up in his big buffalo coat, tied with a bright red Métis sash, wearing moccasins. That alone says he is Métis."

"Yeah, but Grandma and the rest of the family do not like him doing that. They complain about him doing that." **(MISC)**

High School

When I completed grade eight, I was anxious to continue school, but grade nine was not taught at Gerrond school, so I wanted to take grade nine by correspondence and have Mr. Lovell correct my assignments.

One school board member, Alex McLeod, did not want me to attend Gerrond school for grade nine. He felt I should be dismissed from school. Dad was also a school trustee. A special meeting was called about my situation. I could attend the board meeting, but could not express any opinions. However, my presence was intimidating to McLeod. In the final decision, the third trustee voted with my Dad to allow me to attend school for grade nine. This was a great victory for me, as I felt it was my struggle and I had won a victory. [This was the…] beginning [of my struggle..] against the establishment.

Alex McLeod tried to boss the school board with his Nazarene religion. He was a drag on the social life of the Métis. He was always putting his Nazarene religion up front, ahead of education of the local children. He disallowed parties and dances at the school. He worked against the students' [desire to have the…] school as a pleasurable and fun-loving community.

"Hold up, Sid! What in the hell is the hurry? You're no damn scholar hurrying for school. You only waste time watching the girls' legs!"

"Being the teacher's pet, you don't have to study," said Sid. "You cruise through and get high grades."

"I damn well study as long as the coal-oil holds out. I spend hours at home over books. I love school. It's exciting and challenging, but the books are so damn racist. They make me sick in the gut." **(AB)**

Never, at any time did I forget that I was a Halfbreed. But one does not dwell on Aboriginality when three-quarters of the population are descendants of buffalo hunters and there are no WASPs dominating over the social zoo. Mr. Lovell was the only Anglo-Saxon. Apparently, we were indifferent or felt no pain about being colonized, as it was a kind of non-issue. He was never viewed or spoken of as a colonizer. The other one-third of the students were Hungarians and [were] unconscious of colonization. They flowed easily with the ethnic breeze, especially when [...] surrounded by flaming "Rielists".

I enjoyed school, especially [...] high school and then university. I was particularly fascinated by history. I was passionately curious about all the differences and divisions among the people in society [...]. I realized that these creations and transformations did not happen just yesterday. They happened a long time ago. But what were the forces in the world that established them in the order they are today? I was curious to know why I had become Métis—of mixed Indian and White blood—and why the White people discriminated against me. What the hell was so great about them that they were superior to me? They were so damn high and mighty that they made me feel as if I did not belong in a classroom. I was too stupid to understand anything.

At high school, the teacher, Eddy was explaining about the "discovery" of the New World.

"But, it was not a new world," I interrupted, "The Americas and Africa were old worlds. People had probably inhabited them before Europe."

"That is possible," admitted the teacher. "But we don't have any evidence to prove that."

"But what kind of evidence have we got to prove that Europe was a higher or more advanced civilization than the rest of the world?" I asked.

Slowly and with hesitation, the teacher replied. "Well, it is clearly written in all the scientific books. They also had ships that would travel the oceans, compasses and other sailing devices," the teacher answered. I quickly added, "And they had the gun and sword—their symbols of civilization," and my pal, Tony, added, "These were the tools of Christianity. Together, this made up European civilization."

"Do you know how many Indigenous people were slaughtered during the period of the so-called discovery and the civilizing of the savages?"

"No," murmured Eddy.

"In Mexico alone, ninety per cent of the Indians were killed by the civilized White Aryans from Western Europe. Genocide continued throughout the Aboriginal world for the next 500 years of the holocaust."

"Why isn't that written in the textbooks?" asked Tony.

"Because only the killers have written the histories," I answered.

"Then were is the truth written?" Tony questioned.

"It doesn't exist. These textbooks are filled with lies and myths."

The bell rang. It was lunch hour. Tony and I continued our discussion.

"It seems to me that almost any territory of people in the world could have been called civilized," I claimed.

"But we've got to admit that the Whites had superior technology, and by that I mean guns, weapons, and swords," Tony argued. "And also they had the natural desire or instinct to kill or murder all other people."

"And that's how they conquered the world. They captured millions of Indigenous people, transported them to other parts of the world, and made them slaves for their plantations, their industries or whatever. It's as simple as that," I concluded.

"From then on, the history of the Aboriginal people is told by White-European conquerors. That's why history is a package of stereotypes. Those racist bastards had a great imagination."

"After that it was an ocean of piracy eagerly hunting for wealth, mostly gold and precious metals. In Canada, those pirates were chasing the hides of the beaver and other fur-bearing animals."

"Those horny Europeans may have been catching animals, but they were just as busy screwing or raping the Indian women wherever they went."

"So a whole population of Métis soon sprung up across Canada."

"Right!"

School Sports

Dad's command was always the same: "Keep your damn mouth shut and don't run around like an idiot."

"What the hell did we come here for?" I thought as I ran to the playground. "We spent this morning at church silently praying. Isn't that the way we spend Sunday?" I helped unhitch the horses and tie them up to a tree in the shade. I looked excitedly at the crowd gathering along the edge of the lake. Youngsters were gathering at the ball diamond.

The French Catholic and English Protestant Métis regularly gathered at Hudson's Bay Lake on Sunday for a picnic after church services. Many of the families were related, and this was a time for visiting and gossiping. For the youngsters, it was [time for] sport, ball games and swimming.

"Hey, Howard," shouted Angus, "I bet I'll beat you today in the one hundred yard race."

"It's a bet! Remember, you lost last week, and you bitched about it. Blaming me for crowding you."

Uncle Mederic overheard us. "I'll referee the race again. Last week, it was almost a tie, but Howard was a slight bit ahead."

Locally, I was noted as quite an outstanding athlete. I was highly competitive in all races and sports. At home, I usually practiced in the evening when I had finished all my chores. On the road near the house, I had marked off the races and jumps. Although alone, I ran pretend races and jumps. I forced myself to take them in shorter time.

"That damn boy has got to work harder in the day," grumbled Dad. "If he's got that damn much energy, he can fix more fence in the daytime. He's always wasting time with that nonsense of racing and jumping out there by himself. Neighbours will think he's a real jack-ass."

"Ah, leave him alone, Bill," mumbled Mom. "He's enjoying himself. There's nothing else for him to do in this out-of-the-way place. He's got to make up his own games. There's no neighbours close enough to fool around with. He's not hurting anyone or anything." **(MISC)**

The years flew by, and I continued to make good progress at school. The spelling bees were a challenge as I strove to be the winner. I lost one important spelling bee to my friend Cecil because I misspelled "government." I enjoyed these challenges from my early school days. Also, sports became an important part of my schooling, which was encouraged by the teacher. I became a good athlete through the fierce competition at school. At Gerrond, in my beginning years, I began [playing] competitive sports, advancing to major field and sports days in other towns. The sports that I excelled in were fastball, the one-hundred yard dash and the gymnastic bars.

Sid mentioned, "It'll soon be time to get into shape for our big sports meet."

"That's great. I love all those sports games. I am not going to let anyone beat me in the races or jumps this year. I'll be the champion of the sports meet."

"Fastball games are the big winners," said Sid. "With Ross and me pitching, and you catching, nobody's going to beat our team. We'll take all the ribbons."

Mr. Lovell showed great interest in my participation through his own involvement and enthusiasm. For example, on one sports meet morning, he drove to our farm pasture in his car, picked me up and took me to the sports day. It was good for the school's reputation, besides my own, because I won half the total points for the school. According to the students, I was a motivating force for school sports in general.

Mr. Lovell favoured me—somewhat. I wasn't a suckhole, but I liked being at the top of the heap. After the summer of 1938, when all the fifteen-year old boys dropped out, I became the playground commander. I [then] became captain of the fastball and football teams, and the general of the playground. Young Métis students accepted order on the playground from me. But gradually I became too bossy, [and was] always the star on the winning teams. Mr. Lovell realized that I had become a poor loser and a poor sport.

One noon hour, when I had "our" team play against a pick-up one, he came over and umpired the game. Our team had excellent pitchers. Ross McLeod and Cecil Corrigal threw fast pitches with so much spin that a batter rarely hit them. Behind the plate I made all the calls for play. I had continuous rapid-fire balls, shouting and directing the outfield players. Ross or Cecil and I fanned many batters.

Sometimes Cecil would take over the mound. He had a very fast ball, but not always the best control. But we were winners. Ross would fire a fast pitch over the plate and I'd shout, "Strike, he can't hit what he can't see," but to my amazement Mr. Lovell called it a ball. I was outraged. Some were good pitches. According to my eye [they] should be strikes, but the teacher [walked the] batter […]. I was furious. This went on with several batters, until they had more runs than our team. I blew up, stomped around, and threw my catcher's mitt on the ground. In a fury, I threatened to pull our players off the field. It was a horrible scene, the very worst in poor sportsmanship. We finished the game, but I was a basket case.

As soon as we assembled in the classroom, silence fell heavily. Something was forthcoming about my behaviour. I slumped deep into my desk and tried to hide. Mr. Lovell gave a moral lesson on [my] loudmouth arrogance and poor sportsmanship. Although I was dreadfully ashamed, I could not escape or deny my behaviour and poor sportsmanship. It was a lesson that I never forgot, but it had the desired effect. From then on, I was a more reformed player on the playground. I could still play excellent fastball and football, but with a co-operative attitude.

That lesson was one of the most powerful, and it carried forward in all dimensions of my life. That was the outstanding quality of Mr. Lovell. He affected and shaped one's behaviour and attitude towards life. He was not only an excellent teacher: he was a giant in ethical principles […] in every dimension of educating youngsters. I worshipped him. From Mr. Lovell, we learned not only arithmetic and grammar, but proper social behaviour, sportsmanship, cooperativeness and true humanity towards people.

No rich kids came to our school, only dirt-poor English-Métis, except for a small group of Hungarian kids. They were good students, friendly and hard workers. These cultural groups mixed together extremely well. Close friendships developed between the two groups. Later, mixed-marriages happened.

In the winter, snow, sub-zero weather and blizzards were fun if one had no responsibility. During fierce blizzards in winter at forty below, school closed. For us, it wasn't great fun because we were happier at school than mucking around in our two-room shack. Everyone would get restless and grumpy. As kids, we played in the snow, tumbling in snow tunnels four feet deep [and…] were protected by a covering of ice […]. Our tunnels led to different rooms, called "home plate", "dream room" and "war room". "Lordy, we've got a palace down here," said Archie. "Maybe we could reach the school through tunnels."

Each day of school was a big triumph in book learning. Most boys dropped out of school when they reached the age of fifteen. That was good enough for success in a primitive world. No one had ambitions at becoming a doctor, lawyer or teacher. Our aims were low key, like picking rocks or stooking [wheat].

Finally, spring came, and we were back at school full time.

We had to ride horseback for a couple of weeks. Dear Old Queen was a miserable rough ride. Graham sat on the front, and myself in the back. When she galloped, I would puff big breaths and blow into Graham's ear. "If you can't ride any quieter," said Graham, "I'm going to throw you off." I bounced around dangerously. My arse would get sore. Later, when I was the only [...member of the] Adams family attending school, I rode on horseback [since there was] not enough snow for the cutter and too much [of it] for the buggy. Dad crabbed like hell about me using a horse for school. To him, I was just shucking away my time. Every morning when he went to feed the pigs, I would rush to the barn, saddle Lady and race off to school. "Where is that crazy kid? " he roared to Mom. She smiled to herself, "I don't know," faithfully supporting me going to school. Mom didn't have much wisdom about education, but to her it was god-like. She made a religion of education.

"If I catch that crazy kid running off to school, he'll have his arse hanging out." But by the time I came home after school, nothing was said. It was time to look for cows. They had free range, so they could be anywhere in the province.

It was stooped labour from spring to fall, making long ditches in the soft soil with the hoe, and then planting seeds for the vegetable garden. There was almost one acre of potatoes. As soon as they came up, the bugs came in and we went back to stooped labour, picking off the bugs. They travelled in swarms, so it was hard to keep ahead of their destruction. Every bug was removed one at a time and killed in coal oil. The garden was, after all, our storehouse of food for the long winter. Everything was dug up, picked, cleaned, sorted and stored in the shed.

Schooling at Gerrond ended with my completion of grade nine. I would go on to high school in St. Louis. There was no doubt with Mom as a promoter. I said good-bye to Mr. Lovell, the greatest man I would ever know in my life. I had been under his wing for nine wonderful years. But high school was something to look forward to. The girls were my age, [and were] gorgeous and exciting.

School was not that tough, but you still had to work steadily to prepare for the exams in June. But there was still much fun, as most students were Métis. I studied regularly through the year, and then slugged off in June. In July, our grades came from Regina [...]. I didn't worry much because I felt that I had passed the exams. School was my forte. I passed grades ten and eleven easily. **(AB)**

Tony Questions History Textbooks

Right off, Tony questioned why historians called it the Riel "Rebellion." He wasn't challenging Mr. Ellis, but more the scholars who wrote the history books. The teacher gave a simple explanation of Louis Riel leading the Métis against the constitutional government of Ottawa. But this seemed incorrect to the students. In the first place, it was a people's resistance movement against the ruling regime at Ottawa, which was not a constitutional government by the people of the Northwest. Instead, it was an absolute government of eastern businessmen. Tony felt that since the struggle involved both the Indians and Métis, it should properly be called "The Redman Revolt of 1885." Mr. Ellis continued with the traditional explanation of how Métis and Indians were on the warpath about their land, and that Louis Riel stirred up rebellion. Being descendants of Halfbreed families of Batoche, whose ancestors had fought in the "rebellion," [and] in which information [about the resistance] had been passed down, the students were doubtful of the textbooks.

First, the discussion was largely between Tony and Mr. Ellis, but gradually the students became actively involved, as each excited the other towards vigorous discussion. Nancy claimed the Ottawa rulers and their friends wanted the prairie lands for themselves in order to build the Canadian Pacific Railway. To do this, they had to drive off or round-up the Indians and Métis. After the federal government had slaughtered all buffalo in a very systematic kill, the Natives were weak and powerless, thus easy victims for reserves, colonies and country ghettos.

Mr. Ellis interrupted to argue that the buffalo kill was not likely an intentional scheme, but he didn't want to make a case for it. According to Tony, millions of buffaloes had been killed for their tongues, horns and bones, which were never used. The Ottawa regime used this market as a "fence" for getting people to take part in the national animal massacre.

Joan asked, "Why didn't the federal government rulers just kill Indians and Métis, like the British had done with the Beothuks of Newfoundland?"

"Because," answered Louie, "the rest of the world wouldn't have let the Canadian government get away with it. Otherwise, it might've been a blood bath. The rulers had done it before, why would they hesitate to do it again?" Everyone shuddered at the thought.

Mr. Ellis explained that the land was wanted for new immigrants, but Jim added that these settlers wouldn't come to the prairie as long as Indians and Métis roamed freely because Europeans would have the same racial images as Canadians. So, before they'd buy land, the Natives had to be hidden out of the way.

"Do you think the Native people realized these things at the time?" asked Mr. Ellis.

"They sure did," emphasized Tony, "and it frightened them. The government's policy wasn't simply 'Let the Indians die out,' it now became, 'The only good Indian is a dead Indian,' and that went for the Breeds, also."

Irene explained how the Mounties were established and sent to terrorize the Métis in Batoche. Although the police tried to make the Halfbreeds believe [that] they were there for Native's protection, the Breeds were smarter than that, for they recognized the police for what they were: brutes of force. According to Lionel, the "protection gimmick" was nothing but a racist slogan used by White rulers to hold down Native people. Those nonsense stories about the so-called famous Mounties were sweetheart myths written by palefaces who'd never felt the fist or club of the Mounties, like he had, and many other Breeds he knew.

According to Tony, the textbook story about Riel leading a rebellion didn't include facts about White farmers and workers organizing against the Ottawa rulers in 1884, and actually taking up arms against them. This large group of restless White people were the rebels the federal government was really worried about, for fear of them breaking away and joining the United States, or forming their own country. And all these big businessmen of

Ottawa were too ambitious to let the Northwest go, so they organized the Mounties and the army and sent them to Saskatchewan. Since it wasn't easy to get Canadian people to fight against other Canadian people, Ottawa pushed the disturbed Indian and Halfbreed situation into open hostilities. The teacher asked Tony if he had any historical evidence for this explanation.

"Not much, besides what I've read, and what my grandparents told me. But they were told a lot by their parents, who fought against the enemy troops." This was another sore point. The history books told of the so-called loyal soldiers—loyal to the Ottawa regime, but against the people of the prairies. They told of the Métis scout, Gentlemen Joe McKay, as brave and glorious because he fought for the Whiteman. But in the Indian-Métis nation, McKay is considered a dirty traitor; any man who betrays his own people the way McKay did is the lowest.

Mr. Ellis wanted to know that if Tony's argument was true, then why did the prairie farmers and workers stop fighting the federal government?

"Because the federal masters were smart; that is, you can do smart things when you have the power. So they gave in partly to the White people—but nothing that would harm their power or profits—but enough economic advantages were given to quieten them. Ottawa then moved ahead in full force with its troops against the Métis," explained Tony.

According to Paul, it was possible to excite White people against Indians and Métis because Canada is a racist society. In such a society, it is possible to get White people to destroy a minority race because there are strong underlying racial feelings and they need only to be aroused, similar to the way in which Ottawa whipped up racist sentiments in 1885. It was the only racist war in Canada, but as [with] all racist wars, it was exceedingly savage, vicious and hideous. "It will be a big surprise to all Canadians when the real facts are known," concluded Paul.

Mary described how the Halfbreeds throughout Saskatchewan in 1885 were tortured, terrorized and jailed; their homes were ransacked and burned to the ground. Excitedly, she argued that a feeling of hate and hostility burned deeply into the hearts of the Indians and Halfbreeds in 1885, and that it is still there among many today. Lionel, who was interested in weapons, explained how the Gatling machine gun, which was brought from the United States as an experiment, was a powerful and murderous weapon that sprayed bullets [...at] Native people, killing many innocent women and children.

Mr. Ellis was not in full agreement with the students, but he felt they were too determined and [too] aroused to [be] challenge[d].

In conclusion to the day's lesson, Tony said, "The soldiers occupied our Native settlements in 1885, and have done so since that time. The big-shot rulers at Ottawa made us the objects of scorn, ridicule and hate that we have never been able to escape. Making us less than third class citizens, the federal government has used outrageous violence on us almost continuously. When they use violence, they call it law and order, but if we try to protect ourselves, they call it massacres or rebellions." As a final comment, Tony added that *they weren't attacking Mr. Ellis or his textbooks, but it was only fair that he should hear their side of the story. As soon as he'd finished saying it, he was sorry, for no doubt the students would accuse him of "suckholing."*

On the way home from school, Tony thought about the afternoon's discussion, and about how the school teaches such terrible lies about the Indians and Halfbreeds. He could use the word "Halfbreed" freely, now that he was away from the teacher. Tony knew a lot about the Rebellion because his great-grandfather had been one of the leading rebels in the war council as well as on the battlefield. After the revolt, his great-grandfather had been captured by enemy troops, charged with treason, and put in jail for seven long years. But the Parker family were actually ashamed of this fact, so very little was said about the revolt. The government had been able to get all the people to believe that the rebels were savages, murderers and maniacs. Even the Indians and Breeds believed this. **(TB)**

Howard/Tony Organizes Student Protest

Métis feeling was strong. Eddie Vandale, a French-Métis, was an excellent teacher. He taught for thirty years in St. Louis and surrounding districts. I was fortunate to have a Métis teacher in my last years. At the end of grade eleven, Eddie joined the Air Force, so we were without a teacher for grade twelve. **(AB)**

The following Friday afternoon, Mr. Ellis said he had an important announcement. "I joined the Air Force a few months ago, and yesterday I got my call-up, so I'll be leaving right away."

Immediately Tony asked, "Who is going to take your place, sir?"

"The new teacher will likely be Mr. Terry, the retired fellow who substituted here before," explained the teacher. The students groaned. **(TB)**

The school board was very lax in getting a replacement. Days went by and no teacher, nothing was happening. Suddenly I suggested to the students that we have a public protest against the board's inactivity. They not only agreed, but they went into action right away, collecting pieces of cardboard from the cellar, making huge signs with slogans such as "Education: A Right" and "School Board Useless." As a group, we marched around the town, carrying our signs and shouting to attract the attention of local people. It was an exciting [time]. **(AB)**

Tony suggested that they should protest against Mr. Terry being hired as the regular teacher because he was such a poor [educator]. One student complained he was deaf, while others said he couldn't do math.

"We deserve better," demanded a grade twelve student. Some students claimed the school trustees wanted to hire a teacher who cost little money. Anyway, they didn't believe that a high school was very important, and they might take the opportunity to close the school. After a short discussion, it was agreed some action should be taken to impress upon the trustees that students couldn't be pushed around. "Let's organize a protest to show we have rights which must be respected," suggested Tony. However, certain students thought it

might get them in trouble. Ignoring these comments, Tony offered to make signs from junk in the old basement.

"Do not make signs on school time, otherwise it'll look like I sponsored it. And don't demonstrate on school time," warned Mr. Ellis. The following Friday afternoon was agreed upon as the demonstration day. The trustees were holding a meeting in the town hall that afternoon. "It'll be an excellent time to parade around the hall," argued Tony. During the week, the students looked more and more to Tony for leadership, which he accepted. On Friday afternoon, the students assembled in the classroom and discussed the demonstration route. Placards were selected as Tony gave the necessary instructions. Only a few students refused to join. They marched down Back Street, over to Front Street and down it, from end to end, and [then] back to the town hall. They paraded around it, and then stopped for a short rally. After this demonstration, they retraced their march around town and displayed their signs. Since it was near train time, many people were hanging around. A lot of shouting took place, but mostly in good fun. Everyone went home feeling satisfied about the protest. **(TB)**

I enjoyed promoting and organizing the demonstration against the establishment so early in my life. Our demonstration got immediate action. **(AB)**

But, next day, the school board was roaring mad. They phoned Mr. Ellis and demanded an explanation, but, as he had said, it had nothing to do with him.

"Who, which students?" demanded the board chairman.

The trustees wanted to see Tony Parker, but the students argued that everyone was to blame. Therefore, a hearing of all members was necessary. Finally, it was agreed that a committee of three students, Tony and two others, would meet with the trustees. These young people had worked out an arrangement with the local nuns in the meantime, that all of them from the high school would be able to finish out their year at the local Catholic convent—that is, if the trustees insisted on hiring an unqualified teacher. However, as expected, the school board refused both on the basis of high costs. The committee accused them of hedging and using weak excuses. Tony pointed out to the board that if they insisted on hiring a retired teacher, the students might boycott the high school. This greatly angered the trustees.

"That's their loss, young man, not ours," snapped trustee Souci.

"There's a law about going to school for the younger students," barked the chairman.

The board members were greatly agitated about the demonstration, and they certainly didn't like Tony's militant attitude and language. It was his last year, and they were fully aware that he intended to complete high school in a few months. The trustees were sure they had him where the hair was short. Tony knew he had a lot to lose, but he was no pushover during this negotiation. Sure, the board might be able to make trouble for him, but he had an obligation to defend the rights of students. Weren't they entitled to a proper education and a qualified teacher? At the conclusion of the meeting, Tony repeated, "We will not accept an unqualified or retired teacher. We'll demonstrate again or boycott the school. The choice of a new teacher has to be decided [...by] all twenty-four students. The only alternative we'll accept is to be allowed to go to the convent. That is open to us—the nuns will teach us for the remainder of the year. We stand united on these terms."

The chairman was enraged. Pointing and shaking a finger at Tony, he said: "Parker, you're a fool. You're a menace to the school. We shoulda kicked you out to hell'n gone a long time ago. Don't you damn well come here and try to tell us what to do. If you've got nothing more sensible to say, then get the hell outta here right now!"

All three students left without further words. Tony knew that he'd shaken them up, and that pleased him. He walked out feeling victorious and elated. He never expected they'd have a long arm to reach him again, for he'd cover his tracks carefully now.

The old convent at St. Louis, SK where Howard Adams received his high school education, September 1987—a year before the building was demolished. Photograph Courtesy—Hartmut Lutz.

A couple of urgent board meetings were held in the next week. Rumours were flying high, but the students remained firm. Nothing was being settled. Finally, the Superintendent of Education was called in. The students were wild with excitement when it was announced the next week that all students would be permitted to attend the convent for the remainder of the term, starting right after Easter. Of course, Tony was overjoyed with the victory. This gave him great encouragement about his ability as a leader. Politics quickly became his first love. Maybe his mad dream about being a politician wasn't so wild after all. Confidence and boldness were now in every step he made, and in every word he uttered. He'd tasted victory, and it was sweet. His reputation as a militant and radical leader skyrocketed, and he was certain he could live up to it. **(TB)**

The school board went into action. All high school students were to attend the Catholic convent. A great break, as the nuns were excellent teachers. The major objection was that boys were segregated from the girls.

For me, it was okay going to the convent because I was familiar with the Catholic Church, priests and its life. The sisters were super teachers, a good thing because grade twelve exams were mighty tough. I made my highest mark in algebra and lowest in English (damn nearly failed it). It was my luck to have Mother Mary Vanee as my principal teacher. **(AB)**

Tony Steps Out of Place /Tony Finishes High School

Most of Tony's life was now focused on his studies. Although he was a pretty good student, he wanted to do better. He always had a secret desire to beat White students. He never questioned why, and he never felt more confident about doing it than right now. So he decided to study real hard in the next few weeks for the coming examinations.

Mamma protected him from Pappa and Gilbert by explaining that he was not feeling well, or that he'd get upset at quarrelling. It worked, as he was left alone.

Tony got a little more help one afternoon as he was cleaning up the teacher's desk, when he found the Social Studies exam. Quickly, he copied it, and then replaced it. Pappa would've been very angry if he'd known, but Tony said he was studying for a few minutes while resting. On the Easter exams he did very well. Naturally, he made an outstanding mark in Social Studies. After the teacher congratulated him, Tony said the exams were difficult but fair. He dared anyone to call him a suckhole. As soon as report cards were handed out, it was learned that Tony had beaten all White students. At first they didn't believe it, they had to see his report. Obviously they didn't trust him.

"Someone's cheated, that's for sure," exclaimed a White girl.

"Suckholing pays off," shouted Slim.

"Or else he's threatened the teacher," complained another.

"How'n the world could that big, dumb ox get such good marks?" questioned a White pal.

A White girl who was always at the head of the class said bitterly, "Whoever heard of a Halfbreed being smart?" and a student who had opposed the demonstration shouted, "He got those high marks for leading the protest march."

The White kids buzzed around Tony's report, uttering insulting remarks. But words of ridicule and abuse only bounced off him. He stood there like a champion in his moment of glory. But as they walked away, one by one in anger, it began to phase on Tony [...that the] White students become jealous and outraged when beaten by a Halfbreed. It dawned on the other Breeds, as well, for the first time, that school success was the exclusive world of the Whites', a symbol of their superiority, which Breeds must recognize and stay out of. The Redman has his place in school, but at the bottom. Tony had gotten out of place. Would he now have to pay for it? A dreaded thought.

However, at the moment he was riding high—on a winning streak and the students' insults and mockery couldn't dampen his spirit. He seemed unshakable at the top of his pinnacle. He felt he could afford to be charitable and considerate to the lesser and weaker now. Should he rub it in?

He waved his report card around and shouted, "Everybody, everybody, see the workings of a Halfbreed brain." He knew it was arrogance, but he didn't care. "See what a Breed does with Whitey's history. Think what he'd do with his own history—write history books!" He raved on: "Does any student want coaching by a Redman?"

To make sure he drove home the point, he stated loudly, "This report card is the brain work of a stupid savage."

The students became enraged. They tried to answer with insults, but Tony paid no attention to them. They left amid shouts.

Things changed suddenly. Tony never expected to be attacked by the same students who only a couple of weeks dedicated their support behind him. The White kids now regarded him as an aggressive, loud, uppity, smelly Breed. Yes, he wanted recognition, but as a student or a leader. Tony was happy it was Easter holidays. He tried to forget, but the ridicule of the students rang loud and long in his ears. Their mockery plagued him. Maybe the change in schools would help, but that was only wishful thinking.

After the holidays, the students simply took up where they had left off. They tormented and mocked Tony, and made his life painfully miserable. They laughed at his answers in class, and organized systematic harassment. It bothered Tony in the most agonizing ways, to the extent that he began to hate school and even thought of quitting, but Mamma kept after him to finish. His attempts at friendliness were scorned and jeered. Gradually, he was being broken and becoming a pathetic figure. Everything was slowly shattering.

Complaints from local citizens continued to come to the trustees expressing anger about the students' senseless protest. If they had nothing better to do, they should've been home helping their parents. And students who don't want to study should be kicked out. The White people weren't going to stand idly by and let a Halfbreed ruin their school. But Halfbreed parents threw their support behind the demonstration and Tony as the students were now going to the Catholic convent. Local businessmen began to see Tony as a radical agitator. Protestants were heard to say, "I just knew this would happen as soon as we let those Halfbreeds into our schools. I was against it in the first place."

Pappa was very angry and ashamed as he couldn't go anywhere without being told about his troublemaking son. On the other hand, Mamma encouraged her son to continue fighting, as she believed he was completely in the right. That enraged Pappa, and home became hell more than ever. Finally, a public meeting was called by the school board. The powerful White Protestants were there to fight against the masses of Catholic Halfbreeds. Tony was forbidden to attend and Pappa refused to be seen there. Some say it was one of the bitterest religious battles ever fought in the West. It was ruled that Tony would not be allowed to take part in any school activity, apart from his studies. Very definite rules were made for him. Disobedience meant immediate dismissal; no explanation was needed.

The nuns were good teachers. They knew their subjects well, and seemed to enjoy teaching. Sure, discipline was tough, but that was expected. Although there was no segregation of Whites from Breeds, the girls were kept apart from the boys, and this type of segregation bothered Tony as much as the other type. They couldn't even play together at noon hour, so the older boys sat around and swapped dirty jokes.

Tony became very melancholy. He brooded a lot over being rejected and scorned, and finally went into a depression. Because he was so quiet, dejected and sad, Mamma became worried. With some help, she was able to take him to a doctor in Prince Albert. To Tony, the doctor was an ignorant old man who couldn't understand anything about being a Redman. He prescribed some pills and a rest. Maybe it should be a rest from life altogether, thought Tony, for this he could use. Life was quite unbearable; his nerves were raw and jagged. The blues continuously hung like a heavy black cloud over his mind and heart. It was like a ten-ton load on his shoulders. The occasional stroll into the wilderness and [shedding] tears in solitude helped.

The damn Halfbreeds, their ugliness and baseness; their shacks and shabbiness all pulled him down as a disgusting and contemptible human being. He could never be anything else as long as he was one of them, and as long as they and their culture remained so revolting. Yet he could not raise the whole nation and all the people by himself, even if he was educated. **(TB)**

In wintertime, I walked across the frozen river and teamed up with my schoolmates, Louie and Aurore Boucher, to walk the one and a-half miles to school. Then home again. Louie was lots of fun, a practical joker, and Aurore was a charming beauty in her rather shy way.

I got through grade twelve with good grades, except English. The King's English was difficult for the Michif. **(AB)**

Jean's love and tender consideration was indeed a blessing. It was real love, a passionate love, yet not foolish and romantic. It was sincere and genuine. [As was] the beautiful experience of being together, sharing each other's sadness as well as happiness. Tony would always meet Jean outside the school gates and walk home with her. They were spending a lot of time together, mixed between studying and lovemaking. Mother Superior warned Tony about the immorality of his friendship with Jean, but this had little effect. He got along quite well with the nuns, for he didn't blame them for his prison-like school, or for the loneliness and bitterness of life. "It's them," Tony would say with a wide sweep of his arm. "It would serve them right if I burned down their damn public school, but Pappa would get blamed."

He passed his exams with an average grade, below many of the White students. Suddenly they were his friends again. Doubtless he was back "in his place'" and this was the basis of his friendship with the Whites. Maybe the Halfbreeds were smart in not fighting and just accepting their fate. Tony said good-bye to the Sisters and thanked them for their excellent instruction. High school was now behind him. What was ahead was a big mystery, and Tony had reasons for fearing it. **(TB)**

3. Mountie Years

Howard Joins the Mounties

One day at school, we had a visit from [a member of] the RCMP. He gave a convincing talk about the greatness of being a Mountie. He looked so courageous in his bright red serge jacket, blue breeches, high top boots, spurs and the special Mountie hat. How exciting! I knew then and there I was going to be a Mountie. After graduation that summer, I went to Prince Albert and signed up to be a Mountie. I had to pass a tough written exam and equally tough physical. I worried that I might be rejected because I was not tall enough. I just made it: five foot nine.

As I left home on that cold November morning, I knew that to Mom [...], the manner and tone of my voice said I would likely not return. Although she kept her children around her for nineteen years, she didn't expect to keep them nearby forever. But she was not prepared for the day one would leave and begin the rupture of the family.

During that night I tossed in my bed and daydreamed of the glorious world that lay ahead for me. Mom was not asleep. I could hear her soft sobs and cries. I knew what it meant. How very much that pained me. Nothing hurt as much as Mom grieving. How I wanted to go and tell her that I would not leave, but I couldn't. I knew I was leaving. Mom wouldn't want me to stay.

Everyone was up early that morning. We ate our porridge in silence. Words would only bring tears. How close we had become as a family. The years of grim struggle for survival had brought us together as a tight single unit. One member was now shattering that family, leaving a gaping hole that could never be filled. It was very heartbreaking.

On that cold November morning of forty degrees below, I dressed in much of my clothing [...]. Mom helped me get dressed. She couldn't resist bothering and fussing. Tears flowed; it was the loss of her son. A son she had raised to be a local farmer [...], who would raise the best ponies, grow the best gardens and barley crops. He'd marry his sweetheart Irene and raise a beautiful family that would be near her every day. She'd watch them grow up and share their love. But all that was shattered now. She was facing the worst. Her dearest son was leaving her home, going into a foreign world, brutal and cruel. I never really said good-bye to Mom. There are certain things that are too unbearable and painful.

Mom was so right: I never returned. Oh sure, I came home occasionally for a few days visit, but I never stayed. Mainstream [society] caught my fascination and I often spent my holidays with a White girlfriend. My only consolation was that I wrote regularly to her.

Howard/Tony Arrives at the RCMP Depot, Regina, Saskatchewan

On a wet morning, I showed up at the Mounted Police training centre in Regina. All the property I owned was in a small cardboard suitcase. While carrying it up the long stairs, it fell apart from the drizzling rain. Looking down, I noticed my long johns dragging. I nearly ran away and denied they were mine. Quickly, I gathered the woollies and tucked them under my arm. The many huge buildings terrorized me. It looked like I had bitten off more than I could chew. But there was no turning back now. As I pushed against the huge wooden door, the inside sight petrified me even more: Mounties everywhere.

I shuffled to the counter that said "Recruits Admission." At the desk, an officer smiled and asked, "Are you wanting to sign up?"

"No. I'm already signed-up and [have been] accepted into the RCMP." It sounded great. "I'm reporting for training." In a quivering voice, I inquired, "Is this the right place?"

"Yes. Have you got your official papers?"

"Yes, sir. They are right here," as I grabbed my pockets. He glanced quickly over them, and then gave me more forms to fill out. I put my "John Henry" where I was told. He gave me a studied look. His expression said: "My God, the Force is really scraping the bottom of the barrel these days."

"Report to the Khaki uniform room, just down the hall. They will give you all your supplies."

Finally, I ended up in D Block, third floor. It was a bleak, grim barrack room of twenty-five or more iron cots with showers and toilets at each end. What the hell—no outhouse? Can I make the big change so sudden? Several tall men quick-stepped into the room, noisy and jabbering. In our khaki fatigue uniforms, we went to the Mess Hall for supper. I lined up with about one hundred other Mounties. I was scared silly. The Mountie behind me said, "The flunkies behind the counter fill your tray as you go by. Just take the slop thrown in your plate. Don't complain about the pile of saltpetre." "God in Heaven, this food tastes okay." Frightened, I was gawking all around, as if looking for an escape [route]. I thought that I would come unglued before I would get back to D Block and my cot.

Gradually, I fell into the training depot routine. Many things scared the bejesus out of me. So many strange things: 6:00 a.m. roll call, drills and the check-ups. Depot training was hard and frightening—[it was a] new culture, new faces, new everything. I had to drop much of St. Louis' familiar Métis style. Retraining in almost everything was necessary. It almost overwhelmed me completely. I wrangled my way through with a squad of thirty other Mountie trainees. I threw out everything that linked me to [being] Métis. I did not want to give myself away by my speech, behaviour or attitude, so I remained quiet.

I was now a keen student in the mainstream, with middle-class recruits. Thank God, none were interested in each other's family background. Barrack room talk consisted of gossip about brutal instructors and about sex. Soon I became a seasoned Mountie, confident and proficient. I would not know about all the difficulties and problems that would confront me in times ahead. These serious hassles I would encounter later. **(AB)**

The Training Depot was built in a perfect square: each side being about two hundred yards long. Forming the square were rows of red brick buildings. On the west side was a continuous building from end to end. Tony learned this was the main barrack room, which provided his living accommodation while in training. The north side included a complex of buildings of many shapes, which housed all the offices, administration and the huge mess hall (a name that seemed puzzling at first, but after a while seemed very suitable). On the east side were the lecture halls, labs, gymnasium and all training shops, where many hours of strenuous training were to take place. To complete the square, the officers' houses made up the south side. The stables were far to the north, yet not far enough. Within the huge parade square was nothing but a cement and grass surface, used for as the title stated: parades. Depot was a huge place, like a small city situated on the edge of Regina. The Dewdney streetcar, which was the method of transportation to the downtown, came within a quarter of a mile of the Depot. Approximately three hundred men were training at the same time as Tony, and it should've been easy to get lost in such a crowd. Yet Tony was very obvious on many occasions, especially at the wrong times.

During the entire first day, Tony was tense, worried and forever feeling like a simpleton. Much of his time was spent apologizing for just everything. He was also being so extremely grateful. By the end of the day, he had been sworn in as a member of the force, assigned to a dormitory, given an issue of uniform clothing and a set of rules—the Bible of Depot. At suppertime, he was almost overcome with fear, as he had to line up with hundreds of men who moved in a long single line, taking food as they moved, and then seating themselves in a huge mess hall. Tony became aware of his extreme self-consciousness, and was frightened by the nearness of so many strange people.

He was glad when it came time for "lights-out" so that he could be by himself in the darkness and rest, yet he was too excited to sleep. Would he ever catch on to the millions of things that had to be learned, and learned right away? There was so much that was new to him. In fact, it was the first time he'd been in a big city. Everything was so different from the old farm. Even electricity and running water were new. Tony found it upsetting not being able to go to the outhouse. Within a week he'd been forced to make many adjustments and had already become quite familiar with many parts of the routine. Since he was not yet in training, he could dress in fatigue clothes: a smock and pants of brown denim. However, within a month he was assigned to Training Squad D with twenty-nine other young men.

Passing

Now that everyone had the same uniform, there was no such thing as racial and social differences—no big-shot Whites, no low-class Halfbreeds. The uniforms made everyone of the same class and same race—at least Tony hoped this would be the situation. All Mounties were on the same footing, for they all started at the same level. It didn't matter how rich you were before you came in, or how poor, you were treated the same. Only instructors and officers had [a] superior rank. Still, Tony couldn't help but feel sensitive and fearful about his background, for he was sure everyone recognized him as a Halfbreed, and he worried about how they would treat him. Regardless, he was going to play safe, so he remained secret about his racial heritage. He did little talking [...] discussions for fear of revealing himself. If his looks didn't give him away, then certainly his language, his ideas and his behaviour–all so typically low-class Halfbreed—would give him away. This caused him constant worry and fear. Consequently, he remained cautious and defensive, the carry-over mood from the election. Also, Tony felt strange about being in the centre of a Mountie camp, because he knew how they treated the Halfbreeds and [he knew] their attitude towards all Redmen. Would they treat him like that when they found out? Maybe some of the Mounties had been to St. Louis on official duties and had seen him. What would his Halfbreed people say about him being a Mountie? Probably disown him! He hoped so, for he disowned them. He would deny his Redman heritage.

Training had begun, and almost immediately Tony hated foot drill—an army routine of marching and drilling vigorously for one continuous hour in full dress [...], including revolver and rifle. **(TB)**

Desperate to keep my Métis background silent and hidden, I sneaked around. Why? I could not understand, but I knew what was important. The uniform was an equalizing factor, meaning all Mounties in training wore the same type of uniform. One cannot pretend to be better or higher than another. Rich or poor, doctor or lawyer, we are all the same. All of us start at the same place, and all take the same training. I felt comfortable in this equalizing social and military atmosphere. No one could tell the hayseed from the professor.

The drill instructor, Sergeant Savage, was a sadist with an aim to destroy every recruit or terrorize him into self-destruction. He defied a recruit to survive training. Frightfully, he never gave clear commands, just guttural sounds and grunts. As recruits, we jumped at anything that sounded like a command. A mistake was bound to happen. He shouted, "ATTAAMM-SS," which was the "attention" command [...which] I heard [...] as "AADAMMSS." [I...] yelled, "Here," loud enough to be heard in the next city.

A loud snicker ran through the squad.

Abruptly, Sergeant Savage stopped roll call, and in the frosty snow I heard him walking methodically towards me. He stopped directly in front, toe-to-toe, eyeball-to-eyeball, and yelled in my face, "When the hell did your name become 'Aw-tenn-shun'? Don't you know your name? Next time, I'll give you short arm inspection and leave it hang out […when it's] forty below."

"Yes, sir, here, sir!" I nearly fudged in my pants. I thought about going on sick parade for the next few days. **(AB)**

Corporal Howard Adams, Mountie, Red Serge. Photograph Courtesy—Marge Adams.

Corporal Howard Adams, Mountie, Red Serge and Stetson. Photograph Courtesy—Marge Adams.

Instructors always chose the first one or two names on the roll call for their errands and trivial chores. Tony soon learned to run like a gazelle trying to get these chores done on time. As a result, he would fall-in for the next roll call barely on time, puffing furiously. Sergeant Hood would warn him that he was in very poor physical condition and might be assigned extra evening sessions of physical training. Sometimes, Tony would be detailed from the parade square in front of all three hundred Mounties, which made him ten times more nervous. Consequently, he'd fail to understand the bellowing commands. But, without question, he'd come smartly to attention and march rigidly ahead like a mechanical soldier until he disappeared out of sight, then he'd stop and try to figure out what he'd been sent to do. This kind of uncertainty drove him to such extreme frustration and inferiority that he thought of running away. But who ever heard of a Mountie running away? Anyway, he had no civilian clothes, and there were many guards patrolling around the square day and night. He'd signed a contract for five years, and it looked like they intended to hold him to it.

There was only one thing Tony hated more than foot drill, and that was swimming. The instructor, Corporal Evans, was a sadist. Not only did he look like a seal, but he swam like one and gave commands like […] one. Water frightened Tony at any time, but swimming according to rigid rules would almost certainly lead to drowning. As soon as he touched water, he'd lose his breath, often not recovering it for a minute or more. As soon as the water reached his waist, he'd collapse to the bottom like a ton of pig iron. Every high dive was a suicide jump. Tony was warned that if he failed to make the jump, there'd be a rope tied around his neck with the other end fastened to the diving board. In making his dives, he never stopped to look down from the twenty feet diving board—he just ran and jumped. To his amazement, he always came up, and without a cracked skull. Occasionally, he belly-flopped and created a splash that showered the ceiling. It was a miracle that his guts weren't split open; however, it was nothing more serious than a big red belly. Tony prayed regularly throughout his training.

One evening at supper, he took two extra pats of butter, although he knew the rule was strictly [to take only] one. The mess hall corporal saw Tony and followed him to his chair and waited until he was seated at a long table with several others. The corporal shouted, "What's your regimental number?" Tony had a notion to give a phoney one, but what if he gave another Mountie's number. He was frightened, but he couldn't act scared in front of all these Mounties, so he was flippant. He'd heard other recruits act in that manner, and it seemed so clever.

Tony suggested, "You can have these extra pats back, Corporal, they're hardly used." Almost hysterically frightened, he added, "Would you like my phone number, too?"

The next day, Tony was paraded before the sergeant major where he pleaded guilty and was given a suspended sentence, with the recommendation that this offence go on his permanent record. He had no idea what that meant, but he politely said, "Yes, sir. Thank you, sir," and expressed such gratefulness to the sergeant major for saving his life.

For the next few days, Tony was greeted with "butter boy." Back in his dormitory, he couldn't help but feel resentful at the officials for making such a big issue out of two butter pats, but he concluded that the police force probably couldn't have complete disorder among the recruits. It seemed to Tony that most instructors picked on him, and sometimes viciously, but he couldn't figure out why. Did they know he was a Breed? He had difficulty understanding that a different cultural background made a tremendous difference. Most of the things [that were] expected to be known automatically [by all the recruits] were completely foreign to Tony. Even the casual conversations in the barrack room among the recruits were a puzzle to him. He could hear Pappa saying, "stupid," over and over. [...] Feelings of inferiority and mockery [by others], which plagued him, seemed also to cause him to do stupid things. Instead of learning and developing skills, he was making the same stupid mistakes, or [...he could not] answer because of fear. Other recruits seemed to have little difficulty. Many things to them were natural and automatic. Tony couldn't seem to understand that Mountie training was based on White culture, [the culture] where all recruits came from, or at least practically all [of them]. He guessed he was the only Halfbreed in the Depot training. Tony's difficulty was not because of disobedience or rudeness or for not trying. Never did he question official authority, criticize or even complain to the authorities. He surrendered himself completely to the police system, throwing himself at the mercy of the instructors.

From 6:30 in the morning until lights-out at 11 p.m., there was continuous harsh and rigid discipline. All day, Tony was snapping to attention and answering, "Yes, sir." Hour after hour, it was the same: "awww-tenn-shun," "roooomm-shun,""forward march," "on-the-double" and "halt," which echoed loudly in his ears long after he'd gone to bed. By now, rapid, automatic responses should've been developed, instead of awkward and incorrect ones [... followed by] tense expressions of gratitude. It appeared to Tony that the instructors were bent on one mission: breaking him. He was being crushed by the harshness of military life, and was becoming increasingly unsure of himself, if that was possible, for he was totally without confidence now. In his dormitory, when he practiced foot drill and saluting, everything *went well, but as soon as he was in front of an instructor, he became a mumbling cripple, stumbling over his shadow. There seemed little hope, and he was becoming convinced that he must be defective or retarded. Each day kept getting worse, his quivering rarely stopped. The end of the road seemed near.* **(TB)**

Tonight I went to practice revolver shooting. Revolver drill would be happening soon. I was frightened of it. I had never used a gun in my life. Mom was totally opposed to firearms. There had never been a gun in our house during my lifetime. I didn't know which end was the barrel. Now in the Mounties, I was issued with a .45 revolver. It was like a small cannon. The rifle range was deep down in the basement of the gym. As usual, we were lined up alphabetically. Adams was first. From behind the cement barrier, we had to shoot small sliding ducks far ahead. A light would flash on for a few seconds, and we had to fire at the passing targets.

The light flashed. I just stood frozen, totally transfixed. I could not pull the trigger. Quickly the targets disappeared and the lights went out. Then, with a sudden burst by the trigger of my .45, I fired rapidly all five shells in complete darkness. Good Lord, a burst of flame went up like an explosion. Bullets were flying madly everywhere. The waiting recruits ducked for cover. The instructor was shouting, "Stop, stop!" Lights were quickly switched on. I stood at the barrier petrified with the hot revolver in my hand. I had to be physically removed.

My next revolver drill was done privately with the instructor who put me behind a thick cement wall. Before I finished training at Depot, I had become a sharpshooter and won the honour badge as a revolver marksman. **(AB)**

Training was passed the midpoint. Tony had been spending extra time boxing. Besides enjoying it, he thought it would come in handy to him if he ever became a Mountie. Since the spring tournament was coming up, he was spending more time at the gym. The tournament began with the preliminary rounds, and Tony had little trouble reaching the finals. One of his pals from D Squad was the other finalist. They talked it over and tried to make some arrangement, but nothing could be solved as both wanted to win. The situation had to unfold in its own way for there was no other answer—the best man would make it. Not only would winning bring prestige in Depot, but also, Tony hoped, the instructors would act differently towards the winner.

The final match had arrived. The first few rounds were just dancing, and "feeling-out" the opponent. Gradually the fight warmed up. It became serious and brutal punishment, each trying to knock the other out. Tony was hit seriously on the nose, and he was bleeding heavily. In turn, he had damaged the eye of his opponent badly, and kept punching it. He was driving hard punches to the ribs that were having serious effect. Tony could see the pained expression on his friend's face, but he didn't see him as a friend anymore. He saw him as a competitor who was trying to knock him unconscious, and wanting to win and reap all the glory. If Tony lost, this could be the death of his career as a Mountie. So he must go after the final kill, the kill, the kill. He saw his opponent weakening, and immediately flashing in

Tony's mind was: "Finish him, finish him." However, before he could do that, the final bell rang. Tony won by a unanimous decision.

For days his face was a mass of bruises and swellings, but he went on parade, boldly and proudly. Comments about Tony being the new Joe Louis came from the instructors in a good-natured manner—it was their way of congratulating him. No doubt he'd lost a good friend, but it was worth it. Friendship was unimportant compared to winning and prestige, and a new sense of confidence and pride. Tony was recognized as having talent, at least in one way. He hoped to scare each instructor from being such a bully; maybe they'd stop riding him so hard. Conversations with his instructors were now possible. However, his new reputation was not completely satisfying because it hadn't proved that he was intelligent. Nevertheless, it gave breathing room at a time when it was badly needed.

Tony now decided to concentrate on his area of real difficulty: academic subjects, especially criminal law and federal statutes, for these were considered the toughest. **(TB)**

Howard's/Tony's Romance with Edie/Sylvia

I decided to take an evening's recreation before [...studying]. I went ice-skating at the Depot rink. I'm a good skater, powerful and graceful. In the rink there were a couple of young women skating. I picked up one for a skate. I noticed immediately that she was cute, talkative and sociable. She was the first girl that I had come close to since entering Depot training. It was nice to hold her arm. We had a lovely time for the next hour. Then she had to go. I offered to walk her home, but she replied, "It's not possible." **(AB)**

Not knowing anyone in Regina, Tony spent a lot of time at Depot and, lately, in the library studying. However, he took time off to go skating at the Depot rink. One night he noticed two teenage girls skating, who were not only good skaters, but also very good looking. Skating was natural for Tony. He was bold and daring, powerful and graceful, and he knew it. In a rink he was noticeable as an outstanding skater, for with his confidence he performed special routines [...]. In this one area, Tony held himself to be superior to many Whites. For this reason he had no hesitation to seek White girls for partners, but beyond that he remained a Halfbreed. Both girls were cute, but the older one caught his attention. Gliding up beside her, Tony said, "Do you mind if we skate together?" In a soft, quiet voice, she replied, "No, I'd love to."

"My name's Tony Parker. I'm from D Squad." He didn't try to hide that he was a Mountie, but he said nothing about his home.

She introduced herself simply as Sylvia, nothing more. **(TB)**

The final exams were not as bad as I had expected, but to fail would have been a monstrous disgrace to Mom and Dad—they now had high expectations of me. I did very well in all my written academic exams, such as criminal law, federal statutes and justice. Being in excellent physical condition, I sailed through my phys-ed [training]. Of course, I topped the class in typing.

But, for the love of Jesus, I could not pass the auto-mechanics test. In my many years on the old St. Louis farm, all our machinery was manual. The pickaxe, shovel and scythe were the main implements. A car was beyond my understanding. I couldn't tell a radiator from a battery, forget the motor. The instructor puzzled how a rookie could be such a dumbhead in mechanics, and so smart in other subjects. He recommended that I would be fit only for office work or prison-guard duty. I would never be fit for highway patrol. In the oral exam or drill, I was hopeless, even the simplest question [perplexed me]. I could stand up, but no words would come out. In front of White officials I had a constipation of words, a fatal weakness of Aboriginals. […] I had a diarrhoea of words. What makes us so tongue-tied in such situations? It is not biological. It is purely cultural, a part of colonization. **(AB)**

The exams were not as bad as Tony had feared. The only tough one was auto-mechanics. Not knowing anything about automobiles before training, he had to take the course. And now they were having an oral examination. Like all Halfbreeds, Tony had been taught to be naturally shy and withdrawn, so he was now seriously handicapped in oral discussion. Although he was asked the easiest and simplest questions, and he knew the answer, he was unable to stand up and speak out the answer, not even a short one. He tried to get the words out, but without success, and stood there trembling until he thought he'd faint. His friends tried to help, but it was useless. He was torn between an outburst of rage or [shedding] tears. Violence was on the brim of eruption. The instructor was not to blame, for Tony had his tongue torn out by the whole educational system for the Redman, before he came to Depot. Right now, he'd bomb it to hell if he could. He'd blow the head off every teacher of the Halfbreeds, and burn down every damn school. Fortunately, this instructor was easy, and Tony was passed. On all other exams, Tony felt he did well, especially criminal law. **(TB)**

What in God's name had I done that she rejected my friendly offer? She said she was the assistant commissioner's daughter, and that she wasn't allowed to associate with ordinary Mounties in public. God above, what a bummer!

Lately, I had come to see myself as a White man. I had pushed aside my Métis heritage. My Aboriginal culture and life were fading.

I went skating again the next night, motivated by the desire to see that steamy female skater. She had stirred emotions in me and put a fire in my gut. God bless, to my delight she was on the ice. I glided beside her, slipped my arm into hers and squeezed. She smiled and said, "Hello, Howard." I felt a real closeness to her.

"How is the assistant commissioner's daughter tonight? You didn't give me your name last night."

"Edie." Pronounced Edee. Rather unusual, but pretty.

"How long have you been in training?" she questioned.

"Six months."

"Did you enjoy it?"

"The drilling, marching and phys-ed were real bummers. The instructors are brutal."

I was going to say a word, but maybe she talked to the officers.

"How could we have missed each other for the last six months, and meet only now?"

"Puzzles me. Probably you haven't been skating?"

"That's true," she whispered. "But I walk around the parade square a lot."

I was thinking of the many times I had been on night patrol and stable duties. But to tell her that would only be degrading myself.

We skated together for most of the hour, talking and exchanging intimate information. I pulled her closer and was surprised at the quick warm response. I felt the rise of my lustful feelings, especially in my pants. We skated until official time was up. Without a Depot pass, I had to report to guard on duty before 10:30 p.m.

"When can I see you again?" was my anxious concern.

She was struggling with this like I was, but there was no easy answer. Finally she said, "Let's meet here tomorrow evening and see if we can come up with something." That was good enough for me. It convinced me of her affection for me.

God in heaven, I was ecstatic. We were back skating the next evening. I hugged her lightly. Our main concern was how do we get together outside the rink. My mind was raging with wild schemes, but there was no finishing line.

Without Edie, I had become as lonely as a gander at setting time. I lay on my bunk and wondered what in God's name I could do to string out my stay at training Depot. Just last week I could hardly wait to get the hell out, and now all that was changed. Adorable Edie had changed that. To ship out and to not see her was painful. There must be some excuse or way that I could prolong my stay. I had no exceptional talent to offer the Depot. I was strictly a garden-variety constable. If I committed a Depot offence, I'd probably be held back and [would] undoubtedly be put in the jailhouse. To go AWOL, I'd be caught the next day. To hell with it! **(AB)**

Over the last few months, Tony had come to see himself increasingly as a Whiteman. Since he'd rejected everything Halfbreed, and was living up to his personal commitment to [… get Lionel Morin elected back in St. Louis…], he was gradually adjusting himself out of the Redman's world. There was nothing around to remind him of his Breed heritage and nation, and he felt neither lonely nor lost. Nevertheless, he was still self-conscious about his identity. In St. Louis he wouldn't have skated freely with a White girl, as he was doing in Depot with Sylvia. Although the White ideal was still prominent, he found it possible to touch and to hold Sylvia's hand—a White girl. He met her at the rink again the next week.

On Friday night, he helped take off her skates. She was everything he envisioned about White women: elegant and beautiful to the full, perfectly smooth white skin, full deep blue eyes, small lean nose, thin cherry lips, small delicate features without high cheekbones. Her voice was warm and friendly as she spoke with magnetic charm. Sylvia was truly a goddess. She was too perfect and heavenly for the real, earthy world; too gracious and delicate for the ordinary, vulgar society. Simply to take off Sylvia's skates, or to hold her hand seemed unreal, more like an envisioned world. Tony found the actuality of it frightening. As excited as he was about Sylvia, he had difficulty retaining her in his real world. He was greatly attracted to her. It was more than a silent and fanciful admiration. It was a fondness, an emotional response; a passion. How horribly vulgar, thinking of a White woman in such a way! How outrageous for a Halfbreed man to think and feel in that manner about a White woman!

But nothing could discourage Tony from wanting to be with Sylvia and to enjoy her company except for the police rules, which forbade constables from associating socially with daughters of officers. He walked part way home with her, but stopped before he came to the guards on duty, as he was not allowed on the parade square after training hours. Tony asked Sylvia what house she lived in. "The far one in the southwest corner," she answered, and said goodnight. "Geez," thought Tony, as he hurried back to his dormitory. "That's the commanding officer's house. She must be kidding." But he turned around to watch her go into that house.

Tony was with Sylvia as much as his studies would permit, and the relationship affected his outlook and behaviour as he strived harder to fit into the White mainstream, and he enjoyed it. However, he had one serious worry. If he was discovered associating with Sylvia, he could be either imprisoned or dismissed from the police force at once. Final exams were just ahead, but he felt quite prepared for them. Therefore, he could afford to spend some time with Sylvia. Although it was dangerous to associate with her, he didn't hesitate, for it was so delightful to share her company. When he was not with her, he spent a great deal of time thinking of her. He was surely falling in love. Sylvia was not only a new excitement, but [promised] a new world of love with a White woman, and she did much to lift the burden of inferiority and mockery. Being the commanding officer's daughter might have been part of it, but Tony wouldn't admit it to himself. On foot drill and swimming, he chuckled to himself as he thought, "I'm a lot smarter than you instructors." He harboured his love for Sylvia as a beautiful secret.

The next weekend, when Tony had stable duties, Sylvia came over to go riding, but, naturally, had to be escorted by a sergeant. Therefore, he had little chance to talk to her. Although it was against the rules, Tony chased all the horses into the paddock because he didn't see how anything could go wrong when he was watching. When they returned, Sylvia came over to chat, but the sergeant called her back very soon. As he stood chatting with her, he realized how he adored her, and he hated to see her leave. His eyes followed her as she left through the gate and up the sidewalk. He was so completely wrapped up in his emotions that he didn't notice she'd left the gate open and the horses were leaving. Gradually his thoughts returned to the horses and their disappearance from the paddock, but it still caused no alarm. They had little importance to his life. Suddenly it struck him: "Geez, those crazy ponies are breaking lose!"

His first thought was to take the fastest pony and race after the others, but the police force would realize what an excellent rider he is and put him in the Riding Squad, and he certainly didn't want that. He called the officer on duty and reported the situation. The answer almost broke his eardrum. Quickly, several riders were dispatched, but the horses had a good start as they headed towards the legislative buildings downtown. There was a lot of excitement in Depot and in Regina before the horses were finally rounded up. It made news on the front page in the morning newspaper, and so did Tony Parker, but definitely not as a hero. He was paraded before the commanding officer and charged with every offence pertaining to horses and stables. And in case there was anything overlooked, he was charged under the last section of the RCMP Rules, which states that "for any infraction not covered in the foregoing sections the constable can be charged and found guilty under this section for any and all offences committed." Since no defence was allowed, Tony pleaded guilty to all charges, and petitioned for mercy on the grounds that he had a serious allergy to horses, and when near them blacked out.

He was given a long lecture on the seriousness of breaking rules, and how it could lead to his dismissal. A sentence of two weeks open imprisonment was given with a black mark against his permanent record. However, he was allowed to study, but could not leave the dormitory. In one way it pleased him, for he didn't have to do that horrible foot drill and swimming. He could now devote full time to studying criminal law. But on the other hand, he was sad because he wouldn't be able to see Sylvia. On Monday morning he thought of inviting the sadist instructors up to his dorm, and telling them how disappointed he was in not being able to attend their "beautiful" classes, but he would continue to think of them with all his heart. He thought he might cry a little, but maybe that was overdoing it.

During the two weeks he phoned Sylvia frequently and expressed his loneliness. He thought, "What if her father answers the phone?" Out of habit he'd probably snap to attention and salute the phone! Although his emotions were overruling his mind, and Sylvia was becoming the most important fact in his life, he was still determined to succeed as a Mountie.

One day he noticed on the bulletin board that Parker and two others from D Squad were to parade before the commanding officer. His first thought was to head for St. Louis, except the other Mounties were the most conscientious recruits in the squad. Bets were placed among the fellows in the barrack room as to the reason for this command.

"Who's pregnant?" shouted Alex.

Tony quietly asked himself, "I wonder if they've been flirting with the young women of the officers' residences?" Tony's affair with Sylvia was well-known by this time.

"Parker's going to be castrated," laughed another Mountie.

"I'll bet there'll be a shot-gun wedding, anyway," joked Slim. But Tony was too nervous to appreciate the jokes.

The sergeant major marched them in. The commanding officer was dressed in his lavish blue uniform and seated behind the huge oak desk. He seemed friendly and spoke in a sensible manner. "Constables Parker, Hardie and Foster, I brought you here to congratulate you on the excellent scores you made on the final examination."

He went on to compliment them on their wonderful performance at Depot, and wished them every success. Tony thought immediately of the auto-mechanics instructor, and what a great guy he is. He was so relieved of his anxiety for this command that he felt like hugging the commanding officer. All three recruits expressed their deep appreciation, and, of course, Tony kept declaring his gratitude until it was almost embarrassing. He wrote a long letter to Pappa, telling him [that] his son wasn't so stupid after all, for he could measure up with the best Mounties. Tony proved that he was intelligent, and the best in the Mounted Police Force. This, above all else, became an important factor, the one achievement which gave him the proof that he needed. However, it still didn't help when confronted by big shot Whites, where he was still a cripple. But he was now satisfied that he had the intelligence equal to [any] Whitemen. He was more than a smart Breed: he was a smart person.

Tony thought back over his six months of training and what he'd learned. Certainly, there was nothing about the Halfbreeds or Indians. The whole emphasis was on the techniques of catching criminals. "We learn nothing about why a person becomes a criminal or how he's treated afterwards. As Mounties, we don't analyze or interpret anything. All we do is carry out the dangerous work according to the rules already laid down, and we do this dangerous work for a measly twenty-five dollars a month." Tony thought himself a workingman. [This kind of thinking…] didn't fit as a policeman. You worked for the big shot people who ruled the society. You were made to understand these were the important people, and that their interests and property must be protected. There was no doubt about what side you were on and where your loyalty was. But these thoughts were becoming less important as he succeeded more and more with his Mountie career, and as Sylvia became more important to him.

"Hey, Parker, aren't you ever going to kiss that C.O. baby of yours? She's dying to be kissed, and after all the time you've been with her, what's the matter? Assign me to the job!" stated Tim to the whole barrack room. Tim had been out occasionally with Sylvia's sister, and he was speaking the embarrassing truth, probably right from Sylvia's own words.

"What the hell—and get caught by those damn guards marching around the parade square? A guy's got to be ready to run."

But Tony knew he was only making excuses. He'd been unable to bring himself to making love to a White girl. Skating with her and walking her home was okay, but making love was something very different. White girls were to be admired, not for love, at least not passionate love. He was fond of Sylvia and wanted to kiss her, but passion was for Halfbreed girls only. Tony had to force himself through this dilemma, as far as he was concerned. And right away, for he couldn't possibly let all the Depot Mounties laugh at him for not kissing his girlfriend. He'd settle that problem this very weekend. Or was the problem too highly emotional to be solved directly and immediately?

That weekend, he and Sylvia had planned on spending a lot of time together, but things went wrong. Tony was assigned to guard duty. He was furious and tried every way to get out of it, but was unsuccessful. On Friday night, he reported for duty in a fiendish mood. Knowing they'd go through a formal, small arms inspection, Tony had borrowed a few blank shells from a Mountie friend. He never knew why he did this. The six men were lined up for inspection in the basement of the cellblock, grim, dismal and cramped. They formed a straight line against the dark wall, fully equipped with firearms. The officer on duty came in with a great flourish of NCO's [Non-Commissioned Officers] flanking him. He looked like a great Prussian general attending a surrender ceremony. "Present arms," he roared. With systematic flashing movements, all men drew their revolvers and held them rigidly in upright positions for detailed inspection.

The officer moved down the line of men, testing and inspecting the firearms of each as he went. He came to Tony, taking the revolver and inspecting it in the usual manner. He held it loosely in his hand as he pulled the trigger. "Bang, bang, bang!" The whole place exploded with firing sparks and smoke. Everyone threw themselves on the floor. The officer staggered backwards and momentarily collapsed on an old desk. The moment he recovered, he bellowed, "Arrest that man. Arrest that goddamn idiot!"

He was coughing from smoke and trembling from shock. But in one big step, he was in front of Tony, ripping the badges and buttons off his uniform. The sound of ripping cloth shattered the old basement. Grabbing the cap off Tony's head, and pulling off the revolver holder, he pushed Tony towards the cell. "Get into that goddamn cell over there. Cell three, you fool."

Tony did as he was told, saying nothing. The iron gate clanged. Tony was behind bars—[he was] a dangerous criminal. He was amused by the whole spectacle because he knew what was going to happen, and he was prepared for the consequences. Anyway, he preferred to sit in a cell than doing guard duty. On Monday morning, he was paraded before the commanding officer and charged with illegally possessing blank cartridges and endangering the lives of other Mounties. The sentence was amazingly light: one week in jail and two weekends [worth] of stable duties. Of course, it went on his permanent record.

Mounties in his dormitory teased him about trying to pick off the sadistic officer. They offered him real live shells for his next tour of guard duty. Tony claimed the officer had learned his lesson. He'd never do inspection again without first checking the shell chambers. He thought it was a stupid and unnecessary routine, and hoped this incidence would bring an end to it.

Mounties at Depot are not allowed to wear their uniform outside the parade square. Civilian clothes were sparse for those like Tony who came with few because practically none could be bought on the pay received at Depot. Consequently, there was a great deal of borrowing of civvies, and that meant only a few fellows could go out at one time. It didn't bother Tony because he didn't know where to go in the city, or how to behave, so he was glad to spend his time with Sylvia around Depot. He was now quite seriously in love with Sylvia, and was in no hurry to leave Depot. **(TB)**

Maybe Edie would have thought of something. Yes, she put forth a chancy scheme, at least for the moment. Her parents were going out on Saturday night; she and her kid sister would be left alone. I could come over to her house. But what if I got caught? I would spend the rest of my Mountie career cleaning stables. But I didn't have the power to stay away from Edie. I knew immediately that I would be at her house. She'd phone me as soon as her parents had left, and I'd go over immediately. We had to know the exact time, not approximate.

All the barrack room recruits knew I had a torrid romance going with the assistant commissioner's daughter. It was the talk of D Block.

"Why don't you tell the old commissioner directly? Hell, he'd probably make you an officer," said Herb.

"In God's name," yelled Tom, "demand a superintendent rank."

"I'll tell you a sure-fire method," hollered Jim. "Knock up Edie and then tell the old chief that he is going to be a grandfather. He couldn't wiggle out of that one."

"You dumbhead buggers. Edie is a gracious lady and I love her dearly."

"Well, don't get caught with your pants down," warned Bob.

Girlfriend Maxine in Howard Adams' uniform. Photograph Courtesy—Marge Adams.

The Commissioner's Daughter: "Pretty cute, eh!!! In her Dad's uniform. A perfect Doll!!!" Photograph Courtesy—Marge Adams.

Party at Edie's/Sylvia's House

The barrack room phone rang. It was Edie. Her parents were going out tonight at 7:00. "Come over right after. For certain. Check their homecoming time precisely."

Edie met me at the door with an affectionate hug. It was our first serious kiss and, oh Mother of God, it sent hot feelings right to my toes and other places. Edie looked absolutely gorgeous. She had the figure of a model. I had to stop and admire her in her most radiant self. She was so alluring and playful. I was hot to trot. It was a heavy passionate evening. On the chesterfield, I pressed my body against her soft, delicate figure. Love seemed so boundless. It was non-stop. She buzzed, "It's ten o'clock," but it was agony to separate. Yet, the realization of being caught inside the house was unthinkable. There was a noise at the front door.

"Good Lord," exclaimed Edie, "that's Mom and Dad! I jumped up, grabbed my coat. "Is there a back door?"

"No, but the window may be open." I forced it open enough to wiggle through, but not without a lot of noise. I sure as hell wasn't looking back to see where the old commissioner was. I got up and ran like hell through the yard, never stopping until I got inside the guardhouse.

Puffing, I said to the night guard, "Adams, 14329, reporting in!"

"You just made it."

I raced straight for my cot on third floor and covered up hurriedly. My body was still saturated with love, but I wondered how Edie would explain the situation. I would anxiously await her phone call tomorrow. **(AB)**

Sylvia asked Tony over to her house for a party one evening, as her parents were going to a banquet downtown and wouldn't be home before midnight. At first he thought it was a joke, but finally agreed and went over after the parents had gone. There were only a few young people, but in a short time a gay, noisy party was going, dancing, playing records and fooling around. Tony was in his glory, dancing and partying with Sylvia, acting boldly, foolish and mischievous. Suddenly the commanding officer and his wife were heard in the kitchen. It was well before midnight. Sylvia hurriedly pushed Tony into the den, from which he could easily escape through the big window and beat it back to the dorm, as he'd done before. But, just as quickly, another decision came to Tony. He'd go back into the kitchen and meet Sylvia's parents.

Without a moment's further hesitation, he returned to the kitchen. He met Commanding Officer Symmons. Quietly, he said, "Good night, sir." The very fact of using "sir" made Symmons suspicious. Sylvia had no alternative. She introduced Tony, but left out the fact he was a Mountie. She apologized for him having to leave right away. But her father interrupted, "Young man, do you live in Depot?"

"Yes, sir, I'm in D Squad," answered Tony.

Symmons puzzled for a moment, and then asked, "Are you Tony Parker, who was guilty of letting horses get away, and with carrying blank cartridge?"

"Yes, sir," answered Tony, rather apologetically.

"What is your regimental number?" asked the commanding officer in his severe military tone.

"Oh oh," thought Tony to himself, "that sounds like a military warning of something else to come." But he had to answer. "One-four-three-two-nine, sir."

He moved to the door quickly, [and] said a curt, "Good night," and left abruptly.

At 8:30 roll call the next morning, Sergeant Hood assigned Tony Parker to report to the sergeant major. The command was clear, and Tony understood it. The sergeant major saw him right away. He was not in an angry mood, but he was firm and precise as he said, "Constable Parker, you are being transferred to Weyburn detachment. That's about two hundred miles south of Regina."

That seemed like a long way, but it could've been worse. He thought he might be transferred to some outpost in the Arctic. It was possible to get back from Weyburn. Finally, he said, "When do I have to leave, sir?"

"Right away," answered the sergeant major.

"You mean, right away today, sir?" asked Tony.

"I mean right away, right now. Just as fast as you can get packed. And that's not going to be any later than ten o'clock this morning," the sergeant major said slowly and deliberately. "Constable Flynn will drive you there. Take what you need for a few days. Your trunk will be shipped on tonight's train."

"But, sir, I want a little time to myself before leaving," objected Tony, thinking about seeing Sylvia.

"You're not to have any time," stated the sergeant major.

Tony thought the sergeant major was being unreasonable. "May I see the official in charge?" asked Tony.

"You may not. Those are the orders from the top, and you know why they're given. I urge you to do as you're commanded immediately, and don't try any nonsense," concluded the sergeant major.

Back at the dorm, Tony tried to phone Sylvia, but her mother answered and explained that Sylvia could not receive any phone calls and that was final. None of his pals were around to take a message, but she wouldn't be allowed to receive it anyway. Likely she's a prisoner, in a cell. Tony was angry, but he had only himself to blame. He thought, "I could've stepped through that damn window just as I did many times before. But surely to hell people can be more honest than that? Cryz, how horrible!"

It was the longest and saddest journey of his life. Since all his thoughts were on Sylvia, he spoke very little to Constable Flynn. It was a surprise to learn that the police force could be so brutal and merciless. It had no respect for people and their relationships. Tony was certain he was being set afloat by the unfeeling on a sea of inhumanity. But not even a fleet would ever contain or smother his passion for Sylvia. He'd find her again. **(TB)**

A special congratulation from the commanding officer was the greatest thing that happened [to me]. That gave me the confidence I needed so badly to be [the] top scholar of the squad. It was that prestigious award that put me over the top. The entire squad gave me respect. Now I was an official Mounted Policeman of the best quality. I was now an enforcer of the law. The Halfbreeds of St. Louis may not be proud of me in my red coat, Stetson hat, and spurs [...]. Depot training had come to an end.

Our assigned detachments were posted. I was going to Edmonton. I was to be posted out of Saskatchewan. It was my first train ride. It was exciting. I had the top bunk yet.

What a huge city. Geez, I was assigned to highway patrol. "No way," I said firmly to Corporal Muir. "I'm allergic to cars." That mattered little.

"You will join Constable Stewart in the patrol car and he'll teach you to drive. He's a good driver and a pleasant fellow." What a lie! Stewart turned out to be the meanest and most sourly personality that I met in the RCMP. My driving and training was extreme agony. Stewart caused me continued stress and misery. I hated every mile.

We had to bring in our quota of traffic tickets. It wasn't easy to find lawbreakers on those highways in broad daylight. Six months later, I was transferred to guard room duty. That was the end of my social life, as I was on duty 4 p.m. to midnight. Down in the dark, dreary basement, listening to four prisoners snore in their cells was not exactly exciting. But I didn't have to torture people with fake traffic infractions.

Shortly, my life went into a passionate spin when I discovered Bonnie, the almighty beautiful blonde secretary. It was undying love immediately, [but as] passionate as our love became, I was committed to the RCMP for six more years of single life, and so I painfully moved on.

In a fierce cold winter day about four months later, I boarded the CNR [Canadian National Railway] for Rockcliffe (Ottawa), two thousand miles away. What a comfortable and joyful trip for three days and three nights with [my] Mountie co-workers. Rockcliffe Depot differed little from Regina in its training. Six months passed quickly.

Mountie in Weyburn, Saskatchewan

Our detachment postings went up. What a bummer! Sent to Weyburn, Saskatchewan. […]. Ironically, my duties were delightful. Now I was doing all types of police work, dangerous and challenging. **(AB)**

Under normal conditions, Weyburn would've looked like a nice town, but today it had all the appearances of a jailhouse, for Tony was seeing the whole world as a penitentiary. He thought Depot officers should've sent him down in handcuffs and leg-irons. Obviously Weyburn was a farmers' town, and a pretty one. Since he'd heard so much about the mental hospital of Weyburn, he was anxious to see it. Maybe he'd eventually be sent there. Constable Flynn [gave him] a quick tour around. It was huge, much bigger than Tony expected–rows and rows of buildings, almost a city in itself. There were often patients who escaped, and it was the duty of the Mounties to round up these patients.

The police quarters were in the old post office building in the centre of town. They occupied the second floor. All except one room was used for offices, the small room serving as the dormitory for single men. It was as barren as a jail, nothing more than beds and individual trunks. This was Tony's new home. The main office was at the front, while at the back were offices for the sergeant and inspector, and the two stenos. Tony was not allowed to leave the city. He was under direct control of Corporal Simpson, who seemed like a regular guy except that he was obsessed about booze (that is, against it). The Inspector was a huge, roly-poly bull of a man who didn't speak words, just bellows like a jungle animal. He was worse than Sergeant Hood at Depot. Tony was greeted with almost complete indifference, saying hello as if he was an old timer around Weyburn. They were probably told not to make an issue of his arrival. For the first two weeks, he accompanied Constable Hunter, a jovial Mountie of one year's experience.

Farmers in the area had to be checked frequently for purple gas, which was allowed only for farm equipment, and not automobiles. Also, farmers had permit books for selling their wheat, and these had to be checked periodically. It seemed that all farmers were potential criminals. A few young men were hiding out from their army call-up, but with names and descriptions widely publicized there was little trouble in locating them. The huge Royal Air Force (RAF) centre on the edge of town had caused some changes because several hundred officers and pilots threw their weight around, [… being] upper- class Englishmen. Tony was told that the local girls would go out only with these Englishmen, as Canadians were no longer good enough. But this didn't bother him because he was in love with Sylvia.

Occasionally, Tony accompanied Corporal Simpson, a rough and tough cop, but a pleasant and nice guy to work with. He was like an entire liquor squad all in himself, and most of all he hated moon shiners. Simpson claimed he could actually sniff-out homebrew a mile away. Tony didn't have long to wait for proof. One day while out on patrol in the backwoods, the corporal suggested there was a smell of a homebrew still somewhere near. They stopped at a small slough.

"Give me twenty minutes, then drive around the slough and turn in directly across from here. There's probably car tracks there. If anyone tries to get past you, fire a shot," commanded Simpson.

"Okay, corporal," said Tony as they checked their watches. His fingers were already trembling, half scared to death over the mention of using the revolver. He watched Simpson put on some old coveralls, and then proceeded to crawl on his stomach through the wet bulrushes towards the spot indicated. It reminded Tony of the pigs at home rooting in the mud.

On the assigned time, Tony drove the car around the slough. He turned in at the car tracks, making lots of noise, hoping [that] if there were anyone there they'd run in the other direction, towards Corporal Simpson. And that's exactly what happened. The two men were going to run and hide in the bulrushes as they had done before, and [would] then make an escape later.

Simpson jumped up, revolver in hand, and shouted, "Stop right where you are or I'll shoot." The men stopped immediately.

Tony helped handcuff the men and marched them back to the car. His job was to guard them while Simpson drove. He thought they were no more criminals than he himself, yet they were as good as convicted because the corporal had all the evidence he needed, and if necessary, Tony could give evidence to support him. The men were put in cells. Tony and Hunter had to take turns at guard duty.

The next morning, the moon shiners were brought before the court. They pleaded guilty and were given a fine of $200.00 or six months imprisonment. This severe penalty shocked Tony, for they were not harming anyone. He thought back about St. Louis, where there was a bootlegger, and he was certainly no criminal. Instead, he gave a service to the community. The Mounties had tried to catch him, but the people would always warn him in advance. As a result, he was never caught. These poor fellows had to find their way back home and pay a fine of two hundred dollars each, as well as have permanent criminal records.

Simpson was beaming. It was a great victory for him, and it would help [him…receive] a promotion. Tony wondered if the corporal was open to schemes or bargaining. Should he approach him on a deal for a weekend in Regina? There hadn't been a word from Sylvia. Doubtless, she was being watched closely. He tried phoning her, but was abruptly informed Sylvia couldn't come to the phone. His letters had been returned. Although his head was beating against a stonewall, his heart was beating on a wave of passion.

Shortly after, Simpson and Tony were on a bootlegging raid of a farmhouse west of town. This time they were after homebrew, and not the still. They would have to search the entire house. The corporal explained that it would be hidden in the most unlikely of places. Tony was commanded to guard the door and make sure no one ran out with the booze, while he searched downstairs. Finding nothing, Simpson proceeded up the stairs. Just then, a woman came down carrying a chamber pot, holding her nose. She was indicating the worst. Simpson, who was extremely sensitive to such things, stepped aside, giving the woman considerable room, as he certainly didn't want that sewage on him. She did the same at the door with Tony. The corporal continued up and searched the rooms upstairs. A little later, he came down empty handed. They got in the car and drove home.

"They outsmarted us that time," grumbled Simpson.

"You mean they heard we were coming, so they poured out the booze?" asked Tony.

"You know that big chamber pot that woman carried out? Well, it was full of homebrew," explained the corporal.

"Geez," yelled Tony, and he broke into a roar of laughter. "Does that mean from now on, we've got to crawl under beds and smell in all chamber pots?"

"Let's forget it!" commanded Simpson.

"Okay, corporal," answered Tony, as he knew Simpson wanted nothing said about it around the office.

Tony was unhappy in Weyburn, mostly because he was so painfully lonesome for Sylvia. He wasn't interested in the young people of Weyburn or what they did. Sure, there were some beautiful girls, but they held no interest for him.

Imagine being a fully-trained Mountie, and still not having the freedom to leave the city whenever you wished. It seemed like the Mounties were as much in prison as criminals. Hunter was always teasing Tony about being so hopelessly in love, and that he'd soon get over it. They had a lot of arguments about this subject. Of course, sex was the favourite topic during the many hours they spent on highway patrol and checking for purple gas.

Simpson complained they were not bringing in enough tickets, [and that] they were well below the quota, [and that] the inspector would soon be raising hell. In police work, Tony was mostly a passenger. Not being allowed to make decisions, he felt like extra baggage. Whenever the corporal or Hunter were making inquiries, he'd engage other members of the family in conversation, usually on some political issue. Simpson disapproved of this because he believed policemen shouldn't make friendly conversation with people. But Tony was inclined to ignore this, as he thought the corporal wasn't very smart. What he lacked in intelligence, he made up for in brutality.

One time when they were investigating a case of a father who allegedly molested his ten-year-old daughter, Tony witnessed this brutality. Simpson was trying to get a confession, but was getting nowhere, so he took the father around to the back of the house and roughed him up with solid punches to the body. Then he stopped and asked, "Do you have anything to confess?"

The father said pathetically, "No."

Simpson became very angry and really beat the hell outta him. He pounded the father on the face and in the stomach. Falling to the ground, Simpson kicked him with his heavy police boots on the head and back. Every blow sounded like an explosion. Tony was afraid the corporal was going to kill the father. He was tempted to jump in and fight Simpson when he suddenly stopped. Simpson picked him up and stood him against the wall and asked, "Do you want to confess now?"

In a whisper, the father said, "Yes."

The corporal dragged him to the car and threw him in the back seat. A full "confession" was taken and he was made to sign it. At the trial, the father pleaded guilty and was sentenced to five years in the pen. Tony had seen some pretty tough fist fights among the Halfbreeds in St. Louis, but none had ever been that cruel. Tony asked Simpson about the ethics of getting such a confession.

"It's all part of good police work," he explained. "How'n hell would we ever get a conviction on that bastard without a confession? Any other evidence was useless and would never hold up in court."

"Isn't there any danger of getting in trouble? What if he lays a charge against you?" asked Tony seriously.

"Naw," said the corporal, "these bohunks out here are too damn dumb to know anything. That's the only kind of law and order they understand."

That beating really bothered Tony. Maybe the father had done wrong, but did he deserve such a brutal beating? The corporal was a puzzle to Tony because he was a nice guy to work with, seemed friendly and kind, yet he was capable of this fierce cruelty. Was this what years of police work does to a man? Would he eventually become like Simpson? He felt depressed for several days. He hoped he'd be kept on patrol with Hunter, for it was always a lot more fun talking about women and sex.

One evening, the mental hospital phoned to report that a mental patient had escaped. After getting the description, Tony and Hunter went out to find this patient. They searched in the general area where he was believed to have gone, but without success. They extended the search in other directions, but still no luck. They were on their way home when they spotted a man walking alone on the highway. Approaching [him], they could see he fitted the description. They stopped and asked him where he was going. He gave a reasonable explanation about coming from visiting his son across the highway, and was now going to his own home just beyond the bluff. The policemen could see neither house nor bluff. He must be the mental patient.

"What's your name?" asked Tony, who was amazed how much the man looked like Commanding Officer Symmons of Regina. The man got nervous, "Who, me? My name's … my name's John."

"What's your last name?" inquired Hunter.

He didn't seem sure. He must have a disturbed mind. Tony wondered if he had any identification that could prove who he was. But to his sorrow, he did not have any. Finally, he said, "My name's John Dobson."

Tony turned to Hunter and said, "This has got to be the man."

There was no explanation for Tony being anxious to pick up this man, except that he looked like the commanding officer at Depot, and that his son had a big beautiful house and a huge farm, and that he didn't deserve them anymore than Tony did. Tony was already thinking like a Whiteman, in terms of property, wonderful big farms, [and was] jealous of others who had more than him. Tony got out, and ordered Dobson to get in the car.

"But I don't want to go to Weyburn," he protested as he got in the backseat. The two policemen practically had to carry Dobson into the receiving room at the hospital. The attendant received him as the escaped patient.

The next morning, the hospital phoned to explain they had a very angry John Dobson who was brought to the hospital by two Mounties, and that he was not a patient. He'd been kept overnight by mistake, but was now released, and he was insisting the Mounties had to drive him home.

On the way home, Dobson said, "I'm going to sue the RCMP, and you too," pointing at Tony. "I'm going to charge you with false arrest." But Tony just kidded him about spending a free night in the nut house.

"Make sure you get a good lawyer and hit the Mounties for as much as possible. They're worth a lot of money," suggested Tony. He got out and let Dobson out at his house, shook his hand and said, "Now don't forget to sue us. I think you've got a good chance to win. In case you want to get in touch with me, my name's Officer Symmons, my office is in Depot Division in Regina."

A few weeks later, Tony had to go with Simpson on patrol. Tony was getting desperate about not seeing Sylvia. If he couldn't make some arrangement with the corporal for a weekend, he'd just take off. To hell with being caught—he'd been in jail before! Simpson had decided to check cars and trucks, so they were busy checking brakes, license, purple gas, booze, etc. It was monotonous work, and Tony grew tired of it on the second day. Instead of checking, he was chatting and visiting with drivers and passengers. Whenever he saw a beautiful girl, he'd check her registration card, getting her name and address. It may not have been police work, but it was interesting and had possibilities for more excitement.

Simpson checked the vehicles carefully, and if he didn't find anything else wrong he'd nail the truck drivers a fifteen-dollar fine for empty fire extinguishers. At one time, they had several motorists and truckers lined up, so to speed things up Tony was sent down the line to tell the people what to have ready for inspection. When it came to fire extinguishers, the truckers were beat because they were completely dry. Tony let them in on a little secret: "Take the extinguisher behind the bush and piss in it. Then, when the corporal checks, he'll think it's the proper fluid. Anyway, he couldn't prove it here."

Sure enough, Simpson inspected the extinguishers, pumped them. They squirted okay, and he passed them as okay. Except one wouldn't work, so he was pressing on the handle with all his force when it suddenly sprung loose and squirted "fluid" all over his uniform. A great roar of laughter from the truckers rang out, and Tony laughed with them. He didn't feel a bit sorry for Simpson, as he hadn't forgotten the beating of the bohunk father. After the fire extinguisher incident, Tony couldn't seem to bring himself to suggesting a deal with Simpson—at least, not for another week or so.

Hunter and Tony were assigned patrol duty one night on the highway to the RAF base. Almost immediately, a car roared passed. They chased it, but failed to gain on it. Although Hunter put the gas pedal down to the floorboards, they were still left behind. Their car couldn't do any more than ninety miles per hour. At the RAF gate, Hunter asked who had just pulled in ahead of them.

"That was Commanding Officer Williams," answered the guard.

The two Mounties looked at each other, then turned around and drove home. "Well, we can't do anything about that," said Hunter. "We'd really be in trouble if we laid a charge against that old goat."

"Why not?" argued Tony. "He broke the law just as anybody else. What gives him the right to get off free as a breeze? We have a job to do, and don't we have to do it honestly and fairly?"

"Yeah, but we've got to use intelligence about it," stated Hunter.

"Who the hell does a commanding officer think he is—a God or some such thing?" snapped Tony. "Commanding officer" had become a dirty word ever since the Depot incident.

"Old Hexter would really blow his stack if we laid a charge against his real close pal," explained Hunter.

The two policemen argued about it on the way home. Tony was persistent, "I'd love to nail that son of a bitch to the cross. I hate commanding officers!" They decided to ask Corporal Simpson about the matter in the morning. It was the first thing they mentioned to him when he came in.

"Oh good heavens, no," exclaimed the corporal without hesitation. He was speaking as an old, experienced member of the police force who understood the politics in the police force. "Forget the whole matter. Forget you saw old man Williams speeding."

"Come off it, corporal," protested Tony. "A commanding officer is not better than anybody else. They think they're above the law, yet they make everybody suffer under their friggin' law."

Tony persisted with his argument until he annoyed Hunter and the corporal. They said, if he wanted to charge Williams, he could go ahead and do it on his own, because they'd have nothing to do with it.

"Certainly," announced Tony, "I'll be glad to lay any charge against any commanding officer, and right now. And I hope he's put in jail as commanding officers should be." It was obvious that Tony was drawing a parallel between Commanding Officer Williams and Commanding Officer Symmons. Yet that was Sylvia's father. Tony wrote out a speeding ticket and sent a copy to Williams. It told when he had to appear in court.

The next day, a sudden explosion from Inspector Hexter's office announced he'd received a phone call from Williams about the speeding ticket. His bellowing shook the whole second floor. The corporal was ordered to his desk. He explained that Constable Parker had laid the charge against his advice. Tony was ordered to the inspector's office. Hexter was difficult to understand under normal conditions, and was entirely hopeless in a crisis. All Tony could make out were a few words, such as "fool," "stupid," and "idiot."

As usual, Tony was a cripple in front of an officer. Although he tried to argue on the same basis as he had done with the corporal and Hunter, it was useless. Anyway, the inspector refused to let him talk. As he was being dismissed, Tony heard Hexter say, "I may charge you with insubordination."

He joined Hunter and Simpson in the front office. "Next time, you'll take our advice," Hunter said advisedly. "Geez," snapped Tony, "instead of that friggin' commanding officer being charged with flying too low, I'm being charged with insubordination—whatever the hell that is."

"Yeah, but you've got to know when to lay charges, and when not to—and to lay off all commanding officers," said Simpson philosophically. "That is, if you want to get promoted in this outfit."

But Tony remained determined. He'd defy old Hexter and proceed with his charge against Williams. He'd never get a better opportunity to crucify a White ruler. Simpson argued each day, "You're absolutely out of your mind to proceed with this charge. He's getting the best lawyer in town, and he won't even have to appear in court. And so what if he's fined? What's money to him?"

But it never discouraged Tony. "I don't give a damn. He'll have a record against him, just like the courts do to poor people. Let him know that the rules and laws apply to him, as well as all the recruits at the bottom." The corporal spoke intimately to Tony, "I suppose you know that Hexter is giving all this information to the commanding officer at Depot, and that's not helping you any."

"I don't give a shit," barked Tony. "I'm never going to get back to Regina by the looks of it, not even for a visit. This'll let old screw-face Symmons know that Tony Parker's no fool, and not to be shoved around. I ain't going to prostitute myself just to please some paleface officer. I don't give a damn how high and mighty he is. I got principles too." He realized he'd let the word "paleface" slip out. He hoped the corporal would not notice it.

"You talk tough, but you're innocent, green, naïve. You're not dry behind the ears yet! You don't know what the hell the police force's all about yet. Take some advice from a Mountie who's been through the mill: Stop fighting the police force all the time, especially the officers. They can destroy any lowly constable whenever they wish. Live a little, Tony," spoke Simpson in a fatherly manner.

As expected, Williams' lawyer appeared at the trial. As Tony presented his evidence, it was easy to see that the judge was a friend of Williams. He challenged Tony's evidence and at times ridiculed it. He had the same attitude as old Hexter. By the time the case was over, Tony thought he would be lucky to get away without being charged for public mischief, or they might even hang him.

"Case dismissed," announced the judge with finality as if he had made up his mind long beforehand.

The next day, Tony appeared before Inspector Hexter on a charge of insubordination. "Since you're at the lowest level, I can't demote you. You're not fit to be higher than a third-class constable. I hope you've learned your lesson about dealing with important people. But I can't trust you on regular police work, so I'm transferring you to Gravelbourg, where you'll be put on town duty. You'll only be allowed to pound the beat and check doors. You're not permitted to do any other police work until I say so. Any idiot can do that work. And for God's sake, Parker, stay out of trouble. Dismissed."

Hunter and the corporal were sorry to see Tony leave. Simpson was trying to be helpful: "And remember, you'll still be in Weyburn sub-division, so Hexter'll have personal control over you. He'll be watching you." Tony replied, "I'll be waiting for him when he comes to Gravelbourg on his inspection tour."

Tony was sad about leaving Weyburn, for he was going farther away than ever from Sylvia. He'd been here six months and hadn't seen Sylvia nor heard from her. It was like loving someone in a vacuum. He wondered how much longer his love would hold out without a response, for his love demanded responses [...]. Yet, was this not what the commanding officer intended by his action, to crush and smother affection? To Tony, this seemed like the mission of the entire society. He knew police work in Gravelbourg would be the shits. **(TB)**

Mountie in Gravelbourg, Saskatchewan

Corporal Stinson was a tough, burly, but a dynamic and pleasant Mountie to work with. He used the direct approach—little talking and some roughness. First, threaten with a major crime, and then offer a lesser charge for a guilty plea. We had few court cases, [and most of these were...] guilty pleas. He gave his constables lots of independence for their duties. [...].

My own criminal investigations were exciting. They required imaginative thinking and deep exploring. I was solving some mysterious cases. This was exciting work for a twenty-one-year-old. He gave me a good personal report. I was moving up. The year ended with a transfer to Gravelbourg, a French-Catholic town like St. Louis, but bigger. Tragically, this was to be my Waterloo, but I didn't know it then.

Corporal Clifford was a beast; a cruel and a chronically drunk Mountie. He was determined to undermine me from the day that I arrived until the day I left. He was autocratic, very devious and dangerous. He insidiously sabotaged my police work. His personality was gruff, abrupt and insulting. As long as he was half-drunk, he wasn't too bad. But sober, he was horrible and treacherous. **(AB)**

Gravelbourg is a typical prairie town with one main street, with the Wheat Pool elevator at one end and the church at the other end. The streets aren't paved in Gravelbourg, but [...] are gravelled. It is very much like St. Louis, Catholic and French, except it isn't a Halfbreed town—not a single Redman. Gravelbourg is famous for its magnificent Catholic cathedral— the largest and most beautiful west of Montréal. It dominates the town physically, just as the priest, Father Carpentier, dominates the religious and social life of the people. He is very active in politics, being one of the best Liberal party supporters. Since he owns the local newspaper and directs its news, it's little more than a straight propaganda paper. As well, Father Carpentier has his own radio program, in which he preaches the greatness of the Liberal party. Obviously he has an extensive vested interest in this free enterprise party.

Gravelbourg is not as big as Weyburn, but it seems more lively and friendly, for it is a sports town. Economically, it depends entirely on farmers for its business, and most farmers are well off. Many young people live in the town, working either for Father Carpentier or in service trades. Tony soon gets acquainted with many of these lively and seemingly happy- go-lucky French youth.

Politically, Gravelbourg has been a strong Liberal fort, having elected only Liberal members to Legislative Assembly. However, this election, many people have turned over to the Co-operative Commonwealth Federation [CCF], and it has become one of the hottest towns politically in Saskatchewan. The RCMP office is located on the main street, on the second floor of an old brick building. There are just two rooms, or really only one and a half, because the room, which is Tony's room, is barely big enough for a bed and a trunk. It is directly behind the counter of the office and is really not private. Since he is on night patrol and needs to sleep in the daytime, he feels he should be away from the noise of the office. At the moment, Tony is thankful that he doesn't have to sleep on the floor in the hallway.

"Pounding the beat" was worse than Tony imagined. Walking up and down the same grim sidewalk from 4 p.m. to 4 a.m. is tedious and dreadful. If there's anything worse, it's the sergeant in charge of the Gravelbourg RCMP detachment, for he's one of the severest and meanest men Tony has met. It is a mystery how a person so slight and small could contain so much misery and disagreeableness. It could've been partly due to Tony's point of view, for Sergeant Gordon looks like old man Caron of St. Louis—not as old, maybe forty-five, but even his heavy moustache is the same. Like Sergeant Hood of Depot, Gordon is commanding and harsh, unable to carry on a conversation, speaking only when giving orders. He is an Anglo, probably like those of St. Louis, uppity and snobbish. The best way to get along with Gordon

is to stay out of his way.

Being on town beat, and not knowing anyone in Gravelbourg, Tony had lots of free time, especially for politics. 1944 was an election year in Saskatchewan, and politics was a big issue. The socialist CCF party was coming on strong, and it looked like they would replace the old Liberal party. Political literature from the local party offices was free and plentiful, so Tony generously helped himself, reading the latest political arguments, particularly about the latest socialist developments. As a result, several pamphlets and papers were lying around his room when the sergeant came in. Obviously, he got upset at the sight of political material, for he snapped at Tony, "Don't you know you're not allowed to have CCF propaganda in police quarters?"

"No, sergeant, I didn't." replied Tony honestly.

"It's damn well time you knew. You hafta get this damn stuff outta here right away, and don't bring in anymore," commanded Gordon.

"Yes, sir," answered Tony in his customary obedience, but on second thought he pleaded, "I only got it for something to read."

"It doesn't matter for the reason, it's absolutely against police regulations. And what's more, you're not allowed to discuss politics, neither in the office nor in this room. Now get that simple rule into your head," ordered Gordon, looking at the material as if it was diseased. "Most policemen have more brains than to get mixed up with this kind of nonsense. What'n the hell's wrong, Parker, didn't your people teach you anything at all?" said the sergeant sarcastically.

This struck Tony like a bullet, for he knew what Gordon was referring to. He hadn't heard a word about his Halfbreed background since he'd joined, and he thought it was well hidden. It stunned him. "Now get up and clean this shit outta here right away!"

Tony was completely crushed. Under the control of this White tyrant, he found himself an obedient servant, as he replied, "Yes, sergeant, I'll get this political stuff outta here right away. I'm sorry! I hope they haven't caused any trouble. It won't happen again."

Tony was shaken, but also confused. He didn't want to anger the sergeant, yet he was anxious to read about the election. During his meal, he thought seriously about politics, and concluded there could be little harm in it. There should be freedom to discuss politics with his friends, or with the people on the street, just as he had done in St. Louis. The campaign for Lionel Morin [back home in St. Louis] was one of the most exciting times he'd ever had. Now that he was a Mountie, would he be expected to give up all that? That would mean for the rest of his life. Did he want to be denied his political rights, one of the few rights he had? Wasn't he expected to vote? Yet, how could he make intelligent decisions without knowing the facts? Tony knew that Mounties were used in political matters, and that they were not neutral, because in Weyburn they had investigated people who were reported as radicals, socialists or communists.

With the provincial elections drawing close, everyone was talking politics. In fact, it was difficult to get away from it. Doubtless, this was one of the most exciting elections in Saskatchewan's history, and it was mighty hard to sit on the sidelines and ignore it. But Gordon was probably right: to remain a Mountie, he'd have to stay clear of politics. A frightening thought crossed Tony's mind: If he couldn't mix politics with being a Mountie, would he leave the police force? This was the first time, but not the last, that such a question came into his mind.

He pounded the grim and deserted beat that night and puzzled over the whole political situation. He thought of Gordon and his unreasonable rules. No doubt he supported the Liberal Party, as he seemed to support everything for the ruling people and their friends, like the big merchants, doctors and lawyers. Tony was surprised to find how deeply he felt about politics, and that it could come before his Mountie career. However, in the meantime he agreed to keep all political material out of his room, and not get into political arguments on the street. He'd find other ways of keeping abreast of the election. Politically, things were hot in Gravelbourg, and trouble could be provoked any time because there was fear that the CCF would replace the Liberals. Being socialist, the CCF were considered dangerous. Consequently, the Mounties had to be kept ready for law and order. Word came from Inspector Hexter that Tony was to be taken off town beat and given a chance on regular police work.

"You've got to do good work, and none of that child-like behaviour. I won't stand for any damn boozing. You've got to be responsible. I know you people only too damn well, so act like an intelligent man or you'll be back pounding the beat," commanded Gordon.

That rocked Tony; it was like the beating in the boxing ring, only he couldn't punch back here. Every word slammed him like a smash to the jaw. Tony thought to himself, "You sonofabitch, I'd sooner stay on town beat rather than listening to your racists commands." But instead, Tony said politely, "Yes, sergeant, I'll do my best. It's very good of Inspector Hexter to give me this chance." **(TB)**

Howard/Tony and the Grain Theft Case: Two Versions of Howard`s Greatest Feat as a Mountie

On a bright morning while investigating a complaint, I spotted deep truck tracks coming from farmer Grant's granary. The sun had hardened last night's damp mud. The tire track impressions were perfect. It aroused my suspicion, as Mr. Grant did not have a big truck. Checking further at the granary, I found additional clues. A large chip had broken off from the corner of a grain box. It was a splinter that could fit only that box.

Back in town, I checked with the elevator agents for [all the] wheat sold in the last day. A specific ticket had been made out to Joe Pilon, but delivered in Bruce Lefeaux's truck. I knew Lefeaux. He wasn't a thief, but on the other hand he wasn't a saint. The next day, when I was on street patrol, I spotted a truck with a green wooden box that had a familiar chip broken from it. It matched this truck perfectly. The tire mould of mud also matched the tire exactly.

It was ten o'clock Saturday night. Lefeaux was in the bootlegger's lounge. He was known as a huge tough punk. He scared me. But could a Mountie fail to capture a criminal because he was a coward? I walked around the block to get up my courage. Then I boldly stepped into the bootlegger's den. I told Lefeaux he was suspected. To my surprise, he was as timid as a mouse. "I loaned my truck to Pilon last week. I don't know what the hell he did with it." I accepted his answer. The next day, the elevator agent gave me a description of the person who sold Grant's wheat. It fitted Pilon precisely. I had all the evidence I needed to arrest him.

Clifford was sitting at his desk, staring out in a daze. He paid no attention to my exciting discovery of Grant's stolen wheat. He acknowledged nothing, got up, grabbed his briefcase and walked out. I couldn't believe it. This was a breakthrough on a serious crime and Clifford blatantly ignored it.

Walking on the street that afternoon, I bumped into Pilon. I grabbed his arm and said, "You are under arrest." He turned and was about to run, but I held him. I dragged him to the office and locked the door. I felt powerful and victorious. But in a couple of minutes, things changed. His sister, Marie, was shouting at the door, threatening my authority and cursing me: "As soon as Corporal Clifford comes, he'll smash you!"

I shouted, "Shut up and get the hell away from here!"

"You ignorant pig," she yelled, "you don't know all the rotten things about your damn boss."

Marie was no shrinking violet. She was loud, vulgar and would go to any length to get her way. Marie had plenty of sex appeal, and she clearly displayed all she dared. I heard rumours about her and Clifford's relationship, but had given them little attention until now. I knew of the corporal's reputation as a corrupt and immoral person. His reputation as a womanizer was common knowledge throughout the whole region.

I tried to ignore her, but that wasn't easy. During her antics, she demanded the release of her brother. She claimed Clifford was a regular visitor to her house and never left until he was satisfied. She was trying desperately to force me to release her brother.

But I had a solid case against Pilon and could get a conviction easily. Sitting quietly in the chair, Pilon didn't seem concerned. He had probably been in this situation before. Speaking firmly, I said, "I've got all the evidence on you that I need to send you up for a couple of years. There isn't a chance in hell that you'll get off on this charge."

Just then Clifford walked into the office, partly drunk. His offensive manner changed everything. He greeted Marie with a kindly hello and gently recognized Pilon. He pushed my papers to the floor. He took command. That was typical behaviour of him. He had little appreciation of ethical police principles.

Pilon said, "This greenhorn constable claims I stole wheat from Grant's farm, but it's a damn lie."

I quickly interrupted: "I have all the evidence right here!"

Marie leaned over, hugged and fondled the corporal. He looked at Pilon and said, "Get the hell out of here until I call you."

I yelled at Clifford, "How in the hell can you do that? You haven't studied any evidence. You know nothing!"

It was the best police work I had done in my Mountie career, but it had come to nothing and had undermined my credibility. **(AB)**

Shortly after, a farmer named Agnew reported that several hundred bushels of wheat had been stolen from his granary. In great excitement, Tony went out to investigate. Almost immediately in his mind, he was a police mastermind who would receive awards for the brilliant and courageous capture. Tony drove out to the Agnew farm and over to the granary, and parked the car a good distance away so as not to disturb any tracks. He circled and searched very carefully all around the building, checking very seriously every possible clue. A tire track was quite noticeable, so he made a plaster of Paris impression. While he was searching around in the granary, he came upon a short green chip of wood that could've broken off from a grain box. Neither belonged to the owner. Tony persisted with his investigation until darkness fell.

The next day, he returned and took lengthy statements from Agnew and other persons who might help. In the evening, he checked all the green trucks parked in town, and to his great amazement found one that matched the chip and tire track from Agnew's granary. He'd located the thief and he knew who he was—Mike Hardie, a rich farmer, a big shot and a prominent Liberal party member. But, most of all, he was a personal friend of Sergeant Gordon.

Tony was afraid of this huge man of six-foot-six and two hundred fifty pounds, with a reputation as the big-time bully. In addition, there was a political problem, but Tony had no choice. He'd have to "take the bull by the horns" and approach Mike directly. Tony decided to remain firm and official. No one would get out of his police net. He'd solved a big grain theft, possibly one of the biggest in the West, and all by a small chip of wood. What a brilliant policeman he was! Head office in Ottawa would surely recognize his outstanding work and reward him with much publicity and glory. He could already see his name flashing across the news screen. It took a couple of trips around the block for Tony to work up the needed courage. Pretending [to have the] bravery of the greatest Mounties, Tony marched straight to Mike's lounge upstairs and squared off with forced boldness, announcing, "I may have to arrest you for grain theft."

"I don't know what you're talking about," snapped Mike, without turning to look at Tony.

"Agnew's had some wheat stolen, and your truck hauled it away from the granary," said Tony firmly.

"How the hell do you know it's my truck? I'm no goddamn thief."

"Because it's your tire tracks, and you dropped part of the tail-gate in the granary. I've got it."

To Tony's surprise, Mike turned and made a confession, at least partly. "It might'a been my truck, but I sure as hell had nothing to do with it. Young Joe Percy took my truck a few times without my permission." Mike continued to give more information freely, and offered Tony a drink.

His next step had to be planned carefully, for no doubt the sergeant was watching the investigation, and would now crush it at first opportunity. Tony drove out to the Percy home and met Joe, who was working in the garden.

"I want to talk to you about stolen wheat from the Agnew farm," Tony said in a very official manner.

"It's got nothing to do with me," protested Joe.

"You've got another thought coming. You used Mike Hardie's truck and sold it at the Pool elevator on his permit. You left perfect tire tracks and a part of the grain box at the scene," explained Tony.

"You'll never convict me," Joe argued. "Ask Sergeant Gordon."

"What do you mean?" snapped Tony in a surprised tone. "I'm charging you, not Gordon."

Joe didn't seem worried, as he said, "I don't give a damn what you do." Tony issued a summons to Joe and returned home.

That evening, Tony had a visitor to his room, Joe's young sister. Her suddenness and aggressiveness momentarily overpowered him. He was somewhat puzzled by this attractive girl and her exceptional friendliness. She was youthful, about twenty, and had a striking appearance with dark hair, tawny complexion and steel grey eyes. Her snug fitting dress showed she had a shapely figure. Never having met her before, he found her extremely bold and intimate. It was obvious that she was not a naïve farm girl. He found himself being disturbed by her, but in a pleasant way.

"You don't get around very much. I hardly ever see you," she announced with confidence. She stood almost in a defiant position, provocative and sexy. Tony tried to maintain a business attitude, yet being unable to ignore the come-on. Probably for the first time in his life, he held a sexual attitude towards a White girl, and almost immediately. "How do you know whether I get around or not? You don't live in town?" It was more of a question than a statement.

"Oh, I know. I have a way of keeping track of all the handsome and important people," she said. In a playful manner, she reached over and took Tony's cap off, then ran her hand through his hair. She was talking to him from directly across the narrow counter. "Why don't you invite me to your room? I'm good company. Try me and see for yourself."

"I guess I'm always too busy," said Tony, not wanting to be nasty with her. "How come I haven't seen you around town?" His thoughts of himself as a glorified Mountie were momentarily pushed into the background. She walked around the end of the counter and stood directly beside Tony. "I suppose it's because you're so busy with other girls. Do they give you everything you want?" she asked without hesitation.

Tony fumbled nervously with papers on the counter. "I don't know what you mean." Pretending to be officious, he asked, "What's your business in this office?"

"I came just to see you, isn't that enough?" she said, pushing Tony towards his own room. Sure, he was concerned about his police work, but at the moment he was being guided by a stronger urge. The amorous voice and intimate movements stirred Tony's passions stronger than he wished. He allowed himself to be pulled over to the bed.

"Why are you so cautious? Are you afraid of me? I've never hurt anyone. Why can't you enjoy yourself?" she asked, encouraging Tony to run his hands over her body. Excitement was raging in Tony. "I'll stay with you tonight." It was a statement, not a question.

"Do you do this to all the Mounties in Gravelbourg?" Tony asked.

"No, I'm interested only in a handsome Mountie who knows how to enjoy himself," she said softly. There was no doubt in Tony's mind about being able to enjoy himself with her, yet he was puzzled and fearful.

"What's the game you're playing?" he asked, stalling for time while he tried to figure her out. Sure he wanted her, but maybe she'd come back late at night. She got up and took her coat off. Tony's eyes followed her fingers as she unbuttoned her dress. He noticed she was looking at her watch frequently, and that bothered him. In this brief interlude, Tony's passions had cooled slightly, at least enough to think rationally. "What if Gordon walked in?" he asked, more of himself than of her.

"Never mind about Sergeant Gordon, he's out of town on business," she replied. "Maybe we should spend a little more time getting acquainted," sitting on the edge of the bed talking to her as she stretched out.

"What the hell's with your watch that you've got to keep watching it?" Tony asked. He got up and walked over to the counter. At the same time, he heard footsteps on the stairs, and quickly he pulled his door closed. Sergeant Gordon swept in quickly, looked surprised to see Tony working at the counter, walked around the office once, and left without saying anything. It puzzled Tony. He opened his door and saw that she was up and putting her coat on. She seemed annoyed, but Tony guessed it was because he'd failed to co-operate with her.

Disgustedly, she said, "Was that Sergeant Gordon who just came in?"

"Yeah, why?" Her mood had changed very abruptly. No longer was she interested in loving Tony. Slowly, the scheme came clear in his mind. He fixed his eyes on her with a look that could kill, as he said very deliberately, "You little sonofabitch! You came in here to screw me so Gordon would come in right in the act, or you were gonna scream 'rape,' and Gordon would rush in, you filthy whore." Tony stepped close to her and let go with a powerful slap of his open hand that sent her staggering to the other side of the bed.

She got up. Her mouth was bleeding. She looked dreadfully scared as she said, "That's not true. I wouldn't do anything like that to you. Please, Tony, believe me."

Tony grabbed her by the arm and dragged her into the office. He looked at her as she clung to the counter, and said, "You friggin' slut, I should knock the shit outta you. Get outta here. I don't want to throw you out because you're probably so goddamn diseased." But he gave her a heavy shove that sent her out the door and near the stairs.

She turned and looked back at Tony and broke into a shrill laughter, and said, "You dirty Indian bastard, I'd never let a smelly savage screw me. Screw your own filthy squaws!" She took a few steps down the stairs, but turned and shouted back, "Everybody in town's laughing about a thieving Halfbreed protecting their places. They're going to get rid of you, one way or another. You're the stupidest goddamn Indian ever. No wonder everyone calls you the village idiot."

Tony stepped over and slammed the door. He could hear her shouting as she went down the stairs and out. Tony was in a rage. He walked about kicking everything in sight. Ringing in his ears were the shrill shouts of "village idiot." He thought his head would split open. So that's how the town people saw him. He believed it was probably true. Never had he seen himself so low, so inferior, so ugly and debased. He was too ashamed to ever appear again on the streets, and yet that was his job. It would be impossible because he'd be haunted by the roars of laughter, ridicule and mockery that blazed behind his back. He couldn't face the people again, knowing they'd see him as a sneaky barbarian, a child, a drunken Indian, etc. If only he had the courage to commit suicide. He'd never escape being a Halfbreed. It would follow him to the end of the world. Suddenly he got cramps in his stomach. Pain grabbed at his guts. It was like a convulsion. He knew he was going to vomit, but to hell with going to the can, he said to himself, I'll puke on this floor, Gordon's floor, and his bitch and the whole friggin' society. He puked till his guts were about to come up.

The next day, Tony took the police car to go out on patrol, but instead he just rode around in the country, thinking and planning. He didn't want to see people, no one. He had to be by himself to think things out. The two questions foremost in his mind were: How to get even with the sergeant, and would he leave the Mounties? But he was certain he wouldn't leave until the score with Gordon was settled. In the evening when he returned, the sergeant was in the office.

"I got a call from Inspector Hexter today, and you're to go back on town patrol," explained Gordon.

"Geez, I just came off town patrol a few days ago," said Tony annoyed.

"Yeah, but there's no one else to do it."

Tony was sure there was no phone call. He felt like saying, "You friggin' liar, you're the one who's putting me back on the beat." Gordon was probably angry because he took the police car for the day without reporting to him first. He was sorry he hadn't smashed up the old heap. Feeling revolted by everything, Tony said sharply, "I don't give a shit."

Studying the sergeant he wondered about revenge, in terms of violence. He's not big, but for a constable to touch a higher rank would be like committing murder. Inspector Hexter and all the big shot rulers in Gravelbourg protected Gordon, but he must have enemies, even a few. **(TB)**

Howard/Tony and the CCF Poster Scandal

In Gravelbourg, half my time was pounding the town beat from 8 p.m. to 2 a.m. Nothing was more boring and painful than walking up and down two wooden sidewalks all night. The biggest thrill of the shift was checking out four huge elevators at midnight. In winter, at forty below, the patrol was critically piercing and menacing. Regularly, I dropped in at the Chinese café to have my usual free coffee and pie—that was his protection pay.

However, on my regular daytime police […] shift, I worked on serious criminal cases. I had numerous difficult cases that required serious police investigation. My best police investigations were in Gravelbourg. Outside of my police work, I had plenty of social life with the young people in town. They were jovial and reckless types, doubting Catholics.

Politics became important and engaging. Gravelbourg had been a strong Liberal centre. [The town's] big [Liberal] supporters and activists were priests, lawyers and local businessmen. But in 1944, there was a large swing to the CCF, and it was election year in Saskatchewan. I could not stay quiet or neutral. Politics excited me. Corporal Clifford hassled […] me for my political activities. He commanded that I stay completely out of all politics. That was RCMP policy. He threatened to report me to the commanding officer and have me arrested. I worked around him slyly.

The Sunday before election, the parish priest preached a political sermon from his pulpit that was anti-CCF and pro-Liberal. Several church members got up and walked out. A few nights later, a group of young radical Catholics told me that they were going to glue big CCF posters on the Catholic church door, and on the showcase windows of business places and on the lawyer's picture window. They would do it during my night patrol and asked that I not arrest them. I did better. I would join them if they waited until after 2 a.m., when I could change into my civvies and join the group. Maybe it was mischievous, but it was tremendously exciting. With a gallon of superglue, we stuck the cathedral door with a mighty smudge. Next, we smeared the local printing shop as it pumped out a Liberal newspaper. The garage man's huge glass front window was totally smeared and papered. After we had covered the front street businesses with glue and posters, we sneaked off home to bed.

At 7 a.m., Corporal Clifford was shouting at the head of my bed. "Get the hell up, you stupid bugger! Everybody in town is in a fierce rage. You must know about this outrageous glue stunt. It was done while you were on patrol. You've got some explaining to do to these businessmen. If you don't, I'll have the commanding officer arrest you." Looking at the CCF election papers lying around my bed, he grabbed them and tore them up. He walked out and slammed the door. I turned over and ignored the whole storm. **(AB)**

That evening, a couple of young pals came over and talked to Tony as he ate his supper. They had a proposition. "We'd like to glue some CCF posters on the windows of the good Liberals' businesses, like the Imperial Garage, and Gagnon's big store, and certainly the cathedral, with those big two-by-three feet posters. We wanna smear them all over the doors and windows with heavy glue," explained one pal. The other friend continued, "We wanna do this after midnight, and we don't wanna get arrested. I suppose we're asking you to look the other way when you're on patrol tonight. Or maybe you could be checking over at the grain elevators."

This excited Tony immediately. "What the hell, look the other way, I'll join you and give you a hand," he said enthusiastically.

"But what if Sergeant Gordon catches us? You'd get into serious trouble," asked the pal with a concern.

Feeling very reckless and destructive, Tony said, "So what! Maybe we could wrap him up in a poster smeared with glue. How about that?" He was really thinking out loud.

"We have to get a few gallons of real good glue this evening. We're thinking of driving over to Black's Market in LaFleche so we won't be recognized," suggested one.

"I have a better idea," said Tony. "There is a key to Father Carpentier's printing shop in the office, our office, and inside that shop are a lot of tins of glue. I could get some out tonight."

"And that's fantastic glue," said a friend. "I've used it. It sticks to absolutely everything and it's impossible to get off."

The small group met at midnight. Tony had the pails of glue. Manuel had a twenty-six of rye. They went down one side of the street, smearing the heavy glue on the huge plate glass windows of the businesses of the Liberal supporters, and then slapping the huge posters over the adhesive. It was a good job of pasting. This was fun and exciting. The bottle of rye was being passed around steadily. Finally, Manuel had to go home and get another one. As a result, they were getting more reckless and noisy. When they got to the priest's printing shop and radio station, everyone got into the act, and the front became a solid wall of glue and posters. Even the Catholic cathedral was treated, and all agreed it should've because last Sunday, during his sermon, Father Carpentier urged his parishioners to vote Liberal. Many people were shocked that he used his pulpit to preach politics. Several people had gotten up and walked out. Returning on the other side of the street, they did a big job on the door going up to the RCMP office. Tony ran up and changed into civvies. He didn't seem to care if he was heading straight to jail. Tony went down a side street to Mike Hardie's door and fixed it up. They got to the end of the street and congratulated themselves on the great job they'd done. Everybody went over to Manuel's place for coffee, and finally home.

The sergeant was standing in the doorway yelling at Tony. "Come on, Parker, get the hell outta bed! The whole town's in a helluva 'n uproar 'bout posters glued on their windows. There's even one on our door downstairs. Where'n the hell were you when all this violence was going on?"

Sleepily, Tony answered, "I don't know what you're talking about."

"Come on, we've got to look into this mess right away," demanded Gordon. Tony got up grudgingly, but he was going to plead ignorance.

"You got to know what happened. You were on patrol. Several businessmen have been up to the office already this morning, raising hell about their property. We've got to catch those punks right away. If you can't tell us who'n the hell they are, you're in serious trouble,

Parker." Tony began to worry a little, as Gordon was in a horrible mood, and was making some serious threats. Tony tried to play it down.

"Was anybody hurt, or damage done?" asked Tony.

"No, but there's sure one helluva mess, and that's destruction to private property," roared Gordon.

Tony figured he'd have to make it a political issue, and in that way the sergeant would drop it quickly. So, when he went out for breakfast, he called Manuel and told him to get the fellows to contact Sergeant Gordon as CCF supporters and offer to pay the bail if anyone should be unfortunate enough to get charged. They should argue that this is a political issue, and that it would be a violation of political freedom [to press charges]. In the meantime, Tony and Gordon went around and looked at the glued posters. The sergeant complained bitterly and attacked the "punks" for this criminal behaviour, but Tony couldn't help but chuckle to himself and admire the work of the gluers. He tried to convince the sergeant there was nothing criminal in that activity, and that they shouldn't get mixed up in politics. If they tried to arrest anyone, they'd have all the CCFers in town mad at them, and that was a lot of people. Gordon kept raging at Tony for not seeing that this was going on when he was walking up and down these very streets. Tony's only defence was that it must've been done after he went off duty. The sergeant persisted [...] to nail down some specific names. Obviously, he was under pressure from these Liberal businessmen to arrest someone, anyone, as long as an arrest was made.

By the end of the day, the townspeople had become pretty worked-up over this political matter, and it looked as if it could be heading for a much more serious clash. To arrest anyone would virtually mean a call to arms. No doubt, the fellows had contacted Gordon, as instructed by Tony, and this was having a great influence in scaring Gordon off. The incident blew over without further trouble, and the sergeant never mentioned it again. Tony was jubilant about it, as he saw it as a victory over Gordon and the rulers of the town. He'd outwitted them, and, in a certain way, had made fools of them. The fellows had mucked up their windows, and now they were laughing at them. It gave Tony a sense of success, confidence and pride. There were other ways to succeed besides through the usual channels of rank promotion, or what society called "success". However, he still had Gordon to deal with, and his opportunity came sooner than expected.

Tony's Revenge On Gordon

Gordon was a fairly heavy boozer, especially after he got started, and the more he drank, the friendlier he became. A huge ball tournament was being held in Gravelbourg this day. After lunch, the sergeant came up to the office and was amazingly friendly. Tony suspected it was booze talking, but it was a lot better than his usual savage self. Tony brought out a bottle, and they had a drink, then two, and then more. They decided to go to the ballpark and see what was going on. Shortly after they arrived, an official came over and asked Tony to umpire a game. Instead, he talked Gordon into going. He staggered down and got into the pads. He had difficulty seeing the ball, and the batters argued with him, and the fans razed him. Periodically, he'd come to Tony for a quick drink from the bottle of scotch he'd left with him. Finally, Tony said, "You take it with you. Keep it in your pocket, then take a drink between pitches so you won't hold up the game." Soon Gordon was drinking from the bottle, standing in front of hundreds of local residents.

The regular umpire came along and sat beside Tony. He was a big, young man, over six feet tall and weighed two hundred pounds. He looked more like a bouncer than an umpire. Tony recognized him as Paul Green. In a moment, he turned to Tony and said, "Gordon's drunk! How'n hell can he ump?"

"Don't know," said Tony, "he just went down there on his own and started to umpire. I agree. He's making a helluva mess of it." This seemed to satisfy Paul about Tony's attitude towards Gordon, for he immediately mouthed-off an attack against the sergeant. Finally Tony asked, "What have you got against Gordon?"

"The sonofabitch has knocked up my sister, and now claims he doesn't even know her. You can see for yourself what an asshole he is out there." Tony realized he and Paul had one thing in common: a score to settle with Sergeant Gordon.

Tony urged Paul to go down and take over as umpire, but Gordon refused to give up his position. He pushed Paul around and swore at him. Paul was enraged and was ready to tear the sergeant apart. Tony went down and separated them. On the way back to the stands, Paul stated, "I'll kill that bastard if it's the last thing I do."

"Yeah, but not here. Many of these people are his friends," answered Tony.

Gordon called, "Time out." He'd been drinking so much his bladder was full. For some unknown reason, he turned towards the crowd, unzipped his pants, pulled out his tool and let it splash. The crowd was in shock and disgust. The sight of the sergeant's organ and the thought of his pregnant sister was more than Paul could stand: "Bring him for a beer at the Prairie Hotel as soon as the game's over."

On the way over in the car, Tony complimented the sergeant on the fine job he had done as an umpire, and that he was a real favourite with the crowd. They parked far to the rear of the hotel, away behind the skating rink. As soon as Gordon stepped towards the hotel, Paul grabbed him. It wasn't a fight; it was just a straight beating. Every time Paul would knock Gordon to the ground, he'd pick him up and clobber him again. Every punch was enough to smash every bone in his body. His face quickly became a pool of blood. He was being beaten to a pulp, but Tony couldn't sympathize with him. Finally, when he was totally unconscious, Tony went over and stopped Paul. He dragged Gordon into the car and took him home. He said nothing to Mrs. Gordon, except to call the doctor. He would've loved to tell her to invite Joe Percy's sister over to look after him. Gordon was off work for a week. No bones were broken, but he was badly cut and bruised. Not a word was ever said about the entire day.

Tony thought a lot about the beating, and it bothered him much more. He knew this thumping of the sergeant was deliberate and schemed, that it was revenge. The police force *was turning him into a beast—vicious and brutal. Yet, he couldn't help but feel a certain triumph and power over Gordon. He could make a fool out of the sergeant and make a hopeless, bloody mess out of him. He'd reduced him to nothingness. Who was the village idiot now? He'd like to see Gordon try and tell him now about not having political pamphlets in his room. He'd have all the socialist literature in his room that he wanted. He'd make the CCF headquarters in his room, and neither Gordon nor any other police officer would tell him that he couldn't. He'd like to see them try.*

Tony Meets Sue

Being alone on police duty, Tony took himself off town patrol. One evening, he met Mr. Norman, the CCF candidate for Gravelbourg, and his daughter. "Tony," said Mr. Norman, "I'd like you to meet my daughter, Sue."

Tony was immediately excited over Sue's beauty and charm. The sparkle of her deep brown eyes, and expressive smile revealed her elegance and gentleness. Even a short greeting told so much of her loveliness. She was slender, slightly wispy, with a very gracious walk and movement. Her flowing dark brown hair framed her beautiful white face of moderately sharp features, a lean nose and thin red lips. There was nothing Halfbreed looking about Sue—no high cheekbones, no broad nose or thick lips. Her voice was soft and friendly, so refined and steady. To Tony, Sue radiated true beauty and loveliness. She was more beautiful than Sylvia. He guessed she was a couple of years younger than himself.

Mr. Norman, a middle-aged farmer, in his rather brusque but pleasant manner said, "We're just going to grab something to eat before the executive meeting. How about joining us?"

Tony would've joined them even if he'd been chasing a murderer and about to capture him. Nothing was more important right now than lunch with the Normans. "I'd love to," said Tony.

Looking at Sue from across the table, Tony was sure she was the most exquisite girl he'd ever seen. Maybe she was rather shy, but that added to her charm. They discussed politics and, of course, socialism. Tony wondered if the people of Saskatchewan might not be too fearful of socialism to elect a CCF government in view of the frightening propaganda the old ruling parties were putting out.

"They may be a little worried, but I'm sure they're prepared to take a chance on socialism rather than live under the same old capitalist government that gives only poverty and misery," answered Mr. Norman. Politics was a natural subject for Tony, so he was able to converse quite easily. There was little chance for Sue to say anything. Often, Tony directed his answers to Sue, not only to impress her, but to show that he was not ignoring her.

Mr. Norman talked on as he ate his lunch. He explained why it was necessary for the people to set up their own government. By people, he meant workers, farmers and small business owners. The government under the Liberal and Conservative parties was strictly the government of the ruling class, and that was a very small percentage of the people. All the laws and policies were for the benefit of the big corporations and the millionaires. The governments of the past had taxed the people of the province so heavily, and most of it went towards making the big companies richer. Mr. Norman explained how socialism would change that. A CCF government would take some of the wealth and privileges away from the wealthy ruling class and distribute it for the benefit of the people, like free medical care, low cost housing for poor people, and low cost automobile insurance and many other things.

Socialism was exciting to Tony because he felt it would do many wonderful things for the Halfbreeds. Although he thought he'd rejected them, he still had a very deep concern for their welfare. When they'd finished eating, Mr. Norman announced, "I've got to get over to the meeting at Duncan's place. I think Sue's going to her friend's place. Ride along with us if you want."

Tony was a little puzzled and nervous as he said, "I might as well. I've got nothing to do." Mr. Norman got out and said he'd be ready at 10:30. Tony and Sue were left in the car alone. Tony felt that he should get out of the car, but yet he didn't want to. He was uncomfortable. Beside him was a beautiful girl who he'd love to chat with, but at the same time he was being oppressed by the "White ideal." It was crushing him into a position of inferiority. Out of nervousness, Tony teased Sue about her father becoming a member of the legislature, and maybe a cabinet minister, and she'd become one of the ladies of high society. Sue felt that under a socialist government, there wouldn't be a high society because everyone should be reasonably equal. They chatted for a while on politics, nothing very serious. Tony suggested they go for a drive, he offered to do the driving. They drove out to the country. There were no sights to see, so they just meandered around. Tony was talking light-heartedly and joking around. He knew it was a cover-up for his nervousness.

They parked on a small bank overlooking a lazy creek. Their conversation became quieter and more serious. Tony drew Sue close to him and held her firmly. In a soft, low voice, Tony was telling her what a beautiful girl she was, and how very much he was attracted to her. Tony embraced Sue tightly. Their lips met, leaving a soft, delicate kiss. Tony looked at Sue. She seemed so adorable. He wanted to express his tender feelings, but before he could say anything, he was kissing her again and squeezing her delicate body vigorously to him. Her responses aroused Tony, and his powerful arms squeezed even harder, stirring his passions further. But he checked himself when Sue's responses hesitated. Sue suggested they should get back to town, as her father might be ready to go.

Within the next couple of weeks, Tony visited with Sue every time she came to town. She invited Tony to her home the next Sunday. Although he didn't have a car and there was no public transportation to Minto, a distance of about twenty-five miles, he said he'd be there even if he had to walk it.

Tony's mind became increasingly dominated by thoughts of Sue. She was a serious girl, yet pleasant and charming. And, of course, she was a good socialist, which was becoming evermore important to Tony. He was fully aware that Sue was White, but after his experience with Sylvia, White girls had become a natural part of his romantic life. His big worry was that Sue would find out he was a Halfbreed.

On Sunday, Tony had a friend drive him to Minto. The Normans' was a home where friendliness and cheerfulness were supreme, [...and where] politics was the main topic of conversation. Tony found it easy to relax in such an easy-going household. Although it was a very modest house with simple furnishings, it was a lovely place. Almost immediately, Tony liked Mrs. Norman, for she was so spontaneous and sincere. It was easy to see how Sue had acquired these traits.

There was great excitement talking about the upcoming election, and about politics in general. Here, Tony could speak freely. He didn't have to worry about Sergeant Gordon suddenly coming in. The CCF's socialist ideas fascinated Tony. He was hearing for the first time the theories and principles of socialism, and also about capitalism. Mr. Norman explained how the ruling class in a capitalist society ruled the whole country and all the people. These same rulers—a very small group of rich families—took all the wealth of the country through huge profits. Tony wondered how it was possible for such few people to control so much. After all, didn't the workers protest against this unjust distribution of wealth? According to Mr. Norman, the laws and institutions are made to favour the rulers. He claimed that tax laws impose heavy taxes on the masses, and at the same time impose only light taxes on big corporations. This was easy to see simply by looking at the billions of dollars the working people paid on income and property taxes, and on other hidden taxes, such as sales taxes, while at the same time, the ruling elite, with their millions of dollars in profits, pay very little income tax and almost no property tax. It was explained that laws in parliament under the Liberals and Conservatives supported these rich ruling families.

Tony was curious about the laws and courts because they affected him as a Mountie. He agreed that courts were against the poor people—he'd seen that in Weyburn—and how they protected the rich. Courts were powerful and could make people obey whatever law was made, including paying taxes. The atmosphere inside any courtroom was fierce and severe, and overpowering enough to crush and intimidate most people. The judges thought of themselves as gods, but acted like tyrants. Yet they were only local politicians of the Liberal or Conservative parties; often defeated ones who had been rejected by the people at the polls.

After supper, Tony helped Sue with the dishes. It was so wonderful to be in a home again, especially in such a pleasant and relaxed home as the Normans'. He'd lived in barracks and single rooms ever since he'd left home over two years ago. Tony and Sue spent the evening together, and because of his full confidence Tony was able to fool around gaily. He was becoming increasingly convinced of Sue's loveliness and his affection for her.

Secretly, Tony wondered how Sue and her family would react when they found out he was a Halfbreed. Somehow, he thought they wouldn't condemn him, for they seemed to be such an understanding family. They had interests in life, other than petty racial prejudices. But he was just guessing and was being optimistic. Maybe they'd be no different than others.

Mr. Norman and Sue drove Tony home.

In the quietness of his room, Tony puzzled over his next move as a Mountie. In spite of his happiness with Sue, a cloud of apprehension interrupted his thoughts. **(TB)**

Disillusionment with Mounties and Growing Political Commitment

At this point, I was beyond caring. The CCF and politics had become more important than the RCMP. The night beat patrol had killed my [interest in being a] Mountie […]. I had not signed up as a beat cop. The glue and posters incident blew over without a serious flap. They knew there was too much CCF support [in the town] for the Liberals to squeak [about the matter]. Corporal Clifford now made a strong and concerted effort to ship me out as soon as possible. Yet, I had a lot of public support. I was well liked in Gravelbourg. I was a great organizer and supporter of sports, particularly fastball and sports meets. The girls' fastball team were the regional champs. I was a leading hitter and catcher for the local baseball team. We won all the district tournaments.

From now on, Corporal Clifford and me were in a fierce "locked-horn" struggle. What I didn't know then was that he had spread word in the community that I was a slimy Halfbreed. He took that from my personal file. I did not know [how this happened]. The RCMP had no principles regarding confidential information. I realized this […was the nature of] a White supremacist society.

June 1944 was the provincial election. Saskatchewan was in a state of intoxicating excitement. Everyone was talking excitedly about the [possible] new CCF government. At 7 p.m., reporting from the polls started coming in. CCF candidates were winning seat after seat. People were rushing to the town halls—the CCF's headquarters. I was there, front and centre. It soon became a rout. The CCF was winning almost all the seats in the legislature. Liquor was being passed around. Drinks were free and plentiful. The victory [was a] cause for celebration […]. I drank graciously. The next thing I remember was waking up from a sleep in someone's potato patch, cold and aching. The sun was up. I staggered back to the RCMP office and dropped into bed.

I got up for patrol duty. If Corporal Clifford had come in and shouted, I did not hear him. I tried to avoid him as much as possible, but he was still my boss and oppressor.

The second half of the 1940s was a different time—politically active, optimistic and productive. I was now enjoying my police work and [was having] a happy social life.

The next week, I received inspection of my police work by the commanding officer. To my utter disappointment, I was betrayed and trashed. Commanding Officer Ingram arrived shortly for an inspection of the Gravelbourg detachment. I knew it had to do with inspecting me. I was paraded before him. He read the "riot act" to me and made numerous charges about my work. All came from the corporal. He had a mouth like a sewer. Sure enough, within a few days Clifford told me with great delight that I was being transferred out of Gravelbourg. "Where to?" I quickly asked, thinking it may be on guard duty in some remote place.

"To Wood Mountain," he said.

Wood Mountain, Saskatchewan: The End of Howard's/Tony's Mountie Days

In 1944, the Wood Mountain RCMP Detachment was the hellhole for Mounties. He said, "It's for discipline. You'll do police work on Indians, cowboys, bohunks and gophers." What a turnaround!

Corporal Swanson of Wood Mountain was a prince of a Mountie and a splendid man to work with but not for. Geez, Wood Mountain was stark, gloomy and deserted in comparison to Gravelbourg. It was a tiny town, [and did not] even [have] a wooden sidewalk. An old Western Hotel sitting in the centre of a desert. The population was fifty.

But there was real challenging police work to be done every day. I was now a helluva driver and drove police cars over roads with deep ruts. Suddenly Corporal Swanson became ill and had to be taken to the hospital in Regina. There was no replacement, so I had nothing to lose. Some days, I wrote lengthy reports on cases that were still open for further investigation. I used imagination to make them sound good. It worked. Baxter arrived at my station in Wood Mountain one day, inspected it and me. At the end, he smiled and promoted me to constable first class and gave me a pay raise. I was ready to forgive the Divine Bosom of Heaven, but I would not be hoodwinked by Baxter's flattery and sudden change. I was through with the Mounted Police. **(AB)**

Sue's sister was getting married. Sue was the bridesmaid and Tony, the best man. Tony was delighted at the invitation. The wedding would take place in Meyronne. Tony wouldn't ask for time-off to attend the wedding, he would just go.

The wedding was well publicized, as the Norman family was now a prominent family in Saskatchewan. Tony was as nervous as the groom. In fact, both consumed a tidy bit of booze to bolster needed courage. However, the whole affair took place without a hitch. Everything was beautiful. After the ceremony, there was the traditional tour around town in cars with horns sounding.

To Tony's surprise, and everyone else's, there was Sergeant Gordon and two other Mounties patrolling around Meyronne. They knew Tony was part of the wedding, so they came to harass the wedding cavalcade. It was more than embarrassing to have a couple of Mountie squad cars trailing and intimidating the wedding procession. They would like to have given a ticket to the wedding cars. They watched for Tony's police car. Tony was sure they would report him to Hexter immediately. "But if they do that, I'll report them and Hexter to the new attorney general in Regina now," thought Tony, and Mr. Norman could bring his influence to the case.

At the reception, Tony and Sue were teased about their wedding being next. And Mr. Norman, in his speech, mentioned Tony as his next son-in-law in the near future. Tony beamed with pride about it. It pleased Tony to know that he was being considered as one of the Norman family, and this was after they had known he was a Redskin. The parents had fully accepted it.

And now, to get out of the police force! Maybe Inspector Hexter would dismiss him for going away and staying several days away from his detachment without permission. The next week, Hexter informed him that he was coming for inspection. Tony just didn't give a damn. In fact, he thought this would be the ideal time to tell him what he thought about him and his Mounties. He hoped the old man would dismiss him. He didn't care about a dishonourable discharge. To Tony's great surprise, Hexter acted very sensibly and polite. He conducted his inspection as if he was trying to do a favour for Tony. At the end, he came to Tony, shook his hand and congratulated him for the excellent police work he was doing in Wood Mountain. He thought he was one of the smartest young policemen he had under him for some time now. Tony almost fainted away from surprise. This confused Tony, for he thought he might be dismissed for his irresponsible and reckless behaviour under the pretence of doing police work. He didn't regain his thoughts soon enough to state his request for dismissal from the force.

After Hexter left, Tony thought a long time about the situation. Was this the way to get ahead in life? Do as little as possible and keep your nose clean, stay out of trouble? What about his activities with the CCF, his boozing, using the police car for his own social and love life? Maybe it was keeping the people "in their place," and also protecting the ruling class. Maybe life in the Mounties would be easy after all. Maybe he should reconsider it. After all, he had now been in for three years. Only two more years and he could decide for himself. And he could also get married. Would Sue wait for two years? What if he got transferred to the Arctic? But now that he had a taste of success, and individualism, he [developed] greater plans for himself than just being a Mountie—and a third-class Mountie, at that. He could design a better future than that of a cop. But first, he had to get out of the Mounties.

He sat down and composed his application for dismissal. There was no point in saying that he had broken many regulations and had [...engaged in] "behaviour unbecoming to a member of the police force" because Hexter had a chance to see all this first hand while he was here. And he rejected it. He didn't want to get into some legal battle with the RCMP [...] about failing [to fulfil] his contract. He knew they dismissed members for getting married. He had already spoken to them. He stated: "I would like my discharge from the RCMP because I am getting married within a couple of months. I would prefer to have my discharge before getting married, and then be dishonourably discharged."

He signed it and mailed right away before he had a change of mind. Within less than a month, Tony had an answer stating that he would receive his discharge as soon as it could be arranged. Tony started making plans for leaving, and to think seriously about his new ambition and future. He then got an order to report to Depot in Regina [...].

Tony and Sue's Marriage Plans

"Maybe we should wait until fall to get married. That will give me six months to get myself started in something else."

"I agree that we shouldn't get married until fall, but why don't you let daddy help you get a good job. He would only be willing to help you. There's lot of opportunities for good jobs right now," argued Sue.

"I'm not exactly sure what I want to do right away, darling. I think I'm just going home to St. Louis for a while and think about things," mumbled Tony, not really saying anything very definite. There were a lot of things that troubled him. He could feel the pull toward the White world, and he wasn't too sure if that was what he wanted. He wanted to be at home with his own people, where he could consider the whole problem of the two cultures, where he could be comfortable contemplating his career. He didn't like the idea of ambition driving him on, with all that pressure about "getting somewhere," or "organizing for the future." For the last three years, he had enough of order, military order, organization, discipline, structure, meeting deadlines, appointments, inspection, and business obligation.

"I just want to relax from the exactness of work and from the fierceness of competition and from the compulsion of striving. It sucks a lot of real life out of me, darling, I want to be at peace with myself for a while," Tony said philosophically.

"I understand what you mean, sweetheart, and I'm not asking you to walk out of the Mounties and into some kind of office or business job. I'm not trying to crowd you into anything you don't want to do. But when you do decide to look for a job, then let daddy help you," suggested Sue.

Not only was Tony looking at mainstream society for a career, but he was also looking at […] his own ambition. What did he want to be or do, and where was he going? He realized that a lot of his thinking was now […about himself]. He had lost his concern for his people, and his sense of brotherhood. My brother and sister Halfbreeds were not nearly as important to him any more. He was becoming very selfish, indeed. And he disliked himself for this selfishness, as it was unchristian, against the Redskin way of life. Yet, it seemed that if he wanted to make a success of his life, then he must plan and look out for number one, himself. And again, he was excited about freedom just around the corner. He didn't want to surrender it again for another kind of military life. Probably most important of all were Mamma and Pappa.

"I think I'll go home for a few months first and sort things out, and have a visit with my parents. Maybe you should come with me, sweetheart," suggested Tony.

"I'd love to go, but I promised mother I'd help her getting moved into Regina and set up there," replied Sue.

Tony started thinking about the shack the Bruces' lived in and the kind of furniture they had, and their food and their way of life. It made him tremble when he compared it to Normans'. She would only make mamma and the rest of the family very uncomfortable. Maybe it was better that she didn't come, thought Tony. Yes, Tony had decided on spending a few months just loafing around home. He was changing his vocabulary, but also the concept of these words. Earlier, he would never have considered the term loafing. "I just want to say to hell with the future, to hell with a career, to hell with a job. Let them look after themselves. They always do," stated Tony.

On Sunday, Tony and Sue played tennis. This was a game he had learned since becoming a Mountie. This game introduced him into the White world. It was probably the best way that it could've been done. He had now learned a lot about mainstream society, and a more sophisticated way of life. He wasn't altogether sure it was the greatest thing in the world, but it was nice to know it. He could now move back and forth without too much difficulty. He turned and walked smartly, like a soldier, to catch the streetcar. In six hours he'd be home, in another world with nothing—no plans, no money, no job. The only thing he had as a result of his three years [as a Mountie] was a wealth of experience. He knew mamma would be happy to see him. **(TB)**

God Above, that was it! I was leaving the celebrated police force! When I stepped out of my glamorous red serge, I would be on the outside. I would be back in civvies and released from the Mountie contract. I may have some regrets, but their control over my life had been too severe. I had a personal identity, a name and my own humanity, and it was important to me. **(AB)**

Corporal Howard Adams on patrol near Edmonton, AB: "I may have been cheating on the Sandman, but I'm still awake! Really!! Just breaking the monotony out on patrol, one day." Photograph Courtesy—Marge Adams.

4. Drifting Between Worlds

Return to St. Louis

After my decision to leave the RCMP, I went back to the farm in St. Louis. A few days later, I slipped into my work overalls and work boots. Now I was my own Métis person. Quickly, I bought a small new Massey-Harris tractor and an adjoining plough. For the next month, I ploughed every unturned acre that wasn't in crop. I seeded my own scattered crop, and for the rest of the season prayed to God for a bumper crop. By harvest time, I was so far in debt that I sneaked away to look for a job. **(AB)**

Everything was very much the same at home. The shack was three years older, and it showed it. Pappa was still doing janitor work at the school, but his pay had been raised. Gilbert was working the farm and knocking off early to go to St. Louis on train nights. Very little had changed. Marie was now working in Prince Albert and came home only during long weekends. The warm spring weather had arrived, and the hills and fields were rapidly turning green. The family sat around and talked all evening. There was so much to tell, but no one asked Tony what he was going to do now, and [… if he had] a job, and what his future plans were. Tony told them about Sue.

"Mamma, she is just the most beautiful and wonderful girl. You'll like her. You couldn't help but like her," explained Tony.

"Is she a good Catholic, my boy?" asked Mamma.

"No, she isn't Catholic, Mamma, but she's a good Christian," replied Tony.

"Is she French?" asked Mamma seriously.

"No, she's not French, but we're not all French, Mamma. Pappa is English."

"She's one of those White English Protestants, and you know how you feel about them," said Mamma.

"But Sue is so different. She's not mean and insulting. She doesn't try to cheat the Redskins," argued Tony. "She's going to come and visit us this summer some time. I hope you will make her welcome," he pleaded.

"If she's everything you say she is," added Gilbert, "I'll be anxious to see her."

Tony slept in. In fact, he slept in most every morning. This was part of his freedom. He'd go to bed whenever he pleased. He didn't have the horror of early morning rising hanging over his head any more, no alarm clock. The White world can keep that, thought Tony. He did very little work for a while. Everyday was beautiful and warm and sunny. For many days, Tony just wandered around the deserted hills, through the poplar woods, around Gerrond Lake. He wasn't doing anything, just drifting and dreaming. He was very much at peace with himself and the world now. In the evening, he would hunt for the milk cows and bring them home. He had little trouble finding them because Bossy's bell was the only man-made noise in the whole countryside. The wide-open spaces still belonged to the wild animals. He could've taken Gilbert's rifle and shot gophers during the day, but he had no quarrel with the gophers. They weren't fighting him, so why harm them? He walked to town and bought some fishing line and tackle for fishing in the South Saskatchewan River for goldeyes. He watched the fish swim about in the clear water playfully. The hook looked so horrible and cruel, and Mamma now had enough food. He threw it away. Tony roamed over the miles of sandbar between the main bank and the island. For a real trying experience, he roamed through the heavily wooded island.

Nobody nagged him about not paying for his food and for loafing and bumming around. Mamma, Pappa and Gilbert had not changed from their sharing way of life. Often Tony and Gilbert would go into town to drink beer in the evening. Tony enjoyed the rough and rowdy nonsense of St. Louis' beer parlour crowds. His old pals talked him into joining their soccer and fastball teams. He was still in excellent physical shape from the police force, and he was soon taking leading positions in the games. They were travelling to the sports days being held around northern Saskatchewan. They played ball in the daytime and boozed by night. Tony made enough money from the ball prizes to keep him in beer money.

Many of Tony's old Redskin friends were away, either working on war production or [were] in the Army. Sometimes he would be given hell from the White people or a soldier home on leave for hiding out in the Mounties during the war. But he didn't care because he was opposed to war […], and was glad to be given the chance to argue against it.

A local White farmer was looking for a Breed to go and pick roots on his farm. Tony knew that was a tiresome job, but he needed a little cash, so he went. He didn't give a damn if the farmer was a racist as long as he paid. Wages were good now. It was tough work picking and carrying an armful of roots through soft ploughed earth, but Tony was once again a real honest working man, and this made him feel good (or, as everyone said, "the hired man"). The working and poor people received a lot more respect now that the CCF was in power. But Tony questioned whether respect was anywhere as good as wages. And how did it help the workers? He could hold his head high when he knew he was a tough worker. He had prestige among the Breeds, for they were all tough workers.

He worked for three weeks. He now had an excellent suntan and tough muscles in his legs and arms. The rugged outdoor life with no worry [and to him this] was the healthiest thing going. But the pilgrimage was coming up next week, and he wanted to take a week or so off and visit, so he drew his wages and quit. The farmers didn't try to cheat him anymore. They respected the fact that he was an ex-Mountie.

Tony and a few friends decided to go digging Seneca root for a while. They took enough equipment and food for a week. They travelled over the hills, and to good Seneca root areas. They dug up a lot, but also sat in the shade a lot and talked. As usual, there was much talk about sex. They cooked their evening meal in the open, sat around and swapped stories. Joey brought his mouth organ. Seneca root was really just an excuse for spending a week in the open air. The nights never even got cold. Old Mother Earth was warm and sociable. They sold their Seneca root to old man Caron in St. Louis. Tony watched him very closely [… to prevent any] cheating. But he, like the others, now feared Tony. Tony bought a big box of groceries and then had a booze-up. He was still drunk on Sunday, so he missed mass. He was supposed to play for the St. Louis fastball team on Sunday against Prince Albert, but when someone threw a ball at him, he saw several instead of just one. So what, there were other good Breed ballplayers, and also another day for the game.

The next day, farmer Frank came over to the Bruce's. He wanted to hire a Breed to pick rocks off his field. He had just done some, but needed them picked now.

"How much you paying?" asked Tony.

"Sixty cents an hour," replied Frank.

"Oh hell, you're talking nonsense. The Breeds are poor, but not that damn poor. No, sir, I'll work for a dollar an hour and nothing less," demanded Tony.

"That's a helluva price. I'm not a rich farmer like those guys down east," complained Frank.

"Well, those are my terms, and not a damn cent less," stated Tony.

Frank hesitated and grumbled for a minute, then said, "Okay, a dollar an hour. Can you start tomorrow morning?"

"Okay," said Tony, "and I get my pay whenever I ask for it."

What a hell of a hard job, thought Tony. He had a couple of ponies on a stone boat to load the rocks on. Some of them were real monsters. He thought he'd break his back. He took his time, but what a boring job. "We should dynamite these rocks and use them for soil," mumbled Tony to himself.

Tony went with Gilbert on Saturday night to watch the train come, then up to the post office. He was very happy to receive a letter from Sue. He read it immediately. He caught up to Gilbert [who was] going over to the beer parlour. "Sue's coming next week. Geez, that's great. Boy, what a wonderful girl," roared Tony. He had many drinks on that. He bragged to the other fellows about the most wonderful girl in the world. They all offered to make deals with Tony. After all, he was bound to tire out.

Tony quit his rock-picking job after two weeks. Anyway, he'd had enough. He felt sorry for his poor Breed pals who had to do that everyday for a living. He thought he'd drop a rock on his foot and collect compensation.

Sue Visits Tony's Family in St. Louis

Tony met Sue at the bus, and they drove home in the buggy. He was so excited about seeing her that he was doing many stupid things. Sue looked as radiant and gorgeous as ever. There certainly was nothing Halfbreed looking about her. She would be so obvious in St. Louis. She was so White and Protestant-looking. Why was he so hopelessly in love with a White girl? Why had he ignored the Breed girls for a White one? Were they not nice enough or beautiful enough? Had he [... began to look] at girls as a Whiteman? His Breed brothers sure as hell would let him know about Sue. Tony thought Mamma couldn't help but like Sue. But he was wrong.

Mamma was polite to her and tried to make her comfortable, but Tony could tell that she disapproved of Sue [...]. Mamma was looking at Sue as Tony's wife. Tony also knew that Sue was quite surprised at Tony's home, his parents, his relatives and his culture. It was not what she had imagined. Regardless, they had a wonderful and different time. They went on long hikes through the country. They went on horseback rides and Sue was a very good rider. Tony was an excellent bareback rider and he loved to show off. Sue went with Tony to search for the milk cows every evening. In the hot noon, they went swimming in the South Saskatchewan River by the old rock in the sandbar.

Mamma seemed to feel that Tony was wasting a lot of time now. She seemed agitated, not like before when he was alone. It was berry-picking time, so Tony and Sue helped Mamma pick saskatoons and cranberries. They stayed close together and talked, and, of course, "mushed," as Tony called it. He never let Sue get very far from him. Mamma was always yelling at Tony to work harder. Sue slept in Marie's bed, and since it was in the same room as the boy's beds, they had to move right outside. But that was okay because they slept outside every summer. Tony always maintained that it was easier to move than fight the bedbugs.

Tony was free and easy now. He was comfortable with himself because he was home. No White tyrant stood over him and crushed him, so he was able to act natural. Consequently, he was often teasing Sue and fooling around. He was confident of himself, not worried about being crushed and insulted the next minute. Tony took Sue up to his grandpère's place at Batoche. She had a marvellous visit, even though she couldn't speak a word with grandmère. Sue just seemed to fit in so perfectly with everyone, so natural. She was just being her genuine self, she was not pretending. Sue helped Mamma, but Tony wanted Sue with him all the time, so it was difficult for her to help Mamma. She seemed to feel guilty about this, but Tony tried to explain that such was not important in the Breed culture. You did what was important to you, as long as it didn't hurt someone else.

Sue stayed for two weeks. Before she left, Uncle Pierre had a big supper one Sunday evening for Sue. All of Tony's many relatives were invited. There was a lot of booze as usual. Sue saw how Halfbreeds have a big dinner. There was nothing formal about it. Everybody moved about, talked and joked, ate whenever they found a place, drank more, talked to anyone and everybody without introduction. There had been a lot of discussion about Sue among Tony's relatives over the last two weeks. After dinner, uncle Pierre made an announcement about Sue.

"Tony, we have had a discussion about your girlfriend, Sue. We know she will soon become your wife. She is the first White person to come into the family. You'll be glad to know that we like her, and that we have approved of her becoming part of the Halfbreed nation," announced Pierre.

Sue was sitting there, but she was not allowed to comment on the decision.

"I'm sure glad that you have approved of Sue because I would've been in a terrible state if you turned her down, as I don't want to leave my Breed nation, because I love her very

much. I must apologize to my people for bringing a White girl into the nation," replied Tony.

But Tony knew that decision was not approved by Mamma. She said with her eyes, "Go back to your own land and people. Don't come into my boy's life. You have no business here. You will only cause trouble."

Sue was about to leave. "You know your mother has been very unkind to me at times. She has insulted me and called me a White troublemaker. She has tried her best to send me home and drive me away from you," explained Sue.

"I'm not surprised," said Tony. "Don't pay too much attention to Mamma. She's just upset because she thinks you are taking away her dear son from her."

And there was a lot more truth in that statement than Tony realized at the moment he said it. It was not that Mamma hated Sue. It was because she hated every girl that would try to take her Tony away from her. She hated everyone who would cause Tony to put his love first for her, rather than his Mamma. And Mamma could be mean. Nevertheless, Tony loved Sue more than ever, and he knew that Sue was sure of her love for him. Oh sure, there were problems to be worked out between the two cultures and two races, but where so much love existed, it would work.

Over the two weeks, Sue and Tony had spent many passionate times alone. Tony always persisted with Sue, and felt that she was wrong in holding out until they were married. Tony argued they were as good as married now, and what difference did it make? Yet, when Sue had stated her case, Tony was obedient to her. "Was it just another case of being a servant and crushed slave to a White authority," he wondered, but surely it couldn't be with Sue.

Sue had to leave because her mother needed her badly next week. Tony didn't want her to go. He would've liked to keep her. What was so important about the formality of a wedding ceremony and all the celebrations to impress friends? They'd get married in time. She could pick Seneca root and berries with Tony for the rest of the summer. What was wrong with outdoor living? Sure, the winter was tough, but they could always go on relief. The White people became very upset about relief, but it wasn't so bad with the Breeds. Why should it be? There was no work, and no way of living without relief. What's more, it was their right. They had been brutally destroyed by the federal government's troops. Why should they not accept what was theirs?

"But, sweetheart, that just isn't the way the world works. There's a lot bigger world than the Métis–or, as you say, the Halfbreed world."

"But, darling, I am a Redskin, and that's me. That's my way of life! That's my world. Who cares about a career, about a future?" asked Tony.

"Well, I do, Tony, and I won't accept that you stop at being a root picker or a berry picker," snapped Sue.

Tony was surprised at Sue because she never raised her voice or protested. "Look, darling, I went all the way with you in the White world when I was in your culture. Now I'm asking you to consider my way of life, and what do you do but slam it, and condemn it. If you thought I'd accept that, but I won't," replied Tony angrily.

"Please don't get mad, darling, I don't want us to argue. But there's more to your life than loafing around here picking roots," said Sue. Their argument continued, all because Mamma had disliked Sue. Sue came first. This would enrage Mamma. They couldn't solve their problem.

He agreed to see Sue in Regina next month at her new home.

"Darling," said Sue, "I love you more than anything else in this world. You are the most precious thing to me. But I can't possibly come all the way to your way of life. Especially where there are so many opportunities in the White world for you, Tony. Promise me you'll come to Regina and we'll work it out there."

"Certainly," said Tony. "But yet," he thought, "what could be more important than his free and peaceful way of life?"

Tony said goodbye to Sue at the bus depot. She seemed so serious. Tony was full of nonsense and confidence. She seemed so worried. Tony knew that she had not expected the Redskin world to shake her like that. Obviously she had a romantic vision of it, and thought, as a White, she could change it. She didn't know that there were such firm and long traditions about it, which could dictate things to her.

Tony was really confused. There was no doubt in his mind that the first thing in his life was Sue. But there were so many ifs about it. If he married Sue, he gave up Mamma as his most precious love. She would cast Tony out of her life. He couldn't live without Sue, this he understood clearly. He loved her beyond all reason and sense. But Sue was somebody special, and she couldn't be treated as an ordinary person.

"Sweetheart, you'll come to Regina next month," pleaded Sue.

"I'll try. I'll phone you when I'm going, sweetheart," said Tony. "What a puzzle, what a confusion," thought Tony. "I can't live without her, but how can I make her into a Halfbreed?" Tony asked himself.

For the next few weeks, he tried to make up to Mamma. He fixed the buildings for winter for Mamma's convenience because he imagined that he would leave and not come back. Mamma was determined that she would not lose her son to the White world. That fall, Tony worked for White farmers, those who would pay him the best wages. To hell with anything else.

He took time off to go and see Sue in Regina. He spent a week with her. He seemed just as puzzled after the visit as he was before. The wedding date had not been set, yet there was no doubt they would be married shortly. Tony seemed to be stubborn, but yet he wasn't sure why he was hesitating about marrying Sue. She was everything a fellow could want as a wife. His freedom was precious to him. The freedom to come and go as he wished, no one to account to. No one would discipline him again. He'd get drunk whenever he felt like it, and recover the best way possible without nagging. Was he willing to give up his Redskin way of life for Sue? Certainly not! But he didn't think it was a case of either/or. He could have Sue and still remain a Halfbreed. Maybe not as completely as he wished; but in most ways. Yet, he understood that Sue would have a hard time becoming even half a Halfbreed, or even being one part time. What if she turned against Tony's people? The brothers and sisters of the Breed nation were all important to him. There was no love in this world powerful enough to change that. Such a situation would lead to a great tragedy.

How could Tony get Mamma to like Sue? It wasn't Sue that she disliked. But she would have to learn that another woman would come between her and her son. She couldn't fight every girl forever. Tony would eventually turn against her. **(TB)**

Almighty's Depression and Hospitalization

The world seemed totally hopeless and dreadful. The only thing that mattered was death. I wanted to die.[1] Mamma tried every kind of Indian medicine she could think of, but nothing helped. I rapidly grew worse, going into long periods of unconsciousness. My mind became totally irrational. Conversation was just a garble of words, while I cried for death. The family decided that I should be taken to the Indian hospital, even though no one had any faith in that "animal pit hospital." I was kept there for only two days, as the doctor claimed he couldn't do anything for me. He guessed that I had damaged my brain from too much drunkenness. The same old diagnosis! I was moved to the Holy Family Hospital—which is mostly for the White Catholics—and placed in the ward for patients suffering from mental disorders.

I had long since lost consciousness of the life around me. Fortunately, I received strict treatment under a good psychiatrist. At the end of two months, I began recovering. Slowly I improved, and within another month I was almost normal in my mental behaviour. I now was aware of each day, where I was, and what was happening to me.

Apparently, I had had a serious case of deep depression. Some old timers call it a "nervous breakdown". Regardless of what it had been, it was a horrible and frightening experience. I was terrified about falling back into the same situation.

Marguerite (Sue) had come to visit me at the Holy Family Hospital when I was first put there. However, I was in such a violent state of turbulence. She felt so distressed and sickened by my appearance and behaviour that she found it all too unbearable. She did not visit me again until I had recovered considerably. Apparently, during the entire visit with me, I raved like a madman, jumping up and down on my bed, shouting condemnations at the Whiteman. Or standing beside her picking fleas, bugs and worms out of her hair. During the entire hour, I never spoke one sensible word. Of course, I did not recognize her. This was an exceedingly frightening and worrisome visit for Marguerite (Sue).

To this day, I cannot remember that visit. However, once I started to recover and became

---

[1] The "I" in this story is neither Howard Adams nor Tony Parker or Tony Bruce, but a fictional Aboriginal character called "Almighty." Howard Adams probably named him after the famous young Cree man Almighty Voice (Kisse-Manitou-Wayou) from One Arrow Reserve near Batoche, who was hunted down by the North-West Mounted Police and finally killed along with two young relatives for having butchered a free-ranging steer to feed his starving family in 1895. In the original typed manuscript, the name of Almighty's beloved is given as "Marguerite" or "M." but there are later handwritten corrections that insert the name "Sue." The use of Sue would tie the episode in with the time after Tony's return home from the RCMP. The same goes for the use of "Mamma" and "Pappa" in this text, instead of "Mom" and "Dad" as in the autobiographical manuscript. We are not sure whether this may be an experience based on Howard Adams' real life, and if so, to what extent, but we include it here because of what is said about mental disorder and colonization. Thematically, Almighty's story ties in with the passages about Howard's anxiety attacks and mental sufferings during his grade school years, as described earlier.

normal and rational in my behaviour, Marguerite (Sue) came regularly. In fact, I attribute my rapid recovery to her regular visits. There was nothing more important to me than Marguerite (Sue)'s visits. She gave me so much hope and purpose in life. Her love and dedication lifted me out of my depression and gave me emotional strength. She became the very core of my existence, the soul of my life and the light to a renewed mission. I had never imagined that another person could become such a deep and existential part of me. She was so gentle and loving, yet so firm and independent. My love for Sue (Marguerite) was beyond fulfillment. Although Mamma and Pappa came to visit me, and I was always so glad to see them, it did not compare to Marguerite (Sue)'s visits.

I noticed Mamma became very worried about me, and that she had lost weight worrying over me. I sensed she could see that being Indian was part of the psychological cause of my illness. She appreciated my feelings of inferiority and oppression, which had haunted and plagued me to a state of despondency and abandonment. I was merely existing, strung-out in suspension. I knew she had been talking to the psychiatrist because on his next call to see me he drew me into a discussion about inferiority, regression and withdrawal.

"Almighty, do you know what is meant by 'regressive and withdrawal behaviour'?" he asked.

"I think I do," I answered. "Regressive behaviour is retreating from normal society, and from participation in everyday activities. It's adopting an invalid role, where the patient really believes that he/she is sick. It is a kind of escape technique, where the person is unable to face the tough realities of the true world."

"When is a person likely to withdraw and go into regression?" asked the doctor.

"When life becomes too complex, with considerable tension and anxiety, and when facing possible defeat," I guessed.

"Do you think regression and depression are more likely to happen to Indians than other people?" he asked.

"Oh, I think so, because they face so many difficult circumstances that cause personal dilemmas and tension. Also, if they try to do something other than what is allowed or outside of their expected behaviour, they will encounter not only opposition but actual hostility from the Department of Indian Affairs (DIA) or society in general. Simply being pigmented in a quasi-apartheid society automatically creates a hostile situation, which forces the colonized into their subordinate and stereotyped role. That's the Indians' situation," I explained.

The doctor went on to describe how withdrawal can be harmful. "Withdrawal allows a person to isolate himself from social participation in the real environment, which reduces his social skills through lack of practice and renders him less effective in competition and leadership. It causes one to replace an interest in other people and their social and political activities, to an interest in one's self."

"I'm beginning to see how capitalism operates to keep the colonized Indians under control. It is a very subtle psychological way of suppressing pigmented populations, and also a very effective method of control," I said, thinking out loud.

The doctor added that inferiority and invalidism are ways to threaten and control people. He wasn't necessarily referring to Indians. "The very fact of believing that you are inferior limits your freedom of action, causes you to believe that officials will take revenge on you. Also, you will become anxious and self-punitive. Furthermore, invalidism leads to paranoia, schizophrenia and depression. It is the result of interpersonal relationships where other people's attitudes and responses dominate yours." He concluded by asking me another question. "Do you think regression can be harmful in other ways to you?" He stopped and waited in silence for my answer.

"Well, one way is that regression can weaken my own personal security."

Being a psychoanalyst, he explained it in those terms. "We know that security during infancy is, to a large extent, based upon the relationship with the mother. Anything that alters the character of this relationship is likely to cause anxiety and lead to regressive behaviour. Regression in other periods of life has a similar origin in its loss of security. Likewise, homesickness in adolescence, when they have to leave home to go to residential schools—like Indian children do—is characterized by silent preoccupation with fantasies about home life, love, malaise and dependent attitudes towards older, official persons in the new environment. This is a typical situation of how psychological dependency develops among Indian people, whereby they become pathologically dependent upon teachers, the Indian agent, superintendent and other government officials."

I interrupted the doctor. "And of course this situation is encouraged by these colonizers, so they can manipulate and control us through psychological methods."

"It can be even more complicated than that, too," added the doctor. "It may lead into guilt reactions, where the patient attributes threat and blame onto himself from an authoritarian individual. The patient then lives in fear of punishment from the individual he or she has cast in the role of parent surrogate."

"I can surely see the parallel here, doctor," I exclaimed. "The subordinate Indian casts the Indian Affairs official as the parent surrogate. Actually, they do that for us. Ever since they conquered us, made treaties, and put us on reserves, they have always presented themselves as "The Great White Father" or "Protector," which is the typical parent surrogate. The sad part is that many Indians accept that psychological relationship with Indian Affairs. They seriously believe that DIA is sincerely concerned about our health, welfare and protection. That's powerful stuff! But I can't imagine anyone in the DIA being smart enough to figure out these deep psychological theories and then applying them to us."

"Now, don't get paranoid. I don't think the DIA really does anything so deliberately," continued the doctor. "But there are still other factors associated with regression that I would like to explore with you. In infancy or adolescence, if a person is rejected because of his clumsy attempts at social behaviour with his peers, he will likely return to an affectionate dependency upon a parent or familiar adult. Similarly, an adult who is frustrated, disappointed or fails in competition and is disillusioned will likely seek the role of a dependent follower in a relationship where he can recapture that childhood dependency."

As if I had been hit by an electric rod, I exclaimed, "God only knows the DIA keeps all of us Indians frustrated most of our entire lives. Welfare alone is enough frustration to drive us to dependency."

"I don't want you to blame everything on Indian Affairs, Almighty, as you will only become paranoid, as I said before, or you'll develop a persecution complex. I want you to look at dependence in terms of regression before we break up our discussion," commented the doctor. "Children, adolescents and adults typically develop regressive behaviour when circumstances force them to play a dependent role. Their actual helplessness or powerlessness in their environment compel them to adopt attitudes like those they once had in their early impotent childhood. Also, they develop attitudes that support or are consistent with their emotionally crippled childhood. These chronically helpless individuals become clinging, pleading and entreating adults. Often, their adult models of behaviour encourage the return to behaviour that is characteristic of a child who is being trained to be dependent."

"That's it, that's it," I exclaimed excitedly. "That's exactly how the DIA and government officials who deal with Indians operate. I'm damn sure they've been trained to make Indians develop in exactly the way you have described, doctor. They make us helpless dependents so that we are always in a psychological state of supplication—in other words, always 'on bent knees' to our colonizers. Earlier, you said, doctor, that in prisons or concentration camps— and that's precisely what Indians live in—regressive and dependent behaviour is generated by the helplessness of the prisoners, who must depend for their every satisfaction, and even for their lives, upon the good will of authoritarian persons whom they cannot control, and yet who control their lives totally. These situations also promote dependency because of the severity of frustration, which they are designed to provide. Welfare assistance—which most Indians are forced to live on—promotes dependency in the same way because financial aid is contingent upon helplessness and complete subordination. In this way, dependency is bestowed upon the colonized recipient without responsibility. As a result, the Indian is made to feel exceedingly dependent about his assistance."

The doctor interrupted. "You are correct in your analysis, Almighty. Just let me conclude. The role that such a person—and in this case you are referring to the Indian—must play within this situation virtually eliminates the possibility of self-reliance and self-respect, consequently perpetuating dependency."

Shortly after this long discussion with the doctor, Marguerite (Sue) came to visit me. I guess the discussion had done a lot to assist in my road to recovery because Marguerite (Sue) was pleasantly surprised to see me looking so cheerful and confident. "Darling, I just can't get over how very much improved you look," Sue (Marguerite) repeated over. Her beautiful brown eyes were sparkling and her half smile expressed a certain joy. The new dress on her trim frame made her look like a model. After a loving hug, she shyly remarked, "Your hair is almost as long as mine." She squirmed a little, laughed softly and then said she'd braid it for me. After some playful remarks, we cuddled in each other's arms. Our embrace was like we had been apart for years.

We were the two happiest people in the world. As far as I was concerned, we were the only two people in the world. We talked and laughed. Her laughter sounded like tinkling bells and that enchanted me. Time didn't matter; nothing mattered. All my depression, hate and hostility had gone. All that existed was this wonderful and delightful woman. I hugged her closer. I wanted her more than anything in the world. I knew she was bursting to know what had happened, why I had recovered so much. In a teasing manner, she said quietly, "Well, aren't you going to tell me?" She said no more, just waited in silence, implying that I knew what she was talking about. But to me, all I wanted to talk about was her, rather [than] us. Yet, I felt it necessary to tell her what she wanted to know.

"Well, darling," I said, like I was launching into a long story, "the doctor and I had a real good discussion, and I not only know what's wrong with me, but I'm able to understand and deal with it pretty good now. I'm very pleased with myself, about how I got insight into my psychological problems. More than that, into the psychological problems of the Indian people generally! Yeah, including you. But I knew those from my own personal study of that beautiful patient."

"Don't forget, sweetheart, you're the patient," she reminded me.

"We discussed problems around regression, inferiority, anxiety, withdrawal, frustration, depression and other such topics," I replied in a bragging manner.

"My, you'll soon be as educated as the doctor," she chided.

"One thing I think you'll be interested in is resignation and defeatism. People like us—I mean Indians who live in rural compounds—give up easily in our struggle to resist the oppression of the government. There is a minimum of action and no aggression whatsoever by our people once confined to the reserves. We surrender to the situation—I mean psychologically—often accompanied by feelings of depression, and a bitter feeling of defeat. Apparently, we adapt to the dominating situation of the DIA and all other White authorities with completely submissive behaviour.

Although many of us may be frustrated for a while, we nevertheless adapt by adopting temporary islands of security. By that I mean women do routine housework, men do trivial occupational or religious activities. In fact, anything that is safe busy work, as long as it provides a distraction from thoughts and actions of protest and confrontation [is welcomed]. Another consequence of the frustration to our lives is a marked lowering of our aspirations. And still another one is an increase in daydreaming and suicide fantasies. According to the doctor, generally we are inclined to conform to the demands of the Indian Affairs authorities. Because of the particular kind of prison-like environment we are forced to live in, we live under unique psychological circumstances, which cause serious difficulties for many of us. And one of the worst is depression—the one I had. But it seems that I'll live after all." Taking a hold of Marguerite (Sue)'s hand and squeezing it, I said, "I have so much to live for."

"I'm so terribly happy that you are well on the road to recovery now, Almighty. You surely scared me for a while. I shed a lot of tears over you because there was nothing I could, nor anyone else could do for you," said Marguerite (Sue).

"I know it was a very trying time for you and Mamma. For me, well, I didn't know what was happening for a long time. I was right out of it. I can't remember. I must have been unconscious. But I certainly learned a lot from this experience. There are Indians besides me who suffer similar agonies, except that mine was more sudden and dramatic. And I guess I can safely say now that it's a total recovery. I can't understand why, as Indians, we put up with that hideous oppression. Our lives are totally circumscribed by the capitalist government and their agents of totalitarianism. It's amazing that we don't develop revolutionary ideas and violent political movements. Apparently, we expect the worst and most dreadful things to happen to us at all times, so we accept everything, which is often death to many of us. According to psychologists who have studied people like Indians on reserves, they have found that the oppressed colonized do not even develop any antagonism nor do they attack their colonizing persecutors. Instead—like us—they direct all their frustrations and aggression against our own people, rather than against the totalitarian officials."

"It just boggles my mind to think that we will allow ourselves to be subjugated so completely by bourgeois colonizers and do nothing about overthrowing them. In fact, it is just the opposite: we pay homage to our oppressor and attempt to model him. My blood just boils when I think of all the supplicating Indians, the Uncle Tomahawks. And for what? Just a few crumbs. How horrible!"

"Now, now, Almighty, you'll be getting yourself all upset again, and it'll be back into the horrid state of depression. You've got to start thinking about more positive things," counselled Marguerite (Sue).

"There is a lot of education to do," I emphasized. "It is so very complex psychologically. According to the psychoanalysts, racism controls aggression by discharging it on safe objects. And who are the safe objects? Indians, of course! But it doesn't have to be Indians only; any [...visible minority] population in a White-supremacist society is a safe object. We are talking about the bigots again. Although they are responsible for developing the racist settler colony, they cannot adjust to it satisfactorily. Their Puritan morality is so severe that the ego cannot regulate all aspects of social functioning. Even worse, the superego is unable to adapt to the power of the social institutions, which they created and built in their North American quasi-apartheid society. As a result, they are unable to sublimate enough of their aggressiveness in order to get along without encountering difficulty. As a consequence of this difficulty, they are inclined towards sadistic impulses that are directed, of course, onto the subordinate racial minorities. Since the moralistic middle-class society will no longer approve of their sadistic activities against racial minorities—as it did in the slavery period—they have to take place through sexual fantasies of the colonized. As far as they are concerned, this keeps their lives rooted in a dreary and joyless routine. However, danger is always lurking in the wings for non-Whites because the racists' lifestyle cannot always be satisfied simply through sheer imaginative speculation. Hence, [there is always] a perpetual menace. They use this potential sadistic force to keep us in our inferior position. So you see, my dear, our lives are always in possible danger in this White supremacist 'civilization.'"

Sue (Marguerite)'s patience was limited. She interrupted. "Please, at least give me a chance to say something. You're so wound up with all that psychoanalysis knowledge that I can't understand all you're saying."

But I was determined. "Not only is Freudian psychology fascinating, but it provides an excellent explanation of the dominant/subordinate theory of a racist society. It is the only theory that makes sense for the psychology of the colonized."

"Maybe, sweetheart, but don't become fanatical about one theory. Then you'll be as guilty of misinterpretation as the colonizer," protested M (Marguerite/Sue).

"Right, right, darling, but it makes us aware of the dangers of the oppressor. The avenues of fulfilling their infantile wishes and sexual fantasies by being intimate with slave women are not open to them today. Their unquestioned authority, immoral and sadistic activities persisted in slavery days and allowed for the stabilization of the oppressors' personalities," I explained with determination.

"It sounds like you've been doing a lot of reading, dear," Sue (Marguerite) said, questioning me.

"I sure have. But it makes a lot of sense out of the social and economic dilemma that we have to live in. Modern capitalism has forced a new adjustment for the racist colonizers. The rulers are forced into a superficial and hypocritical middle-class lifestyle. They no longer own the bodies of the colonized. But, it seems to me, they own everything else about us." Looking admiringly at Marguerite (Sue), I said emphatically, "There's one damn sure thing, they don't own Sue (Marguerite)'s body."

Quietly, she replied, "Nobody owns this body, not even Almighty. Maybe my heart, but that's all."

"I was only kidding, darling. But I'm serious about the changing capitalist society and the White supremacist in this quasi-apartheid society. The big capitalist or multinational corporate owner has made adjustments by foregoing his dominant racist activities in exchange for greater material wealth. But what about the petty bourgeois White liberals? They have remained powerless. In fact, their power has been seriously reduced. These joyless little men are now forced to realize their fantasies through some sort of violence on the oppressed and colonized. Will there be a greater raping of our women and emasculating of our men?" Marguerite (Sue) slowly put her hand over my mouth to stop me.

"You really must give your tongue a rest, dear. Anyway, I've got to be going home. I'm just so delighted that you are so very much better, and that you'll soon be coming home. You will have to stop from being so involved for a while. I know how hard that will be on you. After all, darling, I want you to live, and live as a normal, happy man."

"But with you beside me, dear, I can be nothing else but happy. I don't know about the part of being normal," I explained with a tone of optimism.

I was now well enough to attend social functions at the hospital for patients who would get along on their own. Movies, dances and public speakers were the most common functions, which were all held at the central recreational hall. The movies were mostly silly

Westerns, but the dances and speeches were usually good. Being a good dancer, I loved the dances. There were some cute young female patients who were good dancers, so it was fun. The speeches were usually related to mental illness theories. Naturally, I always went when the speaker would be a psychoanalyst.

One evening, the topic was "Sublimation and Identification." I sat in the front seat, as I didn't want to miss any of this talk. He included a discussion on racism, including the extreme bigot and patronizing White liberal. The bigot is easily recognized, as he is a worshipper of power, of which he has little. Usually, he comes from the lower middle class. He is a little man who lives off the scraps of the bourgeois class. He is caught in the contradiction of hate and love of his masters above him. Love, because of the power they hold. Hate, because of his submission to them. He fears being swallowed up as one of the colonized and being lost in the mass of sameness—a lingering death. As a result, he despises the oppressed, so he avoids any closeness to them. As far as he is concerned, they must "stay in their place." Likewise, he keeps his distance. He must prevent any familiarity. Because of his fear of plunging into the depths of the colonized masses, coupled with his frantic need for a feeling of greater power, the bigot is forced into a state of dependence on external but related power of the people above him. At the same time, he projects his hatred for these persons with greater power onto those lower than himself.

This explanation gave an excellent account of most agents and officials of Indian Affairs. I had seen these Indian agents give out government rations to the Indians in the same way as you would throw bones to a pack of dogs. At the same time, I could see on their faces the contempt that they held for the Indians. On the other hand, when the agent dealt with his superior, the DIA superintendent, he behaved like a "coolie."

During the question period, I asked, "Would these same psychological factors be involved with Indian leaders, such as chiefs, councillors, presidents of state and national Indian organizations?"

His answer was that these psychological factors probably affected them more than it did the White bureaucrats, especially those who are the head of national Indian organizations, because they deal more with White officials who have power. And on the other hand, these Indian leaders are much closer to the colonized masses with greater chances of falling back into that so-called despised group. They have identified with the White Indian agents, and modeled themselves in their images. They even take on the attitudes of the government authorities, which is hate and fear of Indians.

After the meeting, back in my room, I thought a great deal about the talk by the speaker. I could now understand why the chiefs and councillors behaved the way they did to their own people, why they detested the rest of the Indians on the reserve and why they tried to boss them around as if they were children. They had modeled themselves after the Indian agent. They wanted the agent's position and its power. They did not want to be the Indian agent as a person, but they wanted what he stood for: prestige and authority. Their corrupt mentality and behaviour was parallel to that of the worst Indian agent who had mismanaged any reserve, its funds and people. To these Indian leaders, the relationship with the corrupt Indian officials was their reality. They faded the Indian masses out of their existence, and instead made their real environment the association with the Indian Affairs' officials. **(MISC)**

Tony/Howard Leaves Saskatchewan for Vancouver

Tony finished his fall work. He had money saved up. His mind remained puzzled. It didn't seem to clear up [… his relationship] with Sue. He was doing a lot of boozing around St. Louis. He joined in with some Breed pals [… while they] were going to Saskatoon for a big boozing weekend. Tony liked Saskatoon. It was a lovely city and he had always had good times there. They did a tour of the pubs and got well loaded. They ended up in a flophouse. They found a bootlegger on Sunday. In the evening, some of the Breeds went home to St. Louis, but Tony stayed in the flophouse. He sobered up on Tuesday. He decided to stay a while longer and enjoy the city. In the pub, he met a young couple who were motoring out west to Vancouver in a few days, and they wanted Tony to join them and share expenses and driving. This appealed to Tony.

He phoned Sue and asked her if she'd mind if he went to the coast for a few weeks. Sue was very reluctant to let Tony go, but could she really stop him?

"Okay, darling, I've no objection if you go to Vancouver for a few weeks if you promise to be home by the first of November at the latest," explained Sue.

"I promise, sweetheart, for sure, I'll be home by November 1st, and then we can make preparations for the wedding. Okay, hon, and I'll bring back some of the ocean for you," joked Tony.

Four drivers, and they shared the driving. They stopped only for gas and food. They were in Vancouver the next evening, hardly even time to enjoy the scenery. They dropped Tony off at a cheap hotel in the city's skid row. The next afternoon, when he was resting at the waterfront, a stranger suggested he should stay at the YMCA. Tony had heard about such a place before, but it didn't mean anything to him other than [it being] a hotel. He got a room there. It was cheaper and much nicer.

The hugeness of the big city overwhelmed Tony. He spent days just wandering around admiring the tall buildings and the gorgeous scenery. He went for many walks through Stanley Park. But most of all, the weather was marvellous, sunny and mild. He thought, "Back in Saskatchewan, it's cold and snowy now." He spent more money than he had expected and his cash was running low. The city certainly wouldn't give him welfare. Maybe he should go to work, anyway. He decided to go to the employment office. To his surprise, jobs were scarce. There was nothing at the moment, but he would report back in a day or so. If he could earn a few dollars before going home, it would help in establishing his new home with Sue. **(TB)**

Jobless in Saskatoon, and with the cold weather coming on, I decided to head for Vancouver. A couple of friends were driving to the coast and had space for one passenger in their car.

I didn't know anybody in Vancouver, had very little money and no job. But this was a society of achievement and success. All one needed was motivation and energy. Anyone could make it if you worked hard and saved your money. That was the ethic that I now believed. What a disappointment! In Vancouver it was cold and rainy, no jobs and no cheap places to live. Every morning I stood in line at the unemployment office with hundreds of other jobless paupers. After four days, hopes were fading and expectations dropping even faster. By now I was willing to take any job that became available. Even toilet bowl-cleaning jobs were full.

The next Monday, I lucked out: a job at a Safeway store, stocking shelves at twenty-two dollars a week. It was better than picking rocks on the dusty fields of Saskatchewan. I was to unpack the groceries in the back, pile them neatly on the dolly, wheel them to the proper islands in the store and shelve them orderly and quickly. I was given a limited amount of time for each trip. "Do not waste time travelling around islands. Use the most direct route." I could not understand the importance of quickly pacing around the Safeway floor with a handcart full of cans and boxes of groceries until I collapsed. A farmer's pace was my normal speed.

Egg carton delivery was my big quarrel. I had to cut down one minute on each succeeding trip. An inspector came in and shopped as a customer, incognito, better known as a spy. If you stopped to say a kind word to a nice customer for a minute, you were in trouble. The more I hurried on this job, the more confused I got. Disgusted, the manager tried me at the cash register, checking out groceries. I called out the prices like a hog-caller on the old farm. It was so stressful that I became argumentative and agitated with customers. The job sucked every ounce of energy and pleasure out of me. I became more bitter and hostile.

Although I was scores of years from the St. Louis colony and my Métis life, it was never forgotten. In my grubby room, cold, barren and lonely, my mind would wander back to thoughts of Mom and Dad, and what they would be doing. No doubt everything would be the same. Things changed only with the seasons. What would I be doing if I had stayed? I would never have been satisfied or happy. Returning was not a possibility. Yet my Métisness never really left me.

I was so terribly lonely that I went to church on Sunday, just to be in a social crowd. Soon I spotted a gorgeous girl in the choir. I couldn't take my eyes off her. I went to church the next Sunday, made eye contact with her, and soon got to chat with her. Later, I had a date with her, and life became more pleasant. Days were much happier. My dumpy room in the old rooming house became bearable. The heat was turned off at the end of April. […I needed…] only a light blanket for a covering. I was freezing at night, so I took the old rug from the floor to cover-up. It was so dusty it almost choked me. Under the rug was a huge area of burned floor.

My routine way of life became so damn oppressive and demoralizing. It was little better than subsistence in the Métis ghetto. I became increasingly resentful and hostile about my economic and social life. I could see there was a better life for the rich people, at least in material terms. How did they get all that wealth and good life, and I did not? Damn sure they did not work any harder than me. The misery of big city life seemed unbearable. What British Columbia needed was a CCF government. What the hell was wrong with the people that they had not voted in a socialist government? Did they have no compassion for the workers?

As the days dragged on, the rain continued. The job became increasingly miserable. Twenty-two dollars a week hardly paid for basic food to keep me alive. I was becoming bitter and hostile, and [violent] thoughts [...] began to emerge. The landlady was driving me nuts, complaining about everything—for making too much noise when I closed the door, for not taking my shoes off at the door, for leaving lights on, or for when my alarm clock was too loud. Yet, I was freezing in that room. There was no hot water. She was meddling with my mail, going into my room without permission. Mom wrote regularly, or had someone write for her. Everything [that mattered] was about her Métis life now.

One day, a worker at the Safeway said she was moving away, and I could take over her suite. It was only one block from the store, had two nice rooms, and the landlady was nice. The price was not much more. I moved immediately. I did not let the old lady in my room know that I had left, and I kept the key. I had paid my rent until the end of the month. She kept phoning the store and asking for her key. In the quiet of one night, I returned, took all my belongings, turned on the water tap and left it running, locked the door and left. The next morning, she called the store claiming that she had called the police on me because her ceiling had been ruined. I laughed heartily at her over the phone and then hung up. **(AB)**

Sue recognized that he was deeply involved in union politics, for his letters were filled mostly about the union. Her letters came regularly. She wanted Tony to return to Saskatchewan.

"Why doesn't she come to Vancouver, at least for a visit?" Tony asked himself. "Of course, she could have a lovely holiday here. We could go to the beach every evening. Maybe I could persuade her to stay here," he thought excitedly. He sat down that evening and wrote a long letter to Sue. He concluded, "Come right away!"

His love for Sue had not lost an ounce of its power. It was almost a year since he had last seen Sue, yet he seemed to love her more than ever. He had not been interested in other girls. Not at all, for all his affection was focused on Sue. No one else interested him. She captured his heart completely. There was no doubt that she had a tremendous influence on his life now, as she had in the past year. It didn't seem that she was exerting any serious pressure on him to do certain things. Sure, she wanted him to be a success, but that was only fair. He wouldn't want to marry Sue unless he could properly provide for her. Within a few days, he received a letter from Sue.

*"I'd love to go to Vancouver. I'm ready to go anytime." **(TB)***

5. Mainstreaming in Vancouver

Sue Visits Tony in Vancouver

Tony would have loved to have Sue stay with him. He had room. Anyway, he would argue that he didn't need much room for Sue. However, he knew that Sue wouldn't do that, and furthermore, the landlady probably wouldn't allow it. "Geez, people are fussy," he complained.

Tony rented a "tourist" for Sue in the Kitsilano district. It wasn't far from his apartment. Tony was so excited that he was doing worse things than usual at the store. Sue was on his mind and [… in his speech] constantly. He was boring his co-workers, but he didn't care. To go and meet the train, he put on his very best working clothes. He was there for hours before the train arrived. Sue walked down the platform. Her long hair was flowing as she walked quickly. She was wearing a bright, gay dress and looked absolutely radiant. As always, she was smiling. He had never seen her look so beautiful. If there ever was a moment in Tony's life that he would want to capture and preserve forever, it was now. He could not wait, and he rushed to her.

"Darling, this is a public platform," said Sue.

"There's no one else here except you, sweetheart."

They rode home on the streetcar. Sue told of her trip and the funny experiences she had on the train. But Tony was so excited about being with Sue that he didn't pay much attention.

He'd never let Sue go again! In the apartment, they embraced and they kissed gently. But in a few seconds they opened their eyes. He had to look at Sue, to admire her, to hold her close. "I love you so very much, darling," speaking ever so quietly.

"And I love you, ever so much," replied Sue.

Their lips met again, this time passionately. Tony embraced Sue tightly. Tony's tongue found Sue's. Her affectionate responses roused Tony. He squeezed Sue tighter to his body, everywhere. They sat on the chesterfield, and Tony could not control his hands from wandering. But he checked himself. He wanted to caress Sue, to love her gently. He released his firmness on Sue. But it was impossible to stop: [he was so] passionate. He then released his embrace. Sue straightened up. Tony said with an authoritative voice, "Darling, I never want to let you go again."

Sue replied, "I don't ever want to be away from you again."

Tony's love had never been so great. "You bring such perfect happiness into my life. I'm just afraid to think of what life would be without you now."

Sue was running her fingers through his hair. "But why should you ever think of life without me? I want always to be in your life as much as I am right now." Sue cuddled close in Tony's arms. Looking up at Tony with a serious expression, she said, "I suppose you know you made me very lonely when you left Saskatchewan last fall. I had many very sad hours."

Tony could see the tears in Sue's eyes. It made him feel bad and mean because the last thing in the world he wanted to do was to hurt Sue's feelings. Yet, he had no ready explanation. "Yeah, I know, sweetheart, and I was just as lonesome. I don't know why I did it. But the important thing is that we are together again." Tony kissed Sue so very gently. Sue remained in Tony's arms all evening. "I would just like to stay snuggled right here forever." Tony and Sue claimed they had a lot of catching-up to do on their lovemaking. The evening slipped by, darkness fell. Tony would have liked to simply move from the chesterfield to the bed, but nothing could ever be done against Sue's wishes, and she knew that. She had always controlled Tony simply by asking him. He wondered how he allowed himself to be manoeuvred into a situation, controlled by such a soft voice […].

"Listen, darling, I haven't eaten any supper," she whispered in Tony's ear. He rubbed his hand on her flat stomach. "It doesn't feel like there's very much in there, food or anything else." Sue had learned some of Tony's language, as she said, "But, you've been gone for eight months."

"Okay, we'll make supper if we can't make anything else." Secretly, he always hoped he'd break Sue's resistance, either through passion or persuasion. They made supper, [but it was] not much of a supper. It was what Tony called a "Breed" supper or a "welfare" supper. Tony said they'd leave the dishes because he could do them in the morning to get rid of some surplus energy. They sat on the chesterfield and explained what each had done for the past eight months, and interrupting it with mushing. Finally, Sue said she had to get to bed, as she was tired. "I hate to leave such an inviting bed. I'd like to stay with you, darling, but it just can't be done. There are no reasons, but it just can't be done."

Tony knew it was pointless to argue, so he walked her over to the "tourist" room. He would come over at ten in the morning, as he wouldn't let her sleep beyond that because he wanted to be with her. Tony walked home fantastically happy. Sue was more gorgeous than ever and more adorable. She was as much in love with him as he was with her. They would never separate again; nothing could tear them apart now. They'd talk things over. They'd straighten out a lot of things and also he'd also straighten out.

At ten, Sue was ready. They went out and had breakfast. It was a beautiful sunny morning. "What would you like to do today, darling?" asked Tony. "It's going to be a nice warm day, so let's go to the beach this afternoon."

"As long as I'm with you, darling," said Sue. "You be my guide. I trust you completely."

Tony looked at her quizzically. "Will you give me a declaration that you put yourself in my hands?"

She teased him. "Maybe."

"Stop putting me on," argued Tony.

More seriously, Sue said, "I'd like to see downtown. I've never been here before."

"It's huge, like Meyronne," answered Tony. "Okay, we'll go and window shop."

"Oh no, darling, I have money to spend," said Sue.

They took the streetcar on Fourth Avenue and went down to Woodward's Store. Sue was very impressed with the hugeness of the city. They came home for a late lunch. In the afternoon, they went to the beach. They weren't swimmers. "After all, should a couple of prairie gophers know anything about swimming?" asked Tony. But they played around in the Sandy Beach. Kitsilano was a lovely big beach. The important thing was that they were together, and no two people could possibly be happier. They walked by the ocean in the evening. Tony was a romantic, anyway, so this kind of life pleased him. Each day for the next week that they spent together, it seemed impossible to be together enough. Except for the few hours needed for sleep, they spent every moment together.

Tony argued, "Why not? We're as good as married."

But Sue would reply, "Let me see your license."

Everything about life was so much easier when Sue was with Tony. He didn't find the world so cruel, inhuman and brutal. Sue brought into his world a whole new meaning of human kindness, of peace and the precious sense of love and brotherhood. In the short time he had worked at Safeway, Tony had found the urban world very harsh, fiercely competitive and exploitative. Sue's quiet charm radiated tenderness, understanding and sincerity. During the week, they went to the beach every afternoon. They would lie quietly around in the sun and talked about their plans. One afternoon, they got really serious.

"Darling, are you afraid of marriage?" asked Sue.

"No, why? What a foolish thing to say. Afraid of what? That's like saying I'm afraid of you, and I hardly think that's possible," answered Tony. "Why do you say that?"

"I don't know, but any time that the possibility of us getting married comes up, something happens. You seem to have an excuse for going elsewhere, or you just disappear, like last fall, when you left suddenly for Vancouver."

"I don't know," said Tony. "I never thought of it like that, and I never think of it when I do these things. I just go wherever the urge takes me."

"There's a lot more involved than just an 'urge,' sweetheart. You're a complicated person."

"Boy oh boy, there's a lot to being a Breed, and then coming into White society. And then spending three years in that military police force working under such asses as Sergeant Gordon and Inspector Hexter," argued Tony.

"But you do a lot of things that only aggravate the situation. Sometimes you antagonize people, which just brings you into more trouble, especially with people who are in authority over you," said Sue.

"I don't think I understand what you're saying. A fellow's got to have a little fun once in awhile," argued Tony.

"It's more than that. What caused you to do those things in the Mounties that could've got you in real serious trouble? Was it an urge?" asked Sue.

"Like what?"

"Well, like gluing up those Liberals' windows in Gravelbourg. You were just daring Sergeant Gordon to catch you. You did it so openly and noisily, and you laughed all over town about it being such a great thing. Or down in Wood Mountain. You did all those things that were against the police rules, like going to Montana with a load of young people, or carrying big cooking pails of draft beer across town while in uniform. What was behind it?"

"Nothing! Those Liberals and Gordon had that gluing coming to them, and old man Hexter deserved to have his Mounties play games on him. That's all."

"I disagree with you," said Sue. "It seems to me that you would be telling me about how you had been given 'hell', as you called it. You let that worry you a lot, and then you sort of delighted in getting revenge."

"Look, sweetheart, are you a psychiatrist or something?" questioned Tony.

"Don't get annoyed, darling," spoke Sue firmly, putting her hand on his arm, "I'm very much in love with you, and I want to understand all I can about you. You already [know] so much about me because you've spent a lot of time at our place and with my family, but that's not true for me."

"But you came home with me," Tony said. "I'll bet you analyzed the whole Breed nation."

"Mother and I talk a lot about you. She likes you very much, but she thinks you're reckless and you defy authorities for nothing. That only leads you into further trouble," said Sue very seriously.

"Does she think I'm reckless with her daughter?" He moved real close to Sue. "I'm going to challenge your virginity."

"Tony, be serious. There's nothing wrong in trying to understand as much as I can about the man I'm about to marry."

"Well, according to your philosophy, you'll not be able to set yourself up as an authority, otherwise I'll do something against you, defy you," answered Tony.

"Yes, sort of, if I was sharp and harsh with power and authority over you."

"And there'd be no mistake about you being a White Protestant big shot over me. Boy oh boy, it looks like we're gonna be in for some tough Indian wars. Hey, sweetheart, do you squaw wrestle?"

"No, I never heard of it," said Sue.

"I'll show you tonight after dark," said Tony laughing quietly. "You've got an evil mind."

"I think that's a good point," said Sue.

"You mean about squaw wrestling?"

"No, about big shot White people [lording it] over you; who call you down, and especially when they call you an Indian or a savage. And you've hated yourself for being such a crippled child at the time and couldn't answer them back right away. You always thanked them for bawling you out," explained Sue.

"Hey, darling, that's right, I think you are a psychiatrist, after all."

"They all run together, hon. Listen: You get a bawling out, or somebody disgraces you as a Breed. For the moment, they warn you. Later, it turns to hate, and you defy them to discipline you," explained Sue very slowly and methodically.

"Yeah, I should just punch them in the guts and kick them in the nuts right there on the spot," said Tony pounding his fist in his hand.

"You shouldn't punch them, but maybe it would be better to talk up at the time you're catching hell. Then you wouldn't have to burn with hate and hostility. Then you wouldn't waste so much time daring people and provoking them for nothing," said Sue.

"But it's not for nothing. I like being mad, and I get a lot of pleasure out of showing that I'm not afraid. They haven't crushed me into an obedient and shy Breed," argued Tony.

"I'm beginning to see […] why you came to Vancouver. You remember when we had an argument over [getting married at once,] and I told you that I wouldn't marry you as long as you didn't make something worthwhile of your life? And we continued to quarrel, and I was harshly severe to you? And you know what happened not long after? You beat it to Vancouver! You did this to provoke me into doing something more drastic."

"Wow, sweet, sweet Sue, how can you talk so long without getting tired? You're going to get a headache thinking so deep about such problems. Honestly, darling, I never thought any such thing. I was just boozing," explained Tony.

"But promise me, dear Tony, that you'll think seriously about this, and try to check your daring and provoking behaviour."

"I promise, sweetheart, I swear on a stack of bibles before the White goddess of the world—and the Halfbreed nation," assured Tony. "We better go home and have supper, and whatever else that may be possible."

"You never give up, do you dear?" said Sue as she brushed the sand off.

"Let's toss to see about tonight. Heads, we sleep at your room. Tails, we sleep at my place. How about that, and if it stands on end, we sleep in our own beds," urged Tony.

"I don't gamble on my virtue," stated Sue.

That night, when he was alone, Tony thought very seriously about what Sue had said. Not only was she an understanding person, but she helped him to understand the problems that he faced in the cruel and brutal world. And Tony realized he had plenty. He would [have to] pay attention to White authorities calling him down and his reaction to it. However, he felt that he was getting greater confidence in the White world, and could handle most of these problems now. But they were mighty complex, just like Sue said about him coming to Vancouver. That example bothered Tony a lot because he hated examining his love life with Sue. It was too precious for examination; it was sacred. Yet, he realized there were things about his behaviour that needed correcting. There were so many things that caused him pain, great pain, like being away from Sue. The things that Sue had talked about always pained him, especially when White authorities clawed him. They made him feel so inferior and servile. He became obedient and shy right away. He would lose all his power and confidence. He knew this ate into him. But Tony blamed this [meekness] onto his Breed world, and considered it one of the problems of being a Breed in a White world. He was like most Breeds and Indians: shy and insecure, obedient and grateful.

There was no doubt about it, Sue was intelligent, but Tony [couldn't] admit that she was smarter [than him]. Tony couldn't have a wife who was cleverer than him. He could understand her and often agree with her as long as she didn't want to become smarter. He was touchy about that.

The next day, Tony suggested they make a lunch and go for a walk around Stanley Park. "Put on your best walking shoes 'cause it's a long way around the park, and I'm not going to carry you," ordered Tony.

"If I'm going into the woods with you, I should put on my best running shoes," Sue said teasingly.

"You know, sweetheart, I wouldn't be surprised if you wore a chastity belt."

"With you around, I need one," she replied.

"We'll find out today because we're going to stop deep in the bush for lunch where there's no one around for miles," he said in a playful manner.

"I'll send up smoke signals," said Sue, as she went over and kissed him. Tony hugged her and kissed her passionately.

"Are all Halfbreeds as passionate as you?" she asked.

"Sure, but they've got something to show for their passion—like ten kids."

"I love you more every day, sweetheart. Yesterday, I thought it was impossible to be more in love with you, yet today I love you even more. Maybe each day you create a greater capacity for me to love. And I want to be loved so very much by the most wonderful man from the Halfbreed nation."

These things made Tony feel great. It boosted his confidence to know that he was a Breed and, at the same time, a wonderful man. Under these terms, he liked being called a Breed. They walked on the path along the water. They sat and watched the huge ships move past.

"That's really a different scene from the flat prairie in southern Saskatchewan," said Sue.

"That's for sure. But the prairie is about as flat as the ocean." said Tony.

"And maybe the waves are like the waves in the waving wheat fields," said Sue. "Do you like Vancouver?" she asked.

"I do now, but I hated it when I first came here. The dreary, dull weather and the rain nearly drove me to suicide in the beginning," explained Tony. "Do you think we should live in Vancouver after we're married?"

"I don't know," said Sue slowly. "I'd hate to leave Mother and Dad. Mom's not been too well lately. And your family all live in Saskatchewan. I don't think we should come here now, anyway. Besides, you haven't got that good of a job to keep us here," suggested Sue.

"You're not kidding. On twenty-two dollars a week, we'd have to eat porridge every meal," said Tony.

They walked on. The path was narrow, but they walked close enough together to keep on it. "I sure as hell won't walk Indian style with the woman I love so much," said Tony.

They sat on the grass and watched the cars cross over Lion's Gate Bridge. They decided to count the cars. In a fifteen-minute period there were a hundred cars. "Let's see," said Tony, "that's four hundred cars an hour, and at twenty-five cents a car that's how much?" Quickly, Sue said, "One hundred dollars."

"Just imagine; they make a hundred dollars an hour. Boy, what a racket! At twenty-four hours a day. Hey, we could be rich in a week."

"Tony, you're thinking like a capitalist. I thought you considered yourself a socialist. That money should be going to people for schools and hospitals," said Sue.

"Better'n that, that bridge should be free to all the people," he suggested.

"I think the Safeway and Vancouver are making you into a free enterpriser," suggested Sue.

"I doubt it. They're making me into a militant unionist. I guess unionism and socialism work together. It seems to be all in the same interest, for the workers and people, generally," thought Tony. Sue explained all about the socialist experiments that were happening in Saskatchewan. It sounded very exciting. This is the kind of society Tony should develop everywhere.

"I agree, sweetheart. I want to be back in Saskatchewan, where the people are really making history on this continent and where the people count, and not the rich ruling class. I want to be part of such an exciting change. It's important to be contributing to that new society. There'll be so many changes for the Breeds."

They had their lunch at Brockton Point, and admired the gorgeous mountains on the north shore. "Those mountains are inclined to smother me," said Sue. "I feel crowded in. There should be open spaces to be free all around."

"That's how they affected me at first too."

It took the rest of the afternoon to walk around the park. [...] The walking was frequently interrupted with "mushing." They got home too tired to make supper. Later, they went out and had fish'n chips, something he had learned to like since coming to Vancouver. At home on the chesterfield, Tony claimed, "I'm so exhausted, I can hardly move."

"Can I depend on that, sweetheart?" asked Sue.

"Sure, but you've got to promise not to take advantage of me," said Tony teasingly.

"Look who's talking?" Sue retorted.

"Are we agreed, then, darling, that we're both going back to Saskatchewan now?" questioned Sue.

"Yes, agreed. I've got nothing to stay here for. I want to be wherever you are. And I'm happy in Saskatchewan. That's where the tough and rugged people live, anyway," stated Tony.

"I think you should get a job with some government department, where you can work your way up. You don't want to be a janitor or a street sweeper," said Sue.

"No, I guess not, darling. I should work to be somebody important, and earn big money, like the Safeway manager."

"No, that's not right," said Sue. "There are jobs in the government or other agencies where you don't have to exploit your fellow workers. You don't need to be a big shot, dear. You can have a job that pays a good salary, where you can be contributing something to the new socialist society and for the good of all people. There's going to be all kinds of new things developing in education, social welfare, prison reform, and I'm sure there will be new developments in the Indian and Breed nation."

"Boy, that sounds great, and we'll make the headquarters at St. Louis."

Sue seemed to understand socialism so well, at least when it came to understanding how the people should all benefit from society, not just a few rich families. The wealth and services should be distributed for all to enjoy, especially healthcare. He would depend on Sue to explain socialism to him.

"Listen, darling, I want to ask you a very secret question. Come close. How many kids are we going to have?"

"I don't know. A more important question is when are we going to get married?"

"What about this evening, and then we can start on the first baby," said Tony.

"Seriously, sweetheart, when?"

"I really don't care. Whenever you think it's best. I have no commitments anywhere."

"This is June. What about the middle of August?"

"Okay with me. But make sure it's the right time of the month. I guess I don't have much to do besides getting the booze."

"You leave the booze alone."

"Okay, that's settled. After August 15th, we'll be Mr. and Mrs. Bruce. Shall we invite the king 'n queen?"

"Don't be silly. But we'll invite the premier of Saskatchewan, Mr. Tommy Douglas."

"Hey, that's great. For the best man, I want three: a Breed, a socialist and a unionist," demanded Tony. "They're the best men in the world, anyway."

"Make sure they stay sober; that is all I want," demanded Sue.

"Okay, that's all settled. We're about to be Mr. and Mrs. Bruce. Now, whoever heard of a married couple sleeping in different houses? You agreed to 'honour and obey,' then obey you must. From now on, I give the orders. Okay, Mrs. Bruce, get to bed!"

"Don't be silly, darling. You've got two and a half months to wait."

"Geez, I'll be an old man by then. I'll be over the hill."

"I'm going to bed, but to my own bed, and alone. I'm exhausted."

"Under those conditions, I agree you should be in your own bed. Let's go for a bus ride tomorrow and save our feet and energy."

"Okay, darling!"

Tony walked Sue home to the "tourist" room. He was happy that some decisions had been made. He was happy to be going back to Saskatchewan. It was home. It was the Halfbreed nation, and now it was a province of socialism. And most important of all, there was Sue, the most precious person in the whole world. He would be happier when she was his wife. His life would be less in turmoil. Sue was such a soothing effect in the cruel brutal world.

And Mamma would be happy that he was going back to Saskatchewan. She didn't like Tony being so far away. He'd quit his job on Monday, and then he and Sue could leave for Regina. He didn't have any money, but they didn't need any. He'd get a good job in Saskatchewan. He was anxious to learn a lot more about socialism so that he could make a greater contribution [...]. Also, since his recent experience with the Safeway stores, he was interested in furthering the work of unionism. Yet, his first consideration would be with his own people. Everything seemed so exciting that he couldn't get to sleep, as tired as he was.

Sue woke him up at noon. "The landlady said she thought you had gone out already this morning."

"I don't keep my landlady posted on all the things that I'm doing. She's kind of nosy, but pretty good. Let me tell you, I know what miserable landladies can be like!" Tony told Sue about the one on Nelson Street. Sue made breakfast.

The day was rather dull. It looked like it could rain, so they were undecided what to do for the day. "Darling, what would you like to do?"

"You silly girl! But I'll settle for a solid afternoon of mushing," said Tony.

They had just settled down on the chesterfield after doing the dishes when the landlady yelled, "Tony, a telegram for you!"

"Telegram for me? Must be something wrong. Halfbreeds never send telegrams. Okay, I'll get it!" He went downstairs and to the door. Sure enough, it was addressed to him. He signed for it. On the way upstairs, he noticed it was actually Sue's telegram, sent under his name and address.

"It's yours, sweetheart. Probably from your boyfriend in Regina." He handed it to her.

Sue stood up, took it hurriedly and tore it open.

"Tony, Tony," she said in shocked voice. "Mother's had a stroke!" She dropped to the chesterfield. Tony reached over and took the telegram. Sue was holding her hands over her face and crying. Tony sat down beside her, put his arms around her and held her tightly. There was little he could do but comfort her. Sue's pain and sadness were his too. [...].

"What else does it say?" Sue asked between sobs.

"She's in the hospital, and your Dad wants you to hurry home."

She looked up at Tony. "I've got to get home right away, as fast I can."

"I know, darling, and we'll have to get you on your way today."

"When was it sent?" asked Sue.

"This morning at nine."

"Maybe she's dead by now." Sue broke into frantic crying.

"Sweetheart, maybe she's much better by now. Look, darling, I'll phone home to your Dad, right now and ask him. Then we'll see about getting you home," said Tony, giving all the comfort he could. He was very troubled to see Sue in such agony, but there was nothing more he could do. "I'll use the landlady's phone downstairs. Do you want to come with me, and if we get your Dad, you can talk to him. Here, darling, let me wipe up those tears."

"But I'm afraid of what Dad might have to tell us," cried Sue.

"Well, I'll talk to him first."

Tony was lucky in getting Mr. Norman. He was going up to the hospital. He had been up there most of the morning. Mrs. Norman seemed about the same. She was unable to talk. He gave Sue the phone. Her crying made it quite impossible for her father to understand. "We just received your telegram. Sue will be on her way home today. I'm not sure how we'll get there yet, but I'll phone you or wire you as to when and how Sue will arrive. She'll get home as fast as she can."

"Have you got your return ticket?"

"Yes, I have. It's here in my purse."

"Suppose we are able to get a reservation for you on the train this evening, when will you get home?"

"It took me nearly thirty-six hours to come," said Sue.

"That won't get you home until Tuesday morning."

"Would it be possible to get the plane?"

"I don't know, darling, I've never travelled by plane, but we can find out."

It wasn't possible to get a flight reservation for her, but there was a chance of cancellations just before departure, and she might get on then. They decided it was worth the try. They didn't have enough money for the airfare, but Sue would cash in her train ticket. Together with Tony's money, they could make it. But that meant going down to the CN station first, and then out to the airport. They'd never make it on time. Tony phoned his union pal, Dick, who had a car. He said he'd meet them over at the "tourist" room in about twenty minutes. They were at the airport on time. As Tony went over to buy the ticket, Dick offered to lend him money. Sue was able to get a seat. She had regained her calmness now, and Tony was giving her all the loving comfort he possibly could. He fully realized in this crisis that his love for Sue was the deepest and most intense feeling that he had ever experienced. There would never be anything to compare with it, nor would it ever be possible to replace it. His love for Sue was as precious as it was perpetual. His life without Sue was nothing.

"See you later this week, darling," said Sue. "Now for sure," she added.

"For sure, sweetheart," assured Tony.

They kissed good-bye. He watched Sue go through the gate, and disappear down the ramp. I didn't realize it, but she had walked out of my life forever.[1] **(TB)**

Howard Gets a Job With Vancouver School Board

I took a new job cleaning ditches and raking leaves from the roadside. I met several new friends—university students making extra money during the summer months. Many were communists studying law at the University of British Columbia (UBC). They had many new and profound ideas that seemed to be highly progressive and productive. It was my introduction to communist thought. I became quite excited about it. We

---

[1] This last sentence, in the first person, is a handwritten addition to the typed manuscript.

remained friends and colleagues for many years.

One day a newspaper blew into the ditch. I picked it up and noticed an ad for a job as an attendance worker with the Vancouver School Board (VSB). It was a counsellor [student] attendance job; whatever the hell that meant. It sounded wonderful, but the pay was pitiful. I applied for it and was later asked to come in for an interview. Inside, the boardroom frightened me. Seated around a huge polished table were several well-dressed officials. Such dignitaries with sophisticated language ruffled me. Yet, they were not deliberately cross-examining me. To start, one asked me to "tell them a little about myself and my background." I stuck to the term "little." I talked about my excellent police work and training, emphasizing the counselling procedures that I used. I [had actually] faked a counselling course that I was taking at the University. That was [… what got me] being hired. A long-term employee is what they wanted. I was young, twenty-six, [and had the] appearance of a serious achiever and had an attitude of upward mobility. They hired me. It was a happy day and a turning point in my life.

I felt somewhat like a con man. The one condition that made me hesitate was that I must have a car, as I had to travel to several schools and to the homes of parents throughout the huge city. Vancouver was no St. Louis, but I needed the job. I prayed furiously for a car in both "Anglican" and "Catholic". Finally, I decided to go to the top—the superintendent. In those days, I made myself visible to the important persons around the officials. Superintendent McCorkindale came through like a saint. The head of the local Ford agency was his good friend. On his word, I drove a brand new Ford car out of the showroom. It mattered not if the monthly payments were about equal to my monthly salary. In the next six months, I wrote more rubber cheques than all the rubber in Brazil. Fortunately, the bank manager was helpful and understanding, otherwise I would have had my car repeatedly repossessed.

Things went reasonably well on the job. The work seemed like a natural for me. There were plenty of delinquent students, so I always had enough cases to keep me busy. I enjoyed the work very much and I felt that I was reforming these young delinquents into outstanding citizens. A few years later, when I made a study of my ex-clients, I found that several had ended up in jail, others in juvenile detention and some on parole. However, I did not blink at that record, as I was now well-established in a steady middle-class semi-profession.

I was compensated for the poor pay by […attending] university. I was requested by school board officials to take one course a year in addition to summer school. In the summer sessions, I took two social work courses. In the regular winter sessions, I completed one or two courses. This meant I could not futz around boozing and hustling lovely women.

There was one serious flaw in my duration of work at the school board—a co-worker who had been on the job for a few years before me. Much of her efforts were to undermine and sabotage not only my work, but also me personally. It was part of her nature, [and was] not a personal grudge. To important school authorities, she spread "credible" rumours about my "faults and negligence" in my work. She bad-mouthed me to every person whom she thought would harm me. She must have reasoned that this raised her level of work in comparison to mine. She was a constant threat that plagued my work with the VSB. When I was first employed, she confidently informed me of my duties. In short time, to my dismay, she had misled me on almost everything. The so-called helpful hints turned out to be sly and vicious […]. They were falsehoods that discredited me in the eyes of school board officials. It was a constant worry that she might be successful in totally discrediting me and could thus get me fired. She was a con artist in the sense that she would have me believe that she was my best friend and protector, making me an easy victim to her cruel schemes.

I soon learned that I had to keep all my important information on my casework secret. To protect my work record, I had to falsify information to her. To hold my work record above suspicion, I had to deceive her on issues in which she developed special concern. I hated to think of what she would have done had she known of my Métis ancestry. That type of [personal] information was her specialty. For four years, I had to be on guard against her vicious schemes.

In spite of this employee, my work and study at the VSB was without a doubt the most prominent and foremost platform in my struggles and movement towards […being a] success in the Canadian establishment. **(AB)**

Tony Meets Teddy and Learns About Nepotism

That fall, a new member was added to the supervisory group at the VSB, a young unmarried man named Teddy. He and Tony became good friends. They belonged to the same badminton club. They visited frequently at the office, chatted and fooled around. Teddy was a very jovial and happy-go-lucky type, a practical joker. He was full of fun. It struck Tony, though, that Teddy had never experienced any hard times in his life; otherwise, he would not be so light-hearted about everything all the time. It seemed that Teddy considered life just one big joke. He did not have a care in the world. Tony wondered how Teddy had managed to do so well for himself if he just played all the way through life. He had his B.A. degree. Didn't that require some serious thought and hard work? And to become a supervisor in the VSB system meant that you had to do some good work in the field of teaching. Tony knew that the supervisors who were retiring had made very careful surveys of the possible successors, and recommendations as to who would be the best possible candidates. Tony knew that Teddy had not been among any of the recommended candidates. In fact, no one had known of Teddy at the time the supervisors made their recommendations six months previously.

One afternoon, when Tony happened to be discussing a business matter with one of the assistant superintendents, he suggested that he would like to [...advance his career]. However, the assistant superintendent indicated that it was necessary to have considerable teaching experience in the Vancouver area before that was possible. Tony was surprised by that remark and pointed out that Teddy was a supervisor, and had not taught a day in Vancouver schools, and that any teaching that he had was only one year in northern British Columbia schools. The assistant superintendent, obviously on the spot for what he had said, and tried to cover up by saying "the VSB was under pressure to hire Teddy." That didn't make sense to Tony, so he said, "What do you mean 'under pressure?' Was he going to burn down the schools in Vancouver?"

"No, the Department of Education in Victoria insisted that we hire Teddy."

Tony asked no further questions on that matter. He thought he understood. At least it was none of his business. Tony now realized there was a lot of politics involved in making appointments to top positions in the VSB as anywhere else in the bureaucracy.

Some time later, Teddy asked Tony to come over and have dinner with him and his friend on Friday evening. Tony arrived on time, and was immediately introduced to an older gentleman in the room. "Tony, I want you to meet my uncle, Walter Smiteram."

Tony walked over and shook his hand, trying to figure out why that name was so familiar. Suddenly he remembered: the British Columbia Minister of Education! Tony smiled to himself—so now things added up. That's where the pressure came from for Teddy's hiring, which the assistant superintendent had been talking about. It all began to make sense. Teddy didn't have any responsibility in [...making] his future and working hard to [... to be a] success. It was all made for him. All he had to do was to be present when required. Tony thought that, sometime, he would get Teddy's side of the story as to how he got the job as supervisor. Teddy was honest, mostly because he was naïve about all political situations, and could see nothing wrong with political patronage or, in his case, family patronage. He saw it all as part of the free enterprise system. There was nothing immoral or wrong about it. At the same time, Teddy would argue that competition was the greatest feature of the society, as it allowed only the very best and qualified people to rise to the best positions. Thus, qualified civil servants ran the system. He never saw that he was a walking contradiction of the very thing he was supporting.

One evening after a badminton game, Teddy explained to Tony that he had spent the last year in England studying, and how he really enjoyed the great times that he had there. Tony knew that a year in England cost a lot of money, especially if one was studying there; spending money all the time, and not making any. He knew it was quite impossible to save enough money in one year of teaching to keep oneself in England for the following year, especially if it was the first year of teaching. He was curious as to how Teddy managed it financially. "Did you manage to save enough from teaching to keep yourself for a whole year in England?" asked Tony, knowing the answer beforehand.

"Oh, heavens no, I practically had to borrow money to be able to get through my first year of teaching. The wages were so poor," said Teddy, without giving any other lead as to how he financed the trip.

"I guess Mom and Dad had to foot the bill, then. I suppose that's okay if they can afford to do without feeling the pinch," asked Tony in a sneaky way.

"Mom and Dad might've paid my expenses if it would've guaranteed that I would've never come back to bother them any more, even if they'd had to go to Household Finances for the money. They gave very little help," explained Teddy.

Both men were [playing] games, each trying to impress the other with prestige and academic values. Tony was […] forced to ask […] how did Teddy manage to finance the trip and the year [in England]. But Teddy recognized this and had wanted to make [… his response] as dramatic and effective as possible. He finally gave the facts, but in a very off-handed way, as if to imply that it happened all the time.

"I was awarded the scholarship of the Imperial Order of the British Empire a year ago." Tony knew that it was a rich scholarship and a very prestigious one, as he had seen it when reading over the list of scholarships. He was greatly impressed.

"Geez, Teddy, what a tremendous scholar you must be. Boy, only the best brains in all of Canada ever get that scholarship. Boy, let me shake the hand of one of Canada's great scholars." Tony went over and shook his hand.

"Aw come off it, Tony, it was nothing all that great. Everybody had the same chance. I just happened to be lucky." Teddy seemed so modest.

"How did you know the position as supervisor at the VSB was open, away over in London, England, and how to apply for it?" asked Tony.

"I didn't. I never heard anything about it until I was on my way home on the ship, only about a month before I got the job," explained Teddy.

"I don't understand," said Tony.

"I received a telegram on the boat one day that I had the job as supervisor."

"You mean, you didn't even apply for it?" asked Tony.

"It was impossible, as I didn't know the job existed," answered Teddy.

It wasn't necessary to ask any more questions. Tony could see that being the nephew of British Columbia's Minister of Education explained how he got the job. This bothered Tony for some time. He was quite upset about the whole system, and how it worked. It certainly didn't operate according to the way he was taught in school and university. It was not based on qualifications and having to pass civil service examinations. It was certainly a very dishonest system. He had better learn the shortcuts of the society if he wanted to get ahead like Teddy.

"What the hell kind of crap was the assistant superintendent trying to peddle to me about having to have several years of teaching experience in the Vancouver schools before being able to be promoted?" The assistant superintendent was covering up for the system. He was that stupid about all the exceptions and short cuts, like Teddy. Tony felt repulsed by this official, as he had known him as an honest and honourable man. But now, was he really that? Wasn't he really being just a spineless puppet for the system? Would he really sell his principles and soul for the job as assistant superintendent? Tony developed a contemptible feeling for the man. The next time a good job came up, he'd go right to the superintendent or *to the board of school trustees themselves.* **(TB)**

Attending the University of British Columbia

Part of my agreement with the VSB was that I would go to university to get my B.A. It was important to the school board that I have a university degree. It was only appropriate that their employees have a good education. And for my job, that meant at least a B.A. I would take two courses in the summer session and one course in the regular winter session, as I would be working full time. But they made the provisions that I could take time to attend one course in the winter session, which was three hours a week […]. The request was comparable to a beatification from the Pope. Otherwise, I might never have gone to university.

Oh God, there were so many "what ifs" in my career! There were so many gifts that just fell into my lap, and I was immediately off and running to a higher and better goal.

Although I enjoyed university, it was the most demanding and exhausting work that I had ever done. It was an extremely tight schedule to do a full time job and attend courses at university, where both required my services at the same time. It was very strenuous keeping up with the required reading set out by each professor, as well as the written assignments […and their…] deadlines. During those three years, my social life was almost zero. Saltpetre was a regular part of my diet. No, I did not consider it a sacrifice. Testosterone ebbed away, and I suffered no pain. I considered this a real opportunity to get a university education. Without this deal, I would never have had a university education. Now in my old age, I enjoy intellectual and scholarly pleasures. But I must truly confess that those four years were a dry run, admittedly the most strenuous and tenacious of my life.

This is the most common question asked me: how I rose from an illiterate Halfbreed ghetto in Saskatchewan to a prominent professor and a leader of an Aboriginal liberation movement? […] Feelings of revenge and hostility were forces that constantly motivated me to even the score [with the White establishment].

My experience studying and completing my B.A. degree at UBC instilled the motivation, desire and direction for greater and higher levels of achievement. A great deal of credit goes to the VSB trustees, especially Mrs. Ada Crump, a politically progressive activist, and John Hendry, president of a labour union, who were compassionate supporters as well as firm and wise advisors. I count these two individuals as remarkable persons […who contributed to] my success.

I could not even write the English language properly. At one time, the Dean called me into his office and condemned me for the fact that I could not write or speak the Queen's English properly. Why in the hell did I not tell him that English was not my natural language, and that I could speak Michif? But he wouldn't know what that was. He could speak only about power.

Christmas exams were coming. How does one study for this puzzle? I concocted every possible method without seriously cheating. I wrote answers on my shirt cuffs. Passing exams was the name of the game, not honour. I stumbled and trembled into the exam and wrote it with a frenzied mind. To my utter amazement, I passed it—60%. I was on my road to becoming an academic. It called for a big celebration with my boozing pals. I was no longer an idiot; I was an intellectual. I now felt arrogant enough to tackle a university career.

There was not a Métis among all these hundreds of students. This was strictly a world of European settlers. Although I continued to express ideas that came from the Métis world, few students understood the concepts I was expressing. Everything in class was in the vocabulary and perception of White middle-class society. I had to move into that class. My Métisness was lost. My social life was now completely intertwined with White middle-class students and their lifestyles. As each year went on, I became increasingly involved in the mainstream and moved more in that direction.

There were so many difficult courses, to make a decision on the choice of department. The one real interest I had was politics—meaning courses in Political Science. But a degree had to include several different areas. Sociology caught my interest, as it seemed to cover politics, history, psychology and culture. It was the challenge of intellectual thought that fascinated me. The excitement to speculate and hypothesize on sociological theories was stimulating. These courses led to many mind games. Science and mathematics were limited to the required courses for my degree.

Often, courses were chosen by the professor's reputation. Rumours spread fast and furious about the character of professors and their teaching, but more particularly about the ease of their exams. Social Science courses dealt with society and the general interaction of individuals in society. The professors and authors of these textbooks usually discussed them in ponderous language. As a newcomer to university, I had difficulty understanding the rambling technical language. It required a lot of time trying to make sense out of this rhetoric.

In the basement of the library one day, I came upon Sociology books written and interpreted from a Marxist and socialist view. They dealt with the same "complicated" theories as the assigned text, but the explanations were simplified and straightforward. Theories were so clear and understandable. They provided a key to the "bourgeois" intellectual rhetoric. It was from these readings that I developed a critical mind in my reading. It also made for more interesting discussions with my socialist colleagues.

My first year was pure drudgery, with a constant fear of failing. The results that finally arrived called for celebration—I had passed all four courses. None were high marks, but I was mighty pleased to have passed them. The second year was about the same. I took mostly Sociology courses, as I rather liked the professor. Several students claim the professor had a muddled mind and confused lectures. But this chaotic and cluttered mind seemed to communicate quite well with my thought processes. It was rumoured that we could converse for thirty minutes and not make sense or convey comprehensible thoughts. Professor Topping may not have been the greatest scholar, but he was a true humanist.

I had only one quarrel with him, and not a scholarly one. At the end of one term, he gave an exam of two questions that had not been discussed in class or assigned as reading. Students either failed or got extremely low grades. Of course, we were all displeased. During our class break, it was agreed that we would challenge him and demand a different exam. When we resumed class, most students made critical comments. Naturally, I supported the challenge and was firm in my criticism. He took my dispute very seriously and quarrelled with me. To my dismay, the other students turned against me and supported the professor. It was a bitter disappointment, but a new realization. Students were real opportunists who would quickly turn against a fellow student in order to ingratiate themselves to the professor to ensure good grades. I was dismissed from class and told to see the professor in his office.

It would be a lesson that I would never forget. The name of the game is strictly individualism. Look out for yourself and to hell with anyone else! This episode went deep into me and took some time to be resolved. As a result, it often became an integral part of my character. Hence, after this I became less trustworthy of others, regardless of their friendliness. I was cautious about the potential to find traitors. In my second year, I was again drawn to Sociology courses and Dr. Topping. I worked even harder, read more and studied the theories intensively, and bettered my essays and my academic writing. I cut out words that had reference to Michif. I now had one year of sociological knowledge behind me, and I thought that I would make higher grades. Unfortunately, my final grades were only slightly higher.

During the summer months, I associated with senior students who knew schemes in writing final exams. The first rule was to figure out the main topics emphasized by the professor. Note the issue he underlined in the textbook, listen for the major theme, which he stressed in his lectures. Before the exam, make out an outline answer and memorize it. In my third year, I moved up to the 80% mark. In my fourth and final year, I did better—90%—and I was invited to do an honours course with him. I never looked back on low grades again. This does not mean that I neglected to learn the real substance of the course. Indeed not, I became a serious student.

The snobbish fraternity attitude clashed with the [actions of the] older and practical [war] veterans. Since university facilities were extremely overcrowded, it was a matter of "first here, hold!" Hence, it was constant grabbing of whatever facilities [were available]. What a crush! Some lectures were given in the barn. This made me feel a bit like home.

I would become sensitive about my Métis heritage in the Anthropology courses where Indian culture was studied. They were studied in pre-history times, as savages with all the typical stereotypes. Professors explained Aboriginal people in purely Eurocentric language. It was insulting, but at that time there were few, if any, Aboriginals in university. Racism was evident at the university in the 1950s and 60s. There was always the temptation to question the professor on the ordinary basics on Indian issues, such as land. But the possibility of getting personally involved and the discussion becoming passionate kept me quiet. University was so exciting at all times. The huge crowds of students strolling everywhere at all times made it like a circus.

Speeches on many different topics were given in different halls. Politics was my favourite—I mean radical politics, often socialism or communism. Harry Rankin, a communist, was the most provocative speaker on the campus and would attract the largest crowds. Every noon hour, a whole array of issues on poverty was argued. Tim Buck [Communist Party of Canada leader] gave a few speeches. Labour union topics were popular. Informal education through public discussion was probably outdoing formal classroom lectures. My education was about as complete as any. It was the most intensive period of my life, but also the most enlightening and provocative. Passion for exploring and conquering greater knowledge was raging in my brain. I began to develop some capacity for thinking beyond the basics. Thinking at the intellectual level beyond the basic premise became challenging. I was anxious to explore the ideas and thoughts beyond the surface. I knew enough about politics to know that there was thinking, planning and scheming behind the scenes. Here I was fascinated. Gradually, it spread to other courses.

I also had the good fortune of meeting a Métis buddy who was attending university, which was indeed a great and wonderful surprise. Like me, he had been born and raised in Saskatchewan, similar to St. Louis. He had been in the army and had the advantage of a more worldly experience than me. He had a bright mind and was a good talker–rather unusual, as far as I was concerned. But we became fast friends and quite inseparable. There were so very many issues in common. Our family and community backgrounds were quite identical, so we could compare thoughts on end. We applied the ideas that we gained from lectures, readings and insightful thinking of our own.

Explanations and understandings of the strangeness of the Métis people in our home communities would begin to make sense as we talked them out and related the intellectual ideas to the attitudes and behaviour of the people back home. We soon were deep into the topic of colonization. Now our language and thoughts had expanded beyond the ghetto level. Most of the next year was spent on different ideas surrounding colonization. We rejected the typical concept of Anthropology about Native people and their culture as primitives being civilized by the White colonizers of Europe.

White-European myths were soon exploded. It was not difficult to solve the mystery of the historical myths. It was much more difficult to unravel the process and mechanism of colonization that followed the conquest of the 17th century [the beginnings of European colonization in Canada]. The big puzzle was how our ancestors and Métis relatives became so totally colonized. I didn't even know that I was Métis when I lived in my home. I had some inkling about it, but I was doubtful. It remained a sort of mystery, never being sure who in the hell I was nor how to prove it. It was the same damn thing with many Métis. What a helluva mess! I thought I would go nuts sometimes. No one, not one person talked about being Métis, yet we lived only fifteen miles from Batoche, the [site of the] massacre of the Métis by John. A. Macdonald. Why was everyone so damn silent about being Métis? Hiding it was the greatest shame. Geez, I haven't a clue! Maybe all Métis go to hell! Being such good Catholics, no one wanted to go on that trip. But some may get stuck in purgatory. We really sucked up the monstrous images of the colonizers as savages, lazy, drunkards, cheats, immoral primitives, on and on. Yeah, all of them internalized the totality of those stereotypes. It's amazing how quickly we discarded our own culture and ethos, and in turn adopted false images of the oppressor. The White oppressors dominated the ideology almost the moment they invaded the tents of Indian women.

"Why," said Dan, "do you think that Indian society submerged rather quickly into the colonizers' images?"

"God above, it's a puzzle, but it had to be based on material power because their 'moral' society was certainly not superior. It travelled like a plague throughout our entire nation and territory. It was one of the most powerful weapons in conquering our nation. You know, Dan, it is a complex matter to internalize the oppressor's imperial ideas of ourselves and nation. First, we resigned to our oppression, meaning the oppression by the British and French, and then we adapted ourselves to the structures of domination. By structures, I mean a tribal chief, White administrator, reserve, etc."

Canadian historians have not provided a satisfactory explanation of the racial oppression of Aboriginal people and its subsequent impact on the colonized personality. Once the dominant society has imposed the White-supremacist ideology, there develops within Aboriginal people a desire of acceptance and integration into the mainstream. It is not usually understood or recognized at the conscious level because he/she does not recognize it in his/her everyday thinking. It is a sort of inner force urging Native people towards the dominant stream. The glorification of Whiteness and all its dimensions act as a magnet to our social behaviour and attitudes. At the same time, it causes us to reject and even despise our own culture and nationality. This was a very obvious situation in St. Louis, where most Métis pretended to be either French or English, or any nationality that would hide their Métis [ancestry]. There was not even a small celebration of our Métis culture. All Métis were hiding and covering over every aspect of their heritage. Although we were the largest section of the population around the Prince Albert-St. Louis region, we never celebrated our nationality.

The European French and English [immigrants] were very vocal and aggressive. Each group regularly and loudly proclaimed their ancestry. In doing so, they automatically pushed the Métis to the bottom. But we never resisted or protested. It was the accepted nature of our society. As Métis, we quietly and submissively sat on the sidelines. White supremacy is forceful and arrogant, whereas Métis nationalism is weak and accepting.

The racial stereotypes were well developed in St. Louis in the 1930s and 40s: pseudo-savages, lazy, and no ambition.

No wonder everyone wanted to hide from such images. They destroyed all self-esteem. It fostered the Métis to be shy, quiet and hesitant about expressing their ideas. This results in lack of skills in articulation and leadership. It is a powerful tool in preventing Native people from becoming local leaders. We were inclined to believe that White people are superior and skilled in leadership, and particularly in management. Increased White supremacy on one side and a deepened inferiorization on the negative side constitute a colonial mentality.

On the one hand, mainstream society attracts Aboriginal people to it, but on the other, they discriminate and exclude. An Aboriginal person in a top position is not altogether a positive factor because those below feel that an Aboriginal person cannot lead them into White society. The real power lies in the hands of the Whites. Aboriginals never get beyond [being] the conquered in a nation. An Aboriginal person is marked as being Native by either appearance or lifestyle—these are indelible characteristics. Where Indians are greatly despised, such as in North Battleford, Saskatchewan, the Métis will deny their relationship as part Indian. This is institutional racism because the White ruling class directs the kind of racism in the community. Young people internalize the ugliness of this racism and move into White society. This leads Native scholars away from Indigenous society and into the White mainstream; [they then] become [like the] White oppressors. **(AB)**

Tony Gets Seriously Involved With Judy Knox

Tony was rapidly fitting himself into the whole White middle-class world. He couldn't see himself as a worker anymore. He would never have anything to do with working that required physical labour, nor would he ever work in the fields again, nor would he pick rocks. The very thought of welfare annoyed him. There was no need for welfare; there were jobs to do. He was looking at his success in the mainstream. He'd have to hide his past and his parents. Nobody in Vancouver must ever find out about him being a Breed. His life was now revolving around the university, the Pacific club, nightclub life, tennis, weekends at the beach. He wanted to be well-dressed and sophisticated; he was shying away from the crude and vulgar. He was even giving up beer.

He was spending a lot of time with Judy and he could see that the better way of life made things more comfortable, easy and pleasant. He was thinking of this kind of life for himself. He was no longer thinking in terms of what it would mean for Mamma and Pappa or the rest of the Halfbreeds who lived in such poverty. How could he, Tony Bruce, get ahead, get a good job, make big money, have a nice house in a good district, have prestige and status among his friends? At the centre of everything was he himself. He was becoming a very ambitious Tony. [...]

The Knox family were going on their summer holidays. They were going to motor to California, along the coastline. Judy's young sister was going with them, but the two boys weren't going as they had summer jobs. They were leaving Judy in charge. They had a lovely big car, and they'd be staying at the most expensive motels, so they should have a pretty good time, thought Tony. He kind of envied them to be holidaying like that, with lots of money. But it would be nice visiting Judy with them gone.

That night after supper, Tony dropped around at Judy's place. It was warm and she was in the yard, dressed in summer shorts and halter. She looked cute, had a nice figure, particularly her full breasts. Tony guessed they were at least thirty-eight inches. That evening, Tony and Judy fooled around freely. Tony did not feel that he had to be so careful about proper manners and polite conversation. He felt comfortable and easy in the Knox home. The boys were out fooling around somewhere. They were much younger than Judy and didn't associate much with their older sister. Tony and Judy cuddled up on the big chesterfield in the living room. He was holding her in his arms. "Do you know, darling, I don't think we spend enough time making love. I love being so cuddly with you, and telling you what a beautiful and lovely girl you are. That is probably the most meaningful part of my life," Tony said, talking very low and quietly to her.

"I agree, darling, but it seems there are always so many other things to do. We shouldn't put off such lovely things as being together like this."

"Okay," said Tony, "agreed that we'll put other things off first," and he embraced Judy real close to him. He kissed her gently and pulled her body tightly to him.

[…]

A little earlier, Tony had suggested to Judy that he should stay overnight with her, but Judy's only objection was that the neighbours would see his car parked out there all night when her parents were away. So he went out to her place one evening by streetcar. They played badminton in the early evening, then sat around and had a few drinks and chatted about the future and their careers. They were snuggled on the chesterfield, and Tony whispered in her ear, "Darling, I'm going to stay with you tonight."

"Well, I didn't say you couldn't," she whispered back.

"There's no chance of your parents coming back sometime tonight?" asked Tony.

"Hardly," said Judy, "I got a card from them today, and they are in Tijuana, Mexico. I don't think they could make it back that fast," she explained. Tony would've liked to go to bed right away, but Judy said she had some work to get done, so Tony helped her. They were in love with themselves, but it was not a complete love. It had reservations. They were first concerned with their own ambitions and careers; and love must not be allowed to get in the way of such plans. They loved one another because of the emotional or psychological satisfaction it brought to the individual, and not in terms of a deep human life experience of a beautiful relationship, not something that has beauty and essence in itself.

Judy's bedroom was so delicate and feminine, so much pink, lace and soft fluffiness. Even the carpeting on the floor seemed so soft and feminine that he was awkward walking

133

on it. The entire room had an atmosphere of the soft fragrance, daintiness and tenderness, and all the mystery of femininity.

[...]

The alarm rang at eight o'clock. Judy reached over and shut it off. "Gosh, I think I'm too tired to go to work this morning," she uttered.

"Why not call in and say you're sick? Go tomorrow," said Tony.

"We didn't get many hours of sleep," Judy complained.

"That's okay," said Tony, "it was worth it."

Judy got up, showered and dressed. She had a quick breakfast. Tony got up, dressed and left by the basement door and then down the alley. He caught a streetcar home. He'd think about going to class today. Tony stayed overnight with Judy as often as they dared before her parents got back.

In the last part of the summer session, Tony worked real hard. Judy was helping him study. She was quite a good teacher, as she would question Tony over and over on the important points of the lectures. She helped him write his essays. All the time he was on campus, he devoted his full time to studying. He did not waste any time whatsoever. Both of his final marks were in the low 70s. He was greatly relieved by the mark from the Political Science course. However, he learned a marker marked it, as the professor had left Vancouver right after his last lecture.

The fall work was hard on his job. A nuisance job, but a big part was tracing down the hundreds of students who had registered for school but never showed up. Their whereabouts had to be established before their names could be taken off the school register. Other principals who used Tony's services less frequently felt he was not being severe enough with the child and the parents. They wanted either the boy at school or a doctor's certificate showing he was definitely sick. The superintendent called in Tony.

"I think it might be a good idea if you got a little tougher with some of those students you're dealing with. Maybe the parents should be taken to court," stated the superintendent.

"But I think we can work it out alright if the teachers would be a little more patient," said Tony, not knowing that the principals had reported him. "I'm not satisfied that taking it to court will really solve the problem."

"Talk it over with Ken and see how they're handling these types of cases. But, if necessary, step harder on the parents," suggested the superintendent. He was a pleasant and cooperative person. He did not give sharp, severe orders and condemn you violently if you were not doing the job.

Tony felt that Ken had probably urged the principals to complain to the superintendent about his work, for this was just the type of thing he would do. "If I ever find out that he's tried to cause trouble for me, I'll talk things over with him, but not in the way the superintendent is suggesting."

Tony discussed this matter of cracking down with the principals on the working class and skid row schools. But they didn't want harsher action taken. They were very satisfied with Tony's handling of the cases, and didn't want him to handle them any harsher. Tony had no reason not to believe these men because they had never been dishonest with him. Okay, for the other schools, he took the students to juvenile court. Often this took them out of Tony's hands because they would be held in the detention home for a week or two for a probation officer's report, and then let out on probation to the care of the juvenile officers.

Finally, the chief probation officer complained. "Tony, you're bringing too many kids to the court. You're going to jam the detention home with truants. You've got to slow this down and figure out another way of handling them, than bringing them to juvenile court."

"I wish you'd tell this to some of those eager teachers and principals. Is there any way that I can charge the parents?" he asked.

"No, not unless you can prove a case of neglect, and that's pretty tough to prove unless you've got a lot of witnesses," explained the probation officer.

"Okay, I'll get them all on deep-sea ships where they don't see land for months at a time," said Tony, and he thanked the probation officer. "If that's the way they want it," thought Tony, "I can get tough."

Any kids he found [who] were absent without proper excuse, he'd label as truants and insist that the principal strap them for truancy. If it was the fault of the parents for keeping the kids home without proper reason, he'd cut off their family allowance. And if he really felt dirty, he'd cut it off retroactively, meaning they would lose two or three months of cheques. Tony felt that the schools were made for the benefit of the kids, and why shouldn't they take advantage of it and get a good education? And he'd make the parents understand by touching their pocketbooks. Kids had no right to miss school. There was a law and they had to obey it—and he'd see to it.

This action got some of the principals into trouble with parents. Before they could get their family allowance restored to them, they had to have a form signed by the principal stating that the child was attending school regularly. The parents would blame this on the principal. They would storm up to the office and raise hell with him and threaten him. Many threatened to burn the school down. Tony claimed there were willing helpers among the children whom he knew.

Tony registered for three university courses. He didn't tell the superintendent and he never asked. It meant his entire life was devoted to only two things, his job and university. There was nothing very much wrong with that, as he did not have much money left after his high monthly payments on the car, and rent and, of course, his fees. He settled down to a very serious year of work. He rarely went out, except on dates with Judy. He was beginning to see the value of hard work. But this was hard work of a different kind: books, libraries and the professional work of handling kids absent from school. As the year wore on, Tony began to realize the pleasure he got out of hard work, partly because it was attached to achievement. At Christmas time, he made good marks on his mid-term exams and he received good grades on his term essays. Judy wanted him to take the same Sociology course as her, but Tony refused. He was afraid that she would make a higher grade than him, and he couldn't

135

accept that. He felt it might harm their friendship.

Tony and Judy at the New Year's Ball at the Yacht Club

During the Christmas holidays, there were a lot of parties. And, of course, there was the big New Year's Eve celebration. Judy talked Tony into going to a New Year's ball being held at the Yacht Club, which would include mostly the sorority and fraternity students. Although Tony had become very much a free enterpriser and individualist, he still didn't support the idea of these exclusive clubs. For one thing, he knew that they would discriminate against Indians, and that meant him. But they would never know in a million years.

Judy went to the rental shop and helped him select a tuxedo for the evening. Mrs. Knox claimed that Tony and Judy made the most striking couple she ever saw—Tony with his dark hair and tan complexion and brown eyes, while Judy with glowing blonde hair, fair complexion and blue eyes, both handsome and beautiful. Tony didn't know very many of the people, but Judy seemed to know most [of them]. Judy was popular at the dance. Tony felt left out. It was not his kind of party. He found it difficult to carry on conversations, for everyone seemed to talk about things so common and familiar to one another. They danced with partners according to some arrangement. In fact, the whole party seemed to be structured and organized by special rules.

Tony felt awkward and conspicuous. He said to himself, "At least drinks are not sold according to a special plan," and so he drank more than the rest because he was by himself quite a bit. He tried to make conversation, but it was just fast quip talk, smart jokes and nonsensical sayings. There was no discussion of any kind.

"Look, hon, I can't seem to get the swing of this party. I'm way out in left field. I try, but I just don't know the game. Let's stick close together, and we'll dance together most of the time."

"Don't be silly, Tony. You can't be a deadbeat at a party like this. Come on, everybody's so much fun at a New Year's Eve party. Get in it and don't make me ashamed of you," said Judy firmly.

That cut Tony to the bone. "Is she ashamed of me?" he asked himself. "Well, then, why'n the hell did she ask me here?" He felt his inferiority of being a Breed. These were the White superiors who considered themselves so very much better than the Redskins. "Yeah, and she's having a damn good time with all those boys." And as far as Tony was concerned, they were just little boys. He went over to the bar and had a couple of drinks by himself. He didn't give a damn what Judy said.

He went over to her and said, "Come on, hon, it's time we had a dance together." While they were dancing, Judy said, "I don't want you doing any more drinking. This is a very ritzy affair. Kids from the best families are here tonight, and I don't want to be embarrassed. I've got a good image with these people, and I'm going to keep it that way."

After the dance, Tony had a couple more drinks. He was certainly feeling them now, and it was obvious to Judy. It made Tony a little reckless in regard to his feelings of inferiority, and it loosened up his tongue. Tony was trying to engage some of the people in discussions of politics, and even socialism. Such a topic was about as welcome as the seven-year itch. He had another drink. Judy saw him and came over.

"Now cut out the drinking. You'll get drunk and act like a fool. If I see you with another drink, we're going home before you'll ruin my whole evening."

Tony didn't really care. "That's just too damn bad. But nobody tells me when I can't drink, not even Judy Knox," answered Tony.

"Let's go for a walk in the cold air, Tony. Come on, I'll get our coats." They went for a walk around the Yacht Club, and Judy pleaded with Tony not to do any more drinking.

"Okay, sweetheart, I won't, but how about spending more time with me?"

They went in and danced together, but Judy soon responded to her popularity. The fresh air had helped to clear his mind, so he didn't bother having any more to drink. He was not feeling much pain as it was. But as far as he was concerned he'd had enough of the party. It was after midnight and they had rung out the old and rung in the new year.

"Judy, it's time we went home. I'm tired," he said to her privately.

"Are you crazy, Tony, the party's just going nicely now. If you want to go, go alone," answered Judy sharply.

"That's fine with me, baby, you find your own damn way home," Tony stated angrily.

He got his coat and left. He drove home slowly as he didn't want any damned cops stopping him. He was good and angry. At home, he practically tore off the tuxedo. "If that is formal dance parties, I've had enough already." He was upset about Judy. This told him he was in love with her more than he had thought. He said, "To hell with her. I don't need her to get along in this world. I'll make a big success of my own life without her." Yet he also recognized he was jealous. It was eating at his heart and he didn't want to admit it. "She's my girlfriend. She's not public property for all those damn studs to be pawing," he said to himself. "My baby is mine. What the hell, that's the way Judy wants it, she wants to be possessed. And yet she wants to be the most popular girl on campus."

He wondered how much Judy or any other girl was necessary in his life. He had now set his goals high, and women must never be allowed to come in his way. He had not given up politics altogether. But now he wanted a good university education and a professional position, and he'd achieve that before too many years, but he was going to do that alone. No woman would be allowed to share anything like that with him. He wouldn't have anyone else ever sharing his achievements and glory. They would be his own, single, individual efforts. He didn't want to get his life all tangled up by marriage, and certainly not by children. He'd never allow a woman to trap him. He'd have to be damn good and careful in sex. Judy was right about being so careful.

He had straightened things out with the VSB authorities, and he was getting along very well. In fact, the little incident helped him get better acquainted with the important people there. He'd now make sure that he cultivated the right friendships and played the right game of politics. He wouldn't waste time on persons who couldn't do anything for him professionally. By the time he received his B.A. degree, he'd be in solid with the officials and the trustees, and he could probably move up. He'd keep a few avenues open, and he'd protect them carefully all the way. "It'll be just too damn bad if someone gets in my way. They'll just get hurt, that's all. That's life."

But his thoughts couldn't leave Judy. "What if one of those frat guys takes her home and makes love to her? Geez, what if he puts her [in a compromising position?] I'd kill the pig. I don't care if he kisses her, but, oh boy, if any guy ever touches my woman like that I'll kill 'im. I know I would! That's sacred to me and Judy. By Cryz, I'll get even with her for this. If I let her get away with it, she'll think for sure I'm stupid, an idiot. She'll have no respect for me. But I'll take my time." Yet he was very lonely at the thought of being without Judy. He needed to be loved, although it was on his special terms. To hell with it. He'd let Judy come around. "She can damn well make up to me, and I'll take my time about forgiving her," he thought. He poured a couple of good, stiff drinks and went to bed.

He woke in the morning with a fierce headache. He took several aspirins and it helped. In the afternoon, Judy phoned just to make sure that he was coming for dinner as invited. He said he'd think about it and call her back. No mention was made of last night. He arrived on time for dinner, but as cantankerous as possible. All this formality and fuss in a private home was just too much, just "putting-on-the-dog." He scoffed at it, but not loud enough for Mrs. Knox to hear.

Judy and Tony said nothing about the party and their quarrel. Neither wanted to admit that he or she was wrong. Their personal images were at stake, and they didn't want to tarnish them. They remained very cool and aloof to each other for the day. In fact, it was several days before they let it pass into history and let bygones be bygones.

Tony Is a Serious Student

In the following year, Tony scheduled his time very precisely. He devoted practically every night to studying, with the exception of Saturday night. That was definitely agreed as Tony's and Judy's evening of partying. There was no exception to that rule. They made it a point to always leave the celebrations early enough to give themselves time at Tony's apartment. It was their special time for passionate lovemaking [...]. Tony would take her home some time in the early hours of the morning. On Sunday evening, Tony went to the Knoxes' for Sunday dinner.

At his job, Tony worked hard for the principals of his area, but he made sure to attend meetings and conferences where important officials attended. He made special efforts to promote himself as a bright, concerned and well-informed professional. He was becoming quite aggressive and a smooth talker. He joined a couple of professional organizations where he thought his name would get recognized by the proper authorities, people with power.

Tony did very well on his final exams. They were in the low 80% range. He was indeed very proud, but he was also convinced that he could master the middle-class world of academics. He was confident of his ability to achieve and succeed. The Sociology professor invited him to his office. "Tony, I think you can do very good work in Sociology. Why don't you try the honours program?" This nearly floored Tony. Was he really that good? Was he good enough to be part of the academic elite, even among all White students? He just couldn't say no. The professor outlined the program and the extra work he would have to do. "You will have to do an honours essay, which is quite a tough research project," said the professor. But at this point Tony felt he could handle any assignment. He could hardly wait to tell Judy.

"Geez, hon, this will be great. I'll be able to get into the graduate program on my terms, or I might get a real good scholarship."

"I know, but it's the prestige that it gives you. Then everybody recognizes what a brain you are. You're not just the ordinary or average student. You become much more than what they are. That's real success, darling. I might go on the honours program, too," saying it as if it was already an option to her. But Judy was confident—anything she was determined to do, she could to it, and often did it.

Tony's bed had a coil spring on it, and it made a lot of noise. He had spent several hours wiring down each individual spring he thought was the cause of the noise, but there seemed to be always another. Finally, he had rewired the whole spring down. He didn't want the landlady asking questions about Saturday nights. He tried to convince Judy they'd do their lovemaking on the floor, but Judy said it was too crude, too animal-like. But this was not their first, nor their last quarrel. As much as they were in love, and as much as they tried to keep everything running smoothly, one or the other was often challenging, threatening or clashing with the other. They were unable to work out their love so that it became a "oneness," an "ours." The love had to adjust to their individual goals and future plans [...]. As their sense of love seemed to deepen, their individualism and self-centeredness also increased. Their love was harsh and traumatic. It was as violent in the moments of misunderstanding as it was in the moments of passion, albeit with a different feeling.

During the next year, Tony worked very hard at university. The honours program was a great deal of more work. His studies became easier in one way in the sense that he had a lot of confidence now and didn't waste time in considering whether his approach or ideas were inferior or unsound. He simply went boldly on his merry way and worried little about other considerations. This led him into a serious situation with his advisor, the Sociology professor.

After Christmas, the honours students were called for a seminar with the professor to discuss the reasons why they had made lower marks than the regular students in the same class. "Maybe we've got the wrong students in the honours program," said the professor. The fifteen students were seated around the long narrow table, with the professor at the head in his role as master. No student made a comment. "Well, there must be some explanation for this situation," continued the professor.

"Sir," said one of the students, "is it not possible that it may have to do with the kind of *exam it was?"*

"I don't understand what you mean."

"Well, as honour students we trained ourselves to write essay-type questions and the exam was mostly an objective-type exam which first and second year students prepare by memorizing," she added.

"I think that's ridiculous. You should be able to write any kind of exam."

"Yes, sir, I agree. I was only making a suggestion," she conceded. "Sir, in honours, I thought we would deal more with ideas and issues, and I thought that Christmas exam was rather trivial, so I didn't bother too much with it."

"You've got to know everything in the course, in every way. That was no trivial exam," he assured the student.

"Sir, I didn't mean to imply that, sir. The exam was very good."

Several other students spoke up along the same lines, but were soon crushed by the professor. There was general agreement among them about the exam. Tony hadn't really said anything yet, and he felt he should support the other students.

"Well, the exam didn't provide us with any opportunity to expound our knowledge. It was a kind of simple high school exam."

"Tony, I think you're just trying to find excuses for yourself by blaming the exam. Probably you didn't prepare adequately for it," the professor said, implying that Tony's attack was personally motivated.

"I was prepared, sir, but what could you do with questions that you had to answer with true or false, or in one word? Those tests are no measure of our knowledge," Tony said with confidence. It was becoming a fight between the professor and Tony.

"Maybe I should invite another student as an honours student to replace you, Tony, since you did poorly on the test," said the professor.

"Why pick on me, sir, if all the students here say the test was to blame? Why don't you accept the weakness of the exam and do something about it in the future?" Tony explained very carefully and assuredly.

"But I didn't say that," interjected a student quickly.

"Neither did I," added another. Finally, most agreed. Tony was left holding the bag alone with the statement. They reversed their positions when the professor threatened to replace them as honours students.

"I think that is insolence from a student to say those things, Tony. I make the exam. I control the course, not you," stated the professor.

"I wasn't contradicting that, sir." But Tony was getting angry, especially when the students suddenly turned on him and denied their earlier statements. "I think the whole question of un-academic exams should be taken up with the student council. Students have been putting up with this kind of unfairness for too long."

"You forget, Mr. Bruce, that I am the professor in charge of this course, and I'm the person who decides the exam. The students will do as they're told, and that includes you."

"Well, you asked to come here to discuss the exam, and we're giving you our ideas, and now you reject them outright," said Tony.

"Speak for yourself!" said the other students all together.

The professor realized that all students were against Tony, and that he could discipline him without fear from the class. […] He would show Tony as an example. "Tony Bruce, I will not have any student in my class talk to me like that. See me at my office right after this class. I may dismiss you from honours and from this class," stated the professor angrily.

Tony was expelled from that class, but was allowed to remain in honour [course]. But that mattered little to him compared to his anger over the betrayal of the students. That evening, Tony saw one of the students in the coffee shop. He went over to him and grabbed him by the collar and backed him against the wall. "You yellow pig, you were too damn scared to stand up for your own rights, so when the professor called your bluff, you turned traitor on your classmate, eh? You gutless piece of crap! And you're the kind of crud they call intellectual." Tony let him go, but he felt like spitting right into his pimply face.

The next day, he met one of the girl students who had turned viciously against Tony in order to endear herself completely with the professor. She was a European immigrant. He called over, and in front of his pals he told her, "You bohunk slut! So you want to make yourself lovable to the professor by turning against me. I suppose you're sleeping with him whenever he wants you. I hope he gives you the dose."

Tony was very upset after this experience. He was afraid how the professor would mark his essay and his final exam. He couldn't tell Judy about it because he knew that she was against socialism. But what if he got a poor mark? He would have to explain that to her because she was now taking a personal interest in his career.

Of all the courses he took at university, none of them taught him as much as that seminar experience did. He'd learned his lesson. He'd never stick his neck out again for other students. He'd play the game, suck someone else in, and sacrifice him. He'd get himself in good with the professor or anybody else who'd improve his situation.

At work, Tony saw people […] that would promote him into socially higher classes and bigger promotions. It was his good fortune to get on the mailing list of the administrative officials. This took him to Sunday afternoon cocktail parties where he met the social elite of the bureaucratic world as well as important political personalities and diplomats. He was now travelling in high society. In order to keep in the midst of these conversations, he had become a regular member of the Vancouver Symphony and of the Civic Theatre. He went so far as to attend the visiting opera performances. He truly believed himself to be a genuine member of this type of society. He had cultivated all the niceties and pleasantries, and watched that his language was polite and educated. He had discontinued all association with his former union pals. The life of a worker was for somebody else, not for him anymore. He would've denied any identification with unionists and lower-class workers if confronted with this information, or he'd explained it as simply a temporary situation that was necessary to better himself and move up the [social] ladder.

Tony Becomes White Middle Class and Marries Judy Knox

In truth, Tony was a very different person. His whole value system had changed, and so had his way of life. He had internalized the values of the White middle-class mainstream, and his new attitudes and opinions reflected this. He had become very materialist in that he was driving a new hardtop sports Pontiac with all the extras, and he had moved into a new apartment in the upper-class residential area of Kerrisdale. He had now become a very fashionable dresser. Since his salary wasn't big enough to pay all this, he had charge accounts at the big department stores. It was certain that he no longer saw himself as a Halfbreed.

Indeed not. He saw the Indians and Breeds as the mainstream does: ugly, inferior, lazy bums, immoral, degenerate and as savages. He lived in worry that someone might accidentally discover that he was a Redskin. The Breed nation was no longer any concern of his, nor his own family, not even Mamma and Pappa. He had gone so far as to stop writing to his parents because he had nothing nice to say to them. They were in two different worlds now, and there were no common interests. He would probably never go home again. He had not been there since the summer with Sue. That way of life was vulgar and dirty and primitive. The people were so ignorant they couldn't even carry on a conversation beyond the talk about the farmyard and their neighbours. They knew nothing about world affairs. They were so backward they couldn't appreciate the nicer things of life. All they did was drink that filthy beer. And any letters from home only reminded him of all these horrible things, and he didn't want that kind of eyesores hanging over or around him. His new world was exciting, filled with future plans and optimism, filled with glorious challenges. Someday he'd own a beautiful big house in Kerrisdale or the University district, just like other successful and rich people.

He had become very selfish and egotistical and absorbed in his successes, and in his drive for prestige and fortune. He was very concerned about the techniques and the shortcuts to his greatness. Even if he believed in socialism or unionism now, he had no time to participate in such activities. All his time was devoted to moving himself up the social ladder. Not only his time, but his thoughts. He felt the social pressure of his image, the image he was trying to create. He was deeply concerned that people should regard him as a respectable and ambitious young man, responsible and intelligent. All his energy and concentration was focused in these directions. There was nothing leftover for thoughts or efforts on behalf of the workers or Halfbreed nation. The way he saw it now, it was up to individuals to look after themselves. There were plenty of opportunities, and everybody could succeed if they wanted to. The poor people and the down-and-outers had only themselves to blame. They just hadn't tried. Tony believed this so thoroughly that he began to feel contempt for lower-class people and the workers, and especially for those families he had to work with as an attendance officer. He felt quite contemptuous of the Breeds and the workers.

Tony graduated that spring, but he refused to have anything to do with graduation ceremonies. He refused to go and receive his degree. All because of the fight he had with the

Sociology professor.

Judy was annoyed because she wanted her friends and parents to see Tony in the procession with the other graduates. She was now anxious that Tony should move into a better position than attendance officer. Also, her parents were agitating for Tony to move up. Mr. Knox claimed that three years at one level was long enough; promotion should be due after that. Tony always felt that they were unhappy about the title of his position. It had such a mundane and unprofessional tone to it. It didn't bother him at first, but now that he was concerned about professionalism, he would have been glad about a more refined title. But he liked his job very much, and certainly the VSB and the officials were excellent to work for. And he was getting his university education at the same time.

Judy and Tony had talked of marriage. In fact, they had considered it several times, but it was always a matter of waiting until they graduated, until they got themselves established first, until their careers were further along. [...] Of course, Mr. and Mrs. Knox were not in favour of it. They didn't know anything about Tony's background, or his family. They claimed it was important to come from a "good" family, for you never knew when you might have to fall back on the family or the family name. To them, Tony was a very ambitious and bright young man, but they didn't like the fact that he was an unknown "loner." Also, they didn't want Judy to ever marry a man who might be a burden to her, for she was ambitious for her own career.

"Darling, I don't see that marriage would interfere with our careers."

"We could continue on with our studies for a couple of years more, and you could stay with your job. You're making a good enough salary that we could live comfortably on it. I think we should get married," Judy urged.

"Probably so. But remember, I want to start doing graduate work this fall, so I'll be pretty taken up with that," Tony argued.

"Yeah, I know, but we can still follow our own university programs. We're going to get married anyway, so why wait until next year?" continued Judy.

"I agree, hon. It wouldn't make much difference because we are together most of the time. And I wouldn't have to be bothered going over to your place all the time, especially to take you home," Tony said.

"We could get married about the middle of August and then take two weeks off, right after summer school, for a honeymoon trip," Judy added.

"That seems like a pretty sensible idea, sweetheart. The one thing we must make absolutely sure about: no children. That'd just kill our careers. I just won't have it," stated Tony.

"You know, I agree one hundred percent with that. If I ever got pregnant I'd have an abortion or give the kid away. I'd never keep it," said Judy.

"Sure, children only come in the way of our love anyway. I'm in love with you, and it's you that I want to love, not some dirty little animal that comes into our household," said Tony seriously. "But your Mom and Dad sure as hell won't approve of us getting married. How'll

we handle that?"

"I don't know. I think they're resigned to the fact that we'll get married some day, but they're probably postponing that date as far as possible."

"And they'll probably want a big showy wedding?" asked Tony.

"So will I, darling. I want everything. I want the biggest wedding ever."

"I don't like going to weddings," said Tony. "The formality of the whole ceremony and proceedings bother me. I'd just as soon stay away. Is that possible?" he asked jokingly.

"Of course it isn't, and you know it. I know you'll love the big celebration."

"I won't love it, darling. I'll hate it. Why don't we run away to get married, then we won't have the fuss with your parents, and all the wedding preparations," said Tony, and added after thinking more, "Yes, I think that's a good idea."

"Where do you suggest we go, and when?" asked Judy.

"I don't know. I'm not fussy. Why not Seattle, that's not far," suggested Tony.

"Tony, I think you're mean and cruel. That'd be horrible. It'd be so deserted and lonely when it should be such a gay and happy time," said Judy.

They continued to argue over this issue. The more Tony thought about it, the more it appealed to him. He became completely convinced about it being the only way. And he decided to remain stubborn about it. This argument continued for the following weeks. Judy was undecided and flustered about the whole matter. Finally, she announced to Tony, "Okay, I am willing to go away quietly and get married. And I think we should go the long Dominion Day weekend. It's not a holiday on Friday in the States, and we could get married that day."

Judy left a note for her parents that she and Tony had gone to Seattle for the weekend. They paid little attention to it, other than to inquire who else went with them.

Just as Tony had suggested, Mr. and Mrs. Knox were extremely displeased with the marriage. They said some nasty things about Tony, but he had prepared himself emotionally for this blast. So he took it without saying anything, as Judy had asked of him. "Judy, get what you need for now. We are going home immediately. You can get your other materials later," Tony ordered Judy. They drove away.

"Sweetheart, I'm glad you didn't say anything to mother and dad when they said all those cruel things about you," consoled Judy.

"They didn't say anything that really hurt. They could've said some mighty dirty things if they knew all there was to know," said Tony, not meaning to.

"What do you mean by that, Tony?" asked Judy.

"Oh, nothing. I was just thinking out loud, I guess. I'm sorry, darling," said Tony.

"You were doing more than that. I want to know what you meant by that remark, 'If they knew all there was to know.' Do I know all there is to know, Tony? Answer me truthfully!" commanded Judy.

"Well, you do. You know everything about me. What else is there to know?"

"Don't tell me that I'm already going to regret what I've just done," said Judy. "Maybe my parents were right. I should've found out more about you, your family and your background.

Maybe your word is not good enough."

"Oh for hell's sake, Judy, what else can I tell you? Do you want to know if I wet the bed as a teenager? Are those the kinds of things you want to know?" said Tony angrily.

"Don't be smart with that kind of stupid nonsense. You're not talking to any nit-wit, you know," said Judy, becoming quite excited.

"Come off it, Judy. Just because we're married now doesn't mean you can cross-examine or control my thoughts. I'm still an individual in my own right. I'm not under your command," stated Tony officially.

"Tony Bruce, you're horrible, you're a beast. I'm not going to sleep with you tonight. I'm not going to be your wife just in bed," cried Judy.

"We'll see about that soon enough, Judy Bruce," said Tony.

"I'm glad I left my stuff at home. I will leave it there," stated Judy.

They didn't settle their argument that night. Judy slept on the chesterfield. After all, the bed was Tony's. Their marriage got off to a rough start, but Judy did not go back home. Soon they forgot their quarrel, but Tony had to realize that Judy would surely raise a storm if she ever found out that he was a Halfbreed. And to be sure, the Knoxes would disown him completely. But he would cross that bridge when he came to it.

Judy graduated in the spring. She had done outstanding work. She was highly recommended by her professors. She devoted almost her entire time to studying. Her life was quite independent from Tony's. She had her own little car; she kept her own bank account. Actually, she and Tony got along reasonably well, for they didn't get in each other's way too much. As long as neither got in the other's way in terms of their own career and success, they remained friendly. They were much too interested in their own ambitions to notice anything about the other. They motored to Mexico City for a holiday one summer and had a grand time following all the romantic tourist attractions. After they returned home, they invited their friends over and told of their holiday. They had rented a nice apartment in a nice address, and therefore felt they must invite friends over occasionally in order to show off their place, especially to Judy's friends because her sorority sisters were getting married to lawyers and engineers and doctors. And Judy felt her inferior position very deeply, but she always excused it because both Tony and she were still studying.

Tony's salary was never able to keep up to the expensive life of Judy's friends, so they became selective in the activities they went to, and only to those that promoted them. Often, they had to do with [...] journalism, Judy's interest. Gradually, they got back on good terms with Mr. and Mrs. Knox, but Tony knew that he was not a big favourite with them. They would tell Judy that she did not have to put up with any misery from Tony. Just come home.

That spring, a good job came up with the VSB. In reality, it was a public relations job. It was to promote the VSB's image, give short talks and discuss the issues with the news media. It was a sort of a selling job for the VSB as a great institution. It was among the top administrative jobs with a big salary. It appealed to Tony. Since he had been an employee of the VSB for the last five years, he thought he stood a good chance for the job if he wanted it. He was now working on his Masters degree. At least, he could have a talk with the superintendent about it, and ask about it. Most of the time, the superintendent was very friendly to Tony, on a first name basis. But as soon as Tony opened the discussion about the new job, and that he was interested in it, the superintendent became very, very official and aloof. He repeated the same old argument about having to teach in the Vancouver schools for years first. Tony immediately recognized this was a lot of crap, and it immediately annoyed him. The superintendent was pulling the same old crud as the assistant superintendent had done the other time because this time it was so obviously a lie that was followed only when it was to their convenience. The superintendent tried to explain to Tony that he was too valuable in his present job, and that they'd have difficulty in replacing him. But Tony realized this argument was about as honest as the line about teaching experience.

The interview revealed much more than Tony had originally intended. He observed how the superintendent regarded Tony, in terms of his present position, and in terms of any future position with the VSB. He was as qualified as any other person for this job, and he certainly knew the VSB as well as anyone. But he was being outright rejected, without even a possible thought of being considered. Why? Was it because he was an unsatisfactory worker? Not well enough qualified? Because he was politically influential? Or could it be that because he was a Halfbreed? "Oh my God, surely not," thought Tony. They could have a file on me just as the Mounties. Why was the superintendent so opposed to considering him for the job? At least he could've shown interest and suggested that Tony submit an application. But he seemed to be afraid of that. He was determined that Tony should be kept in his own job and move to no other position in the VSB.

"I suppose what I'm saying, sir, is that I don't want to stay all of my life as the attendance officer, that I'd like to move up in the VSB. I'm very happy working for the VSB and would like to continue working in this institution. If I don't get this job, I'd like to apply for the next one that I could handle." Tony was really just talking the matter over rather casually with his boss about his future, in a friendly way, and trying to get some idea about how the superintendent saw the possibilities. But the superintendent's negative attitude shocked Tony. He seemed to be totally opposed to Tony in all respects. He even seemed uncomfortable talking about it, and about Tony being in the office. This surely threw Tony into a dilemma. He was practically in a daze. He had been shown such consideration and encouragement by the previous superintendent and board. Now, what had happened? Had he hit a dead end? Was he at the end of his line in the VSB?

Feelings of inferiority began to plague Tony. He was unsuccessful as a professional worker. He just didn't have it. Maybe he could never understand the complex problems and then work to their solutions. He was so tortured by it that he was performing poorly on his job, losing weight. He decided to ask one of the other officials from another department whom he was well acquainted with. But maybe he would turn out the same as the superintendent. He would chance it.

"I want you ask you a confidential question, Les, but you don't have to answer it, except that it is pretty important to me, and I think you can give me some advice on this problem," explained Tony. He related the interview with the superintendent and his reactions and attitude, and now Tony's dilemma about his whole future with the VSB. "I suppose, what I'm saying is, do you know of any confidential or special reason why the VSB officials wouldn't promote me to higher positions?"

"Well, your name has come up for consideration in terms of other positions, and I know it was rejected. But it's kind of hard to explain, Tony. They consider it a poor policy to promote you," explained Les.

"You mean, ever promote me? Is it because of my politics? Is it because I'm not as White as the rest of you?" asked Tony nervously.

"I don't understand what you mean by that. I've never heard anything about such expressions. No, it's a different kind of thing," continued Les. Tony was glad to drop the subject of Whiteness. At least he knew it wasn't because he was a Halfbreed. At least they didn't know that.

"Could you give me some clue as to what it's all about?" persisted Tony.

"Well, when you first came to the school board, you came from a lower-class background, and apparently you showed it and talked like it, and you had ideas that were consistent with the lower-class way of life," Les said.

"Geez," said Tony, slapping his hand over his forehead, "I can't believe that. I was no different than anyone else. But so what? Hell, now I'm better educated than most of the trustees and many of the officials. I'm no slob or uneducated pig today. What are they holding against me?"

"Sure, your value system today may be very similar to the rest of us. But since the whole educational system is based on the firm middle-class values, they've got to have officials who are genuinely middle class through and through, who can be depended on in any crisis. You're a bit of a risk in that you can drop back or change your ideas and ways to another class too easily. I sure hate to tell you this, Tony, but I've always been honest with you before, and you have never betrayed that trust, so I feel I must tell you so that you can govern yourself accordingly," Les continued.

"Cryz, it's too fantastic to believe. Anybody knows how I hate the lower classes and how I think they're to blame for their own circumstances. I could never be part of that trash again," declared Tony.

"When you first started with the VSB, you identified too closely with the lower class and worked hard to defend them, rather than doing the things demanded by the teachers and principals. Your sympathy for them was so great that you were in trouble with some principals shortly after you started. You might get out of step again with middle-class values, and that would create serious trouble if you were in an important decision-making position. It's too risky in the educational system because that is the basis of the schools."

Tony was trembling. He was crying, at least inside, if not outside. He just couldn't believe what he was hearing. Yet he certainly could believe Les because he had always told him the truth in the past. It was absolutely too fantastic to make sense out of it. He was prepared to argue that no one in the whole world could be more middle class than him. What more was there to prove? He would've burst into a torrent of swearing, only he knew that he was lower class. But why shouldn't he? This was how the world saw him. He was speechless. He just sat there paralysed, staring at Les.

"There's no more to say, Tony. Unless you want to ask me some questions."

"No, nothing. Thanks, Les, you've been honest. I guess you know it's been awfully goddamn painful," mumbled Tony loudly. He left quietly.

The next few days were hell. He never said a word of this to Judy, for she would only raise further hell about his lower-class background. But the whole thing gnawed at his guts. Hadn't he done what they had asked: go to university and get a degree? Not only had he got his B.A. degree, but he was on the verge of getting his M.A. degree. What more did he need in order to prove himself, in order to move up the professional ladder? He was living in an excellent residential district. He had married the daughter of a well-to-do accountant. He had good credit rating at the department stores in town. He had no police record. Surely these were adequate testimonials of his dedication and membership as a professional middle-class citizen? "I thought this was a free society that allowed for social mobility? Is this just the VSB, and their peculiar rules?" Tony could only conclude that his future with the VSB was at a dead end. He was going no further with them, and he was now at the conclusion of his university studies. Next month, he would start on his Masters degree. At least he was quite well qualified now, although there wasn't much he could do with a Masters degree in Sociology.

"But before I leave, I'll disrupt that situation. I'll expose the whole administrative set-up, as to how it's a Family Compact arrangement, [based on] family patronage. How the place is filled with friends of friends, and the fantastic salaries they pay themselves. And how they create all kinds of phoney jobs with elaborate titles, and how the principals are promoted on the basis of how well they are acquainted with the superintendent and his chiefs. Then I'll publish this for the taxpayers of Vancouver to read and see how their tax money is being wasted. But first I must collect my data very carefully. I'll do that around the office in the next few weeks," said Tony.

That summer, Tony started working towards [finishing] his Master's degree in Sociology. He would take Judy to work before he went to class and then pick her up after work. Her parents didn't invite them up all summer. Tony didn't care. **(TB)**

6. Turning Points

Mamma Is Sick in Prince Albert; Judy Shows Her Racism

Marie asked, "Are you going out to St. Louis?"

"Yes," said Tony, "I think we'll go out to the old place and stay with Pappa while we're here. It's not far to drive."

"Be sure to be back at seven o'clock, as Mamma will be expecting you. Is Judy going with you?" asked Marie.

"I think so. I haven't asked her, but I imagine she'd like to come out to the old place," explained Tony.

He picked up Judy at the hotel, and they drove out to St. Louis. Tony was travelling slowly as he was reminiscing, for he hadn't been home for many years. Judy was quiet, but Tony was so wrapped up about Mamma that he hardly even noticed Judy. Pappa was in the yard peeling posts. Tony rushed over and shook hands. They looked at one another, and recognized they were meeting at a time of crisis. Tony didn't see any hate or anger in Pappa's face. He seemed to be downright glad to see his son. "You haven't got very much older, Pappa," announced Tony.

"Geez, boy, you're thin. That city life doesn't agree with you. You'll have to come back and work outside again in some real, tough work," said Pappa. Judy stayed in the car until Tony called her over.

"Pappa, I want you to meet Judy." Pappa seemed to feel a little awkward. He just said a quiet hello, and paid no further attention to her.

"By God, boy, I think we'll go in and have a cup of tea," Pappa announced. Everything was exactly the same as when Tony left, except much older. The old cook stove had a few more cracks in it; the ashes were spilling out of the bottom onto the floor, [… and weren't] swept up. The stovepipes looked like they might fall any moment. The old kitchen cabinet had lost most of its doors. A couple were still hanging, twisted, with the glass gone. The backs of the old chairs were all gone. The old linoleum was worn through; only spots of it were left.

"Things haven't changed much in the old shack over the last few years," said Tony.

"No, we couldn't do a damn thing since your mother got sick," explained Pappa. But Tony could see that not much had been done since the very first day he could remember about the old shack. Tony was busily looking around and reminiscing about all the things and places that were so familiar to him all the twenty-two years he lived here. A flimsy partition had replaced the old curtain that set off the bed from the rest of the room. Pappa poured tea into three old cracked cups that were sitting on the old wooden table, but Judy said she didn't want any tea.

Tony sat down on the old bench behind the table and remembered how it was when he had been a youngster here. He began telling stories of his experiences and all the funny things the family used to talk about. He began joking with Pappa, and telling the story of breaking in Midnight. Pappa just loved to talk of old times. At noon, Gilbert came in from the field. Gilbert had aged.

"Geez, Tony, that fellow was drunk for two years. He never sobered up one day. I thought he'd kill himself," Pappa said, speaking of Gilbert.

"The old man's bullshitting you, Tony, don't believe that." Gilbert had not left St. Louis or the old place in all these years. He was still eking out an existence, with things getting worse and worse all the time. But that didn't seem to worry Gilbert. For the rest of the day, Tony, his father and brother wandered around the old farm, talked about the animals, neighbours and old times. No one mentioned Mamma. All knew it was a death situation.

That evening, outside the hospital in Prince Albert after visiting hours, Pappa, Tony, Marie and Gilbert were gathered around talking about Mamma and her illness. All were very sad, as all realized that Mamma was on her deathbed, and that it was only a matter of days now.

"How long are you going to stay?" Pappa asked Tony.

"I don't know. I guess as long as Mamma wants me," answered Tony.

"I want to go home now," interjected Judy. This startled everyone, as no one would even consider leaving Mamma at this crucial time. It was unthinkable. It seemed like a wicked thing, almost murderous.

"But, dear, I just can't possibly leave yet, nor for a while yet. I don't know when we'll go home. You don't have to be at university for another two weeks, anyway. And I can phone the VSB superintendent for extension time."

"I don't care what you're going to do, but I'm leaving. I want to leave tonight. You brought me here and you can drive me home. It's up to you to get me home," demanded Judy.

This angered Tony. At this time, he was exceedingly touchy about anything connected with separating from Mamma, and to suggest that he should leave Mamma right now was like tearing out his heart.

"I'm just not going, Judy, and that's final. If you want to go that badly, take the bus home," said Tony.

"I will not take any dirty old bus. Who do you think I am, anyway? I'll fly home," said Judy.

"You haven't got that kind of money to fly, and I haven't got it either."

"Get it from your family here. They can lend you the money. That's what they're for," demanded Judy.

Tony knew that his family didn't have a cent of money. They were barely able to find enough money to eat. And now, with Mamma, they had spent every cent on the extra care for her.

"Wire home for money from your parents if you want to go home that badly. I'll drive you to Saskatoon and you can take the plane from there," explained Tony.

"I'm going home tomorrow morning, and that's final. I'm not hanging around this place any longer. And what's more, I'm not going out to St. Louis with you tonight. You can go alone," said Judy.

She said these things with a tone that clearly said she couldn't stand being with the Bruce family. They were not good enough; they were not her kind of people. She certainly insulted Pappa about his St. Louis home, as he was proud and happy with his home, even if it was a shack. Tony could see that the others were ready to let Judy have a piece of their minds and let her know the score around here. Tony knew Marie very well, and he knew Marie could really blast Judy with a fierce tongue-lashing. He tried to prevent any further conversation from Judy, but she persisted.

Finally, Tony said, "Okay, I'll take you to the hotel here, and then I'll go out home for the night. Tomorrow morning, I'll take you to Saskatoon, and you can catch the plane home."

In a very antagonistic manner, Judy said, "Am I not going to see your mother before I leave?"

Marie spoke up quickly. "No, you will not see Mamma. Anyway, Mamma doesn't want to see you." Tony agreed with this statement. Judy continued being quarrelsome.

"The reason you don't want me to see your mother is because she's an Indian."

A gasp went through all of them. That was an outrage, blasphemy. Tony stepped over and slapped her solidly across the face. She screamed, started walking towards the car, while at the same time condemning the Bruce family as being nothing but a tribe of dirty savages.

In an enraged voice, Marie proclaimed, "Don't you ever bring her around this hospital again, Tony, nor bring her out to St. Louis again."

The other members added their warnings. Tony was still part of the Bruce family and still a Halfbreed, and he had serious obligations to these relationships. The family was going to see that he lived up to them. If he had problems with his White arrogant, racist wife that was his problem. They weren't going to tolerate her for one second. Get her out of here. The Bruce family was first, and his wife would be second, but a very poor and far down second. Tony knew where his first loyalties were.

In the hotel room, Judy was almost hysterical. Between sobs, she kept screaming about Tony being a "filthy savage", "an uncivilized animal."

"Don't come near me, you sneaky primitive," she shouted as she moved around the room to keep as far away as possible from Tony. But Tony was not seriously disturbed about Judy's actions and shouting, probably because his whole mind and heart was wrapped up over Mamma.

"Tony Bruce, I don't want you near me again. Never again! I couldn't stand you touching me. You make my flesh crawl. I never want to be in the same house with you again. I'll die of shame if my parents and friends ever find out that I married an Indian."

"Oh for Cryz sake, stop this damn nonsense. Geez, you'd think I wasn't a human being the way you're raving on," complained Tony.

"But you aren't. You're an ignorant barbarian. Whatever made you think you could go to university? You belong in the zoo. And that's where you can live from now on as far as I'm concerned."

Tony was getting angered. "Just because you're a blonde, blue-eyed Anglo doesn't make you a damn bit different than me. Just because the racist society tells you you're superior doesn't make it a fact. And don't get stupid ideas that you're better'n me, baby."

"You touch me and I'll call the police," shouted Judy.

"Sure, and those pigs would protect you—White racists of the same kind," said Tony.

"I should've known all along because you were a drunkard when I didn't watch you. And you probably were down in skid road sleeping with your diseased sisters, the filthy sluts," cried Judy.

"That's enough of that crap, you arrogant little White whore. Just because it's done in a beautiful home in a rich district and in a luxurious bed doesn't make it any different morally. One is a skid road whore and the other is a ritzy whore."

Tony and Judy Separate

When they arrived back in Vancouver, Judy insisted on being taken to her parents' place. It was useless to argue with her. Anyway, he was too tired for any argument. He dropped her off and went to his apartment. His mind was burning like a branding iron. He tried to make sense out of the whole madness of everything. Mamma was dying; there was no doubt about that. It was just a matter of time. Now Judy had left him, and she would not likely come back again. He was still very much in love with her, and he hated to see her go. On top of all that, he was rejected by the VSB for any promotion because he was a […] sympathizer [for the lower classes]. It was impossible to fall asleep.

He had three-quarters of a bottle of rye in the cupboard. He poured himself a generous drink. He became quite furious when he thought about Judy creating the scene she did outside the hospital in Prince Albert. He would never forgive her for that. He had seen Mamma for the last time. He thought he would never live through the misery of her death and the funeral. Tony's whole world was collapsing. The very things he had struggled for over the past few years were turning against him. Everything that seemed like success was now a mess, a tragedy. He poured himself a few more drinks. Since he had been married, he had drunk very little. Judy was very opposed to Tony doing any serious drinking. There were more important places to put money than in the liquor store, she argued. The booze helped to ease all the pain. It didn't clear up the dilemma, but it took the fierceness out of it. He thought of Judy casting him aside because he was "Indian," how he was an "outcast" and not to be touched. She treated him as if he were a disease, the Black Plague, repulsive, repugnant, offensive, loathsome and nauseous. She wouldn't even sit near him anymore, let alone sleep in the same house with him. This was the woman he loved. Yes, he still loved Judy. Maybe not in the way that he had loved Sue, and his thoughts for a moment drifted back to Sue. Nevertheless, he loved Judy. She was his wife. Tony would've drunk more, but he fell asleep.

Although it was springtime, with all the season bursting forth with excitement and new life, Tony's spirits remained low. He worried constantly about the news that came about Mamma. He kept hoping to hear from Judy, at least a phone call explaining about the furniture. But nothing, and he was too proud to call the Knoxes. Judy would probably refuse to talk to him, anyway. It was now June, and his work with the VSB was slowing down. He was trying to figure out what he would do during the summer months. He didn't have to go to university this summer, as he now had his Master's degree. The memories of Sue were growing stronger in his mind and in his heart. He tried to push her out, as he had to be realistic she was history. He wasn't interested in going on a holiday.

Alone

It was a long and lonely road home. Two of the most precious women in his life were leaving his world forever. When he walked into his apartment in Vancouver, there was nothing. Judy had cleaned out all the furniture, drapery, linen, dishes, pictures, just absolutely everything. The emptiness and nakedness of the apartment hit him like a lightning bolt. It was like real life: empty, bankrupt, deserted, barren, desolate. He felt there should be a cold north wind whistling around the rafters of the apartment, echoing the desperation and loneliness of the world. The only furniture left was an old green chesterfield in the second bedroom, which was Tony's before he was married, and his personal belongings. He guessed Judy wouldn't touch the chesterfield, fearing that it might be contaminated with "Indianness."

Tony wandered through the rooms but couldn't even get a sense of life in the apartment with Judy because there was nothing but four barren walls. There was nothing with character or [was] reminiscent [of anything]. She had had the decency to leave his bottle of rye, but she probably didn't give a damn what happened to Tony now. He could drink himself to death. She wouldn't care. He poured a drink. He sat on the chesterfield and thought seriously about Judy. He still loved her. She was still very much a part of his life. But there was no doubt about it; she would never come back. She would never be his wife again. There was no use pretending otherwise. He lapsed into sad thoughts about Mamma. She would never recover. The racist society was killing her slowly. The doctors were useless. The CCF government was not doing its job properly. What about their programs and improvements for the Indians and Breeds of Saskatchewan? What had Mr. Norman done about these things? Where was the socialism that Sue had talked about?

Yeah, what about Sue? He had not even thought about Sue on this trip back to Saskatchewan. But why should he? "Sue, dear Sue," mused Tony. She came into his thoughts. He wondered where she was, what she was doing, what had she done with her life. He poured another drink. Sue came back into his mind stronger than ever. He recalled the days she spent in Vancouver, and the wonderful times they had together, and the great plans they worked out together for their future. He could see Sue as she was, so very beautiful, radiant and understanding. All of those, he needed now.

"It was on this very chesterfield that Sue and I made our plans for the wedding," he remembered. "It was right here that I experienced the great love of the most wondrous person in the whole world. The girl that I held in my arms, and loved so tenderly." Tony spent the next hour reliving the precious times that he spent with Sue, and trying to recapture that same precious love. By midnight, he had killed the bottle. He stretched out on the chesterfield and was asleep almost immediately.

Mamma's Death

One morning, a telegraph boy came into the supervisor's office at the VSB and asked for Mr. Tony Bruce. It read: "Mamma died at eleven o'clock last night."

Tony just burst out crying. The others knew the story, but they could do nothing. They had to leave Tony alone. He burst into a barrage of vicious swearing. He went down to the furnace room and cried his guts out. For the next few days, Tony didn't really recognize anybody or anything. He simply wandered around in a daze. He was numb.

"There is no God, there is no justice, there is no humanity, there is no Christianity," he repeated over and over. He resolved that somebody would pay for this someday, even if the whole nation has to pay. He would figure out the method over a period of time.

Breakdown, Drinking and Obsession with Sue

He moved out of his apartment and continued drinking steadily. He was thrown in the drunk tank at the city police station every few nights a couple of times. He was living on the edge of skid row. He seemed to be unable to drive Sue from his mind. She plagued him almost constantly. During the day, he drove around at work, trying to figure out where she would be and what she'd be like now. He almost crashed his car. He kept puzzling over why Sue had come back into his life so powerfully. He studied the old pictures he had of her and tried to imagine how she would look now, seven years later. "Maybe she is living in Vancouver," he asked himself. He watched the women who passed by. By chance, could any of them be Sue? "But I don't even know that she's alive or maybe she moved to another part of the world, like Australia or China." Tony bought records that were popular when he and Sue were in love and played them over and over. He built up fantastic images of Sue, of her beauty and charm, more beautiful than when he first knew her. She was incomparable.

At nighttime, Tony found it impossible to sleep because his heart and mind were so turbulent. He was sure Sue would be married, have her own home and family, but that didn't stop his passions and thoughts from running wild about the most gorgeous girl he'd ever known. It didn't matter that she was somebody else's wife and that she probably would not even remember Tony. He was madly in love all over again with her. He couldn't accept that he was in love with history and with images. He couldn't seem to separate the two—Sue of 1944 and Sue of now. He turned it over and over in his mind, but the madness for Sue was uncontrollable. In the long hours of the night, he paced his room. He cried for Sue. He talked to himself continuously about Sue and tried to explain that she was part of somebody else's world.

In his hours of turbulence, Tony wrote pages and pages to Sue. He wasn't sure what he was trying to say. When he read it over, it was all so illogical and confusing. He wanted to write intelligent things to her, to make an impression on her. He would like to have said all kinds of beautiful things about her. It would not have been dishonest because he knew that Sue would be just as lovely and adorable now as she was seven years ago. Tony's endless pages to Sue circled round and round the old story of "I love you." He couldn't possibly say this, but he said everything except these words. He admitted this to himself, yet he wouldn't want Sue to know. It was wrong, morally wrong. "No doubt, Sue has married a respectable man, and now lives a respectable life with her family. Everything about her is bound to be honourable." She was in a very different world than he, and she could never be a part of his world, now or ever again.

But he couldn't drive Sue from his mind. He didn't want to. In fact, he spent hours and hours of recreating her in his thoughts. He pictured her with that lovely disarming smile, her soft and friendly voice. He wanted so desperately to hear her again, to talk to her, to listen to her understanding explanations, but most of all to sense her love. He couldn't explain why Sue had come to be so important in his life again, why she dominated his every minute. He couldn't tell Sue this, for it would seem outrageous, and he didn't want to do anything that would make Sue think he was foolish or seemingly mad.

Tony lived in a world of dreams and speculations—imaginary scenes of where he would find Sue, how he would greet her, what he would say, what he would wear. He was sure he knew what she looked like. She was the same girl from Meyronne, only seven years later. How she would greet him, and what she would say! Every one of his scenes was always so delightful. It was almost like the old days. But then he controlled the scenes, and he would not have control over the real situations. He wondered and worried, and wondered and worried more. He thought he was going out of his mind. Yet the pain and the agony of not knowing where Sue was, and not being able to contact her, was more than he could bear. Even to be able to send the many letters that he had written to her! It would be so satisfying to know that she was at least reading his thoughts. It would be a way of communication. It would mean so much just to have her know that he was alive.

His letters to her piled up, higher and higher. He began to see his mission in life as a dedication to Sue, to immortalize her. In his sleepless hours of anguish, Tony wrote a commemoration to Sue Norman. In fact, he wrote one almost every night. He knew he had no right to impose upon Sue, to ask her to see him, but if it meant his sanity, should he not prevail? She would understand. But he didn't want her sympathy. No, he wanted her love. "But, that's impossible." It seemed that he had never been in such turbulence in his life. He was driving himself to madness. He would have to find Sue. He would never rest until he did. In the daytime, he walked the busy streets looking for her, even though he wasn't sure what she looked like now.

He wrote a letter to the postmaster in Meyronne and asked him where he could find Sue. Almost immediately he waited anxiously for the postman to bring an answer. Each day became more anxious, but also more agonizing. No answer, no answer, day after day. Did the postman ignore his letter? Did he send it to Sue, and she refused to answer Tony's request? "Oh God, no." That thought was enough to drive him to suicide. He researched the libraries and directories in Vancouver, but could get no trace of Sue. There was no way of tracing her. Mr. Norman was no longer an MLA [Member of the Legislative Assembly]. Sue's sisters had married, and he didn't know their [married] names. He couldn't remember the names of anyone in Meyronne anymore. What more could he do? He decided to send letters of inquiry to as many people as he could think of—to the bank manager, to the church minister, to the school principal, even to the Mounties. Of the replies, none gave any clues or leads to Sue's whereabouts. Tony worried obsessively that Sue had probably learned of Tony's inquiries, and had informed all people to not give information about her to Tony.

He was through at the school board for the summer. He would not be attending university. He was losing contact with his old friends, his middle-class friends, because he was drinking heavily now, and drinking alone much of the time.

"I've got to find Sue. That's all there is to it," Tony told himself over and over. "But where else can I look? I've researched every possible source book in Vancouver and provided nothing. Cryz, they don't even report on Saskatchewan. How can I ever find Sue's name without some good reference?" Mumbling to himself, in his reminiscing he said, "I'll return to the scene of the crime." He repeated it to himself a few times. Suddenly he said aloud, "Of course, that's what I'll do! I'll go back to Meyronne and search for her in person." He became all excited about the idea. "Tomorrow, I'll get things ready and leave for Saskatchewan, and I'll find Sue before I come back or I'll never come back."

Searching for Sue in Saskatchewan

But Tony couldn't wait. That evening, he threw a few extra clothes and his sleeping bag in the car and left for Saskatchewan. Although he was in a great rush to get to Meyronne, his drive was not long and weary as his daydreaming went wild with imaginary scenes of finding Sue and meeting her. Frequently, he had to check his speed, as he would find he had moved up to eighty and ninety miles per hour while his mind was not focused on the road or car. Somehow he ended up in Regina. He had not planned that. It was beautiful, sunny, hot weather. The city was friendly and easy.

The first phone booth he came to, he stopped and checked it frantically for Mr. Norman's phone number, but it was nowhere to be found. There were no Normans in the phone book at all. It was obvious they did not live in Regina. He stayed at the YMCA, but thought it stank with a White middle-class atmosphere. He felt like mucking it up. In his room that night, he planned his strategy. In the morning he would research the directories at the public library and at the Legislative Library. If he found nothing, he would drive to Gravelbourg and make inquiries there.

He was there before they opened in the morning. The librarians helped him and went through every possible book they could think of, but all in vain. He was working and moving as desperately as the most wanted criminal. He found it impossible to quieten down his frenzy.

Gravelbourg had changed a lot. He couldn't find anybody he knew when he had been there as a Mountie. The young people with whom he had associated had all left. Anyway, he wasn't coming for a reunion. He preferred to remain unnoticed. He made a few casual inquiries at the gas station where he bought gas and at the café, but they had never heard of the name, "Norman". He checked in at the hotel and then bought a bottle. In the evening, he sat in the beer parlour, drank slowly, as he wanted to make inquiries about the Norman family. Nearly everyone recognized the name, but knew nothing about Sue. As the evening wore on, Tony took more to drinking than questioning. Up in his room, he drank himself into crying and finally into a sleep.

The next day, from his systematic investigation, he managed to find a couple who moved from Meyronne to Gravelbourg. "Oh yes, we know the Norman family quite well," said the husband.

Immediately, Tony fired a question: "Do you know Sue, and where she is?" At once he was afraid that he frightened them with his show of urgency. He wished he had been easier with his questioning. He added, "I'm an old friend of the Normans. That was a long time ago, though. And I've lost track of them."

"I suppose you know that Mrs. Norman died soon after Mr. Norman got elected to the Legislature in Regina," explained the wife.

Slowly, Tony answered, "Yes, I knew that." But he didn't know that. Yet he had to give the impression of knowing something so important about them after he had stated that he was an old friend. His thoughts immediately jumped back to Sue leaving Vancouver at the time of the telegram. But before the pain overcame him, he asked, "I suppose Mr. Norman is living back in Meyronne now that he is no longer an MLA."

"Oh, no. He died just a few months ago. It was a very big funeral in Meyronne. He was well known, and certainly a very well-liked person. He had done a lot for the people of southern Saskatchewan."

"Did you people go to the funeral?" asked Tony, thinking about seeing Sue.

"Yes, we went. Everybody from all around went," answered the husband.

"No doubt, the family were all there," Tony asked.

"Oh yes, his three daughters. They're all married and have their own homes now," explained the wife. Tony was almost out of his mind in his madness to find out Sue's name, her whereabouts and how she looked.

"The old man was well-fixed, you know. He had a lot more money and property than most people realized. He left a fortune to his girls," the man went on rather philosophically.

That seemed to be startling news, but it wasn't as important as finding out Sue's married name.

The wife talked freely. "The girls all married well. One's married to a good farmer in Meyronne. She teaches school. Doesn't have to, but I guess she likes to be doing something. She's a hard worker for the community. Sue, the one you're asking about, went into nursing. She's a very lovely girl, liked by everyone. She's such a sincere and pleasant girl. Made a wonderful nurse. She went into Regina General Hospital several years ago."

Tony interrupted her. "I wonder if she's still in Regina." He could drive back to Regina tonight and find her, he thought.

"I really don't know. She was in Regina after she got married. They may have moved to another city, but I don't think they've moved out of the country. She married a nice young man by the name of Knechtle."

Tony virtually collapsed in his chair and breathed a tremendous sigh of relief. It was like suddenly letting all the steam [escape from] a pressure cooker: At long last, her married name. He could trace her. Tony felt so much easier and more comfortable. Now it'd just be a matter of a few days. He could take his time now. As he would say in his Mountie language, "I'm closing in on her." Tony sat and chatted with the couple more casually now, joking about the "good old days" of being a Mountie in Gravelbourg.

That evening, he drove around the outskirts of town and recalled his experience when he was here in 1944. He drove out to the spot where he and Sue had parked. That night in the beer parlour, he drank many to the health of Sue Knechtle. He tried to understand why it was so almighty important to find Sue, why had he been so doggedly persistent and compulsive about finding her? Why was he in such frenzy about making contact with Sue? He had no other answer, and he tried to excuse it. It had to be affection, and yet a love based on imagery, old flames, not on fact or realism. Of course he was a sick romantic, but how had he allowed himself to get trapped into it? He couldn't surrender it right now, for it was his meaning to life, because of the emptiness of middle-class existence. It was the very passion and power of his life. His heart pounded for Sue Norman, not Sue Knechtle. Yet, how was it possible to separate them? Wasn't it Sue Knechtle he was pursuing? He knew there was no Sue Norman.

"Surely to hell that isn't all there is to love except romantic images," Tony asked himself over and over. But he couldn't seem to get any other answer. He drank and chatted gaily with customers all evening.

The next day, he decided to go to Meyronne. What for he didn't know because Sue wasn't there. He'd probably get so emotional over the days he spent with her in Meyronne that he'd only cry. "It will be deserted without her. It will be like death. It'll be so damn lonely that I'll want to die. The trip will be like one big funeral." He turned around. He would never interrupt the beautiful images and memories of Sue in Meyronne. He would preserve them till eternity.

Back in the Regina library, he got all the city directories for the major cities in the Prairie Provinces and checked the name Knechtle. There were a couple in Regina and Edmonton, *but none under Sue Knechtle. "Damn the husbands of this society. Obviously she's [listed] under the name of her husband."*

Tony prepared very carefully the things he would say to Sue when he got her on the phone. He didn't want to be lost for words or sound stupid. He dialled one number in Regina, but was so nervous that he hung up before the phone rang. He tried later again. He stuck with it until he got an answer, but it was not Sue's home. He was getting close. The next call could be Sue. He couldn't get up the courage the first evening.

That evening, Tony took a few good shots of whisky. It was one of the few times that he was nervous about talking to anyone, and especially on the telephone. A lady answered and the operator asked if this was Mrs. Sue Knechtle. The lady answered, "No, it isn't. She won't be back for another hour."

Tony interjected, "Is she the former Miss Sue Norman of Meyronne?"

"Yes," came the answer.

"I'll call back in an hour, operator," said Tony.

Tony now knew where Sue was. He was joyous. It seemed so completely satisfying and comforting to know this. Now he wasn't sure what he wanted to tell her. She would never understand the revived feeling in his heart, and it was madness to even think of it, let alone convey it to her. If he spoke to her, he might not be able to control his thoughts as well as he imagined. He certainly didn't want Sue getting the wrong nor a bad impression of him. How could he tell her that she was still so very important in his life without sounding stupid or ridiculous? Maybe he should just write to her. In this way, he could control the words. Maybe he should send her the hundreds of pages that he had written to her in the last few weeks.

Brief Return to Métis Land

Tony didn't call back in the hour. He didn't call back at all. He met a couple of Breed friends from St. Louis and they went for a beer. In fact, many. The next day, they talked Tony into driving them up to the Halfbreed community of Meadow Lake. He was no longer a Breed. He was a middle-class Whiteman—dressed like one, spoke like one and acted like one. Tony visited in Meadow Lake for a few days, then picked up another acquaintance and went north to the Breed towns of Green Lake, Buffalo Narrows and LaLoche. Then back through the [...] Halfbreed towns of La Ronge and Île-à-la Crosse. The weather was beautiful, so he camped out much of the time. Tony was not recognized as a Halfbreed, nor accepted as one. To his brothers and sisters, he was just another Whiteman. He lazed around and chatted with whoever came along. He was in no hurry and going nowhere in particular.

He felt there was something exciting happening in his Halfbreed nation, even though he couldn't describe it in objective terms. There was a new spirit stirring, a new sense of concern over their plight and who they were, while at the same time there was a worry taking place among the White officials who dominated the Redskin ghetto. Tony made extensive inquiries, but could not find any Breed organizations developing within the nation, nor were there any Breed leaders emerging in the Redskin nation.

In the few weeks that he spent with his people, Tony found a new sense of brotherhood and an authentic humanity. There seemed to be a real meaning to life here. Certainly there was poverty in the most extreme, but that was material poverty, not spiritual poverty. His people were not unkind to him, but they were hesitant and remained somewhat aloof, and Tony could understand that. But in the short time, he recognized it as his world. It was pulling hard on Tony, especially now in his sea of loneliness and sadness.

He had to accept that Sue would never be part of his life. Mamma was gone, and Judy was as good as gone. The things he fought so hard for over the past few years seemed so cheap and phoney here: a B.A. and M.A. degree—no one was even concerned with university here; his nice big shiny Pontiac was no prestige symbol here; his expensive apartment and furniture; his membership in nice businessmen clubs.

Return to British Columbia

Tony left for Vancouver in a very confused state. Sue was still in his mind, but he would write to her. The Halfbreed nation was drawing him like a magnet. He was becoming contemptuous of the White middle-class world. He didn't seem to have any further interest in trying for success in it. To hell with the VSB and the university degrees!

He didn't contest the divorce. He even paid the costs. He considered himself [lucky] to get out of it so easy, but he knew Judy would never accept Indian money.

He rented a little three-room house in Kitsilano district. He felt it was the only way of being totally free from landlords who were always listening and watching his activities. This would be his last year with the VSB, so he might as well make [… the best] of it. He made arrangements to take his teacher training course that would give him a professional teacher's certificate next year. He didn't know what he would do next year. He kept his job, but worked at a bare minimum. The principals were not giving him many referrals now, so he had little to do. That pleased him because the less he had to do with school principals the better. They were such strivers, status seekers, they were almost disgustingly so. The superintendent didn't bother him, and he stayed out of the way of all officials. The coursework at the teacher's college was not difficult. Besides, Tony had set his mind on just getting through. He was no longer interested in high marks, for scholarship or for prestige. There were other things in life.

He was now drawn to extreme social and political groups. He became part of the Beatnik crowd. They had coffee houses in Vancouver that catered to the [Beatnik way] of life. On campus, he joined the public speaking and drama club, for it was a club that attracted the "way-out" people. The part that Tony liked was that they had frequent parties, and there was always a lot of boozing—not real hard drunks, but good time boozers—and there were a lot of attractive young girls at the parties.

He started associating with young married couples who practiced sharing of partners for sex. Although he didn't have a wife, he always managed to find a girlfriend who would go along with such activities. Generally, these organizations and activities were either protesting against the morality of the society or ignoring it. Tony came to find White middle-class society and its value system oppressive and intolerable. He hated it, he attacked it, he condemned it, and he tried to deny its existence.

His relationships with women became brutal and arbitrary. He seemed to be unable to get along without their company, but he was now measuring it in terms of cash value. If he took a date to a movie and then to lunch, the expected return of loving would be small. But if he took his date to dinner in an expensive restaurant or to a nightclub with all the trimmings, then he expected a full return of loving from the girl. If he encountered resistance from her, Tony would tell her where she stood. Companionship was sex, and he was willing to pay for it. He had gone so far as to make out a schedule of payment for each type of social function he went to.

Tony's heart seemed to be turning to stone. He was incapable of loving in a true sense. Possibly, it was because he was afraid of being stung, and having to suffer the pain of loneliness again. Yet he seemed to be addicted to female companionship. He found it painfully lonely without women, but he refused to love. He enjoyed women who were different from the nice, virtuous, respectable type. The extrovert, the foolish type, and the immoral, violent and dramatic types fascinated him. In fact, he developed a great contempt for the Girl Guide type, the churchgoer, the sorority, the conformer, the housewife type—the submissive and obedient women, the one who wanted to be dominated by a husband. He found these contemptible and disgusting. "Women who can't stand and take their place on their own, shoulder-to-shoulder with men, don't deserve anything better than to have ten kids and bare feet." Those girls who subordinated themselves to men weren't worth saying "hello" to. They were totally uninteresting and unimaginative. They were nothing more than doormats, and Tony treated them as such. He thought to himself, "I may [… have an inferiority complex] and [may be] colonial, but I'm still not as subservient and pathetic as you!" Tony rarely lived alone on weekends. He had many names in his "black book," but he had few friends, either men or women.

Tony was anonymous in the big city of Vancouver. He often thought that if he died suddenly, his body would only be found when the stench became noticeable. This is what urbanization, sophistication, the middle class, social mobility, education and success had damned him to. And secretly he hoped it would foul up the whole damn rotten city or, even better, society. If he was sure this would happen, he might have been prepared to sacrifice himself. Yet the free-enterprise world had taught him to emphasize the aspect of selfishness and individuality so that he must strive towards his own greatness and betterment. Of course, it had to be at the expense of the other people. It wouldn't matter if they died as a result of his gain. It would just be too damn bad. The best men rise to the top.

Meeting Thea Dean

In the spring, the drama club put on a play. Tony helped out with scenery and makeup. He had fun putting on makeup on the girl's legs since they were dressed in tights. During these rehearsals, Tony came to pay special attention to a young, dark haired girl with a rather dark complexion. She was quite attractive, with a high forehead and with extremely beautiful brown eyes. They were unusually attractive and had the extraordinary ability to look at you with the most magnetic look ever. She had a very nice figure, and of course beautiful legs. He considered himself an expert here. She was rather smallish, but well-proportioned. She was always pleasant and quite playful. She seemed mentally quite sharp, for she certainly held her own in discussions and never surrendered to the "expertness" of a man. Yet she seemed the innocent and virtuous type—the type who'd obviously be a bore. She puzzled Tony. Tony drove her home a few times.

There were other things that attracted him as well. She looked a lot like Sue—had the ready smile and sparkling eyes, the fighting spirit and politically, she spoke a lot like Sue. But the underlying magnetism and fascination was that she looked like a Breed. He wondered and wondered about this, but he was always afraid to ask her. Gradually, he was taking her to parties and out on dates without demanding "meat" in return for his expenses of the evening. He couldn't prove anything by her home, a very modest working home in Kitsilano.

Her father was a longshoreman. Obviously, she had worked hard to put herself through university. Tony was curious, but he was taking his time. Likewise, Thea was playing a cool game. If she was interested in Tony romantically, she certainly wasn't letting him know in any obvious way. Yet they were more than good friends. The friendship was developing. They were seeing more of each other all the time, but it wasn't the type where they became possessive and exclusive, and planned things. Their lives went from day-to-day, and they made no demands upon each other. Tony found that he was not as all-accepting of women being equal as he thought he was. For Thea was certainly no colonial woman, nor career woman. She was simply Thea, an equal and liberated woman, and insisted on standing firmly on the same footing as men. Tony found this threatening at times, and often realized that he had to back off from his male-supremacist position [...].

They had a lot of serious discussions. Sure, they quarrelled politically, but they rarely quarrelled over personal things. Yet they found time for parties and nightclubs, movies, dances. They were becoming very attracted to one another. Tony found that Thea was beginning to have a deep meaning in his life. In spite of her attitude of equality, she represented a sense of tenderness, love and understanding. It was a pleasure just to be with Thea, to be in the same room with her, to be near her, to experience the pleasure and comfort of her presence. She was like a new humanity. Tony was convinced that she must be a Redskin. He would question Thea frequently about her family background, trying to connect her with a Breed heritage. She claimed that her ancestors on both sides were Scots, although it was several generations ago they had come to Canada. She didn't look like what

Tony thought a Scot should look like.

"Are you sure there's no Indian in your background?" Tony said very apologetically, fearing to insult her, but yet in a way he meant it.

"Oh, that's possible," she said agreeably, with sincerity. "They've always lived on the West Coast, and there are many Indians in this area. Why do you say that?" asked Thea.

"Oh, nothing, just making conversation," but Tony knew he was doing more than that.

She added, "When I was young, we lived on Vancouver Island in a community where there were Indians."

Tony hoped to hell that she wouldn't say, "Some of our best friends are Indians." He couldn't question her about Halfbreeds because that word seemed to be unknown on the West Coast. And in Vancouver, the word "Indian" immediately brought up the image of the Indians on skid row. Thea didn't seem to express any hatred towards Indians, yet she was no sympathizer. They were just people.

Thea knew a lot about union politics. Her dad was a vocal unionist in the longshoreman's union. He was very active among the membership. At home, he talked continuously about unionism. He had always been deeply involved with the union and its struggles. But his way of discussing unionism seemed always so involved and complicated that it left the ordinary person confused.

The Dean home was markedly a worker's and unionist's home. Mrs. Dean worked as a telephone operator and managed to look after home, in addition. Tony was greatly impressed with the great qualities of Thea's mother. She was so sincere, frank and kind. She was not full of pretence and show. She did not make ridiculous demands in terms of the middle-class values. She was a very flexible and liberal person. Thea's home was certainly a sharp contrast to Judy's home. But Tony swore that he would never be associated with that rigid type of middle-class people again.

Tony was now spending a lot of time with Thea, but there was nothing compulsive and obsessive about it. Yet Tony knew he was falling in love with Thea. **(TB)**

Howard at the University of California at Berkeley

My last year of study at the University of California at Berkeley was the most remarkable year of my life. I would receive my doctorate of philosophy degree in June 1965. That was part of the pleasure. But the real excitement was the great turmoil that was taking place on the campus among the thousands of students. It was the year of the famous Free Speech Movement and of the liberation struggle of the students against the rigid, conservative "Dinosaur Board of Governors" who had dominated the university for many years as their fiefdom. The famous chief of the board was Randolph Hearst, the chairman. In the long history of the university, it had run as peacefully and orderly as a church.

All at once, on a warm September day, all hell broke loose. Thousands of students were gathered on the "Quad" listening to a student speaking from the top of an illegally parked car. In radical terms, he was condemning the despotic rule of the university administration. Quickly, the police moved in to arrest him, but the masses of students held back the police. It was obvious that speaker Mario Savio had mass support from the students. Every effort was made to stop Mario from his very critical speech, but without success. This was the beginning of the famous Free Speech Movement at universities throughout the USA in 1965.

In a short time, most of the students were involved in a liberation struggle against the domination of reactionary board members. It became an intense and harsh struggle for most of the year. Almost immediately, I knew that I was involved in the struggle with the students. Every kind of civil rights action was taking place on the campus. I was excited about "storming the Bastille." I helped organize groups for sit-ins, for picketing, for mass demonstrations, militant confrontations of every type that advocated the progressive ideas and movements of the students against the reactionary authoritarians. It was rapid learning on the spot because the campus became surrounded by hundreds of police and paddy wagons [police vans]. I threw myself into the struggle and quickly learned all sorts of tactics and strategies that we must adhere to in order to outwit the police and still win our battles.

Suddenly I had to stop and make a very thoughtful decision. A rule was made by the university hierarchy that all foreign students who were caught involved in any student activity struggle would be immediately dismissed from the university and deported to their home country. I had spent three years working towards my doctorate degree and was now in the final stage of it. In a few months, I would have that very cherished document, a Doctor of Philosophy degree from Berkeley. That would be the greatest achievement in my life and bring my status to a level that I had never anticipated. But at that moment, I was preparing with a group of students who were about to sit-in and occupy the offices of the president, the most guarded office.

The leader took a moment to caution us in our final move before we went into action. He warned us that if we had any hesitations about the confrontation, or might back-out later when the action became critical—and that we would likely be arrested and thrown in jail—then we should remove ourselves from the group right now. That was indeed a tough decision to make. Many of these students were racial minorities like myself—Black, Chicana/o, Mexican and Asian. Yet I would probably throw away the most precious thing I had dreamt and worked on for many years, my Ph.D. degree, [which was] only months away. Finally, I turned and walked away in torturous guilt. I continued to work in the movement, but only on relatively safe, marginal projects.

In June, I received my precious degree, and since those years, long ago, I have realized it was the best decision. I was able to be much more effective at home in Canada with the Aboriginal liberation struggle for much of my life. With my degree, I had received not only my degree, but considerable knowledge and strategies on the civil rights and national liberation struggles. The recognition of my doctorate degree also carried considerable prestige and weight in my capacity as a radical organizer and promoter of struggles of oppressed people.

During the year, there were some notable speakers at Berkeley campus. The one that I was most impressed with was Malcolm X. His speech was on the topic of nationalism of the Black people. It contained the most penetrating and insightful thoughts on nationalism. He was a spellbinding speaker. After his speech, I was so wrapped in the thought of nationalism. I sat for a while and thought about how and where nationalism fitted in with the Indians and Métis back home in Canada. Dr. Martin Luther King gave a most memorable speech on the topic of civil rights struggles for freedom. My thoughts turned more and more to the subjugated Métis and Indians at home, and their horrible state of impoverishment and powerlessness.

I had now concluded that as soon as I had finished my degree, I would return to Saskatchewan, my home province, well-populated with Aboriginal people. In the 1960s, jobs for Ph.D. graduates were plentiful, but I would find something in Saskatchewan. A week later, I arrived at the University of Saskatchewan in Saskatoon and inquired about a job. The only vacancy was in the Community Studies Department. It would involve travelling to Métis and Indian communities to conduct studies. It turned out to be the perfect job. As I made my visits, I talked about politics and the discrimination against them. They were anxious to discuss possible plans to challenge the semi-apartheid rule [of the White colonizers].

The Politics of Language: Michif vs. the Queen's Standard English

The form of language that is used to write a book about the history and life of Indigenous peoples is very important. […] They have been deeply colonized since conquest [Contact]. Their language, speech and expression have been critically destroyed, deformed and distorted by the White-European colonizer. Over the years, he has distorted Aboriginal languages into a type of pidgin. In speaking to Aboriginal people, the colonizer will speak in child-like language. In the pub, the Indian will call out, "Waiterrr, bing me a beeya."

Yes, I have to take pains with my words and language in this book because I shall be judged by it. My Aboriginal comrades with great contempt will say to me, "He doesn't even know how to write or speak the way he did when he lived in the ghetto with us. Now he speaks the fancy, high-flown words of the citified Whiteman." The Halfbreed knows that in the big city there is a stereotype of him and his type of language, that it is a caricature of the Queen's Standard English. They say one or two words of Cree and then mock and laugh about it. As Aboriginal persons, we are mocked and laughed at as we try to move into the arrogant, aggressive, mainstream White society. We are subjugated, subordinated and [are made to feel inferior…] in the most direct and powerful manner.

How well I remember my first horror of embarrassment when using my Pidgin-English amid a group of White-supremacist youngsters, when I told them that "Ee be'aved like a dun-key." Fresh from my peasant ghetto, "dun-keys" were commonly used for farm work. The crowd stopped talking suddenly and looked at each other in a moment of silence, and then broke out into a rage of laughter, shouting at the same time "dun-key, dun-key. Tell us again, Howard." I repeated, and they laughed louder and mocked me more. The depth of the contempt and scorn they poured on me still rings in my ears forty years later. I am still hesitant and fearful of speaking out casually and unthinkingly, fearing the horror of scorn that will sting my sense of dignity because I know the vivid stereotype such White people hold of Halfbreeds […]. "Ah come fron San Wee. It's the first time ah've eveh come to Sass-toon"—only halfway between pidgin Michif and English.

I know it's only White people who come closer to being real human beings than me—they look and speak like a White person. I'm totally aware that I'm not a complete person because I have only to listen to myself. The individuals who possess the Queen's Standard English possess the world and are part of the White-supremacist Aryan race.

The Aboriginal person has two sides. One is with his Aboriginal fellows; the other is with the colonizer Whiteman. We behave differently among our own people and with the White settler. This division is a direct result of conquest, subjugation and colonization. It is the formidable eternal wall that never diminishes. It locks us in the racist vice of a colonized society. It quarantines us from being ethnic folks. Make no mistake about it: Indians and Métis are colonized, Aboriginal sub-humans. To White fundamentalists, we are still in the stage of slow evolution from monkey to human. To speak means to use the correct verb and to have the full understanding of the subordinate adjectival clause. The closer we come to the Queen's Standard English, the closer we come to being a real human being.

In every colonized person an inferiority complex has been created by the burial of his true culture. "The colonized is elevated above his jungle status," argues Fanon, "in proportion to his adoption of the mother country's cultural standards." The more he renounces his Indianness and tribal identity, the Whiter he becomes.

My father, being English Métis, could not speak nor understand Michif. Yet he married a French Métis woman who spoke almost no English. As the children arrived, and Mamma was the sole caregiver for the children, of course she spoke Michif to the children. Hence, ignorant Pappa demanded that the children be taught English.

In looking back and understanding racism, Pappa forced the children to speak English so we would become more [assimilated/integrated into the world of] the White colonizer and less of the Halfbreed world. Thus, he not only divided the children between Métis and White society, but divided each child from their Métis soul life against the White mainstream. Such a paradox and complexity simmered through our household and community. Since we did not enter another country until adults, we could never visualize or imagine any culture or language except our Métis customs. There was no other "mother culture."

But, lest I forget, let me return and linger over some of my earlier years following the ghetto. Obviously wanting to enter a tantalizing city of the mother country, I enrolled and studied at evening classes—after work—education classes. Why? No one urged me to attend. No one cared about my speech. I had no ambition to speak publicly as a politician or preacher. Then why speech lessons, and after a full day's work? My co-workers were all of the educated English class. Obviously, I was stinging from the inferiority of my language, its coarseness and crudeness. I was timid and easily stung by reproaches on my speech. […] Why had I been so stupid and ignorant? I had slowly and carefully edged my way into the precious White mainstream society for years. Yet I stumbled and fell heavily on a single word. The next week I was taking evening elocution lessons twice a week. The next year I was taking regular classes in public speaking. Never have I suffered such anxiety and fright than when I had to give a presentation to the class. It was my test of good public speaking presentations. I trembled but persevered. If only I could have given myself a sense of reality that I was condemning those ugly White racists from my childhood, but no. My value system had become a total confusion. I stumbled and stuttered through it, and returned to my seat in a state of shame and inferiority. Back to square one in the ghetto. Such insults and bitterness drove me on until I could speak as well as any White.

As a young man mainstreaming it in the city of "Sass-a-toon" among the White settlers, I was suspicious of my own tongue, continued to watch ever so carefully my Michif accent. Desperate to talk exactly as the Mother Country Aryans, I would practice for hours each evening locked in my tiny dark room. Yet I longed so much to go to the pub and meet my buddies and drink beer at the National. But that would only drag me deeper and deeper into my ghetto dialect. I resolved not to fit the stereotype of the typical Métis Halfbreed.

I had been imprisoned for twenty years on an island of Aboriginals, lost in a community that offers not the slightest outlet. All four walls were insurmountable. Maybe it was not exactly at my fence, nor even at the school fence, but somewhere nearby was the Great Wall that abruptly halted all Aboriginals from the mother country. When the Aboriginal arrives in the mainstream, he changes because to him the new country represents the temple of […] Europe. There is a kind of magic of distance from the reserve.

How well I remember the cold November morning when Pappa took me to catch the bus that would take me far away into the training for the armed forces.[1] As the bus drove away, and I looked out the frosted window, I felt the entire amputation of Aboriginal being.

How correct I was! As soon as I entered the Regina barracks, I was stripped not only

---

[1] Howard Adams may have been conscripted during the Second World War under *The National Resources Mobilization Act*.

of my name, but my identity and heritage. I became a number dressed in a dingy khaki uniform that was exactly the same as all other recruits. We had been transformed into zombie[2] draftees. I spoke only to questions asked. Before long, I no longer understood Michif. The fierce drills and marches quickly drove out all my peasant behaviour. I deliberately ignored and sidestepped all Aboriginal recruits. I, like all other recruits, betrayed myself in our culture and speech. I denied everything of our background. Uniforms and hats made everyone the same; only our numbers were different. We were already used to being dehumanized, so it was easy to go the extra step. This new national culture quickly intensified a deeper inferiority. At the same time, we became ever more silent and withdrawn, the typical Aboriginal hunters of the woods. We heard the Aryan barrack-room buddies condemning the Aboriginal languages in the most vicious racist language possible.

Everyone today will readily claim that racist discrimination is strictly out of order and that it must be eliminated, yet it flourishes among the Ku Klux Klan, bikers and fundamentalists. By all means, it gags and mutes the Aboriginals. There is still an Indian and Métis problem. Yes, even more so. But what else can you expect when it says so in the Bible: "the separation of the White and the coloured races will be continued in heaven as on earth" (Fanon). There still exists the pattern of imprisoning the Aboriginals, making them primitive, de-civilizing them. Of course it insults us. It is like treating us as if we suffer from dementia.

When I meet an Italian or Asian, I do not forget that he has a language of his own, a country, and is probably a well-educated person. I treat him and talk to him in the usual dignified conversational manner. But when I meet an Aboriginal, I wonder if this imbecile is still stuck at the stereotypical ghetto level. Immediately, I recall the tough and fierce struggles against the Anglo-Canadian apartheid government in order to Aboriginals up to the level of the 1990s. But nothing can be taken for granted because the quasi-apartheid politicians and bureaucrats have not changed an inch in those three hundred and ten years. The sixty million dollar *Royal Commission Report on Aboriginal Peoples* after six years came up with recommendations that were readily discarded as toilet tissue. The report was written to please the colonizing dinosaurs that sit in parliament. These dinosaurs have a fixed stereotype of the Indians and Métis, and nothing will change their stereotype. They have not changed in five hundred years. Why should we be hopeful that a few additional years would have caused them to change? They must be driven from parliament. Destroy the medieval stone castles and then rebuild a new structure and government. Feudalism and capitalism are history. They must be pushed aside for a new caring human society.

Doubtless, the Royal Commission's report was written in the beautiful Queen's Standard English. It contains no Michif, nor pidgin Cree language. Then surely it has the

---

[2] "Zombie" was a term of derision for those men who were conscripted (and thus did not volunteer) into the Canadian military during the Second World War.

respect of the great, learned parliamentarians. Does it matter that the Aboriginal has to wear the livery that the colonizer has sewn for him, leather fringes and feathers? Out of the mouths of the Aboriginal collaborators comes the ritual: "The Aboriginals in the remote areas are still very colonized." Of course, there may be some Indians and Métis who are drunks, drug-users, lazy and careless about the state of their house. […] Do we say that all Whites are child murderers because Clifford Olson is one of the Whites? To make us all drunken Indians is to ensnare or imprison us into a false generalization or category.

Because the colonizer still has control over our minds and behaviour, we are still vulnerable. He perpetuates his racist images of us at school, in the movies, TV and all media venues. These are the products of capitalism, and will persist as long as there is no free socialist-type democratic society, regardless of the pain and outcries. The Queen's Standard English and Robert's Rules of Order are only serious obstacles that serve to deceive and oppress us. Such pretence sophistication should not intimidate us any longer. We know they are only scarecrows. Nothing is more astonishing than to hear an Aboriginal person express himself accurately and tastefully. You shock the White settlers. They are in disbelief.

Dr. Howard Adams, Métis, Returns to Saskatchewan

During my last year at the University of California, the Berkeley campus was the explosive site of the Free Speech Movement, in which I had actively been involved. This gave me a great education in the oppression of racial minorities. In Berkeley, it was the [oppression] of Blacks and Chicanos that was parallel to the Métis in Canada. Saskatchewan had a large population of Aboriginals. Although they were not at the university yet in 1965, they would be on the university campuses in a short time. In my mind, I thought the university officials would be concerned about having Aboriginal students on campus, but I had not realized how deep and complex colonialism had penetrated into the imperial psyche of the Caucasian people. The psychology of imperialism was still deeply embedded in Canadians. It was still a matter of going on bent knees and cap in hand to the master […].

As soon as I had completed my doctorate degree, I would return to Saskatchewan, […I] hoped to obtain a teaching position at the university. No other place was even considered. It was my homeland and it was where I felt a strong pull. Why? I was not exactly sure. Was it to prove [myself] to those White supremacy people who had degraded me in my youth?

The university explained that they did not have an opening for me, but I did not accept that. I knew that a Métis with a doctorate from the University of California-Berkeley was unique and would have no trouble obtaining a university position. Indigenous professors were rare. In 1965, the universities provided opportunities for

Aboriginal professors.

When I returned to Saskatoon after obtaining my Ph.D. at the University of California-Berkeley, the Aryan population absolutely refused to believe that I was an Aboriginal. To them, I was a total contradiction to the typical stereotype of a Halfbreed. How could I possibly be mentally capable of obtaining a Ph.D. degree at one of the best universities in North America? No Aboriginal has that much intelligence. I spoke like an educated and professional person. I was aggressive and walked with my head held high. The society was in a flap. Oh no, they did not dare to confront me or criticize my credentials. But when I bad-mouthed their apartheid society, and how it continued to oppress and discriminate against Aboriginal people, they had to attack. I simply could not be a Halfbreed from a ghetto of peasants.

The media and racist officials drove out to my old ghetto home and looked it over. They talked to my brother who looked Aboriginal, spoke and behaved like an Aboriginal stereotype. They saw the long shack with mudded walls. For the first year of my "coming-out" as a protesting Aboriginal, these frenzied racists motored frequently to my old Aboriginal home and to the town of "San-Wee" to talk to most of the population, trying to get some locals to disclaim my Indian heritage and Métis upbringing. Try as hard as they must, they never found a word to disprove my claim of being a Halfbreed. To them, it was completely impossible that a true Aboriginal person could possibly achieve the level that I had. Aboriginals are incapable of such achievements. They are inherently stupid, lazy and without any ambition or goal.

Much paper and ink and TV propaganda was used in attempting to bad-mouth me in any and every way possible. These racists will fight to the death to prove that their stereotypes are correct. Also, there is the great danger that educated Aboriginals may push them out of their soft, cushy, high-salaried jobs. I had not only taken elocution and public-speaking lessons, I had practiced them often as a leader in organizations. I was a protest leader against the semi-apartheid society, had learned to use organizing skills and leadership skills. I was well-practiced in the verse of confrontation politics against my White racist enemy. Oh, sure, I was accused of every imaginable form of manipulation, deception and cheat. I was accused of self-aggrandizement, playing dirty politics, exploiting my Aboriginal qualities for personal gain. And on and on it went. The mainstream media were sure they had destroyed me as an Aboriginal success. They censored me finally. I was prohibited from speaking on TV and on some radio shows. Newspaper journals either blanked me out or gave false quotations that would disgrace me.

My fellow Aboriginal people supported me and refused to give White lies to the reporters. My Aboriginal brothers and sisters embraced me. That alone destroyed the White mainstream's efforts to destroy me. They were defeated at every turn. I spoke and behaved like a true Halfbreed. **(MISC)**

7. Métis Leader in Saskatchewan

Dr. Adams/Dr. Bruce Is Hired as a Community Development Officer by the University of Saskatchewan/Redfield College

"Couldn't a position be opened for me?" I insisted. "The university should have an Aboriginal professor." The dean wrote back apologetically: "We have no Aboriginal students on campus."

"There should be. What's wrong? Saskatchewan has the largest Native population of all the provinces."

"Maybe [we] can get a position opened in the Extension Division."

"Doing what?" That sounded like part of the barnyard.

"As a community development officer." I had never heard of it [and had] no training, much less being an expert in it.

"You visit the Indian reserves and Métis communities, develop viable projects." I wasn't sure what "viable" meant. After my Berkeley training, I wondered if that meant to make it an activist movement.

"No, no, you work with the people and motivate them to organize and develop economic projects in the community-like building a skating rink."

"In summer?"

"Then fix up the school and paint it. Or get them to cut and haul wood."

"They must have ideas and projects they want to do! After all, they've lived in these communities for all their lives. I don't want to go in their neighbourhoods and tell them what to do."

"Okay," said the dean. "Professor Wilcox is going on a trip to the northwest area visiting these communities on community education evaluation. You go along with him, see for yourself what needs to be done. And talk with the people. They need improved educational programs and many other things."

"Yes, I like the education issue." Types of projects and programs were developed in the minds of the White bureaucrats at head offices, and not from the local Native people. As professors, we could suggest community programs and have discussions with the people. Maybe we could help them. They need better schools and teachers, and improved welfare. When people are hungry—worse than that, starving—they know what they want—better farming methods, finding transportation to root-picking jobs in the next province. They want food on their table right now. I understood that. I could relate directly to the Native people and their demands. I was in tune with them although I had left Saskatchewan twenty-five years earlier.

The Extension Division boss, Harold Baker, decided that I should be introduced to the Indian reserves and Métis communities in northern Saskatchewan. One of the extension program professors, John Smith, was making a trip to the northern part of

Saskatchewan to visit these communities on evaluation business, and decided that I should go along with him and be introduced to the communities and the Native people. We would visit six communities. I was pleased to go along and meet the Métis people.

I went as a White university professor and was accepted as such. At each town, we visited White officials. We were accepted as semi-celebrities at each visit. At the schools the teachers, who were all White (several were nuns), treated us to a special reception. After school, they invited us to their homes—nice, fully modernized homes, as compared to the Natives', but all within a strong steel fenced yard with a padlocked gate. That was Fourth World, a South Africa township of the 1950s. The teachers held a communal tea and cake visit, and talked continually about the savage students.

A child of a teacher got out of the fenced yard. Immediately the mother raced after the child to drag her back inside. I asked her what was the hurry. She said that the Métis child was diseased and would pass on a plague to her child.

This was complete segregation of the most rigid type. In the evening, we went to a town council meeting managed by the White bureaucrats, except it included a couple of elected Métis officials. One was called "the mayor." I quickly observed that it was an apartheid meeting. The Métis mayor was a totally co-opted individual, known as a collaborator. He was completely powerless and almost speechless. The White officials did all the talking and made all the decisions. Decisions were made for control and management of Native children. They bragged about carrying guns and keeping themselves well protected from the savages. Obviously there was hostility between the Whites and Aboriginals. This was evidently a recent happening. The Métis fishermen had blown up the Mounted police plane just recently, as the Mounties continuously hassled the Métis fishermen on their boats while on the lake. The town of Buffalo Narrows was the most obviously hostile and had greatest potential for violence. The racial atmosphere was fierce and touchy. A visit to the local priests' palace shocked me. He spoke of the Métis people as children that needed to be controlled.

Racial tension was even worse in the next town farther north, La Loche. It was administered in much the same as Buffalo Narrows, except that Father Mathieu was a serious dictator. We had supper at his grand palace overlooking a beautiful lake while the nun-servants fed us the most lavish dishes of exquisite food, while I knew that the Métis population of the town were half-starving. In the evening, he held a picture show at the local town hall. He made it his personal business to divide the people into Whites on the main floor and the Natives upstairs. He stood at the door and personally divided them, guarding the people as if by law. He was a pompous, arrogant and cruel ruler.

The next summer, I made a trip to the same towns and Métis settlements. I was now widely and publicly known as a Métis who opposed the White quasi-apartheid rule of the Aboriginal population, and who supported them and their causes. In each Native community, I was happily welcomed by the Native people and, of course, condemned and hassled by the White-racist rulers. At each town, there was a big public meeting held by the Natives. Not one White person attended these meetings and the crowds of Natives. I did not fear for my life, as no White person would dare attack me in a fully Native town. He would be caught and maybe dealt with on the spot. Yet those same Whites of past year were still at their jobs in the village.

I spoke to the Aboriginals vigorously, and urged them to take matters into their own hands and make decisions that improved their conditions—to oppose and to deny the White authorities the right to manage or command them. I urged them to replace the nuns and White teachers with Natives. I suggested they should elect their own town councils of Aboriginal people and get rid of the White officials. The two tough problems were to transform the Hudson's Company Bay agent and the Catholic priest. There were Métis men who could manage the Bay store. It was suggested that we drive the Bay manager several miles out of town, and then leave him to walk to the city, which was many miles away.

It was a tougher problem to deal with the priest because most of the people were of the Catholic faith and they did not want to go against their church or priest. The only action was to spread ugly rumours about the priest that would cast a distrust or suspicion on him. In the long civil rights struggle, priests turned out to be the most vicious and troublesome and the most persistent in colonial oppression. This was consistent with my expectations of the role of missionaries as a major partner in imperialism and oppression. That is their function.

I needed to spend the night in the town of Buffalo Narrows, but the motel operator refused to rent a room to Howard Adams, and I knew he had the right to do that. I suggested sleeping in my tent in the park, but my Métis brothers insisted that it was too dangerous. I would undoubtedly be shot. So I had to travel through the night to the next safe town.

I continued to travel to other Métis settlements and Indian reserves throughout the province. I wrote a long report on the conditions of the Native communities and detailed the racial, social, political and colonial conditions, etc. I submitted it to Harold Baker and expected that it would be submitted to higher authorities for consideration and action. But it never saw the light of day again, and I stupidly failed to keep a copy. I knew that the university and the White imperial establishment did not intend to make any improvements for the Native people of Canada. This imperial racist country was not going to change, at least not without considerable struggle.

The Aboriginal people throughout the province were becoming organized. They were holding mass meetings and complaining in a single voice [about] the hardships and deprivations they were suffering. Gradually, the media began to give attention to the actions of the Natives. White liberals in an oppressive racial society began to feel the political pressure and suffered a certain sense of guilt. Thus, in a patronizing manner, they made efforts to push to the front the voices and faces of Aboriginals that would proclaim their generosity, the volunteering and the gifts these Whites dedicated to the

Natives. Also, the university was giving me some recognition as a Métis professor.

A happening took place that hit the Métis world like a bomb. I was interviewed on the local Saskatoon TV station as a Métis activist. This station had a wide audience and, of course, reached St. Louis [...], my hometown.

I was questioned about my ancestry. At this stage of my life, I was very proud of being Métis. I was asked to explain specifically what constituted a Métis. My answer was: "a mixture of European and Aboriginal; usually one parent was Indian or part Indian."

He asked directly, "What part Indian makes you a Métis."

I stated clearly, "My mother is part Cree."

This rocked my hundreds of relatives in St. Louis like an earthquake. The phone board at the TV station lit up, and angry calls roared in. Most were denying that my mother was part Indian. They accepted that we were Métis, but not Indian. That could not make sense, but it mattered not to the irate callers. But my statement affected the Métis beyond my relatives. They were overjoyed with the knowledge that a Métis was a professor at the university and had a doctorate. **(MISC)**

Tony applied for a teaching position at Redfield College in Saskatchewan. He got a reply in early August that he had been accepted. He and Thea packed what goods they had [in] the old car and shipped the rest by CNR. They rented a small house. Tony started teaching the next month. He was happy to be back home. It wasn't a Breed community, but it was Saskatchewan, and he was a next-door neighbour to his brothers and sisters.

Every weekend they drove out to the Breed ghettos and Indian reserves. Tony was re-establishing contact with home again. He was almost desperate for his own Halfbreed way of life, to share with his brothers and sisters the spirit of the Breed nation and culture. On the long Thanksgiving weekend, they went on a big tour of the Breed communities in the north. This time he had contact with the Redskin people of the communities so that he felt more readily accepted as one of his people. Tony now had a great political sensitivity to their problems. They were speaking out in strong language against the racist system over them. They were complaining about the schools and what insults they were to the Breeds. They were protesting against the provincial government officials, especially the Department of Natural Resources [DNR] and welfare officials, who had such wide powers over them, and who were abusing it. Of course, there was the usual dissatisfaction with the Hudson's Bay Company, which continued to cheat the Breeds in every way possible on groceries, furs, clothes and even their mail.

Tony didn't know how to answer his people. There was no use telling them to take their problems to the government for consideration and, hopefully, improvement. The government was the very part of the power structure that was oppressing them, and holding them in a colonial situation. It seemed to him that the only way was through organization, unity and power. He had followed the civil rights movement of the African-American people in the US over the last few years, and he had studied their movement. Also, he had read extensively on the national liberation movements of the Third World people throughout the colonial world. Tony had read about the Black people of Africa, the Asians, South Americans and other conquered people. The Breeds were facing an identical situation. They and the Indians had been conquered by the White Europeans from the 16th century on, and had been systematically colonized ever after. There was no way out other than a united struggle by all the Native peoples of Canada. Therefore, he became interested in combining the struggle of the Breeds and the Indians as one united struggle. **(TB)**

Howard/Tony Organizes a Radical Conference on "Indian, Eskimo and Métis Education," 1967

In the spring of 1967, the university sponsored a unique education conference whereby presenters would be exclusively Indian, Métis and Eskimo—no White speakers. White people would be the listening audience. It was a national conference with speakers selected from all sections of the nation. The topic was Aboriginal. Within education, they were free to choose the content. Aboriginal education having been under the control of churches, clergy and government bureaucrats since colonial times, the colonial managers felt "all heart" towards the heathen savages. Thus, they had made the decision to have Aboriginals do the speaking and the supreme intellectuals [would] listen. I was assigned to being chairperson and selecting speakers. I was given the freedom to select the speakers without any interference [because...] university officials felt safe in allowing speakers free choice. I had been in my position for nearly two years and had become acquainted or had heard of politically radical individuals throughout the nation. Hence, I selected speakers who I knew would speak clearly on the politics of education. Of course, being the chairperson, I made the opening speech and outlined the program. I opened the conference with a clear, confident voice on the issue of oppression and racism.

The terrifying part to the White semi-apartheid society of Canada was that the CBC media crew was covering this conference, as well as local media. I prepared carefully for this type of media coverage, as it was the greatest opportunity to bring a strong message of the oppression and racism [facing] Native people into the living rooms of the White people. I opened it with an accusation of the rigid racism imposed on the Aboriginal Indian, Métis and Eskimo populations for centuries. That powerful statement gave the other speakers confidence and power to put their strong messages on the politics of educational oppression across, speaker after speaker. If the audience expected soft-spoken, mumbling apologies and gratitude, they were surprised.

It was my intention to guide and provide the speakers with assurance. The first speaker, Mary Ann Lavallee, a Cree mother from Cowesses reserve, a passionate, emotive and moving speaker on any platform, presented a brilliant and eloquent talk. It was spellbinding. Her talk was so great that it gave her national stature as a renowned spokesperson. She elaborated on the faults and failures of past education for Native children. However, the White-Eurocentric listeners criticized her. The next speaker, Rod

Bishop, a popular Métis leader, emphasized the racism of the curriculum and teachers in Métis public schools. It was a profound statement of the factual situation currently existing in the Métis schools. Another forceful speaker was Kahn-Tineta Horn, a Mohawk Indian, who denounced the nuns, priests and the Catholic Church in a strong manner.

All speakers for the two days kept up [their] powerful speeches. Of course, this was very disturbing to the White audience. University officials had become enraged. What was this? [There were] complaints from high government authorities. I had planned on giving the sum-up speech with a ringing condemnation of Canada's apartheid education system and its apartheid society in general. The director of the Extension Division, Harold Baker, was afraid of what I would do. He caught me in the hallway and told me very firmly that if I did, I would be fired. Those were not only inappropriate words, but racist. The CBC radio host happened to be standing closely with his microphone. Upon hearing Baker's words, he dashed over to broadcast them. Immediately, Harold retracted these comments. Fortunately, I seemed to have things working to my advantage.

Howard Adams speaking in the late 1960s or early 1970s.
Photograph Courtesy—Marge Adams.

Besides the media, the Aboriginal people and many young White people were supportive of the tone and content of the conference. After all, it was new, provocative and stirring, in harmony with the mood of the 1960s. I was thoroughly enjoying the conference. I was comfortable in front of an audience, confident of my command of the microphone. The conference clearly established me as a good public speaker with an excellent stage presence. I was now a public figure, but at the same time a condemned professor at the University of Saskatchewan.

I felt quite good about my new image. I liked being a rebel Métis. It gave me an opportunity to "get even" with the imperial government that had tortured my ancestors in the 1800s. Indians and Métis were ready to join a radical cause that might right some of the wrongs done to them. A movement for Native liberation spread quickly, and soon we were gaining public attention. We were gaining in confidence about confronting the establishment and attacking the institutions of the government, such as courthouses, welfare offices, police and schools.

Although the Métis had been on the move in terms of civil rights actions, they had not been organized or mobilized for an effective and ongoing struggle. They lacked effective and powerful leadership. It was the role that I would fill very quickly. The reasons were obvious: I was a highly educated Métis (no other Aboriginal at that time had my educational qualifications); I was an impressive and forceful speaker; and I had skills and talent for mobilizing Indigenous people. It was necessary to keep in constant contact with a few sub-leaders and, for the sake of democratic decision-making, obtain feedback from the masses participating. We made very few poor decisions or moves.

One of the most effective was to organize actions in the local community or neighbourhood because there the violation or misdeed was immediate to the local people, and they could be pulled together as a group in a hurry. The cause for the action was understood clearly and immediately by all. It was a matter of discussing the type of action to be taken, the tactics and the target of the action. This was extremely effective in developing a politically aware consciousness among the people in a matter in which they felt involved. The language was always kept simple and in terms that uneducated Aboriginal people could understand. Make the issue as personal as possible. Have as many people as actively involved as possible, [and inform] that they had a commitment. At the end, they would feel a sense of accomplishment. Have some designated as the leaders in chants, songs or shouts. After the confrontation, gather in the community hall or friendship centre for a victory celebration. It was important to congratulate the people on their victory, [of their] confident activities against the oppressor. A feeling of victory was instilled. This was necessary for people who had been powerless, conquered and colonized.

In my first visits to the Aboriginal communities, there would be a general meeting to explain the way we should organize, the kinds of problems we should attack and give them a feeling that I was an Aboriginal brother, and would work with them in their interest. They became quickly aware that there were many problems that were similar to Native people in general, regardless of where they lived. This notion helped to bring them together in the struggle. CBC radio and TV were most helpful in promoting our cause. They covered many of our confrontations. They made good news reports as we were new items and we were potentially explosive. However, I never felt that the news coverage was exaggerated. The reporters, Mike McCourt, Barry Hussey and Craig Oliver, were most honest and fair in their reporting. Canadians were seeing their racist society and actions for the first time. It was ugly, and they were unhappy about their bigotry being exposed. Without this news coverage, the political awakening of the Native people would not have developed so fast and far.

Another factor that made Saskatchewan Natives [advance] to the front were the actions and comments of Premier Ross Thatcher. He intended to administer the Métis in a very patronizing manner and as peons. His programs were racist and defeatist. His program, AIM: Adopt Indian-Métis, was not only a disaster, but cruel for the Native children who were adopted because these Aboriginal children were adopted by White families who had no knowledge or comprehension of Indian/Métis culture. As a result, these children suffered from day one to their release, and in every dimension. However, it is unfair to condemn every adopting family, as there were a few who did an excellent job. **(MISC)**

That winter, some professors from the university planned a conference on "Indian, Eskimo and Métis Education." They had been given a grant of five thousand dollars by the federal government. The plan was to have Native speakers, with the White officials and public as listeners. However, the professor in charge claimed it was to bring in a "bunch of Natives," and show them a big time for the weekend—in other words, a big drunk, and then send them back to the ghettos and reserves. Fortunately, he got sick and was unable to continue as director of the conference.

Tony was asked to take over, and he did. He got the rundown on the most militant and radical Natives of Canada, and contacted them [and asked them to be...] speakers for the conference.

The conference went well as far as Tony was concerned. The speakers denounced the racist system of Canada, exposed it as the country most notoriously oppressing its Native people. The White authorities and the public had to listen to what their society really was—apartheid. The Natives spoke with the passion and fury of a raging fire. Tony made a passionate speech from the bottom of his heart about how the racist schools were inferiorizing his brothers and sisters, that it was an insult to them, and that the White power structure had better start giving over some of its power to the Native parents in the local communities. His Indian and Breed brothers and sisters hailed Tony as a champion, but at the same time the White officials, especially the university and his college boss, condemned him.

The director came over to Tony immediately after he had stepped down from the speaker's stand, and guided him off to one side away from the crowd. "Tony, those are outrageous statements. They are irresponsible and foolish. You know perfectly well they are false. If you want to act as a spokesman for your people, and make speeches like that, you'll be fired from your job."

Tony was annoyed with the college director for pushing him around, and certainly for threatening to fire him. "My people can speak out as much as they wish, and they can have whomsoever they wish as a spokesman. No Whiteman will shove them around anymore," said Tony angrily.

"I don't care whom they have as a spokesman, but they won't have you. If you speak tomorrow at any time, you're fired. Understand that. It'll be final. We've talked it over," ordered the director.

Tony thought, "So that's the way the Whiteman controls us! As soon as one of us steps forward to lead or direct our people, Whitey just cuts him down, one way or another. In the early days, he shot us down; today, he fires us. What a pig! To hell with him and all his pig friends."

Tony told his Native brothers and sisters what the director had said to him. They called a meeting immediately and decided that if Tony were fired, all the Native people would leave the conference immediately and picket the hotel. The whole situation was getting a lot of publicity as the CBC and the Canadian Press were covering the conference. Publicly, the director and the university denied any interference with the conference leadership. The White audience felt insulted by the way the Native speakers told them the real facts about Indian, Eskimo and Métis life and education. They had expected to be told what they had always been told, i.e. that they were doing a wonderful job. This conference shook them up fiercely, and Tony was pleased that he had a major role in it.

As a result of this conference, Tony was established as a militant and radical Native, and as a controversial troublemaker. But he had already learned who the enemy was for his brothers and sisters-the government, the White officials in all the key positions who governed the Native people. They were racists who were fearful of their positions. The most vicious and racist of all were the professors of the provincial university and their assistants who controlled Indian and Métis education. Yesterday's champions of the Native people today were now the vicious racists. In reality, they had always been basically the worst type of racists and oppressors, but they had cloaked it in the guise of helping the Natives. This was a lesson that Tony learned, and that he was not to forget. This kind of Whitey was to be watched closely from now on.

The professors went so far as to publish an extremely vicious personal attack on Tony in their special Indian-Métis journal. They said the most notorious things possible about him, which they hoped would destroy Tony forever as a leader. Tony sued them. He tried to sue the Saskatchewan Teachers Federation and the College of Education as they sponsored the journal and used their staff in producing this journal. Tony won his case easily—so easily, it was settled out of court. He was sorry that he had not sued for a million dollars, rather than just a public apology.

Tony could easily see how the White oppressors had kept his brothers and sisters under such absolute control and in such ghetto conditions for so long. He had found his enemy a lot faster than he had expected. And the enemy was much more obvious than he thought. He wouldn't have to look for him. Tony learned important lessons about oppressed people's struggles. In a civil rights movement of Native people, where a leader emerges from within their group, the establishment's news media moves in to destroy the credibility and sincerity of the Indigenous leader. In this case, the Teachers' Federation and the College of Education tried to do the hatchet job for the establishment. Tony saw that these people and their organizations were the first to rush to defend the power structure. It was pretty obvious that the whole [...education system...] was racist [...]. And it was also the most oppressive. The big task that lay ahead was to educate the Natives about the racism of the school system and the phoney White racist officials who were at the head of it. This would take time.

Growing Political Commitment of Tony and Thea

During the winter, Tony attended several conferences on Indians and Métis that were sponsored by the government or some big organization. They wanted to find out about the "Indian problem," and so they always held meetings and conferences at the big cities, like Regina and Saskatoon. At the conferences, Tony always met the same Indian and Breed people and listened to the same discussions. It was always what the government or power structure wanted to hear. It was easy to see that they were not getting any of the ideas from the grassroots people. Tony was often called on as a speaker on behalf of the Breeds. He spoke very frankly and harshly about the terrible conditions and the fact that the brothers and sisters had to mobilize for a greater struggle. His ideas were not always welcome. In fact, they were embarrassing. Gradually, Tony began to be dropped from the conference-circuit list. But he was glad, for conferences were only a clever scheme of keeping organizers and leaders of Native people busy at safe and useless things. Conferences were the Whiteman's sophisticated game of deluding himself into believing that changes were being made, but in reality they were preventing all changes. His brothers and sisters, he hoped, would not get involved in that type of Whitey nonsense. It looked like the activity of a dying society.

The provincial government stated that there were forty thousand Métis and thirty thousand Indians in Saskatchewan. He had many brothers and sisters in the province, and he tried to figure a way of organizing them into one single group so that they could have some power. As soon as college was out, he planned a provincial tour of the Native communities in his little black Volkswagen. Big new shiny cars were no longer part of his life. He and Thea were able to pack along enough camping stuff.

Most of the settlements had heard about Tony Bruce, so he was welcomed in each town or ghetto reserve. He held meetings with the people and explained how important it was to organize the local settlement and to get as many people as possible involved in working together on things that concerned the Indian and Breed way of life. "We will never get fair and just treatment until we all stand together, shoulder to shoulder against our enemy, the White power structure." Tony tried to make the people politically aware of their circumstances by explaining how they were controlled and who controlled them. Each settlement organized a local and promised to work together for the improvement of their situation.

Tony and Thea saw for themselves the horrible ghetto conditions the brothers and sisters were living in: no plumbing, no electricity, no decent houses, mostly log shacks, very little furniture, no health services, no doctors, no hospitals. Just about as bad as things could be [...]. And in every settlement, the White officials, the teachers, priests, Mounties and Hudson's Bay Company officials, lived in their own protected area in lovely new homes, fully modern, electricity, even TV. His brothers had told Tony that the White people of the settlements were very opposed to him coming there and talking to the Natives. In one settlement, they prevented him from meeting with his people. The priest and the government officials warned the Breeds that if they went to a public meeting where Tony Bruce spoke to them, there would be violence. Tony knew that racists do not hesitate to kill to keep control over "their Natives." So he left that settlement unorganized, but he knew his brothers and sisters were at work just the same.

That winter, Tony got together with several of his brothers and sisters throughout the province and drew up a constitution and formed a provincial organization to include all

Breed settlements throughout the province. Tony would've liked to include the Treaty Indians, since he felt that it was necessary to bring all Indians and Breeds together, but the Indians already had their own organization and it would be poor business to raid their organization for members. The government offered to give the Métis nation a small grant, providing it did all the things asked. Tony did not agree this was a good thing to do, but the others argued they needed the money.

"Okay," said Tony, "as long as they don't put too many strings on it. Also, I don't like the idea of a lot of structure in the organization. Why should we have a president, vice president, secretary, treasurer and a board of directors? We have never organized in that manner. We are Halfbreeds, not White bureaucrats. This will be so organized, we won't be able to work in it," argued Tony. "It is not a Halfbreed way of doing things. This arrangement makes everything so permanent. It's not good because our movement changes every day. And if we have all this structure, we won't be able to change. We should use only committees whenever we need them. I am very opposed to any central and individual leadership," he argued. "Colonial people are inclined to look towards a messiah type of leader, and then not to do things enough for themselves. They want to depend on their leader for everything. In that way, it prevents them from developing their own skills and abilities to run their own settlements. Also, the news media always [likes to identify] a great hero-worship type of leader, and then, whenever they want to stop the movement, they just destroy the leader."

But the others argued there was a need for central and individual leadership at this stage, since people needed direction and inspiration. But they agreed with Tony that as the local committees developed and became skilful in making decisions and managing their own local leadership, then the central leadership would gradually disappear.

Tony and Thea rented a nice small house near the college. Thea was now working at the library. So they were both very busy. Their social life was practically nil. Thea became involved with radical women's work and the union. She took part in a lot of Tony's activities with the Indian and Breed movement, but she did not take part in the actual meetings, partly because she was [not] a legitimate member of the Breed nation, and partly because she was so involved with her own political work that she never had the time. They were solidly supporting one another in their endeavours.

Whenever the government or power structure attacked Tony, threatening his career or existence, Thea threw her support behind him a hundred percent. In fact, it was Thea's dedicated affection and moral support that gave Tony so much courage and power to fight the way he did. Sometimes he was alone, and it looked like a disastrous conclusion for Tony, but Thea gave such love and encouragement that Tony was able to withstand the brutal treatment of the establishment.

Even during the time that the racist establishment plotted to assassinate Tony, Thea treated it as a threat on her life, and fought back with all the wisdom and courage only a brave warrior could. They hired a good bodyguard for Tony and extra guards for the house. The plan was to either to throw a bomb in the Bruce's house and blow it up when Tony was in it, or to stab Tony to death when one of them went close to say hello to him, or to catch Tony as he walked from the conference hall to his car and club him to death. A committee of brothers and sisters stationed Breed guards throughout the crowd every day and frisked or "shook down" any suspicious-looking characters. Tony made speeches during the two days, argued on panels, encouraged his brothers and sisters to speak up and express their ideas as angrily as they wished. He led every assault on the Whiteman's racist society and on the power structure.

Death-defying situations like this drew Tony and Thea ever closer together. It forced Tony to do a lot of soul searching and come to terms with himself that he must be prepared to face death any minute, and Thea had to realize she could be without Tony any second. But Thea would never ask Tony to back down or withdraw from the front line of political action in the movement. She knew this was his full meaning in life. He had finally found a full purpose in life, and he would not settle for anything less now. He was a very proud Halfbreed and a very dedicated fighter for his nation. As his love for his nation deepened, so did his love for Thea. Tony no longer found it threatening when his wife became a liberated woman.

Because he had grown accustomed to male chauvinist attitudes and manners, he had a hard time to make the adjustment to accept her as an equal. In the past, Tony had always made jokes about himself and booze and women. But Thea objected to those jokes because he was classifying women as things, just like booze, that could be had if men wanted [them]. She argued that women were human beings equal to men, and not playthings or property. Tony had to take a lot of words and concepts out of his speech because he had built up a male chauvinist vocabulary. Tony never resented Thea straightening him out on this problem. He felt she was a brilliant analyst in that she saw right through the main issues of women's lib, and not the superficial issues. She had gone through the process of decolonization, and Tony was pleased with this, for he grew to despise colonial women, just as he hated the whole system of colonization. Through these experiences, their love deepened.

Tony Speaks at Batoche

The weekend of the huge rally and annual meeting had arrived. Thousands of Indians and Breeds were camped on acres of prairie. Tony was to speak to the huge crowd in the afternoon. The speaker's platform was on a mound, and all around it the people sat on the ground in the hot, dry afternoon. Tony didn't need an introduction, for most of the Native people knew him.

"Brothers and sisters, this is the happiest day of my life, to be here with so many of my own people, to discuss with you the important issues, to be able to sense the excitement of our new nation, the stirring among our people of every age, the warmth of a new humanity. We know that someday we will be free people once again, and that day may not be too far off. Of course, we have many sacrifices and sufferings yet before we achieve our liberation, and we know it will not be an easy road. But anything that is worthwhile is not easy. We have to understand colonization."

Tony continued to stir their passions to nationalism, to unity and pride for the Indian-Métis nation, and their eagerness for liberation. National flags were waving by the hundreds. Tony gave an explanation of how the conquering imperialist, in this case the English, came into a country of Native people, conquered them by sword and gun and used violence of the most notorious way, and then imprisoned them in prisons called reserves, Métis colonies, ghettos, etc.

"On top of that, the imperialists destroyed our culture in every way possible. In the first place, the missionaries came in with their arrogant, superior and racist ways to 'civilize the heathens.' They murdered many they couldn't convert. There has never ever been a more notorious creature or, worse, saboteur to come to our nation. No one else has ever done such subversive work in the whole world as the missionaries did to us and to our culture. They did everything so deliberate and systematic in undermining and razing our culture. Every priest and minister in our reserves or settlements today should be tried for treason before a jury of Indian and Breed citizens.

"The White rulers at Ottawa murdered our brother Louis Riel for treason. Well, now let us turn the tables and judge all those traitorous palefaces who have betrayed our people and nation. In an indirect way, they have been guilty of the death of thousands, if not millions, of Indians and Breeds throughout the years, and for butchering the spirit and the vigour of a nation, its sense of pride and dignity and honour."

Tony was interrupted frequently by extensive applause. His people loved to hear him talk so boldly and honestly. They admired his courage and ability to articulate so well the ideas that most of them wanted to say but couldn't express in public.

He went on to explain: "The Whiteman degraded our culture by injecting into it such bizarre things as scalping and massacring. These were the things that the Whiteman used against the Indians, or paid the Indians to scalp others. But he made this a part of the Indian culture, so that Indians and Breeds would crouch and squirm whenever scalping was mentioned—and believe me, it was mentioned constantly! To make them feel so inferior and uncivilized, for they had come to believe this is what their ancestors did. This is how vicious the Whiteman is! So we know what to expect from him. Whitey has mocked our God and our faith, and he has made us the objects of ridicule. He has degraded our nation so badly that most of the brothers and sisters are ashamed of being an Indian or Breed at some time in their lives, and some are ashamed all their lives. How often our children cry because they are Natives.

"But this is what White supremacy is all about, and that's what it's like being a Native in a racist-colonial society like Canada. They hold us up to the world as shiftless primitives who prefer to beg and steal, rather than work. They say we are lazy and irresponsible, without ambition and industry, after they have broken our spirit, imprisoned us, and denied us all opportunities of getting ahead. Whitey says that we lack all morals, and that we are a nation of stinking people. It's simply a racist way of saying that we're not capable of running our own affairs and we need protection. After all, can immoral, lazy and dishonest people administer a nation of people? In this way, he can oppress us with a clear conscience. The White rulers have infused into our culture ugly and hideous distortions that barely make us human beings. We are denied any decency, beauty or heritage. Is it any wonder that Whitey's laughter makes us recoil and shudder, which is fully intended to remind us of our inferiority? This form of debasement is an effective way of crippling us and keeping us in our places. But it also reminds us of the bitterness and hostility that surrounds us.

"Teachers and priests drum continuously into our ears that we are shy and withdrawn by nature until, finally, we come to believe them, and grow up in this kind of obedient and subservient way. What hate and frustration is seething within us! We have our hostility but are unable to express or articulate it. If Whitey knew the hate he has generated within us, he would now clear out while the going is good. But don't worry, he is too arrogant and racist to understand, now or ever. The racist schoolteachers treat us like we were retarded Aborigines. Of course, every IQ test shows us up as being ignorant because these are racist tests based on the White middle-class culture. Every time we are given one of these tests, we should tear it up. I ask you to do this.

"The racists justify their racism by saying that we love living a free and easy life by nature. And then they romanticize about the Indians and Breeds having such a wonderful life in the wilderness, free from the dirty cities. But they are only saying that we love poverty, deprivation and misery, oppression and racism, that we are satisfied with just a few paltry things of life because we don't know how to enjoy the finer things. I suppose we are too crude and vulgar.

"After the White imperialists and missionaries emptied the Native nation of its essence and vigour and force, they ossified it. Many things were changed to the Whiteman's ways. Of the many traditional Indian things kept, many were made useless and powerless. But they were necessary because they were needed as an effective way of controlling the Native masses. They were kept because it would coagulate our civilization and preserve it in an archaic way, thus arresting all development towards progress and a dynamic and powerful nation. They didn't want any competition. They disfigured the Native culture and developed a caricature one.

"Imperialists rarely exterminate an entire nation, but they will not allow it to develop normally with the changing world. For example, the position of chief is an archaic institution without any power. The White rulers wouldn't let it die because they needed it for ruling the Natives on the reserves. Yet, today it is little more than ritualistic and ceremonial. He is only a puppet for the colonial White officials. It becomes a sordid mockery when the Indians make a so-called "White dignitary" an honorary chief. It is the same with the Breeds. We are allowed to trifle in all kinds of traditional ceremonies, such as pilgrimages, but as soon as we translate it into political action, like we did in 1885, they massacre us with their troops. Imperialism never allows the real authentic culture to grow. Instead, it promotes a caricature culture. It smothers creativity and productivity; it prevents progress and development. Colonialism freezes the culture and nation, where there is no inspiration, no hope, no culture, just despair and fatalism.

"From the present struggle, we will snap the chains of oppression and colonialism. We will be the people who will determine the direction and the speed of our liberation. And we will make it free from the racist and imperialist masters.

"I want to outline a plan to you that I think will lead to our freedom! It is a plan to take over our own Breed and Indian settlements and reserves. The first thing we will do is to educate ourselves as to the political circumstances of administering the community. Then we will start training our own Native people for the jobs that will require particular skills. Some time in the coming year, each community should get the people together and decide on who would like to run as council members. Then in the spring, you should hold elections for Natives to the local council. The only qualification they need is that they are Indian or Breeds, and that they have an interest in our Redman nation and its liberation. Once the council is elected, you will then go about setting up a whole administration for your community. You will start training certain people for the position of Indian agent, DNR agent, or welfare officer-actually, for every government position in your community. We would want you to have all this done by next spring because when we meet here next summer, we want to have our Indian and Breed nation well organized and in the control of our brothers and sisters. Because, if the government has not turned them over to us, we will hold our annual meetings and festivals in the legislative building in Regina.

"When we have our councils elected throughout every Breed and Indian community, then we will go to the government and demand that constitutional power be turned over to us. If the government refuses, we will put pressure on them. We have eighty communities organized so far, and by next year we will have eighty more. And never forget, there are seventy thousand of us in this province and increasing rapidly every day. If the government refuses to act on our demand for constitutional power, we will be prepared to act. Of course, we are not going to tell them how we will act, but we will.

"This will not be easy because I have already argued with the government authorities on this issue. The Minister of Indian and Métis Affairs in Regina refused to grant us power to run our communities because he said we are not responsible. But racists like him and all the government will use this argument till doomsday. As long as one White paleface is alive, we will have to wait for his definition. So we are going to say, 'To hell with you, Whitey, and your racist decisions! We are going to take over our communities right now. And if you don't transfer power to our truly elected councils, we will ship your racist agents out of our settlements by the best damn way they can get out.'

"If necessary we will do one reserve or settlement at a time with the forces we have here today, and all those many more that will be here next year. But remember, we must have trained Natives to take over those positions. By trained, I mean only that they know how to administer the local situations. We are not concerned about all the rules and the procedures of the bureaucracy or the government. If the DNR people and the other officials won't teach us how, then we'll set out a plan for ourselves.

"By demanding that our councils be given constitutional power, we are asking for no more than participatory democracy. If we make up ninety percent of the population of our settlements, then it is only democratic that we should be the people to govern our communities. As Indians and Breeds, we don't go over to the all-White communities and put ourselves at the head of their councils and in all the important positions. Yet that is what they do to us. The Whiteman wouldn't stand for it, why should we?! Well, we won't anymore.

"The other things we are going to take over are the schools. We will elect a school board from the Native population, and this Indian-Métis school board shall have all the powers of the present school board. We will demand from the government that our boards be given this power. They will have the right to hire and fire the teachers, the right to decide on the textbooks, to select the curriculum, and all the general business of the schools. If the government refuses to do this, we can boycott the schools. Keep our kids home from school. There'll be nobody at school, and then they'll see how many Native kids go to these schools. We will appoint the principals of the schools. Before too long, we will have our own Native teachers.

"Certainly we can do these things. We can do them in the same way that we held area meetings and demanded that the government officials and cabinet ministers come to our communities and talk to us about the dirty deals we are facing all the time. We made these meetings a real thing simply by insisting and demanding, and not accepting anything less. We can do these things in the same way that we made the government recognize our welfare committees as part of our legitimate rights, the rights of those who would fight on behalf of their brothers and sisters. As long as we continue this political pressure, we have a very good chance to win the things we will demand. But always bear in mind that all the time we are politicizing and mobilizing our brothers and sisters. It is only through national unity that we will strengthen our Indian-Métis nation. So remember, if we do not have constitutional control of our reserves, settlements, school boards and all official positions by this time next summer, then we must be prepared to go into action. Maybe we would decide to move this many people from each community and simply take over. With five thousand people, we are powerful, and not even the Mounties could stop us. We are asking only for the things that rightfully belong to us. No more.

"Then, when we have formed councils in many of our settlements, and have taken our constitutional power, we will form one central governing council for all local councils. It will act more as a coordinating council body or federation for the Indian-Métis Nation of Saskatchewan. We will make all decisions about the towns, streets, lighting, electricity, water system; building highways, community halls, taxes, about how we want the Mounties to police our settlements. Maybe we won't want them at all in our communities. The people will decide these things. Always remember: it is the people who will be the rulers, not the White capitalists. And the people are you!

"We will have a true democracy, just like Gabriel Dumont and the Métis nation back before 1885. And after we force the government to transfer the power back to the local people of the communities, and they develop them in the interest of all the people in that area, then we will bring other things under the control of the people, like the Hudson's Bay Company store (applause), the private garages, hotels, cafes, fish marketing firms, furs, the northern freighting companies and the airplane companies. We won't give a cent to the owners for these things! They are ours!

"Over the many years that they have been in business in our settlements, and the millions of dollars they've made by cheating and exploiting us, they rightfully owe us money. They'll just turn everything over to us, and all they'll get will be a receipt.

"Don't let Natives from other provinces or White bureaucrats come to you and try to talk you out of it. They'll say we have programs for self-determination for the Native people in our province. Don't be fooled by that crap talk. They'll tell it's self-determination for the Natives. It is like hell. Big rich fat capitalists, like the banks or insurance companies, invest money in certain industries, like in southern Alberta, that involve Indians, but it as sure as hell isn't for the good for the Indians. A capitalist invests for the good of profit. Period.

"Sure, the Native people are probably involved in a small way. Tokenism! Allowed to sit on boards or in high positions, but they are all without authority or power. The real power rests in the hands of the White capitalists. Instead of leading to self-determination, it leads to greater oppression and racism, the very basis of racism. Here in Saskatchewan, we are planning, mobilizing and moving towards national liberation. That will give the complete power to the local people, and they will decide how the resources will be developed, and for the good of the whole community and all people, not just for the pocket of one rich man.

"In our progress to liberation, we will be travelling all in the same direction, national liberation, and there is only one way! But the seventy thousand of us may be travelling at different speeds or levels. Some will not even be concerned about it! They will be still asleep in the state of colonialism. Others will be working at the level of education, having discussion sessions and meetings. Still others will be taking more direct action through confrontations, such as demonstrations, sit-ins, etc. Others will be circulating petitions and making demands from the ruling class, others will be out mobilizing the masses, others will be doing what I have suggested: forcing the government to surrender its dictatorial powers back to the local people.

"And it's possible that others, who are very impatient, may want to operate a higher level of revolution, and do such things as kidnapping and hi-jacking. For instance, I could see a group kidnapping some ballot boxes during a general election and destroying the ballots. That would ruin a whole national election so fast. Also, it would help to point up that elections are just a phoney bourgeois game to make the people pretend they are involved in changing the society, when in reality the same ruling class is always in power. That sounds like a marvellous scheme. It would also show that we, as Indian and Métis, won't stand for the nonsense of political parties and the ridiculous nonsense of voting.

"We should never condemn any of our brothers and sisters who become involved in liberation struggles. We should always work together to help each other at all times, even though we may disapprove of their methods. We should always be prepared to shield and protect and keep secretly our brothers and sisters when they are in trouble in the liberation fight.

"But we must be careful not to be adventurists or elitists or opportunists and do something that could wreck the whole nation at this point. If you do something that would bring the police and all the racist judges and all against us, as well as the news media, and finally all the White people, then we could be in for the same type of treatment we got in 1885. The government would isolate us from the rest of the Canadian people, and then turn racism wild on us, and the whole nation will be out for blood, and they'll spill our blood once again, just for sport and vengeance. So you see why it is important to have many friends.

"We should make as many allies as possible among the White people of Canada. There are groups who join and support our struggle, for they are involved in a similar struggle, such as the farmers of Saskatchewan, the students (high school and university), the women's liberation, and even to link up with the French Canadians of Québec. Basically, the vast majority of us are French and Catholic, just as the Québécois.

"And never forget our wonderful brothers and sisters who are locked up in the jails and penitentiaries. They are working towards national liberation as [...we are to our] own liberation. We should be working closely with them and help them organize programs in the jails, so they can take their places in the leadership of the movement when they come out."

Offer to Become Deputy Minister; Refusal to Be Bought Off

While at a meeting in the legislative building in Regina, Tony was invited to the office of a top authority.

"Tony, you've been doing a lot of good work among your people, and you're a very able person. I want to offer you the portfolio as deputy minister to work with your own people. The government will make a lot of money available for grants for the Métis and Indians, and I think you could do a very good job of administering it. What do you say?"

It hit Tony like a bolt of lightning. He had never anticipated anything like that. In fact, he had not even been nice to the government officials. "This is so sudden, I'm stunned by the whole thing. Let me think it over for a few days, say a week or so, and then I'll let you know my decision. I really appreciate your offer, and that you have faith in me to do the job you're asking for."

Tony would talk it over with Thea. He would never make a serious decision like that without a serious talk with her. She had ways of seeing things that Tony could not perceive. She had a brilliant analytical mind, particularly in political matters.

Within a week, he answered. "I'm sorry, sir, but I've decided against accepting the position as deputy minister." He gave no reason.

But Tony knew the reason. You cannot sellout when involved in a Native movement.

The brothers and sisters would see you as an opportunist who jumps at the first opportunity to better himself, and at their expense. After all, what would he be without their support, without the support of all the brothers and sisters? Nothing!

Tony thought, "Before I can accept anything, it has to mean a big improvement for all the brothers and sisters, and not just for me. Everything for the movement! Once you sellout, the masses will never let you back into the movement. And well they shouldn't. There is no room for selfishness and individualism in the movement, and any leader that doesn't recognize that principle is in for trouble."

As far as Tony was concerned, it was a deliberate effort to buy him off, to co-opt him. It was a mighty tempting offer. And the president of the college was urging him to accept. His classes would be looked after, there would be nothing to worry about—just go and all will be well! He knew the president didn't like him, so he suspected this promotion.

The next week, when Tony was in a discussion session with his brothers and sisters, they raised [the issue of] the deputy-minister position, and gradually talked about being co-opted, not only Tony, but any other leader who is effective.

"There's more than buying our leaders off," said Tony. "The ruling class is buying them off all the time. The DIA buys off our Indian brothers by giving them jobs in Ottawa, or even on the reserve, maybe just collecting garbage. But these aren't jobs: nobody works on them. It's just a way of giving money to our leaders to shut them up. There's getting to be so damn many garbage collectors, they'll soon be loading one another on the truck!"

"And the reserves are crawling with band administrators, recreation advisers, physical directors and community development workers," said another.

"And so many of our brothers are suddenly showing up with new cars or a new house, and with no explanation and not having worked a day in their lives. But they've been active in the movement for a few months. That's the business today. It's to get in the movement, and the power structure will buy you out almost immediately. But they can't continue to buy out everybody."

"Hardly," said Ed. "There are seventy thousand of us in the province, and increasing rapidly every year."

"But there are other ways of co-opting us," said Tony. "Just like with the welfare committees, when the government offered to hire several Breeds to work as welfare worker aides and make them part of the establishment. The idea was to put these Breeds in official positions to administer welfare and make them the new oppressors of our own people. And the other thing, these employees soon get a vested interest in their jobs, by their salary and prestige. They become concerned with themselves, and not with the masses, and the nation, and the movement. Then they are doing the dirty job the White racists have been doing. In a sense, making House Indians out of them, to rule over the Field Indians. No sir, we won't have the nonsense! We must always be on guard for that type of co-opting.

"This other way, where the brothers and sisters are supportive and defending each other against the oppressive welfare system and the government, it serves as a unifying force."

"By hell, fellows, if the establishment offers me enough, I might take it and turn all you crumbs in. Of course, I'd want more for that job! Say, if they offered me a hundred thousand a year," said Jim jokingly. But he was expressing the idea that many may have felt—that if enough was offered, they might sellout. It was only a matter of principle.

"This is one place where principle has to come before selfishness or money," said Tony. "You're involved here because of the principle and the convictions you have about your brothers and sisters and our nation. You should be able to say with complete sincerity, 'I'd be willing to lay my life down for the cause of the Indian-Métis movement.'"

"Hey, do you know that the government could be trying to co-opt us by giving our organizations a lot of money?" said Slim.

"That's for sure," said Tony. "It's more than paying us money. It's co-opting into the whole way of the White middle-class life. You see, every ruling class that can bring in the masses of lower-class people into traditional middle-class life make it very safe for themselves because the middle class is in a slave mentality to the ruling class. It worships and glorifies their rulers and their system. More than that, they become the passionate defenders of the whole rotten system. Mostly because they get a few crumbs from it, and they feel so grateful for being better off than the lower classes. Being middle class is like being a squirrel in a cage, trapped into all kinds of debts, payments, credit notes, purchases of all kinds of junk like a second car, boat, motor cycle, trailer, a cottage, holidays to tourist traps, etc., etc.

"We mustn't let ourselves be trapped into that kind of mentality or activity! I notice already that some of our leaders are beginning to think in terms of staying only at the most expensive hotels, holding conferences at the big ballrooms with thick carpeting, and driving shiny new cars—how do these cars look, going into our settlements where most of our brothers and sisters are on welfare? Eating at expensive restaurants, eating steaks, wearing the latest fashion in clothing."

"But hell, Tony, we don't have to live in tents at forty below just to prove we are Indians and Breeds. What's wrong with a little bit of comfort, just like the Whiteman?" asked Henry.

"Nothing," answered Tony, "as long as we don't get trapped in that way of life and start thinking like Whitey. Then we'll start looking down at our own people for not doing better, and then start doing things only for ourselves. We have to always keep in mind that the masses of our people are at the welfare level and in the lower-class bracket. That's nothing to be ashamed of. We'd be trapped into the system already if we said we're ashamed of being low class because that is strictly Whiteman's middle-class language.

"We are part of the Indian-Métis nation, and that has nothing to do with class. We cannot become dependent. At any minute we should be able to leave all these middle- class luxuries without feeling we're making a sacrifice. We've got to keep resourceful to make our living by traditional and resourceful methods. If you can't feel comfortable without central heating, boy, you're hooked.

Prince Albert: Tony Becomes President of the Saskatchewan Métis Association

In the spring, a Métis nation meeting was held in Prince Albert. A couple hundred of delegates were brought in from the northern settlements. Other Breeds came from parts of the south. Tony explained that they, as Breeds, would never be able to achieve their freedom in any other way than through national liberation struggles, just like other conquered people who live in apartheid systems in the world. He gave a historical account of how the Canadian power structure had conquered the Natives several centuries ago.

"It's even longer than that," Tony went on. "About two hundred-fifty years ago, the Whiteman from Europe killed all the Beothuk Indians in Newfoundland. He slaughtered them one by one, partly because he wanted their land and resources, and partly for sport. He claimed the Indians were only animals, anyway."

A brother added, "And now Whitey tries to hide the historical facts about the Boethuks, or if they do talk about them, they say the Micmac Indians killed them."

"Well, when you control all the machinery that tells the history of a people, you can make up the most outrageous lies about them you want. And more than that, you can claim that these are objective historical accounts," said Tony. "And here on the prairie, our ancestors had the most flourishing and strongest Native culture and nation ever developed, based on the buffalo and horse. But when Whitey wanted our land for the Canadian Pacific Railway, he just came along with his guns and murder instinct, and did another mass slaughter job. He killed every buffalo moving. When he had finished, the miles and miles of beautiful prairie were littered with dead and rotting carcasses. In summer, the stench was unbearable."

"What use did he make of these buffaloes?" asked brother Ray.

"Very little," said Tony. "The power structure paid money for buffalo bones, hides, horns, and even tails, but that was very little. Just gave a legitimate excuse for rapid slaughter. In this way, the White people of the Prairies made a little money, and this kept them from rebelling against the government."

"Why didn't the Whiteman wipe us out instead of the buffalo, just like the Boethuks?" asked sister Anne. But she answered her own question when she said that the Whiteman would've done it if he could've gotten away with it, but by this time the entire White society might now protest against slaughtering innocent people, even if it were the Indians and Breeds. They ended the buffalo blood bath as quickly as possible to prevent [the development of an independent Native nation.]

Mederic, being a socialist, explained, "The men in the government and in the establishment—for they were, in reality, the same thing—were anxious to make millions by seizing our land, and then dividing it up to sell to the new immigrants. Men like Lord Strathcona, the Canadian Pacific Railway, and the Hudson's Bay Company gave themselves the best land, and especially where they thought a city would emerge."

"Yeah," said Tony, "they had to clear all the Breeds and Indians off the land in order to get the White people to buy it. Because these newcomers were the products of western civilization, they had racial stereotypes and attitudes. It was no longer to 'let the Indians die out.' Oh no, it was violent extermination now. Ottawa became desperate. So they sent out troops to Red River to wipe us out. Except Riel and Lépine were too smart for them."

"It was more than that," interrupted Mederic. "The bourgeois historians have deliberately lied in the interests of their masters, the ruling class, by saying that the war in Manitoba in 1869 was a rebellion of Métis led by Louis Riel. In reality, it was a civil war between the federal government and the [... British] owners of the Hudson's Bay Company."

"If you're so smart, Mederic, how do you explain the so-called Riel rebellion of 1885?" asked sister Marion.

Mederic was not stuck. "In the beginning, it was a struggle between the White people— farmers and workers—and the federal government. Ottawa was exploiting and cheating the prairie people so badly, they had decided to rebel. In fact, they had taken up guns to fight at one time in 1884. The Indians and Breeds came into the revolt only at the end, to fight for their land and freedom."

"And in a racist society," Tony added, "it's easy to turn the White population against a racially oppressed group. So Ottawa just turned the White Canadians on the Indians and Breeds and virtually massacred them. It has been so bad that we are only beginning to recover now, after eighty-five years."

"And we want to be careful that we don't get trapped into the same kind of a massacre again," said brother Rod, "because the same racism exists today as it did in 1885."

"As long as we have capitalism, we will always have this kind of racism and dangers. We've got to change to socialism," expounded Mederic.

"Hear, hear!" shouted many, and applauded Mederic.

Tony decided it was an excellent place to explain how "the White-ruling class had not only destroyed our economy, but also made us beggars and prisoners, made us so dependent that we could never get along again without the charity and support of the government. We would never be allowed to be independent.

"After the buffalo massacre, the Indians were forced on reserves at the point of the gun, either Mountie or soldier, and the Métis [were] broken to be dependent children in their northern settlements. All this was done under the typical imperialist slogan of 'protection.' This is the most racist and apartheid slogan that can be used. The only people we have needed protection from are our so-called protectors. They seized our land, massacred us in our homes, terrorized and stole from us, violated our rights and humanity, and then have the nerve to say they must protect us! From whom?" asked Tony. "First they put us on rations and crushed our nation, jailed all our leaders and intimidated us for years just to let us know they were master over us. Through their schools and media they inferiorized us. They forced us into a state of dependency, to handouts, rations, relief and welfare. And now they say to us we are lazy, shiftless, irresponsible, without ambition. Over a hundred years they have practiced this policy of inferiorization and dependency, and then they complain that we have no self pride and independence."

"Any Whitey that talks out of the historical circumstances is a fool. He's just letting us know what an idiot he really is. He doesn't know the historical circumstances of his own country," explained Jim.

"All White ruling-class regimes do the same thing in all countries—China, Africa, South America, USA., and Canada. And they develop and control all the power in the nation, like the police and the army, navy and air force," explained Tony.

"And they commit all the worst kinds of violence against the Native people."

"That's for sure. Like massacring us in 1885 with guns, cannons and machine-guns, burning our homes, torturing the women, raping," said Tony.

"And that's not only historical," said brother Joe. "Look how the Mounties beat our brothers in the local settlements."

"Boy oh boy, police brutality is really a serious thing in our nation," added brother Rod.

"Yeah, look how the Mounties shot and killed brother Napoleon last month, just because they said he looked like an escaped prisoner. And nothing was done about it. Just pulled out his gun and shot a Breed in the head, and practically given a medal for it. To all the racist Canadians, though, a Breed or an Indian is nothing. No different than the Beothuks two hundred-fifty years ago."

"And why are the jails' and pens' population more than sixty percent Indian and Breed? We sure as hell ain't sixty percent of the population—at least, not yet. And in that new women's jail in Prince Albert, over ninety percent of the inmates are Indians and Breeds."

"That's because the judges and the whole court system are so damn racist."

"Boy, we should do something about those bigoted judges. They call our brothers 'savages' and 'animals' in their fascist courts," said Tony.

"I just hate the sight of a damn lawyer," said Jim.

"They got brains that are only good for the ruling-class regimes," concluded brother Tom.

"Hey, fellas, don't you think that we need to know our legal rights, so that we can fight for our rights through the courts?" asked sister Evelyn.

"No," said Tony, "I don't think we have much hope in that direction. The courts are set up to serve the ruling class, and they can never serve the people, especially the Breeds. To go through the courts means we have to go through their routine and play their games, and according to their rules. As far as I'm concerned, that's a total waste of our money, time and energy. We have to move as a mass movement on the outside of government institutions."

"Yes," said Mederic, "everything within the ruling class and government is geared to serve the rich people only."

"Not even the political party system is of any damn use to us," shouted Ed. "It is strictly in the interest of the capitalist class of rulers. The Liberals, Conservatives and Socreds [Social Credit] are the same damn thing. They never make any real changes in the society. Oh sure, funny little things like building more roads, raising the taxes on the people. They don't represent the people. And even if they did, it's strictly impossible to bring about changes in society through a parliamentary system. That's just a big, phoney, farcical circus to make the people believe that changes are taking place. Parliament is strictly in the interest of the ruling fat cats and nothing else. The NDP couldn't even bring about any significant change!"

"Hold on just a darn minute," shouted Mederic. "The NDP are socialists and they stand for helping the poor people, and for real changes."

"But how is that possible?" asked sister Kathy. "We had them for twenty years in Saskatchewan, and what did they do for the Breeds? We were no better off at the end of those twenty years than at the beginning. They're no better than the other parties."

"They brought in medical and doctor insurance, which was the biggest thing that ever happened in North America. Also auto insurance. And they improved welfare," argued Mederic.

"But," interrupted Tony, "those things have never really changed the structure of society. We still have political parties, parliament, a premier and all the White officials in Breed settlements that hold absolute power over us. They are still a bourgeois party, working within the framework of the capitalist system. To be truly socialist, they would have brought in changes for a true socialist society, such as giving the people on the local level more power, not this phoney representation through members of [of legislative assemblies and] parliament. Because these people only work in the interest of the wealthy class, who control the country, and the rich Americans. Again, it's a waste of our time to fool around with partisan politics and elections. Let's not get trapped like all the White people into that nonsense of elections. As Breeds and Indians, we were never seriously involved in them anyway, and why start now? We should work towards a new kind of society."

"Parole or probation is not good enough anymore," said sister Kenny.

"Not even reform. Reform just keeps us quiet. Pacified like a baby with a sugar tit," argued Tom. "Reform keeps the whole bourgeois system in perfect shape. It gives a few crumbs, but never hurts itself."

Tony was elected president.

Tenure Decision

That spring, the college had to decide whether they would give him tenure—a permanent appointment—or fire him. The dean called him into his office one day and said, "Tony, if you'd be interested in going to another campus, we'd be glad to give you excellent references."

"But I don't intend to go anywhere," said Tony. "I'm perfectly happy here." And got up and walked out.

As the weeks went past, he had invitations to seek employment elsewhere. He took his case to the Faculty Association, for there were no professional or academic reasons why he should be fired. It was based entirely [... for] political [reasons], in that he had become a militant, radical leader among the Breeds and Indians, and they claimed he was giving a bad name to the college. Tony argued this was a free society, and he should be allowed to express his ideas without being threatened or fired. He knew this was no free society, but he was using that as an argument since the rulers shouted about the freedom and democracy of Canada.

The board of governors and the college administration used every method, dirty and otherwise, to get rid of Tony, but he fought back. He had some of his Breed brothers and sisters go in and speak to the president of the college, and state they wouldn't accept their brother being fired without taking some action on the matter. Tony was called into the discussion. They would give the most beautiful academic jargon-type of explanations to the Breed people. And they would just pretend they never heard his long tale of rhetoric, and say, "Yeah, that's fine, but if you fire our brother, there'll be trouble around this campus."

Tony had never experienced such excellent guerrilla tactics in all his life. Another time, several of his Breed brothers and sisters, dressed in their roughest outdoor garments, came to the campus and pretended they were surveying the campus grounds for a demonstration or a sit-in. It was a beautiful piece of guerrilla work again.

In the meantime, the Faculty Association fought vigorously for Tony, and were ultimately successful because they got Tony a permanent appointment on the faculty. The dean was outraged when he found out that he had to keep Tony on his permanent staff. But apparently the board of governors felt that they couldn't afford to fire Tony at this point, as he would cause too much trouble. He might even create another Berkeley incident. And Tony was preparing for a final showdown, as he realized that ruling-class administrations are capable of the worst kind of action, and to destroy a person meant nothing to them. But Tony had power—the power of the Indian and Breed nation—and support from the students and faculty, and the news media were anxious to report the bitter struggle between Tony and Redfield College.

Tony always talked things over with Thea, so that their final decisions were mutual efforts. Even though Tony was now on permanent appointment, his positions could never be guaranteed, for he would never draw back from his political activity, and as long as he was involved politically, he was [always in the] grazing danger of unemployment. They could not plan their careers like other people who could plan to settle in one city for years, or work on the same job until retirement. If Tony should slip, or lose his grip for just one minute, the ruling-class administrators would pull the rug very quickly, and he would be looking for a new job. They made no permanent plans. The idea of a pension plan became a joke. They had to plan their retirement privately if they wanted one. But that was unimportant.

Election Campaign at Meadow Lake, Saskatchewan

It was the year of a general Canadian election. Several Indians and Breeds got together and decided to run a Native candidate in the northern constituency of Meadow Lake where hundreds of Native voters lived. There were many important things to be decided immediately.

"What will be our platform?" asked Fern.

"Who or what organization will back our candidate?" asked Len.

"And one of the biggest problems, who will be our candidate?" asked Ed. But Tony realized there was also the problem of money. Where would they ever get money to support them? And there was the organization to the whole campaign, such as lining up speaking engagements, canvassing from house to house!

"Our candidate should run on Red Power," argued Slim, "or at least on Indian Power."

"But it has to be both Indian and Breed power," argued Tony. "I suppose the word Red Power might frighten a lot of people, especially White people."

"Let's just call it Indian-Breed Power."

But the others didn't think the word Breed would be any good for trying to get votes, so it was agreed to call it the Indian-Métis Power program.

"Okay, what are some of the things that we should include in our platform?"

"For a start, I suggest we should argue for the control of our own Native communities. To give the power to the local people," said Tony.

"And improved marketing of fish and furs for the Natives of the north."

"And more beer parlours in the reserves and Métis settlements," joked Tom. "It would probably help to get votes, anyway."

"Rather than argue for better welfare, shouldn't we include a demand for a guaranteed annual income?" Anne argued.

Within a short time they had more suggestions than needed for a good, sound election platform. Now, who for the candidate? Immediately, everyone agreed that it should be Tony.

"No, I don't think it should be me," said Tony. "In the first place, I think my public image is too radical and militant. I would scare away a lot of potential voters. Another thing is that I can do more effective work behind the candidate and platform scene. We should involve as many as possible, rather than concentrating on one—that's what the ruling class wants us to do. Why not Ken, here? He's good in politics, and he's a pretty good speaker."

"But, Tony, I don't think I should because I've been in jail a few times for drunkenness and fighting. As far as I'm concerned, it wasn't my fault, but I was still convicted and served time," explained Ken. "But I'd like to recommend Bob Eagle, sitting across the room."

"I'm in the same damn boat as you, Ken. I've got a jail record, too, and for the same things," Bob explained.

"Well, I guess the quickest way would be to ask all those who have no jail record to put up their hands, so we can see who can qualify," said Tony. Almost all the men stood up, plus three women. Those who remained seated would not run. This sent up a roar of laughter.

"Cryz, we're nothing but a bunch of jailbirds, and not even political prisoners."

"The Liberals at Ottawa have nothing to fear from the Indians and Breeds getting their own political party elected. How'n hell are we gonna get a hundred and thirty three members elected to form the government at Ottawa when we can't even find one?" asked Tony.

"But is that important?" asked Ken.

"No, it isn't, at least not among our people. But it probably is important to the Whites because they don't understand the racism of the police and courts of Canada," explained Bob.

"Okay," said Tony, "let's think about a candidate over the next week. And we'll meet again next Friday night and pick our candidate. Let's hope we've got one to chose from," suggested Tony. "The big question: How are we going to raise money? That is, legally!"

"Who'n hell cares about legally? It'd probably be a helluva lot easier to raise it illegally," suggested Jim.

"Sure, we've probably got some experts right here," added sister Anne.

"Seriously, fellows, let's try the White liberal reformer—small "l"—those types who are always wanting to do something for the Indians and Métis," said Tony. "Let's run a big ad in the city newspapers of Regina, Saskatoon and Prince Albert, asking for donations. Also, we should send out letters with appeals for money from the well-off people, such as professional people, doctors, lawyers, professors. Let's draw up a big list of names."

A committee was formed for each city. Lists were prepared, notices were sent out and big display ads were put in the daily newspapers. A few weeks went by and only a few donations of five and ten dollars came, obviously from workers. In the whole campaign, there was one single donation of $200 from a professor. The committees were frantic. What would they do? There were bills, bills and hundreds of bills to be paid. Tony kept paying out of his own pocket and was soon taking out of his savings. In the end, Tony had to withdraw all his savings of $1,800. He made some serious analysis of the White people and their lack of financial support. He would never depend on them again. He knew they were [not] serious about wanting to help the Natives. At least not in a way they didn't control. It would've been alright if they were in control of the election platform and the candidate. They weren't going to support anything unless it was along their nice, patronizing, paternalistic and racist ways that fitted into the White middle–class system. Obviously they weren't going to put their money where their mouths were. None of the brothers and sisters could pay a cent toward their election, as practically all were on welfare.

The candidate agreed upon was a young Indian woman who had completed her high school and was planning on training for a teacher. She was a good speaker and an able politician. She was a good choice. Tony did a lot of campaigning in the constituency. Bob was the campaign manager, at least until the Mounties kidnapped him.

Forest fires broke out in the north, and the Mounties rounded up several young Indians and Breeds from the beer parlours. In Green Lake, there were many young Breeds lying around town doing nothing, but the Mounties never touched them. Instead, they came over and picked up Bob.

"Get your gear, you've got to come fire fighting," demanded the older Mountie.

"But I'm working on the election. I'm campaign manager," Bob tried to explain.

"That doesn't mean a thing to me. Be ready in two hours when I come back to get you,

or we'll take you to jail," ordered the corporal.

In two hours, they came back and took Bob to fight fires. No one knew where he was taken. Tony was outraged.

"Geez, the pigs, the Gestapo," shouted Tony. "Did they kidnap the campaign managers of the three other candidates in this constituency? Of course not!" He called for a mass meeting in Green Lake to mobilize the Native people for action if Bob wasn't returned immediately. He wired the Prime Minister in Ottawa about this injustice. He got CBC television news interested, and condemned the whole ruling class system as fascist, dictatorial and rampant with racism. He issued a warning that if Bob wasn't returned by the next evening, the other three campaign managers would be kidnapped, except it wouldn't be by the Mounties, and the forests in the north would be kept burning "as long as there was anything left standing." Tony wasn't sure that he could get his brothers and sisters to support these threats, but it was worth a try. The next evening, campaign manager Bob was back home.

"How did they bring you back?" asked Tony.

"They flew me from where I was by plane. I don't know where it was, but it must've been a long way because we flew a long time. Then we put down here in Green Lake, and I walked from the lake," explained Bob.

"The rotten pigs," said Tony. "They got orders from the top to bring back our campaign manager. The government's just like the mafia."

Tony did a lot of campaigning in the White communities, as Bob and Fern worked in the Native settlements since they spoke Cree fluently. Tony encountered vicious racist audiences wherever he went. In his speeches, he argued that it was unlikely their Indian-Métis candidate would get elected. The White people were very fearful of this. They just couldn't accept that an Indian should represent them in Ottawa. It was unthinkable that a savage, a barbarian, should be their representative. What an insult! For they had all the racial stereotypes, and they came out when cornered. They would shout at Tony, "The Indians and Métis are nothing but drunks, lazy, irresponsible people, living on welfare. They won't go and work in the beet fields in Alberta. Instead, they lie around and collect welfare."

Tony asked the man if he had seen the living conditions the Natives have to live in, and the wages they're paid.

"No," he said, "but I have a picture of one here." Obviously, if it was in the beet fields, then it had to be the master's house.

"If the work is so good and pays such high wages, why don't you White people take the jobs then?" Tony asked them.

"But that's Indian [work], not for Whites. It's okay for them because they don't do anything else, and they're not qualified for anything else," the man explained.

These people were using two different standards for working and living when it came to the Indians and Métis. Tony tried to get these people to see their racist attitudes, but it was impossible. He could see that he would never get these people to analyze their racism. It was completely irrational.

Fern ran into trouble with the government officials in the Breed settlement. The only way of communication was through the radio phones that were under the control of the DNR government authorities. These men from the DNR refused to send messages for Fern so that the campaign was seriously handicapped by the fascism of these government despots. And at every public meeting, where it was almost all Natives, the White schoolteachers, priest, and other White people would come and sit at the front, and then insult, intimidate, heckle and disturb Fern so that she would be unable to speak.

At least the election revealed that racism is a serious thing in Saskatchewan and particularly in northern Saskatchewan. It was going to be a big job to wake up the brothers and sisters so they would fight shoulder-to-shoulder with the others already in the vanguard. The White oppressors were stepping up their oppression, and they had all the legal and social machinery and the power to use it on the Natives. The worst part of all this was that the White population really thought these White officials, including teachers, were sympathetic to the Native people, and were trying to help them. In reality, they would help them only as long as they "stayed in their places" as Indians and Breeds. The College of Education may talk all the beautiful language in the classroom to teachers about the "lovely, modest Native children," but in reality, at the Native settlements, these teachers were vicious cops and the brainwashers of inferiorization. To Tony, they were contemptible.

Their candidate, Fern, received six hundred votes, which they considered quite a success.

Would they run a political candidate again? And should it be on one of the established political parties, like the NDP?

"I would object to running on a political party ticket, either the Liberals, NDP or Conservatives," said Tony, "as it would turn away all our brothers and sisters who are opposed to that party. We've had Indians and Breeds elected to parliament over the past many years, and what'n hell have they done for the Native people? Nothing! They have to do what the party tells them. They can't do whatever they want or think will help the Natives. In most cases, they are working for the ruling class that keeps us oppressed. Sure, running our own candidate helps to raise the political awareness among the Indian-Métis nation because of all the publicity we get, and the fact that the racists expose themselves, then our people are able to see who their enemies are. All this is important," argued Tony.

Book Burning at Duck Lake, Saskatchewan

That summer, a big sports day and festival was held by the Indian-Métis nation at Duck Lake. This location was chosen because of its historical importance. In the battle between the Halfbreeds and Ottawa's troops, the Breeds under the leadership of Gabriel Dumont won a battle against [...the North West Mounted Police and the Prince Albert Volunteers] at Duck Lake. It was a gala two-day affair with all sorts of Native sports and social activities.

"I can't understand why we don't have a beauty queen or princess pageant?"

"Because," said Tony, "it's a stupid thing to do, and certainly among the Natives. There was no such thing as titles, social ranks or royalty in the Indian world before the Whiteman came, and there sure as hell was no such thing as royalty among the Breeds. The Whiteman put this phoney notion in our mind and in our world. And we should have enough guts to stop it right now. And why should anybody have prestige in a society simply because of the shape of their body? There's no talent or skills involved in that. That's an injustice to all the others who don't happen to be born as pretty. Should they be condemned because of their god-given appearance? And it's strictly a bourgeois idea. It's purely a gimmick of the ruling class to exploit beautiful women as sex symbols, to promote the sale of their rotten goods, such as cars. And I don't think our girls should prostitute their bodies anymore on skid row or on the advertising market. The White women are opposing these beauty queen contests now, so why should we start on something they themselves are throwing off? It doesn't make sense in any way."

"I disagree. I think beauty queens do contribute something to society with their shapely curves and sexy looks," said Jim.

"Sure, for horny old men like you it gives you some sexual excitement. But shouldn't a new society be looking to something more profound and meaningful than cheap sexy thrills?" asked Bob.

"And I thought I was going to be a judge. Boy, and was I going to look real close," said Slim.

"Somebody ought to nut you!" snapped Jim.

A big fire was burning brightly in the centre of the big baseball diamond in a huge steel drum that had purposely been arranged for this affair. Tony got up and spoke from the platform through the microphone.

"We are now going to proceed with our book-burning session. Those books that have been written by Whitey, and which insult our ancestors and heritage, and which continue to inferiorize our kids in school, should be burned here. This will let the White people and the ruling class know that we have had enough of their hate stories and racist writings. There is no possible improvement that can be made in these books. They are completely racist from beginning to end.

"We can follow in line, and as you pass the mike, name your book, the author and anything else you want to say about it.

"The one I have is considered the daddy of all histories of the Métis. It has a great reputation among the White scholars because it is supposed to be objective. But to the Indian and Métis nation, it is the greatest outrage against us since the massacre of 1885. It is called The Birth of Western Canada by George Stanley."

Tony threw the book into the fire with all the power that hostility could generate, and that was plenty. Everybody shouted in jubilation.

Bob followed next. "My book is by the same author, George Stanley, and it is called The Biography of Louis Riel. It is the worst insult to [Riel] and contains the most vicious lies that could ever be told. Sister Anne followed. Her book was [...] Brother Jim was next with [...] And on and on went the parade of book burning until over thirty books were burning. It was a fire heaped with hostility and hate, the kind of hate that is built up from the moment a Native arrives in Whiteman's world.

A fight broke out a short distance from the fire. A couple of White people became enraged at the book burning and started to condemn the Natives. But the brothers and sisters jumped them right away. Tony rushed over and was pushing his way to the centre, but the police were right on the scene.

"Let'em fight! Let'em fight," a brother was shouting.

Tony would have liked to let it develop into a big fight. The palefaces would've got massacred there. "What a helluva lot of nerve they have, coming to an all-Native celebration and still wanting to push their filthy, racist superiority on us. It's a damn sure thing they've a helluva more gall than sense. Sure, they'll cause trouble in here, and we'll have to take the blame for it. We know how the police act when it's a matter between Whites and Natives."

Thea was pulling on Tony to get him out of the crowd. He could hear shouts of "Dirty Indian racist," "A hatemonger," "A lousy communist," "He's a traitor, like Riel. Hang'im!" Tony knew these shouts were aimed at him. But that's exactly what he wanted, to get the Whiteman riled up, raging mad.

Getting Even With the Mounties

Tony had a chance to get even with the Mounties not long after. Brothers Cliff and Tom called him up and explained they had been followed, searched and humiliated by a Mountie just outside of Saskatoon. If Cliff was telling the truth about the circumstance, it certainly looked like a good case against the Mounties. Tony drove right down and met Cliff and Jack in a café near the Mountie office.

"Now, when the Mountie first stopped you, he just gave you a routine check?"

"Yeah, except he asked about the extra battery in the car on the back seat. Luckily, I had the bill of sale for it or he would've taken me in, right there."

"And then he let you go, after you assured him everything was okay?"

"We never saw him again until just after we stopped in the little town of Estey in front of the garage. He pulled in like a mad driver, jumped out and made both of us lean over the car with our hands held high. Then he searched us right to the skin and down to our boots. It was damn humiliating in front of all those people. They must've thought we were tough criminals. Then he told me to open the trunk of my car. But I told him I lost the key."

"So what'd he say then?" asked Tony.

"He said to damn well open that trunk or he'd put me under arrest and take me into jail immediately. So I borrowed a crow bar from the garage and forced up the trunk door."

"I guess you really damaged it, eh?" asked Tony.

"Yeah, I took it to the body shop, and they said it'd cost a hundred dollars."

"What'd the cop say when he found nothing?"

"Nothing. He just buggered off without saying a thing," answered Cliff.

"Okay," said Tony, "let's go in and ask to see the cop and his chief, and ask for an explanation, and tell them we want all damages paid for."

The corporal in charge of the patrol came to the front office and spoke to the Breeds, but they wouldn't let the cop come out. The corporal took a full report of the incident from Cliff, and said he would look into it. Tony explained that this was a case of discrimination and brutality against the Indian and Métis, and that he wanted an apology in writing.

Cliff, Jack and Tony talked about it after they came out of the Mountie office.

"He's not going to do a damn thing," said Tony. "He's just going to try and protect that smart aleck cop. What would you say if we organized a demonstration of the Indians and Breeds and around this Gestapo office?"

"That's okay with me," Cliff consented. "I agree that the corporal isn't going to do a damn thing."

"Okay, you get as many of your friends as you can, and I'll organize all the people I can. We'll demonstrate tomorrow. Don't tell any more than you have to, as these Mountie boys are liable to cause us more trouble," said Tony.

Tony had all the people meet in the union hall. He told them, "Everybody keep in line behind the other. Don't stop and block traffic. Don't walk on the street, just the sidewalk. If they come out to arrest us, don't resist. We'll get your bail right away, that's all been arranged. Don't engage in conversation with the pigs. We'll parade for exactly one hour and then return here, hopefully."

They took the Mounties completely by surprise. They didn't react to the demonstration because they were entirely disorganized. The inspector was so enraged that he pushed a reporter right out of the building. All the news media were there to report on the situation- radio, TV and newspapers. This would really hurt the great honourable image of the Mounties. Signs read: "Redcoats Unfair to Redskins," "Welcome Mississippi to Sask.," "Pig brutality," "Storm Troopers," "Long live Riel."

The next day, the inspector agreed to see a delegation of Indian-Métis and Whites about this situation. But he was so nervous he couldn't arrange his own seat. The committee wanted a guarantee that the Mounties would not discriminate against the Natives, use brutality or intimidation. And if this happened again, they wanted a public hearing with the Mounties involved. They wanted full retribution for all damages done to the car.

The inspector tried to explain that the two men had criminal records, and they were not picked on just because they were Natives. "Cliff Anderson served a jail term in the Regina jail, and the young Indian boy is up on a criminal charge at this moment," implying [a] grave situation.

Cliff immediately asked, "What was the crime I was jailed for, and how long did I spend in jail?" The inspector hesitated, but Cliff persisted.

"You were in jail for being drunk, and you served a weekend in jail, and that was over

twenty years ago."

"Geez," said Tony, "and that's what you been calling a major crime and criminals with a record. Then ninety percent of the Indian and Métis nation are criminals. And that's why that smart aleck cop took after Cliff and Jack?"

"Yes. He radioed in from his car for information, and we told him they had criminal records," said the inspector.

"Did you say they were dangerous criminals?" said Fred jokingly, sneering.

The committee informed him they would be watching the Mounties from now on, and they would also take this matter up with the attorney general and the Human Rights Commission, and he was expected to do his part in checking his Mountie boys. "We should work towards putting the Mounties under the control of the Indian reserves and Métis settlements," said Tony.

Co-optation of Native Organizations and Leaders

A special meeting was called to discuss the things that were happening in the Indian and Breed world in terms of the Native organizations springing [up] in every province with extensive government grants.

"I think we have to assess these organizations with respect to what they are doing for our people. Is it good or is it bad?" posed Tony.

"Well, I can't see how they can do anything but good, with the big money they get," commented Roy.

"Yeah, some of these organizations get grants of half a million dollars a year."

"And all that comes from the provincial and federal governments. The governments must have a very good reason for paying out that money. They're not doing it because they love the Breeds and Indians," argued Tony.

"It's one way of saying they are doing something for the Native people."

"Yeah, and they get a lot publicity on it, so that they give a good impression to the White people."

"I think we need to look at how they're structured and who's running these organizations, and the things they are accomplishing and the methods they use. For one thing, they are structured exactly like Whiteman's bureaucratic organizations, with a president, vice president, secretary, treasurer and a board of directors. That's no Indian or Halfbreed way of organizing. We have never had anything that highly organized. And when it's organized along Whitey's lines, then there's going to be a lot of thinking and acting along his lines, too," said Tony.

"And that idea of getting representatives elected by the local people and send them to a big central conference is another Whiteman's nonsense," said Tom.

"As well as being damn well bourgeois. If Native organizations are still operating along those lines, then they sure as hell haven't progressed any from their beginning. Anybody

knows how phoney that deal is, and how easy it is to rig or manipulate those representatives' arrangements. My God, we had them here for a while, and it was criminal the way those things were being arranged. Too many Breeds behaving like those palefaces. That kind of phoney [management] doesn't teach our people anything about involvement and participation. It's a trick for manipulation from the top. That's why representative arrangement remains part of the ruling-class system," said Ed.

"But what do these organizations do?" asked Roy.

"Well, they carry out government programs mostly, and act as the government's public relations agent to our people."

"What I don't like," said Tom, "is that they are too damn friendly with the government. Look at those beautiful pictures they display on the front pages of their Native papers, showing their leaders real buddy with the prime minister, the premier of the province and with the minister of Indian Affairs."

"Yeah, hell, they're so loving, it's almost embarrassing."

"And those White pigs are the ones who are oppressing our people and promoting the racists' capitalist system."

"And just listen to their speeches and comments! They're so sickeningly patronizing and bragging the government, it's laughable."

"The leaders are all 'yes men.' They do exactly as the government tells them. In fact, they're so obedient that the government authorities [don't] even have to tell them. They can anticipate the commands before they are ever given."

"They have become the real sweethearts of the ruling class at Ottawa. Notice how these men are promoted so vigorously by the news media, in TV, radio, magazines and newspapers? These people are exceedingly dangerous for our people because they will never become freedom fighters for our liberation."

"Indeed not. They are part of the loving 'establishment' and are the new colonial oppressors of the Indian and Métis."

"They certainly are that, alright, because they are now carrying out government programs which should be rightfully done by government. But the politicians are smart enough to get these organizations set up, choose the leaders, then give them grants of money to implement the racist-oppressive programs, and keeping our brothers and sisters in the same starving ghettos."

"This is bad because these outfits are given so much publicity that the White people think so very much is being done for us, when in reality it is mostly in administration."

"Sure, these organizations and leaders are well known among the White world, but are hardly known among the Native people because the majority of our people are beyond the realm of the news media."

"Yeah, I was told by one of their field workers that the leadership won't even let the workers handle any of the welfare problems because that work is too messy for their organization. That means they've ruled out about eighty percent of our people."

"Two of these Breed 'dandy bureaucrats' spent about five minutes at a meeting in Ottawa arguing over a 'dangling particle.'"

"And they call themselves Métis. That's Whiter than Whiteman could possibly [... be]."

"These so-called leaders are real opportunists. They're interested only in their own ego and selfish interest. There is no place in the Indian-Métis movement for individualism and self-glorification. These people can never be sincere enough or genuine to ever work for the masses."

"Okay, okay, we all agree they're nothing but a bunch of useless tits, but what are we going to do about them and those organizations? Remember, those organizations are well-supported by the government, and also well-protected by the establishment and the news media, and they're all going to support those phonies."

"The whole leadership of Native organizations is entirely reactionary and conservative. In fact, they're so far to the right they make the John Birch Society look radical."

"But they are always shouting off bold statements of protest and defying the government, making them sound so radical and militant."

"But it's all done in such a nice safe place, and where there's no danger of stirring any radical thought or action. Like at a conference in the swankiest hotel in the city."

"And yet the news media give it a lot of play and time, knowing perfectly well it's only hot and stale air."

"I know these organizations and their leaders have refused to give any kind of support to radical or militant Native groups or persons."

"You bet. Behind the scenes they are more oppressive than any government branch has been. That's why they're dangerous. It's the old trick of having slaves rule the slaves. And there's nobody more brutal and cruel than an Indian or Breed slave ruling his brothers and sisters. It's because of the oppression and colonial mentality that has seethed in hostility and hate, and then it is released on his brothers and sisters. We've got to watch out for those fellows."

"And these damn fascist organizations came into their present colonial functions only since we Breeds and Indians started to raise hell here in Saskatchewan on a systematic movement basis for national liberation."

"Sure, the other provincial governments took their lessons from Saskatchewan and said we don't want any trouble with those goddamn Indians and Métis, so let's arrange a new set-up whereby we can get some reliable puppets to rule over the rest. And now there's two or three organizations in every province from Halifax to Victoria."

"Okay, well, do we do anything about them, or just let them run their course?"

"Well, there are two ways to think about it. One is just the way you suggested: Simply ignore them because they don't have any legitimate existence in the Native world, anyway. By that, I mean they are irrelevant and meaningless to the masses. They reach only those very few who have made it successfully in the White middle-class world. The rest of the poverty-stricken masses of Indians and Halfbreeds, they don't even know these organizations exist.

[...] It's possible that the grassroots people are organizing at the local level themselves, but we would never hear from them as all the news is focused on the leaders. Here in Saskatchewan, because our movement is grassroots, we have continuous contact with our people. But another way to look at them is this way: They are the official Native organization for that province. They are registered and administer large sums of money. They are official and legal. The ruling-class government would be very protective and defensive about its neo-colonial Indian departments. They've got nice cozy little arrangements over the masses of Natives, and they'll keep in good order as long as possible."

"But we can't stand idly by and let the government and these 'uncle tomahawks' oppress our people like this any longer. They have to be awakened to the seriousness of their plight, just as we in Saskatchewan have."

"This would mean a direct confrontation with these organizations and the puppet leaders."

"Sure, but I think they're paper tigers, anyway. They'd fold up the moment a little pressure was exerted on them."

"They are the worst enemy of our people, and they will become even worse yet if we don't encourage the people to kick those neo-colonial regimes out of the way and get on with their own people's movement. The masses may need some help at the beginning, but not much. Once they catch on, they can direct and master their own situation."

"They can seriously mislead our people if they are checked into thinking that they can integrate into a racist society—impossible! Or that the masses can succeed if they will only get a good education in a racist school system. To follow their plan would mean the loss of our people and nation in one generation. How dumb can those guys be?"

"But they're having a nice time now, giving themselves nice big salaries of fifteen or twenty thousand a year, plus other members of their families and relatives. Sitting in beautiful luxurious offices with carpet and a couple of personal secretaries, while the masses of our people are living in shacks, on welfare. Some leadership!"

"They conduct their meetings exactly like the palefaces' business meetings and they're always having conferences in the luxury hotels with the top government officials. They're so damn busy doing that trivial stuff they never get to the real meat of movement work, even if they knew how."

"Well, I've been to Native meetings from Nova Scotia to Victoria, and I've spoken to the people from the ghettos and settlements and reserves, and they are plenty dissatisfied, not only with their economic circumstances, but also with their leadership. Our people look to Saskatchewan for inspiration and leadership, and we should be able to provide that to them. They see the impressive impact that we are making on the power structure, and how we're gaining rights and moving towards a new kind of society [...]. Not just tokenism or phoney community development programs. Here in Saskatchewan, we, the people in the ghettos, make the programs and send them up to the government to finance them, and we administer them. With every program goes a full program of political education. Our slogan

is 'Radicalize and mobilize the masses.' We don't want community development programs controlled by the White bureaucrats and politicians. We insist on nothing less than complete and constitutional control of our reserves and Breed settlements through our own council chosen by the local Native people."

The Starvation Issue and Its Consequences

The Canadian Farmers' Union were holding their annual meeting in Saskatoon, so they asked Tony to speak to their delegation. He explained about the extreme poverty of his brothers and sisters, and how they were trying to organize to form a power base, just like the Farmers' Union, from which to operate. They were working in the same way and wanted to politicize the brothers and sisters, and work at the grass-roots level in order to form a broad base for operation. In conclusion, he asked that farmers reconsider their offer to give wheat to the starving people of the world, in order to redirect it to the starving Indians and Métis of Saskatchewan: "My brothers and sisters of Saskatchewan are just as starving as any other hungry people of the underdeveloped countries. We are living in some of the most underdeveloped settlements in the world, and in the most oppressed and apartheid situations in the world."

The next day at the convention, the farmers passed a motion to donate several thousands bushels of wheat to the Native people of Saskatchewan. A committee was immediately organized to look after the distribution of it. The Indian and Métis organizations solicited names from among their own people as to who needed flour and how much. Within a few weeks, much work had been done to get the wheat into the mill and the flour distributed. When suddenly everything came to a halt.

"A permit is required from the Canadian Wheat Board to grist the wheat into flour. No mill can grist it without first having a permit," stated government officials.

"What the hell?" yelled Tony. He immediately wired the federal government authorities and [...] to cut out the damn nonsense. But that was the truth. And even worse, the Minister of Agriculture had refused to grant a permit to the Native people of Saskatchewan. Tony argued permits were granted for poor people of other nations but [not] Canada's own. By this time, the Native committee for the wheat had collected a great deal of information from their brothers and sisters about their extreme poverty. Tony had tracked down very carefully the death of a twelve-year old Breed girl who was supposed to have died of pneumonia. In checking back on all the evidence from the doctors, hospital, nurses, home, there was no doubt about it—she died of starvation. "Cryz Almighty," shouted Tony, "this ruling class at Ottawa tries to make itself as the great humanitarian and benevolent charitable and kind government to all the people of the world, and it has people starving to death right on its own back doorstep. What a vicious fascist bunch of rulers." Tony couldn't see the logic of allowing his sister starve to death while Ottawa bragged about all it did for the poor people of the world, and at the UN. This sounded like a Nazi regime. He wrote to the MP for the northern constituency of Saskatchewan, Mr. Cedoux, and told him the story. He managed to get the news media people interested in the story. He shouted "Starvation."

In the House of Commons Mr. Cedoux raised the issue in Parliament, and immediately a cry went through the nation: "Starvation in Canada." The Liberal government, in power both federally and provincially, were humiliated and fought back to protect their nice, shiny image of affluence to all classes of people. A committee of Liberal politicians was dispatched that evening for Saskatchewan, not to look into the poverty and starvation of the Indian and Breed people, but to publicly show that there was no starvation in the nation, and to prove that Tony Bruce was a liar. And they were successful, mostly because the news media people reported as the Liberal politicians told them.

This phoney committee went into one home in the north and said they did not see starvation, and that was definite enough for a conclusion. It was obvious there was no sense of humanity or brotherhood in these politicians. They were the typical middle-class "niggers" of the establishment, fully aware of their servant duties, racists and oppressors of the most vicious kind. Tony studied them from across the table and concluded, "These men would make Hitler's SS look like kindergarten kids." In their attack on the Native people, he was right.

But the defeat of the wheat and starvation issue made Tony the biggest champion among his own people like nothing else ever did. The ruthless and brutal stamping out of this request wakened the Native people of Saskatchewan like a prairie fire. Likely it was because they were involved in it personally, at least to some extent. They saw how their leader, Tony, was trying to help them out, and how the government and the big bosses worked against them. They knew that it wasn't Tony's fault that they didn't get the permit to grist the flour. More than ever, Tony was entrenched in their minds as a real leader who sacrificed his name for the sake of the Indian and Breed cause. They saw how the ruling power made Tony out as a liar and a fool, but that only endeared him more to the hearts of his brothers and sisters.

Also, the issue of starvation of the Halfbreeds was a mighty touchy and tough statement to make about his people. He felt it had to be told some time, and now was as good as any. It was a tough blow to the pride of many because they knew the White people would only say, "They are starving because they won't work, or they're too drunk, and that is their own fault." And they would have to live with this image, not Tony. But there were many more who were glad to admit they were starving. It was the fault of the Canadian system, not theirs.

Tony argued that, "As long as we are ashamed of our poverty and try to hide it, then we'll always be trapped in that kind of a starvation hell hole. When we admit it to ourselves and to the world, we are then able to say boldly that it is the fault of the system, and not ours, and we want the system changed so that we are not kept near-starvation all the time. Then we will go out and organize and fight politically for a change and improvement. But as long as we try to hide and pretend we're too proud to admit we're on welfare, then we're dead because we'll never do anything politically to change the system, and we'll always be actually where we are today."

The Indians and Breeds stirred right across the province and spoke out so boldly and vigorously that they practically shook the legislative building in Regina.

That summer, Tony was called to Ottawa to present a report on poverty of the Métis of Saskatchewan to the Senate Committee on Poverty. He was glad to have the opportunity to present the economic conditions of his brothers and sisters and argue on their behalf, and to officially condemn the capitalist system. It would be a real pleasure to tell those "fat cat" senators what capitalism is [all about].

That fall, it was decided to hold small group discussions in the local Breed settlements to further their political education. Tony would attend any sessions that were possible. Since he had to teach every day at the college, it was not easy for him to get away from Saskatoon. By now, he had given up an automobile altogether. He argued that it was too expensive, caused too much pollution, and it only made Ford or General Motors richer and it made him too dependent on the establishment. What if he ever came to guerrilla activities and someone stole his car? He'd be like a cripple. He'd be better in a wheel chair. No, he'd learn to get around without a car—ride the bus, train, ride a pony, hitch a ride or walk.

Meadow Lake Discussion About Nationalism

On a weekend in October, a session was held at Meadow Lake and Tony attended. "What topic should we discuss today? We discussed welfare and housing last time. Maybe we should discuss something that is a little more theoretical, rather than the practical things all the time," suggested Tony.

"Well, the one subject we've been interested in, but don't know anything about, is nationalism. We hear you talk about nationalism all the time, and we're not sure what it means," said Tom.

"Yeah, something more than just Canadian patriotism," said Joe.

"I suppose there are many ways of looking at nationalism. We're concerned about Indian-Métis nationalism. By that, we mean what we identify as our culture, things that are particularly Indian and Breed ways, and that are different from the Whiteman's culture. Simply to say that the Redman is beautiful, or that the Indian or Métis is beautiful, is being nationalistic.

"We have declared our pride through our own Native leadership. No longer do we want Whitey to act as our leader. We declare ourselves separate from White Canada in that we don't want assimilation or integration. We will live in our own Indian-Métis nation.

"Nationalism says simply that, as Natives, we will control our own settlements and reserves. The constitutional power shall rest firmly in our hands at the local level, and not in Ottawa or Regina in the hands of the White ruling class. This is known as revolutionary nationalism, and it's the only type of nationalism that we want. But we must always be prepared to fight reactionary nationalism. This is a kind where people go backwards and believe in tribalism and old traditions."

"But isn't that part of our culture, to be proud of culture and to restore our tribal or old ways?" asked sister Anne.

"Yes," replied Tony, "there is nothing wrong reviving the traditional ways, providing you don't make it a kind of religion or cult, and have it serve no other purpose," explained Tony.

"You mean, something like the Black Muslims in the States, or the Doukhobors?"

"Yes, I suppose that would be true. Nationalism must serve the revolutionary cause or the new society that will emerge. For instance, it's okay to restore the powwow, providing it continues to serve a social and political purpose for improving our conditions or working towards our liberation. But if it is a strictly religious thing, worshipping mythical gods, or a ceremony just to come out and wear Native dress, then that is reactionary nationalism, because it is getting people to believe in a type of nationalism that involves and busies all in trifles and nonsense, and that doesn't do anything towards improving the understanding of our circumstances in our colonialism and the way of freedom from it."

"But people in one or the other would dress the same, in their Native clothes, and yet not know whether they stood for reactionary nationalism or revolutionary nationalism," asked Joe.

"That is right," said Tony. "The only way you would know would be through their activities, conversation and understanding, and what they were contributing to liberation. Revolutionary nationalism plays a very important role in our liberation. That is one of its main functions. Once we are free, free from the imperialism of Canada and America, then our Indian-Métis nationalism may disappear. This, we don't know. It sets our culture in motion once again because it has been static or fossilized for so many centuries thanks to Whitey's imperialism. It will help to decolonize our minds, our mentality, and our whole psychological make-up. It fosters a new humanism and opens the doors to a new creation.

"Unless a culture deals with the politics of national liberation, it is worse than useless. It is dangerous, for it can lead our people into blind alleys, thinking they are recreating their genuine Indian and Métis ways of life, but in actuality leading them into bourgeois nationalism, which means greater oppression. It is the collective building-up of our culture from our daily living experiences that makes the kind of nationalism we need. Revolutionary nationalism means freeing ourselves from the domination of the racist capitalists, and the changing of the society to a new system," said Tony.

"Wow, that seems like a helluva lot, and a helluva lot of deep thinking."

"Like our organization is now busy collecting and writing a history of Gabriel Dumont, and will then erect a monument to his memory this summer. That's a form of nationalism. Now, couldn't that be reactionary nationalism?" asked Ted.

"Oh sure, it could be if we didn't watch the direction of it. If Breeds and Indians just dressed like Dumont and made pilgrimages to a Dumont shrine, and made it strictly a religious form of nationalism. But instead, the memory of Dumont will serve as a spearhead to revolutionary action, just as he did in his life. It must give our people a sense of dignity, pride and unity. The monument must stand as a memory to our liberation," explained Tony.

The discussion carried on for hours, going over much of the same material for the sake of clarification. There was a new nationalism stirring in the people. **(TB)**

8. Looking Back and Taking Stock

Howard Adams, Reminiscing After Seeing the Movie *Out of Africa*

I went to the movie *Out of Africa* the other night. Before I went, I had already made up my mind about certain things. That it would be a picture portraying Indigenous people of Kenya as savages, sub-humans. The aristocracy of England would be the dominant ruling class, exploiting the people, their land and animals. It would show a sharp and rigid division between the Indigenous people, their culture, as against the dominant White western colonizers and their particular western way of life. I knew the story was the point of view of the colonizing White WASP and would thus have a very distorted view.

As I sat in the viewing room, trying to enjoy it, enjoying the scenery shots, I tried to get drawn into the story or identify with some character so that I could be involved in the movie. Gradually, the movie stirred my emotions, and I found myself feeling saddened. Soon, a few tears began to flow. But my sadness turned out to be a different notion, and I was sad and weeping about something that I had not anticipated or expected. Slowly, it became increasingly clear to me that I was watching not two different racial groups—the Whites and the Blacks—but I was watching the interaction of two different civilizations, different racial peoples, different nationalities, two very different worlds. So different that they would never come together as an integrated culture. […] The differences were so great and the outlooks were totally different. The totality of character of each culture was so different that it was clearly water and oil. They would never mix, regardless of the Herculean attempts that may be made.

Oh sure, there would be occasional individuals that pass into the dominant White society, but that would make no difference. The masses of the Indigenous people would be condemned to live as inferiorized sub–humans that would be held separately by the Whites. The very fact that Indigenous people have a dark pigmentation—are Blacks—and they are forced into another civilization, a subordinate, racist, powerless and oppressed one, where they would have all the disadvantages.

The story was written by a White woman in 1910, and since that time many wars and many Black Kenyans have been slaughtered. The Mau Mau war was fought, and finally Kenya won its independence. And Kenya is liberated, is its own nation. Its own decision-makers determine its destiny and control its own society and state. It is now a sovereign nation, as equal as England, Holland, Germany. And today there is no mixture. Almost all the colonizing Whites have gone back to their homelands and left the Indigenous people to their devastated land. The few Whites that remained are not Aboriginal or Indigenous people. They can never be that. They have to remain White and western for the rest of their lives and that of their civilization. They can never become Aboriginal people. They would never want to, anyway. So why even mention it?

That in itself was not a surprise, not unexpected. Thus, why weep? It was the expected—it was normal for the time and the situation. But the sadness brought me to the realization that I, like a Black Kenyan, an Aborigine, colonized Indigenous, was also a separate member form the White western civilization. I could never become a member or an integral part of it in any way. I was Indian and that meant I was not part of the western civilization. I did not have the consciousness, the mentality, the soul and heart, the nature, the physiology of the westerner. Although I looked relatively White, and became highly educated in the western universities, and had a career in the western institutions, I was an outsider. And that I had been fooling myself all along for these many years that I was an integral member of that WASP society. I did become legitimated by the mainstream.

My great-grandfather [Maxime Lépine] clearly established the fact that there were two diametrically opposed civilizations and they could never be an integrated or acculturated one. They would have to remain two separate civilizations forever, and that we could not share with each other. We had to go our own separate ways and be our true natures to our particular civilization. In the final war between the White colonizing British and Canadians in 1885, he was one of the main Indigenous leaders against the [assault of] western civilization. He took a firm position that the Aboriginal people had to remain Aboriginal and had to have their land and their nation, liberation and freedom [to determine] their destiny. They could not surrender it, nor could they live

Howard Adams, the Thinker, 1990s. Marge Adams' favourite photograph. Photograph Courtesy—Marge Adams.

as autonomous people. He saw clearly the distinction between these two civilizations and the fact that they had to remain forever as two. He helped organize and lead our people against the colonizing White western oppressor. He understood the situation as millions of oppressed colonized coloured people of conquered colonies saw it, and he fought in the way that he could. He knew that he had to fight with the gun, and he understood that if he didn't kill the White westerner, he would be subordinate captive and treated as a savage for the rest of his life […]. There was no alternative. Either we win our independence from the White westerners or we would be prisoners. He knew the consequences. He made a commitment to himself and to his people. But the western colonizer had already infiltrated our civilization too far. We had allowed subversive agents, popularly called missionaries, to operate as full members and free members in our society, and their ideology had penetrated the perverted minds of some of our people, so that they became collaborators and spies on their own people and worked for the enemy. Our leaders and our society were seriously undermined ideologically and culturally.

As Indigenous people, if we want to remain free from western civilization, we have to fight these White colonizers in the exact same way they war against us: violence, guns, explosives, torture, terror, and guerrilla warfare. That is western civilization. My great-grandfather fought with all these methods. But, unfortunately and tragically, we were to lose the war. My great-grandfather was a hero, a hero whom only we, as Aborigines, understand and feel the pride and the glory for. He was killed. No, not in action! He was taken prisoner by the colonizer and imprisoned in the colonizers' jail for savages who fought against being western captives. They did not even kill him in prison. They could not break his spirit, or his Indianness. Marked on the little wooden peg above his grave are dates of his birth and death. He died from a broken spirit. Three years after release from the colonizers' jail, he was dead as a young man. Dead because his civilization had been killed. He returned home from jail to find that the White colonizers had taken over the Natives' land and resources, and had smashed their nation. Oh sure, lots of Indigenous warriors live after losing a war, and live to fight again. They fight again and again until one day they defeat the westerner and drive him out of their land, or kill him and shove his dirty body off their soil. But he was different. He had fought once. He fought as a leader and a brilliant guerrilla. He fought with all hope and confidence that he and his warriors would win. He had no doubt. He was well acquainted with the westerner, and he knew that he could not live together with the westerner. He fought to kill the westerner or to drive him from his land. He had sensed clearly the sharp boundary between the Aborigine and the westerner, and there was no compromise, no negotiation, and no plural society.

As I sat in the movie and watched how the White Europeans treated, humiliated, tortured and mocked the Natives, I understood why my grandfather had stepped out as a leader, picked up his gun and mobilized, and proclaimed that we will fight till we kill the

Whiteman or until we are killed. There is no alternative. Because, in western civilization, we can['t] be ourselves. We can have our consciousness, though we can never again have our nationality, our loyalty to our nation. But in western civilization we can never be equals. We can only be patronized.

Out of jail and back home in his old neighbourhood, he found his people all driven from their homes, their land. Their houses burned to the ground, their livestock killed. The sight pained him so much that he wished that he had been killed during the battle. The Native people—his old friends and relatives—were, in a sense, still hiding out. Hiding from what? Hiding partly from fear, but hiding largely from humiliation and repression.

In the movie, I wept as I saw a defeated Black native of Kenya walk slowly and painfully across his precious soil to see that the westerners had desecrated the land, the resources and the creatures of his noble land. Those creatures that were precious to him because they are part of his nature, he is a co-creature with them. Now the White colonizers—English, Germans and Dutch—had indiscriminately slaughtered much of those beautiful creatures as sport. The land stank with dead carcasses. The noble Native Kenyan strolled ever so slowly and dejectedly. He stopped and surveyed the extending plains, turning slowly and studying, all ears with studied expressions. He radiated an understanding of the nature of western civilization, and he could never cross over, whether he wanted to or not, or whether they wanted him or not. It could not be done. These are two diametrically opposed civilizations.

Identifying him with my great-grandfather, I wept deeper. I felt the feeling of my great-grandfather. Life is over. I'm dead. In reality, it's just my body that is alive. What caused my great-grandfather's death? No one knows. There are no records. The old timers say that he just quietly slipped away, a saddened and broken man. Everywhere, our people were silent, full of shame, starving, frightened, tortured in soul, disorganized, disorientated. I wept for the agony of my great-grandfather, that he suffered those few years he lived after his prison term. I cried because I hurt from his agony, his suffering. How he must have tried to explain to our people that it is impossible to live as Native people in a western civilization. And how so many of our poor people would not understand because their minds had been screwed up by missionaries. Christianity is the biggest curse, the greatest psychological torture of all aspects of western civilization.

I wept with bitterness when I thought about how I had never heard about the great hero my great-grandfather was, and the noble guerrilla warrior that he had been. A man so courageous, so knowing, so committed. His history was hidden from me. I was as ashamed as all my relatives were of him. I didn't know why, but obviously he had done something terribly immoral. I dared not ask. And he had lain and rotted in that little unknown grave for eighty years before I discovered his greatness and what he had stood for as leader of Native people.

And as I ran back over the trail of my life, I realized the hideous things that I had done, in some ways that had disgraced the great deeds of my great-grandfather. I was horrified to think that I had not come to understand earlier in my life that there are two very different civilizations, and that I had walked between the two of them for years without noticing the crossovers. **(MISC)**

I had lived the first twenty-two years of my life as an Indigenous person. I was born to Halfbreed parents in a Halfbreed ghetto that I never left, even for a visit, even for a full day. I lived fully and totally inside my Aboriginal ghetto for more than nearly eight thousand days without knowing the outside, without associating with the western civilization. **(AB)**

Part Two

MEMORIES

OF HOWARD ADAMS

BY HIS CONTEMPORARIES

Let Me Tell You[1]

Marge Adams

Let me tell you about the Howard Adams I knew. We first met in the fall of 1953, as new members of the UBC (University of British Columbia) Players Club—a fun loving group of would-be thespians who loved to party. Howard and I were cast in the same play that fall. I can't remember the title, but Robertson Davies wrote it. Howard played a citizen of Rome and I a chick (as in "chicken"). My only spoken words were "peep peep peep."

Our dramatic endeavour soon blossomed into romance. This glamorous person with the wavy black hair, natty moustache and unforgettable voice enthralled me. He declared his love for me on our first date. I wasn't quite that impulsive. Our relationship soon developed into a very close and loving partnership. Of course, there were the usual misunderstandings and tiffs, but Howard was an excellent conversationalist and could be very persuasive. He could always smooth troubled waters.

Two years after we met, Howard needed a change from his counselling job at the Vancouver School Board, and chose to take up teaching. Once he was accepted into the Ontario College of Education (OCE) at the University of Toronto, he sold his prized maroon-coloured Pontiac and we rode the CNR east.

Toronto was a very conservative city in 1957, especially at such institutions as the OCE. It is hard to believe today, but unmarried couples living together could result in expulsion from the college. So, the fact that we were not married remained a deep, dark secret. I have always thought that that trial period was one reason why our marriage was so successful. We learned to respect each other and cooperate, knowing that neither of us was legally bound to the other, and therefore free to leave the relationship at any time.

Once the second term had begun, we were convinced that we were right for each other and wanted to make the relationship permanent. So we were married very quietly on Saturday, February 9, 1957 at Glebe Road United Church. Since we had no close friends in Toronto and did not want to reveal our secret (and thus disclose that we had been living together unmarried before), the church secretary and the custodian witnessed our signatures. After the ceremony, we went out for coffee and then rode the subway back to our bachelor suite. We often chuckled about the quiet simplicity of our wedding. To have eluded all the trappings of society's demands on a traditional wedding was very satisfying.

Howard was a wonderful marriage partner. He believed in and practiced gender equality. Fortunately, our basic values were very close, even in the early years. There was never any question about each of us pursuing his or her interests independently. Our careers—I am a teacher and librarian—required much time and energy, and sometimes

---

[1] This is the text that Marge Adams wrote for the memorial service held for Howard Adams at First Nations Longhouse at the University of British Columbia in Vancouver on November 9, 2001. At the time, she was unable to give this speech. We are grateful to her for letting us include it here.

extended periods apart. But such separations only sweetened the time that we were together.

There are many adjectives that come to mind when I think about my husband— loving, kind, patient, hardworking, helpful and exciting come to mind. He had an exuberance for life that was extremely attractive. I remember so often how, when we were entertaining, a room full of people would gradually quieten down and everyone would be focused on Howard. Whatever he was talking about seemed to be more exciting. But I must admit that he was not the best host in the world. He was always the designated bartender, but the wine glasses would be empty and forgotten. Old friends soon learned to help themselves. At the dining table, Howard was so concentrated on discussion that the serving dishes, filled with food, would halt when they reached his place at the table. But his end of the table was always filled with the liveliest conversation, and I was probably the only one concerned about the ignored dishes of food.

I was indeed blessed to have this person as my closest friend and partner for so many years.

In closing, I would like to move to a more serious topic. In recent months, Howard was very concerned about the phenomenon of globalization, which he saw as an expansion of the capitalist system leading towards world domination by the corporate elite. He was concerned about the masses of people whose very survival is in jeopardy. The present so-called war on terrorism would have him more determined than ever to work towards the overthrow of our present economic system that exploits all people, particularly Aboriginal people.

I'm hopeful that Howard Adams' legacy will inspire others to join the struggle for the equality of all people.

The Old Farm

Marge Adams

No place had a greater impact on Howard Adams' life than the farm where he grew up in St. Louis, Saskatchewan. During the forty-eight years that Howard and I were together, I doubt that a week passed without him referring to the "old farm." He never tired of relating stories of people and events from those early days.

The prairie climate, with its hot, dry summers and bitterly cold winters, made him very aware of the changing seasons, and his emotional state was closely tied to the weather. Although he lived for many years on the West Coast, where the weather is mild, a seasonal gloom would descend upon him as the summer days shortened and fall arrived. He found the dark days of winter so depressing that he always located his desk in the sunniest area of our home and then installed additional bright lighting. The days that he most enjoyed were those when the sun shone and the trees were bursting into blossom. "Wouldn't it be great," he would say, "to spray the trees with glue so the flowers would stay forever?"

The Adams' farmhouse was located just a few yards from the South Saskatchewan River bank. One can easily imagine Mrs. Adams fearing for her children's safety, and frequently reminding them of the dangers of going near the water. That is probably why Howard rarely swam or sailed. On the rare occasion when he did go into the water, he was careful to avoid venturing beyond the shallow areas. However, once, while we were bathing in California, Howard suddenly realized that he could no longer touch bottom. Panic immediately set in and he started sputtering, choking and sinking. Fortunately, an attentive lifeguard was at poolside within seconds and pulled him out.

One of the greatest motivators in Howard's life was the grinding poverty that he experienced in rural Saskatchewan during the Depression. It not only filled him with powerful resentment against people in high places, but it created in him a determination to free himself from poverty and change the system that caused so much suffering. In his mind, a combination of hard work and education was the only way to accomplish these goals.

There were two people instrumental in getting him started on the path to success, his mother and his grade school teacher. In spite of their extreme poverty, Olive Adams made her home a loving, caring place for her children. She wanted the best for them, and when her younger son showed interest and ability in his schoolwork, she provided plenty of encouragement. Although there were always chores waiting to be done on the farm, she made sure that Howard attended school regularly and had time and space to do his homework assignments. Howard was deeply distressed by his mother's passing in her early fifties, and blamed her untimely death on the deprivation and poverty that she endured most of her life.

Gerrond School, a one-room schoolhouse located four miles from the farm, was where Howard received his first nine years of schooling. Mr. W. C. Lovell, his teacher for all of those years, had a profound influence on him. Through Mr. Lovell, whom Howard greatly admired and respected, he gained the desire, confidence, skills and knowledge necessary to complete high school and go on to university.

The last person I'd like to mention is Mederic McDougall. "Uncle Mederic" was a role model for Howard from his earliest years and throughout his life. Mederic could fill a room with his energy. He had an enthusiasm for life that far exceeded that of most people. He earned his living through physical labour, first by working on neighbouring farms, and later by grading and snow ploughing the roads for the Municipality of St. Louis. In order to feed his family in hard times, he would hunt on horseback. These experiences provided exciting material for the fascinating stories that he told so well. Mederic, who described himself as a French/Roman Catholic/socialist, spent much of his life educating and politicizing his Métis community in the hope of bringing about an improved quality of life. In 1986, Mederic was recognized for his years of dedication for his people when he was awarded *The Order of Canada.*

Howard Adams achieved great success during his lifetime. Perhaps this success was not gained in spite of his humble beginnings, but because of them. Granted, he was blessed with many fine characteristics: a splendid speaking voice, strong body, personal charisma and a good mind. But without his early years on "the old farm," I believe that he may not have developed the other qualities necessary to become a successful public speaker, writer, Métis leader and professor. I'm grateful, as well as proud, to have shared his wonderful life.

Howard Adams[1]

Rose Richardson

Today, we celebrate the life of a visionary, activist and scholar. Howard Adams spent the majority of his life in the pursuit of justice for his people, and to do this he went to extraordinary lengths. Howard, however, was a down-to-earth man. Sitting around the table, drinking coffee, we generally told stories and, at times, made up funny stories, usually at someone else's expense. Howard was no exception. One of the strengths of the Métis people is our ability to laugh at ourselves and make jokes about each other.

The following was told by Mederic McDougall about Howard's attempt at farming, and why Mederic was so happy that Howard went on to further his education, instead. Howard went from door-to-door every day, selling fresh milk. Long ago, fresh farm milk was sold without running it through a separator, and the milk that Howard delivered had about two inches of cream in the bucket. One day, the cows did not produce as much as normal, and he was a bit short of making an extra gallon. Howard felt that he had a way of dealing with this—he added a bit of water to the milk. No one seemed to complain, so the next day, he added a little more water. One day on his sales route, someone asked him, "Howard, every day when you delivered milk, it had about two inches of cream on top. How come there's only one inch now?" Immediately, Howard knew that relying on farming as an income was too risky, so he decided to further his education instead!

Later, Clovis Regnier told us that Howard failed at farming because he had such a little tractor. When I saw Howard, I told him that his farming failure was due to the fact that he had purchased a small tractor. The size that Clovis had described was the size of a toy tractor.

Leaving Saskatchewan to pursue an advanced education, Howard went to university in Berkeley, California, and was there during much of the student unrest during the

---

[1] This is the text of a speech given by Rose Richardson at the memorial for Howard Adams in Saskatoon on September 20, 2001.

60s. Upon his return to Canada, he brought many new ideas that he had developed as related to the organization of the people and motivational education.

In his public speaking, he was exuberant, and used all parts of his body to make his points very clearly. You had to watch as well as listen to get the full impact of his speeches.

Entering the world of political activism, Howard made numerous trips to many remote areas, including Green Lake, and was able to attract audiences of several hundred people within an hour to hear him speak. He taught us how to set up communication lines in order to create an awareness of the many issues that affected the lives of Métis, and other oppressed people. At one point, he even got the Farmers Union (of Canada) and the Aboriginal people to stand together in a common cause.

He knew that all his activities were being monitored due to the unrest throughout the nation in respect to farm unrest, the FLQ (Front de libération du Québec) and unrest in both the Aboriginal and non-Aboriginal communities. So he set up a word communication code system. Radiograms were common in the north, although there were a few phones. Howard would call us about upcoming meetings, sit-ins, etc. We would send out radiograms with two words, "Pac Sac," to key individuals, who, in turn, would relay messages in their assigned areas.

Talk about government confusion and frustration! Like, is that all? When you sent a radiogram, you paid by the word, but the person receiving the message knew that within a day or so someone would be picking them up for an important meeting.

In the 1960s, Howard, along with other Métis, formed a provisional government. As he stated, "We will be the vanguard against oppression!"

Howard Adams was an individual who did not need to use politics or political office to provide for his income. When he attended meetings in far-flung places, he did not require per diems or accommodation funding. He would stay with friends, of which he had many, and he felt that the issues he was promoting were more important than a means of earning a living.

He was always able to obtain employment outside the political arena to support his family and the cause, thereby allowing him to focus his attention on dealing with the issues at hand.

When he was fairly new in his position at the University of Saskatchewan, an attempt was made to scale down university staff in order to get rid of Howard. A group of concerned Métis met with the president of the university, threatening to grind the university to a halt if they should fire Howard!

The plan was that I'd walk into the office and check if the dean was in. I walked in as a shy, timid Métis woman and asked if the dean was in. The lady at the desk informed me that he was, but that I needed an appointment.

"Do you wish to make an appointment?"

I said, "Wait!"

I walked over to the door, opened it wide and waved at everyone to come in. We walked straight past the secretary, and into the dean's office.

Howard was called into the dean's office and was asked, "Who are these people? Are they serious?" Howard stated that we were very serious!

On that day, the university guaranteed his contract.

Howard had a strong personality. It is easily understood that such a strong personality as his needed a very strong and supportive woman to stand beside him. Marge has shared her strength with Howard for most of their lives, and must be given a great deal of credit for any of the achievements that may be looked at as his. It has only been through such powerful partnerships that balance and accomplishment came about.

In terms of politics and leadership, Howard learned early on that politicians holding office are often restricted by having to follow agendas that are created to reflect "party lines". While he did, at times, hold elected office, his contributions to society were more often made in his role as an educator, researcher and writer. As well, he felt that if politicians remained in office too long they would lose touch with the people whom they were elected to represent.

He recognized that it was through grassroots efforts that real changes could be made. Howard was an organizer and a planner. His research abilities and his gift for writing enabled him to bring heroes and role models to our attention. He raised to national and international awareness the plight of Native people, always stressing the importance of bringing the oppressed and Third World people together to stand against oppression. The powers that be recognized the impact of his work and strategically divided the Aboriginal peoples into various distinct groups, with specific funding that we were intended to fight over. It is sad that many Aboriginal groups continue to fight over "soft dollar" funding to this day, and that financial issues continue to keep us divided.

As a result of Howard's great insight into the plans to divide us, he was sent into exile by his own people. He left Saskatchewan and moved to California, and, ultimately, British Columbia, where he continued to attempt to educate the public in matters that were closest to his heart.

Materials written by Dr. Adams have been included in various curriculums, and will continue to educate and motivate people concerned with the betterment of life for all people.

The spirit that inhabited a man such as Dr. Howard Adams cannot be extinguished, and will continue to dwell amongst those who strive for a better life for his people and for all people.

About five or six years ago, Howard made his last visit to Green Lake. We had, at the time, many stories going around about one of our Native politicians, who was being charged with sexual harassment. I was acting really appalled by these stories.

Howard looked me straight in the face and said, "I wish they would charge me with rape! Cripes, at my age I'd go to court and plead guilty, regardless of whether I was guilty or not. And I would not allow medical evidence or Marge to try to prove otherwise!"

There were many questions, in Howard's mind, regarding the disappearance of a Métis leader, James Brady, and the leadership loss of Lionel Deschambault. Today, he knew what happened, but it still remains a mystery to us.

When my former husband, Rod Bishop, had kidney failure and lay dying in the hospital, with medical bills as high as the hills, who called to help? Howard sent me over a thousand dollars to pay for Rod's medical needs. Who called to check if I was okay? Howard did. Howard *cared*!

The day before Howard's passing, all we talked about was Howard. There was a need to talk to him. I met his sister, Isla, and we talked about Howard in a general manner, but I failed to call him. I failed to check. Marge, we won't do that to you. No man or woman need be forgotten. He didn't deserve it, and neither do you.

Thank you, Marge, for bringing Howard home.

We love you!

Thank You!

He Could Have Been Successful in Almost Anything
Craig Oliver

I met Howard in the 60s at a Native event at which they were outlining some of the problems that Indians and Métis had and have in Saskatchewan and elsewhere. I was impressed with his intelligence and his drive, and especially with his single-minded commitment to the cause. Howard was a charismatic guy in any league. He was also strong on television. He was well-trained in the art of the news-bite, long before a lot of other people were.

While all that about Howard impressed me, my own background also leaned me toward liking Howard because I'd grown up in northern British Columbia with Native people. My best friend, with whom I lived together for a year, was a Tsimshian Indian, and when I started reporting in the Prairies, I was shocked at the state in which Aboriginal people were living. I was shocked at how little at that point Canadian governments were doing for them, and how badly organized Aboriginal people were then to defend themselves.

The issue of Red Power was being raised in the States, and the FBI was all excited about it. Howard was picking up on a lot of the same verbal cues and the same kinds of issues. He was warning society that this whole thing could explode if Canadian governments did not get a handle on it. He was right, of course. And Canadian governments did take on Aboriginal issues in a big way. They may not have gone as far as people wanted them to, or as far as they should have, but Aboriginal affairs is a major issue on the Canadian agenda now. And I think that Howard had a lot to do with that.

He scared the hell out of the Mounties, who followed him all over Saskatchewan. I'm sure they bugged his phone. They must have on their files any number of phone calls between Howard and me, as he would advise me when he had an upcoming event, and I would make a judgement about whether to cover it or not.

At the time, I belonged to a social club to which a number of Mounties also belonged. It was a shooting club, for pistol and rifle shooting. So, I got to meet a number of these folks socially. And then, occasionally, I would see them at some of Howard's events, hiding behind a newspaper, wearing old clothes, or otherwise trying to look casual, as if they were just ordinary citizens.

At one occasion, one of them asked me whether I thought Howard was a threat, and I said, "Absolutely not!" I did not think Howard was a violent man. I know he wasn't, and I told the Mountie that. And I was glad to tell him that because I was telling him what I believed about Howard. And somewhere, I'm sure, there is probably a RCMP file which has me down as an informant. But it was the only such conversation I ever had. It wasn't a case of being called into headquarters, but of being at one of these social occasions and one of these Mounties pretending to ask me just "causally" about Howard Adams, knowing that I had seen a lot of him.

I covered many of Howard's events, and since that time I must have covered more than five thousand stories. So it is hard to remember any specific events, but I do remember one, though, at which Howard positioned two axes in a sort of cross, and we had a shot of Howard through these axes. That upset a lot of people, and Howard loved it! It was somewhat editorial in the sense that it suggested, "If you don't deal with this problem, you may have some similar problems as are happening with AIM (American Indian Movement) in the United States."

This was before CSIS (Canadian Security Intelligence Service) existed. Those were the RCMP security guys, whom I found to be neither a particularly inspirational nor very bright lot. So I agreed when that famous commission recommended getting rid of the RCMP Intelligence Operation. It was not intelligent! And when they sent Howard to Rockcliffe, Ottawa, as he mentions, it seems possible that they may have wanted to use Howard as an agent within the Indian and Métis movement. But I have no idea. There are so many other things here that they may have been training him for, like drugs. But if that's what they were trying to do, it sure did not work because I know that they were very worried about Howard and kept a very close eye on him. He also really upset the Saskatchewan government, who did not like to have to admit about the state Indians and Métis were living in.

I had a very high regard for Howard. He also had a sense of humour. He could have been successful at a lot of things. I think he was successful in drawing public opinion to what was then, more so than now, a crisis in Aboriginal and Native affairs. And I am sure that would satisfy him. But if he had gone into business or media, he could have been successful in almost anything. He was bright and he was a good scholar, too. But I am a reporter, and scholars don't impress me.

An Appreciation of the Late Howard Adams

Ron Bourgeault

When I learned (a week later) of Howard Adams' sudden death on September 8, 2001, it left me with a deep feeling of emptiness. I felt empty because, for that week, I had been following the news coverage of the attack on the World Trade Center in New York City, which coincidently occurred three days after Howard's death. Already, one could see the rise of reactionary nationalism in the United States, and that it was going to be directed with a vengeance against the Third World. The death of Howard Adams, a Métis Marxist intellectual and anti-colonial activist, represented to me the passing of a generation in Canada of left-wing Native activism at a time of growing reactionary sentiments towards Native peoples.

I first met Howard in the early 1970s, when we were both active in the then-Métis Society of Saskatchewan and the "Waffle wing" (left formation) of the New Democratic Party. Over the years, we did not maintain a great deal of contact for no other reason than that physical separation and because broad political directions absorbed our energies. The last time that I had personal contact with Howard, apart from the odd telephone conversation when I happened to be in Vancouver, was in 1996, when he was touring Saskatchewan to launch his latest book, *A Tortured People*.

Over lunch, we talked about the growing social racism, and manipulations by the federal government of the self-government issue, particularly as a product of New Right direction adopted by all levels of government. While Howard had no sympathy for the exclusivist and narrow nationalism expounded by the official state-sponsored Aboriginal leadership, at the same time he saw it as a logical consequence of a long ongoing policy of state-cultivated identity politics and control of Aboriginal national self-determination and marginal economic development. Without reading into Howard's thinking, my sense is that he saw the current self-government issue as intricately part of the overall New Right agenda of dismantling universal social policy rights, fractionalizing the country into regions and throwing labour and wages, with reduced regulation, into the operation of the free market, in which self-governing areas would be a part. In this reworked arrangement, the treaty would become the new Indian Act and political conduit of suppression.

As a political person, Howard Adams did not emerge in a vacuum, nor was he personally isolated from radical history. Howard could trace his family heritage to Ambrose and Maxime Lépine, who, along with Louis Riel in the tradition of radical 19th century liberalism, were leaders in the Métis agrarian rebellions of 1869-70 and 1885 for liberal democracy, national self-determination and liberation from colonial capitalism. Originally from the Métis community of St. Louis, Saskatchewan, Howard, after a brief stint in the RCMP, found his way in the early 1960s to the radical Berkeley campus of the University of California. While there, he was exposed to the thinking of Third World Marxists and nationalists who were applying Marx's ideas of historical materialism and class struggle to Third World national liberation. At Berkeley, Howard formed his basic ideas about class-based radical nationalist politics as a means of liberating historically colonized Aboriginal peoples from class and racial oppression within an advanced capitalist Western society.

After completing his doctorate at Berkeley, Howard returned to Saskatchewan in the late 1960s. Once back, he became active in Métis politics, connecting with the then-Métis Association of Saskatchewan and the legacy of Jim Brady and Malcolm Norris. Brady and Norris, as Marxists influenced by the CCF and the CP (Communist Party of Canada), had been organizing the Métis going back to the 1930s in Alberta. Not surprisingly, Howard's ideas of class and national struggle were not greatly different from those practiced by Brady and Norris. What was different was the context in which they now operated. The 1960s and '70s were a period of profound social and economic transformation in Canada, arising from the expansion of monopoly capitalism and associated social and economic policies by a moderate Keynesian welfare state. For Indian and Métis peoples, it meant that they were subjected to liberal policies of reform, which, to a degree, changed the circumstances in which they lived, but did not address the fundamental historical cause of their inequality within the then unfolding capitalist economy and society.

In northern Saskatchewan, the Indians and Métis were gradually freed from two centuries of exploitation and servitude as trappers by backward commercial capitalism and associated institutions like the Christian churches. In turn, and in a somewhat similar fashion, southern Indians and Métis were released from the formal and informal policies of Social Darwinism—the segregated development by the federal and provincial governments imposed since the rebellion of 1885. Overall, the great majority of Indians and Métis were formally proletarianized and unequally incorporated into the wage labour market, constituting, in the process, an impoverished and marginally employed labour force.

Over these years, in the midst of great reform, what was at one time state-sanctioned and -administered racism gave way to state-supported social racism, all of which created profound inequality between Indians and Métis and the surrounding white population. To Howard Adams, this transformed social state was the basis of a new colonialism and national oppression in the post-WWII period.

Against this background of profound change and continuing class and racial inequality, a generation of radical activists emerged from the overall White and Native population. Many of whom were rooted in the experience of class oppression and, in conjunction with opposition to the Vietnam war, called for a new internationalism for the world and socialist order for Canada. It was in relationship to this overall social movement that Howard Adams and other Indian and Métis activists, like Rod Bishop, positioned their activism with the Indian and Métis people. As a socialist, Howard, as did Bishop, broadened his base of activism by joining the left-wing of the New Democratic Party (called the Saskatchewan Waffle), which was where much of the 1960s new social movement was crystallizing with students, trade unionists and farmers.

In a series of popular initiatives, Howard attempted to forge a link between broad-based Native activism and the larger New Left social movement in the Waffle, including farmers and trade unionists, all the time trying to bridge the gap between racial oppression and class consciousness. No different than Brady and Norris before him, Howard saw the necessity that in order to advance the nationalist struggle, there had to be a united class basis to overcome the racial divide. For no fault of his own, these initiatives did not necessarily take root. The difficulty was that the labour movement was racially divided, which made the task of mobilizing a broader class movement difficult. In part, these difficulties were augmented by the fact that trade unionism and the working class were being transformed by the welfare state, from class-based unionism, with the politics of class struggle, to business unionism and the politics of economism. The state had intervened into society to gain control over and diffuse as much as possible all forms of class conflict. This included Indian and Métis and trade unions.

Perhaps Howard's hardest fight came over the independence and integrity of the Métis political organization. Social unrest amongst Indians and Métis precipitated both the provincial and federal governments to initiate funding of all Aboriginal political organizations. Howard was a staunch opponent of any state influence let alone control over the political organizations.

With government funding came the politics of opportunism and compromise, which was not necessarily in the peoples' best interests. This was a fight that Howard lost. Harassed and isolated by the government-funded leadership and their allies in the new Métis Society of Saskatchewan, Howard was driven into political exile in the United States. From that point on, all political organizations came increasingly under the control of the federal government.

To the very end of his life, Howard remained a committed Marxist, socialist and internationalist. In his last book, *A Tortured People*, Howard steadfastly believed that new struggles would emerge in the future to justify the socialist alternative to capitalism and its bellicose imperialism. He consistently emphasized the particularity of the Aboriginal struggle and the importance of linking it to broader (class) struggles, nationally and internationally, against world capitalism. Howard's early ideas of the dialectical relationship of culture and class to the national struggle for liberation from capitalism by colonized peoples were refined over the years. Drawing upon his experiences in Saskatchewan, he saw locally-based struggles, where all contradictions are reduced, as the starting point for creating a revolutionary consciousness. Linkages, in turn, could only truly come about when, in the greater racial divide, both parties, in terms of their political development, would come to see the other in themselves.

If one were to assess Howard's thinking over the years, what he was doing was excavating Marxism from the doldrums of what can be called metaphysical economism or dogma, to which the old as well as the post-WWII New Left degenerated. From my experiences, the Left in North America refused to see the relationship of the Aboriginal struggle with the greater class struggle, something that Howard constantly strove to bring about. That blindness, unfortunately, is just one of the Left's failings. While Howard continued to analyze and explain the national struggle in terms of the dialectical relationship between the colonized and greater working class within a changing society, many of the New Left returned to liberalism, with its cynicism, identity politics and the current New Right intellectual fashion of post-modernism.

It can be said, in looking back at Howard Adams' life of political activism, that it was a life well-lived.

Being Howard's Officemate at the University of California-Berkeley

William Johnson

Dear…,

Carol told me of your interest in Howard Adams. I responded joyfully that I had known Howard in Berkeley. But when I scoured my memory, I could find nothing that would be of interest to you.

For a while, we shared an office in Tolman Hall at the University of California (UC) at Berkeley. This was during the 1963-64 academic year, my last year at UC. The way I can date it is that we were there together the day John F. Kennedy was shot. I remember talking with him about it. But what did we say? I can't remember a word. I don't even remember who told who about it, or how I or he found out about the shooting. I only remember the shock, and sharing it with Howard.

The reason I can recall so little is that we were living in entirely different worlds at Berkeley. I was in the Sociology department and was president of the Sociology Graduate Students' Union. I was working halftime as a research assistant. And I was living with a woman and had just had (in April, 1963) a son.

Howard, as I recall, was in the Education department. I knew that we were both from Canada. But other than that, I really knew nothing about him. I didn't even know until years later that he was Métis!

He was big, handsome, jovial. I have a vague memory that he was much interested in women and successful as a womanizer. But I can't remember a single specific detail. He always seemed in good humour and we laughed often. I was skinny and full of anxiety. Our relationship was entirely superficial, made up of cordial greetings and small talk. We never spoke about our preoccupations, our lives away from Tolman Hall, our past lives or our objectives for the future. I was intense and, while at Tolman Hall, I would be engrossed in my studies.

So you can see that I "knew" Howard the way you might "know" someone whom you saw fairly often on the bus as you traveled to work, but without ever sharing true confidences.

Best of luck in your research. I will be most interested some day to read the result of your work.

Howard Adams and the Revival of Métis Nationalism

James M. Pitsula

Howard Adams played a pivotal role in Saskatchewan's history, especially in the revival of Métis nationalism that occurred in the 1960s and '70s. Both a thinker and a man of action, he helped reshape the relationship that exists between the Aboriginal and non-Aboriginal citizens of the province. His book *Prison of Grass* (1975), a penetrating analysis of colonialism and its effects, can still be read today for insight and illumination. But Adams was not content merely to write about the problems that he saw around him—he entered the political fray and gave practical leadership. Confronting an uncomprehending Saskatchewan government, he succeeded in reorienting Métis policies away from subordination and assimilation to cultural pride and self-determination. A new paradigm based on Aboriginal rights replaced the old colonialist regime.

A number of factors came together in the 1960s to create an environment conducive to Aboriginal activism. The civil rights movement was underway in the United States, and the Quiet Revolution had taken hold in Québec. Around the world, former colonies threw off foreign rule and claimed their independence, while university campuses in North America and elsewhere were alive with student power and political protests. The anti-poverty movement drew wide support both in Canada and the United States. At the same time, demographic pressures gave new prominence to Métis and First Nations issues, particularly as the birth rate increased and large numbers of Aboriginal people moved from rural areas to seek economic opportunities in urban centres.

The Saskatchewan government led by Liberal Premier Ross Thatcher established an Indian and Métis branch within the Department of Natural Resources in 1965, the purpose of which was to accelerate the process by which Indians and Métis became "an integral part of Canadian society."[1] The main focus centred on job placement, with little attention being paid to other issues, such as education or counseling. Howard Adams called for a more comprehensive approach. He said that Métis people had a growing awareness of and pride in their distinct identity. They were not willing to be aggressively assimilated. A policy based on placing them in jobs, without any acknowledgement of their culture and values, was doomed to fail.[2]

Adams based his critique on a thorough analysis of colonialism that he developed as a student at the Berkeley campus of the University of California, where he completed his doctorate in 1966. He was struck by the parallels between the experiences of African Americans and those of Aboriginal Canadians. Both groups faced social discrimination, economic oppression and political powerlessness. While at Berkeley, Adams had the opportunity to attend a lecture given by the African-American leader, later martyred, Malcolm X. The words struck a chord, and Adams later wrote, "The ideas he expressed about black nationalism were so important that I could not put them out of my mind. I kept trying to fit them into the Indian/Métis situation at home. Nationalism seemed to be the spirit that motivated black people to a new sense of pride and confidence. Like the black people, I began to reject my feeling of inferiority and shame, and to become proud of my Indian heritage and native nation."[3]

Struggling to come to grips with this insight and integrate it into his worldview, Adams wrote *Prison of Grass*. He argued that the Europeans who had come to North America in pursuit of economic gain had reduced Aboriginal peoples to a subordinate status so that they could be exploited as cheap labor. The racism that originated in the fur trade had become deeply entrenched in Canadian society, permeating the institutions of government, church, school and the courts. Images of white superiority were inescapable in movies, television, books and the cultural media. First Nations and Métis children internalized negative perceptions of themselves, which led to feelings of shame and self-hatred.[4] Aboriginal people were not even allowed to have their own history. Adams recalled that, as a young boy, he and his friends were never told about the Métis heroes of the 1885 Resistance. Their parents and grandparents were too ashamed to claim their own history. The schools taught the language, literature and history of the colonizer, forcing Aboriginal students "to deny their language, culture and essential being." This led to what Adams called the inculcation of the "white ideal," the tendency

---

[1] Saskatchewan Archives Board [SAB], J.R. Barrie Papers, R-10 VII 53b, W. Churchman to John Cuelenaere, 22 March 1965.
[2] SAB, Cy MacDonald Papers, R-64 VI 151, Inaugural meeting, Saskatchewan Task Force on Indian Opportunity, 9 August 1968; Saskatchewan Task Force on Indian Opportunity, 13 September 1968.
[3] Howard Adams, *Prison of Grass: Canada From the Native Point of View* (Toronto: General Publishing, 1975), p. 176.
[4] Ibid., pp. 3, 5, 8, 9.

for Indians and Métis to seek validation through acceptance in white society. Everything white was considered beautiful and valuable; everything non-white was judged ugly and unworthy.[5]

A central tenet of Adams' thought was that the colonialism of Canada's past continued into the present. Its persistence led to poverty, lack of employment and low-paying, menial jobs. Until this colonialism was addressed, measures to overcome racial inequality were futile. Adams drew a distinction between what he called "revolutionary nationalism" and "radical nationalism." The former had emerged in Cuba, Vietnam and other Third World countries where liberation forces took up arms to free their territories and secure independence from colonial rule. He did not endorse revolutionary nationalism of this type for the colonized peoples of Canada because, as he realistically observed, First Nations and Métis lacked the power to overthrow the Canadian government, reclaim their land and set up a separate state. Instead, he advocated radical nationalism, the goals of which were "economic, social and cultural autonomy, and control over all political affairs concerning the natives as a nation, beginning with complete local control of Indian reserves, Métis communities, and native urban ghettos." He pointed out that since the Canadian government was willing to give millions of dollars in aid to Third World countries, surely it could do the same for underdeveloped communities at home.[6]

Although Adams rejected armed force as the preferred means for Métis liberation, he did not rule it out altogether. He said that "there may come a time when guerrilla violence will be necessary and appropriate, and we must not hesitate to use it."[7] On another occasion, he was even more definite, predicting that in the struggle for justice in Canada, violence was "inevitable."[8] Such comments helped to make Adams an object of fascination for the media, who invariably referred to him as a "militant" and "red power advocate." In April 1969, reporter Eric Malling interviewed Adams at his Saskatoon home. On the wall of his study, there was one picture, a portrait of Louis Riel. Adams, in the course of the conversation, took three books from the shelf: the diary of Che Guevara, a manual on guerrilla warfare, and Frantz Fanon's The Wretched of the Earth. When asked what tactics Métis people should used to take the power to run their own communities, he answered, "The first rule is to never let the enemy know your tactics."[9] Adams did not entirely disavow comparisons made between him and Riel: "This comparison is made continuously by my own people and by white people because—they even say I look like Louis Riel-because, in emotion I'm sort of the evangelistic type of leader, and because I am a militant…. There's no doubt about it. I'm a revolutionary."[10]

Statements of this kind were not calculated to endear Adams to the Thatcher

---

[5] Ibid., pp. 152, 167.
[6] Ibid., pp.150, 193.
[7] Ibid., p. 214.
[8] First Nations University of Canada Library, "Red Power," The Pierre Berton Show, #1304, Interview with Howard Adams, 9 January 1969.
[9] Regina Leader-Post, 2 April 1969.
[10] Leader-Post, 10 May 1969.

government. Indeed, he emerged as one of the foremost opponents of the government's Aboriginal policies. In August 1968, the premier launched the Task Force on Indian and Métis Opportunity in order to enlist the support of the population at large for his jobs plan. Dr. Howard Nixon, dean of Physical Education at the University of Saskatchewan and chair of the task force education subcommittee, stated, "The culture of native people is dead. There is no foundation for it in hunting, trapping, fishing. Their society, as we know it, must change to be the same as our society. They must adjust to our white society."[11] This type of thinking was anathema to Adams. He rejected the notion that Métis culture was dead, and that there was nothing left for Métis to do but assimilate into the dominant society.

When he returned from Berkeley to take a teaching job at the University of Saskatchewan in Saskatoon, Adams became aware of the cultural and political awakening that was occurring among Aboriginal people. He prepared a report on social conditions in northern Saskatchewan and found that the state of political activity was surprisingly high. People were talking openly about problems and confrontations— police brutality, poor housing and the need to take action on these issues. Adams took the plunge into active politics and in 1968 became head of the Saskatchewan Native Action Committee (SNAC), a vibrant organization that challenged the policies of the Thatcher government.

The government responded by attacking SNAC and giving grants to the rival Métis Society. The strategy backfired, however, when in April 1969 Adams won the presidency of the Métis Society at the annual convention in Prince Albert. Premier Thatcher, who was invited to give the banquet address, was asked whether it was true that, if certain persons were elected the government would take away the Society's $20,000 annual grant. "I don't think so," Thatcher replied, "I'll wait and take a look." Hearing groans from the audience, he added that he expected the Métis Society "to give us officers we can work with." Despite the veiled warning, Adams won a narrow victory and declared, "We will not be pushed around any more. I consider that we are now the vanguard or the forefront of a liberation movement."[12]

Under Adams' leadership, the Métis Society began publishing *New Breed,* a monthly newspaper that celebrated the rebirth of Métis nationalism. The Métis would no longer accept discrimination and humiliation or sit back passively and accept their fate. The paper declared in capital letters: "HELL—NO! We do not want to be integrated into the white race. What we do want is to be recognized as an individual race with a unique, true Canadian culture; a people well able to govern our own affairs."[13] On July 19-20, 1969, the Society sponsored a mass rally at Duck Lake, the site of a Métis victory over the North West Mounted Police in 1885. The festivities featured a field day, square dance, fastball games, chuck wagon and pony races and the ceremonial burning of school

---

[11] "A Better Citizen-Both of Us," Armadale Productions, 1970.

[12] *Leader Post,* 29 April; 10 May 1969.

[13] *New Breed* 1, no. 3, February 1970.

history textbooks that were deemed "racist and inferiorizing."[14]

In February 1970, Adams charged that Indians and Métis in northern Saskatchewan were starving because of the provincial government's inadequate social assistance programs. Despite Welfare Minister Cy MacDonald's insistence that the accusation was baseless, the story received nation-wide publicity. The federal government dispatched a four-man delegation to investigate. Following their whirlwind tour of northern communities, the inspection team found no outright starvation, but reported malnutrition and confused welfare policies. They condemned "shocking" housing conditions and questioned the practice of cutting northerners off welfare in the middle of winter.[15] Thus Adams had succeeded in his objective of focusing attention on the neglected problem of Métis poverty and the lack of government action to address it. Shortly after this episode, Adams announced that he would not seek re-election as president of the Métis Society. Premier Thatcher, who in 1969 had thought well enough of Adams to offer him the position of deputy minister in the Indian and Métis department (Adams had declined because he thought accepting the job would be a sellout), now denounced him as a "strange person," who could have accomplished much had he not been so preoccupied with "stirring up trouble."[16]

Quite the opposite was true. Adams' willingness to "stir things up" was the very reason he was able to accomplish so much in reviving Métis cultural pride, national identity and self-determination. The acuity of his analysis of colonialism and his courage in confronting the "powers that be" enabled him to play a decisive role

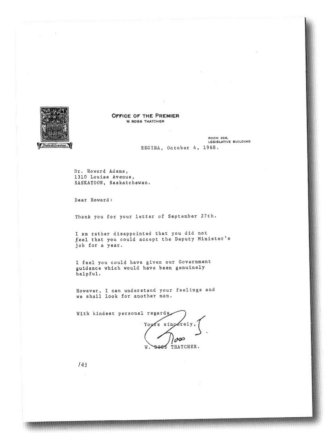

Howard Adams declines to become Saskatchewan's Deputy Minister for Indian and Métis Affairs, September 27, 1968. Document Courtesy—Library and Archives Canada.

---

[14] *Prince Albert Herald*, 6 August 1969.
[15] *Leader-Post*, 23, 27 February 1970.
[16] *Debates*, Legislative Assembly of Saskatchewan, Ross Thatcher, 12 March 1969; *Leader-Post*, 25

at a crucial moment in Saskatchewan's history. The 1960s were a time of social change when Aboriginal and non-Aboriginal Canadians re-examined their relationship and charted a new course based on mutual respect and cooperation, rather than coercive assimilation. Howard Adams not only understood what was happening, he played a decisive role in making it happen.

Remembering Howard Adams

Rhoda Kaellis

Moving from the New York City area to Saskatoon was a big leap for me. It was 1967 and the American war in Vietnam showed no indication of ending. Many Americans were escaping to Canada. I had never heard of Saskatoon until my husband accepted an offer of a university job there, and I had no idea of what to expect in the way of amenities, social life, culture or political atmosphere. But I was a savvy New Yorker, and perhaps I could find some Canadians who would join me in anti-war actions. During our first month in Saskatoon, we connected with a group of peace activists who easily equaled the degree of commitment and understanding of the people whom we had left behind.

Howard Adams was among them, distinctive in his astute understanding of twentieth–century political circumstances, and his readiness to grapple with the forces of society in general and in his immediate Métis world.

With typical American arrogance, I was gratifyingly surprised at the cosmopolitan sophistication of the people we met in this little prairie town of 100,000. I was particularly impressed with Howard and his wife Margaret and the activities of which they were a part or initiated. My family soon became friends of the Adams and I was flattered when Howard invited me to be a guest speaker at some of his university classes. My respect for Howard grew geometrically as I got to know him better. Here was a man who had all the disadvantages of race flung at him through his youth, who had not only overcome and beaten them, but who had come out the other end with the following almost unbelievable attributes:

- physically good looking, extremely intelligent and charismatic with no pretensions or signs of self-congratulation;
- principled and steadfast in his belief of the need to struggle for justice for his own people and for all people who are degraded by the social system;
- incorruptible with integrity that was as natural to him as breathing air is to all of us; and
- always good-natured and cheerful. Even when Howard complained, it was with a smile in his voice.

Howard could so easily have climbed the ladder of self-interest to end up with material benefits or in politics—he was offered many opportunities by the establishment that wanted to buy him and get him out of their hair. Some very large carrots were held under his nose. And when he told us the stories of the offer that he got for a deputy ministership in the provincial government, he did it with eyes and voice spilling laughter, at the wonderful, outrageous stupidity of those attempting to seduce him.

Howard was that rare combination of some of the best characteristics of the human race. He never faltered in walking the path he chose, even when it meant challenging those among the Métis who served only their own selfish interests.

Throughout his whole life, he remained faithful to his high principles. It was a privilege to know him and count him as a friend.

Remembering Howard Adams

Eugene Kaellis

I have to admit that when I hear the word charisma, I think of public figures, usually politicians or theatre people, who project a persona that they believe will enhance their careers. Their charisma is a conscious and deliberate effort, and, when done well, can achieve the desired results among the many who know only the image. Rarely, however, does a public figure come along who is truly charismatic, i.e. attractive in a special way, and who gives every indication that what you see is what is real.

Howard Adams was one of them. A very good-looking man with an engaging manner and a remarkably captivating speaking voice, Howard did, indeed, have a presence. But, as I discovered and had repeatedly confirmed over the years that I was his friend, behind the image was a person of genuine substance. Howard cared, above everything else, for justice. He willingly took all kinds of risks and turned down all kinds of offers so that he could continue his struggle for that elusive goal.

Yet, in spite of his being conscious of the injustice and misery in the world, and feeling especially concerned about his own people, Howard never became a "heavy," someone whose social conscience and its attendant frustrations have turned him into a grim, angry person. Although Howard was militant and uncompromising in his principles, he was a kind, warm-hearted man who was able to see the humour in human foibles. Howard enjoyed life and really cared about and for people.

I'm very glad to have been his friend.

The Man That We Knew: A Conversation between Maria Campbell and Donna Heimbecker[1]

Maria: I met Howard in 1969. There was a Senate hearing in Ottawa on poverty, and as a representative of the Métis Association of Alberta, I submitted a brief. I was excited for two reasons. First, I was young and naïve, and I believed that the Senate would make all kinds of changes, maybe even put an end to poverty. And so I put a lot of time and effort into researching and putting that brief together. My second reason: I had never met Howard Adams, but I had heard all kinds of amazing things about him. He was the radical intellectual Métis leader from Saskatchewan. He had been educated in Berkeley, people said, and had been mentored by Malcolm X. So I was excited and flew off to Ottawa, thinking the Senate would change the face of poverty, and I would meet Howard Adams.

My plane was late getting in, and so I was late getting to the hearing. As I rushed into the room, Howard was speaking to the Senate committee. He was as eloquent and dramatic as only he could be, wearing a fringed buckskin shirt and beaded choker. As he spoke, he gestured with his hands, causing the fringes of his shirt to fly. I remember looking at him and thinking, "He looks just like Louis Riel!" Then I looked at the senators, sure that they must be just as impressed as I was. All of them, except for two, were asleep. One, a man, was reading a newspaper, and the other, a woman, was listening attentively and taking notes. I learned later that she was a famous parliamentarian and senator whose name was Thérèse Casgrain. But the others?! They were old, and any ideas I had about them changing poverty went out the window. When it was my turn to present my paper, one of them actually snored. That was my first disappointment. The second was Howard.

When we were all done and leaving the chamber, the other presenter, Reverend Adam Cuthand, who was the president of the Manitoba Métis at that time, introduced us, and the first thing that Howard said to me was, "You've got to be the most beautiful woman I have ever seen." And that was about as intelligent as our conversation was all evening. I had so looked forward to having a political discussion with him, but it never happened. We had a pleasant dinner, the three of us, and he had the political discussion with Adam. I knew that Howard didn't believe I had anything substantial to contribute.

Donna: I met Howard in 1990 as a student in my first year of the SUNTEP (Saskatchewan Urban Native Teacher Education) program at the University of Saskatchewan. Métis History was a compulsory course as part of the program, with Howard Adams as professor. I had heard numerous comments and stories about Howard through the SUNTEP faculty and other professors and colleagues, who touted him as a renowned Métis leader and radical activist. Being a first year mature student, I was a real

---

[1] This conversation took place in the spring of 2004.

keener, and I was extremely enthusiastic and eager to learn all I could about Aboriginal peoples, and to learn more about Métis history and culture. I was very excited to meet Howard, and I could never have been prepared for the extent by which he would affect my life.

I remember the first day of class, and Howard was late. He made a very flamboyant entrance, and appeared very eager to share his wisdom and knowledge with us. During that first hour of class, I began questioning how this man could get away with speaking the way he did about the state, the church and the institutions that were our oppressors and colonizers. He spoke with such passion. I remember watching his arms flailing about as he spoke with conviction, confidence, strength and power. This was no "ordinary" professor, and I knew then that this learning experience would change my life, and perhaps influence my way of thinking. I wanted to get to know this man.

Howard introduced the required reading for the class, *Canada and the Métis, 1869-1885,* by D. N. Sprague, and, following a discussion, we collectively decided that the book was a distorted and inaccurate account of Métis history. Howard suggested that we either (a) burn the book or (b) use it as a means to delve into colonialism, colonization and imperialism, and thus we would be critiquing the publication from a Métis perspective.

Although Howard had his Ph.D., he did not like being referred to as "Dr. Howard Adams," at least not by his students and his friends. He loved it when "white" people called him "Dr."—in fact, he encouraged it and enjoyed the prestige that came with the title.

Maria: My first impression was, like I said, he reminded me of Louis Riel. Remember the photograph of Riel in the courtroom? He has his hand up and appears to be speaking. From that photograph, and from what I've read, and from all the oral stories I heard, he was eloquent, powerful and charismatic. Well, my first impression of Howard was all those things, but my impression was also that he didn't really like women to be to be smart, political or outspoken—at least not with him. He wanted me to listen, not talk. I was disappointed, but what the hell, that was not an uncommon occurrence in those days, especially in our community. Women were not for talking.

I heard Howard speak on several other occasions after that, and I always liked what he had to say, but I never really got close to him until many years later, and then it was as a friend, not as a political colleague.

Donna: I recently found a letter that Howard had written to me, and he was reflecting on the first days we met. He talked about a time that he was invited to make a presentation at a gathering of Métis people at the Gabriel Dumont Park downtown. I recall watching him with such pride as he stood up and spoke with passion and conviction about Métis identity and pride. Using his ever so confident body language, shaking his fist high up in the air, he spoke with such authority as he motivated and inspired the crowd of Métis youth, students and community members.

I was invited to respond to Howard's presentation as one of his students. I was honored to do so. Although I was extremely shy at the time, I was very moved by his presentation and quickly got up and praised Howard's commitment to the struggle of Métis people, and I thanked him for sharing his wisdom and knowledge with us. Howard was moved by my response, and we knew then that we were destined to be friends. Howard and I spent a lot of time together during his visits to Saskatoon, and we spent endless hours together playing tennis, sharing meals and drinks (Howard loved his beer) at one of our favorite gathering places, Alexander's restaurant.

Howard was like a father figure to me—the Métis father I never had. He was a true friend and a mentor.

Howard loved beautiful women, and, more so, women who were educated and intellectual. He made no qualms about openly stating his feelings to me and to other women he met, but he rarely included them as contributors to any serious discussions or debates. I recall feeling a sense of uneasiness with that, and it was reaffirmed one time when I was having dinner with Howard and my good friend Harry Daniels.

Harry was an avid political activist. He always talked openly about his views on the political arena. Harry and Howard shared their love and passion for women. However, Harry was always respectful and inclusive of women in his conversations and discussions, something he often corrected Howard on. But I was Howard's student, his friend, and I believe he saw me as his protégé, and I referred to him as my mentor.

Howard made a very strong impact on me. I felt I had to work twice as hard for him. I wanted him to be proud of me, and to respect my thoughts and opinions, and to see me as a colleague of sorts. But I always remained a student, never a colleague. It was a struggle and a challenge being his student, but I think he respected that and our discussions around my papers and the research that I was doing for him on his autobiography reflected his appreciation and respect.

Maria: As I said, I got to know Howard much better years later, and I believe I had a good friendship with him. We talked about writing—you know the way that we write—and we talked about books. Sometimes he'd go off on a political tangent, but we did have a political discussion. Not like the ones I had with Harry [Daniels] or Paul [Chartrand], whom I could and can sit with for hours and talk and plan strategies. They always treated me as an equal, respected what I had to say. I just never got that from Howard. I always felt my job was to listen to him, and to make him feel he was okay.

He was a very fragile man, and it would have been easy for me to get after him for being so chauvinistic, but I could never do that to him. I think that maybe it had something to do with my generation. I think he was afraid of strong Métis women, you know? Maybe that is just my thinking.

I read a book once called *Soul on Ice* by a man called Eldridge Cleaver. He was one of the leaders of the Black Panther party in the United States. He wrote a chapter—I believe the title was "Oh my Black Sister." I remember thinking about Howard when I read that. It was very sad and very true, not just about him, but also about many other Native men.

I respected what he had to say. But once when I told him that I, too, had come through the 60s, done my stint with Karl Marx, Lenin, Frantz Fanon and all those guys, and I dropped out because their tidy impersonal analysis just didn't work for me. It was just another "ism," and it was more important for us to look at our stuff from our own place. Well, that was the end of what may have been a discussion.

But in spite of all that, I always I admired and respected him. He was not afraid to say what he felt, even if it meant he might be shunned—and he was for a while. You know how often people have to be in a pack before they will voice their own opinions. Howard was never afraid to do that. But on the other hand, it was also a way to keep himself separate from his community. Métis people were not really a part of his life, at least not his everyday life, except maybe on the page.

Donna: Our relationship grew into one that mirrored a father/daughter relationship. I would discuss personal and confidential matters with him, but Howard never really opened up with me about his personal life or struggles he was having. We knew each other a year before I found out he was married. We were lunching one day, and a friend of his, whom he hadn't seen for a while, stopped by to say hello. The friend asked Howard how Marge was doing, and much to my surprise, he was talking about Howard's wife.

Of course, I began grilling him with several questions about Marge, whom he spoke very highly of as his friend, lover and life companion. When I asked him why he didn't share that with me on the onset of our friendship, he didn't really have a response, other than that he thought it wasn't important.

The next year, I had the pleasure of meeting Marge when she came to Saskatoon during Howard's teaching term for a visit. Marge turned out to be a wonderful person who was totally committed and supportive of Howard.

Maria: But he didn't mention her to any of us. I didn't know her name was Marge until he passed away. I knew he was married, and I just assumed she was non-Native, because why else would he never mention her.

Donna: When I think about the impact that Howard has had on my life, firstly, I think of the love the two of us shared as friends. As many Métis people were, I was inspired and motivated by his passion for his work, his accomplishments and achievements, and the impact his efforts had on the development of First Nations and Métis peoples of Canada. Howard encouraged me to continue my education. He offered to pay for my graduate studies, and for me to pursue a doctorate degree. Howard held formal education in very high regard, and he was willing to invest in my future and what he believed was an investment in the future of the Métis.

Mentors and leaders like Howard, Harry, you and others have made profound impacts on people and communities. Like all of you, he was an educator and a leader in his own right. I, too, have always made the analogy of how Howard resembled Louis Riel, given his preacher-like style of communicating his thoughts, his physical appearance and charisma. Flamboyancy came naturally to him, and I know that he loved overly dramatic moments. I don't think that he rehearsed his presentations. However, from an artistic perspective, he would have definitely been in the running for an Oscar!

Maria: He loved attention, for sure, and, yes, he inspired students. Many of them speak very lovingly of him, and I can believe he was probably an amazing teacher. He loved to tell stories, and he was a born orator, but I don't know what kind of impact he had on the communities. I know he made an impact on a lot of individual people, and he certainly contributed to a better understanding of our world.

Donna: I coordinated a national book launch for Howard's first edition of *A Tortured People*. I was making attempts to secure community-based sponsorship to support the promotion and tour. I approached our esteemed Métis Nation of Saskatchewan leadership, who, I thought, given the extensive work Howard had done for Métis people in Saskatchewan and across the nation, would be eager to support the project. Little did I know that aspects of Howard's book were not well received by some of our Métis leadership, in the sense that he was writing about the internal struggles of our leadership, about collaborators, compradors and those bought off by the money that flowed through the leadership's coffers. Needless to say, they refused to sponsor the book tour, which was no surprise to Howard. In fact, he was even a little miffed that I had approached them to begin with. In spite of their rejection, the tour was a remarkable success. Howard spoke to thousands of youth, academics and community people throughout Canada.

Howard contracted me to do research for his autobiography. I completed personal interviews with Howard's family, friends and colleagues from across Canada. It was obvious that Howard had impacted individual people in both positive and negative ways. Some of the positives included how he instilled a sense of Métis pride, his willingness to work as a mentor and his dedication as a leader. Some of the negative impacts were made mostly by women (ex-girlfriends) who truly despised him for one reason or another. From my summation, they were mostly jealous that they hadn't won his love. A couple of his distant relatives who lived in Saskatchewan were obviously in total denial of their Métis identity, and thought he was a disgrace to the community, and would not speak with me about him at all. I also spoke with one Métis woman who had a political run-in with Howard that ended up in a physical battle, and Howard ended up with his shirt ripped off his back!

Maria: I often wondered, "Why didn't he stay?" When I first heard that he was living in exile in the United States, I thought, "In exile? Give me a break! Get the hell back here, we need you!" I've always believed that you have a responsibility as a leader, but I came to the conclusion that maybe he was not that kind of leader. His leadership was perhaps as a writer and teacher. I often felt he left us high and dry. He could have stayed to help make political change. But on the other hand, what did I want from him? Did I want him to get hung?

I loved *Prison of Grass,* and I have used it in many of my classes. But I did have difficulty with *A Tortured People.* What he wrote was true, but it didn't have the power of *Prison of Grass.* It was just not very articulate, I think.

Donna: I found his book *A Tortured People* to be an academic piece of writing that was challenging to read and, for the most part, went over my head, but *Prison of Grass* was a powerful and passionate book that I fell in love with. I believe the book spoke to the truths of Howard's life and the struggles he went through in achieving a true sense of his own identity. And in that way the rest of us, and me in particular, really identified with it.

Maria: Yeah, it is a well written, eloquent and powerful book.

Donna: And controversial.

Maria: He invited me to speak to his class at the university once to talk about the early movement, and I remember thinking, "Holy! Something has happened to this guy. He's changed, he wants me to come in and talk about political stuff." But when he introduced me, he spent most of the time telling the students how I looked like I'd stepped out of *Vogue* magazine when he first met me. He didn't tell them I was an elected leader at the time, and that I had also submitted a brief on poverty. He was such a contradiction.

He never talked about his life in St. Louis, or his family, other than to say the community was a ghetto and that his family tried to pass as white. He also never spoke about his home in Vancouver. I always thought that he lived very modestly; that he was probably quite poor because of the way he acted. Until he phoned me one night and said he had a favor to ask. He was very apologetic—you know how Howard was when he was apologizing. He said he didn't want to lose my friendship over this, and I thought "Good heavens, what did he do?" When I said "Howard, just tell me," he said he wanted me to sit on a committee with two other people whose politics he could trust. (Remember, this was the first time he had ever acknowledged that I had any politics!) He went on to say, "I've got all this money and I'm really embarrassed to talk about it." When I asked, "How much?" he said, "Over a million dollars, and I want to give it to students to further their studies." He went on to say that he wanted to make sure it went to the right people with the "right politics." When I asked, "What do you mean about 'right politics?'" He said, "No right-wing people, and I trust that if you sit on this committee you will make sure that doesn't happen." We had a long talk about it, and he kept apologizing until I said, "Howard, stop that! I think it's wonderful that you have a million dollars and even more wonderful that you want to give it to Métis students." I tried to convince him not to wait until he died, that he should start giving the money away now. I said, "Howard, do you know what it would mean to have a student take a cheque from you personally? There would be so much pride, especially for the student. Our young people need uncles like you." Anyway, we had a long conversation about this, and I told him to also think about the arts because artists have a hard time getting money. He listened, then asked me again if I would sit on the committee. I said yes, but never heard from him again about it.

I saw him many times, we had dinner often, but he never talked about that committee again. A scholarship was set up at the University of Saskatchewan, but I understand that the bulk of his money is destined for animal rights in Vancouver. But that was Howard, a total contradiction.

Donna: Given my discussions with Howard regarding the legacy he hoped to leave behind, I was certain that he would have set up a foundation or scholarship fund while he was still alive. He talked about this often, as one way that he could make an impact and support Métis students pursuing a higher education. Another thing that Howard was very concerned about was his collection of books, writings and papers. It was his wish to create a non-profit organization, which we (Howard, Robert Doucette and myself) did. *The Howard Adams Archives* was to house his personal collection and the collections of other Métis leaders, like Harry Daniels. Howard's greatest fear was that his documents would end up in some government-run institution. Unfortunately, in his final years I think he lost focus, and thus the organization fell by the wayside. I believe his documents are now housed in Library and Archives Canada in Ottawa. Like you said, a contradiction.

Howard cared about the arts, and he knew that could be a strong vehicle for change. He was extremely interested in my pursuit to establish the Saskatchewan Native Theatre Company (SNTC). Although I'm certain he would have loved to see me pursue my graduate studies and doctorate in a more "academic" genre, he was genuinely proud of my accomplishments and wanted to support SNTC in whatever way possible. We discussed a new performing arts centre and the potential for him to make a contribution toward the capital campaign. Of course, he was extremely excited about the project and the potential for him to leave a legacy of sorts through this cultural/arts facility. Unfortunately, we were not able to complete our discussions because he passed away.

Howard spoke often of his growing up in the ghetto of St. Louis, and the poverty mentality that he had developed throughout his younger influential years. He speaks of this in his writings, and it was evident in his humble lifestyle, at least here in Saskatchewan. My perception of the "ghetto lifestyle" was altered somewhat when I was invited to visit Howard's home in Vancouver. They resided in a very upper middle-class part of West Vancouver in a lovely home. Howard was initially shy with me about his dwelling and felt that apologies were in order upon my arrival. I told him that this was not necessary. We all struggle to live a good life, and that he should not feel embarrassed by his wealth and success. I did not criticize him. However, I did question the contradiction by which he led people to believe that he lived a humble lifestyle in the "ghettos" of Vancouver.

Maria: I guess one thing that I worry about in this dialogue is that I don't want people to think that I didn't respect him, because I loved him. He reminded me so much of all of the sad things that we don't talk about in our community. The things that happened to our men. And those are the things that he wore. And when I say he was vulnerable, I mean he wore the humiliation that many Native men have had to live with in our history. I saw my father go through this stuff, and I saw what it did to him. It is very hard when your spirit has been humiliated. I think that's why we see so much dysfunction and horrific violence in our communities committed by men who don't know how to overcome all the ugly, so they can move ahead. Howard was somehow able to stuff it away and get through it, but he paid a price. I don't know how long it will be before that legacy of humiliation is no longer a part of us.

Donna: I don't know if there is any one person who really knew Howard Adams. It's been an interesting experience reflecting on my relationship with him and the contributions and impacts he made on my life and the lives of many. I think it is important that people know that Howard was a unique and dynamic human being who had struggles of his own. He struggled with his own identity, with love, relationships and the politics that made up the world around him.

Howard changed my life, and I know I am a stronger, more confident and focused individual for having shared those special times with him. In memory of my dear friend, Howard.

Maria: Yeah, in memory of you, Howard.

The Howard Adams I Knew

Ron Laliberte

When asked to write my thoughts on Dr. Adams for this book, I jumped at the opportunity because I wanted to tell others what he meant to Métis people like myself who knew him on a personal level. However, my interaction with Dr. Adams was most likely an anomaly in comparison to others because of the way our paths crossed at different times and places.

My first encounter with Dr. Adams was during the early 1970s when I was sitting in the bar of the Baldwin Hotel in Saskatoon, Saskatchewan. I didn't saw him again until the mid-1980s, when I became a graduate student at the University of Saskatchewan. Thereafter, I learned to know him as a colleague and friend during the late 1980s and 1990s, when he would travel from his home in Vancouver every spring or summer to teach in the Department of Native Studies at the University of Saskatchewan.

The Howard Adams that I came to know was a complex individual. He was generous with his time, passionate about his beliefs, devoted to the Aboriginal cause, witty and humorous, particularly in a social setting, and a person who vigorously resisted the neo-colonialist policies of the Canadian state. I found him to be impeccable in character. In many ways, he was a product of the anti-establishment period of the 1960s, and yet this was a big part of his appeal for many who sought him out.

In my office above my desk there is a photo of Dr. Adams, or "Howard", as I called him. It's a wonderful photo. There is a huge, somewhat mischievous smile on his face, and a twinkle in his eyes. This photo is a constant source of inspiration for me, particularly when I feel down. It quickly snaps me out of any self-indulgence because it's a reminder that it was political activists like Dr. Adams who came before me and fought vigorously for social justice for their people who really had it tough. Moreover, such leaders did what they did without a blueprint to guide them or footsteps to follow in. I'm keenly aware that it's because of the past struggles of individuals like Dr. Adams that people like myself have many of the opportunities that we have today. The photo also reminds me of what a character Dr. Adams was. You know how sometimes you hear someone describe someone else by saying "God broke the mould when that person was born." Well, I think this applies to Howard because he was a unique character, and he definitely had his own style of doing things.

Dr. Adams was articulate and a gifted orator. Whether you were in class listening to him lecture or in the bar having a few beers with him, he had a certain charisma that held your attention. I remember coming across those who identified with his 60s radicalism and hung on to his every word as though he were a Métis guru who could lead them to nirvana or reveal to them the path to a utopian society. I also saw a few people who angrily chastised him for his intellectual perspectives, particularly when it came to the topic of racism and non-Aboriginal society. However, I often thought that Dr. Adams was deliberately provocative and outspoken on controversial issues in order to stimulate conversation and debate. All kinds of people from all walks of life seemed drawn to him for various reasons. Many people, I think, were touched by his enormous passion for doing something for the downtrodden in society, even when his solutions to social problems were somewhat idealistic or too radical for contemporary reality. Still, many people, myself included, liked the fact that he stood up and said what many of us only thought about and kept to ourselves. Moreover, it was his outspoken "tell it like he saw it" and "damn the consequences" attitude that made it exciting to be around Dr. Adams. And there were times when he would get quite worked up when he was speaking. During those times, you could always tell when he was about to make an important point. He would position himself by planting his feet apart, place his left hand on his hip, raise his right hand in the air and then state the point while waving a pointed finger. Given his delivery while speaking to a large audience, you can understand that he had a tendency to generate a nervous tension in a crowd, which, in turn, seemed to electrify the air.

I would like to relate the story of my first encounter with Dr. Adams because I think it speaks volumes about what type of person he was. I think it will also provide insight into how he was able to generate that nervous tension and to electrify the air around him as described. While I hadn't met Howard Adams until I attended the University of Saskatchewan in the mid-1980s, I knew who he was even prior to attending university. Let me explain.

Before becoming a university student, I used to work in construction. Occasionally, I would patronize a bar in downtown Saskatoon called the Baldwin Hotel. Back then, the bar in the Baldwin was typical of a number of pubs in the downtown area of Saskatoon. In particular, it was characterized by spatial racial segregation, having Aboriginal people sit on one side of the bar and non-Aboriginal people on the other. This division between the two groups was quite common in bars throughout Saskatchewan at the time.

One hot, late summer afternoon after work, I was sitting in the Baldwin with some friends, chasing the concrete dust down with a few beers, when all of a sudden we heard this loud commotion. When we looked to see what was going on, we saw this large group of Aboriginal people come into the bar shouting, singing and pounding drums. Before long, we found out that the group was holding a demonstration to protest the Baldwin's policy of segregating Aboriginal people to one side of the bar. Then I saw a svelte individual standing at the front of the group, dressed in a buckskin jacket with long frills hanging from its sleeves, who, as I later found out, was Howard Adams. He was shouting out slogans and rhetoric that accused the bar of being symbolic of the segregation and oppression of Aboriginal people in Canadian society. Of course, while all of this was going on, the bar manager in post-haste called the police, and before long they arrived. Immediately, they moved in and attempted to break things up.

But, just when it seemed as if the police were about to exert their control over the group, attention focused on Howard, who yelled out to his followers, "There, you see! This is how the oppressors maintain control over Aboriginal people and keep them in their place—through the use of police force!" Then, as he placed his hand on his hip and raised his other arm, he pointed to one police officer in particular who was standing nearby, and he yelled out, "Look at that cop! Do you see how he's got his hand close to his gun? Well, why do you think he's doing that? It's because he would like nothing better than to pull his gun and use it on all of you!"

Needless to say, after Howard's harangue the group eyed the police officer and gave him some seriously mean looks. Things then got quite tense for a few minutes while the group seemed to become more agitated because what Howard had said resonated with them.

Years later, when I got to know Howard personally, I mentioned that I was in the bar when he staged this political protest. His response was that he remembered it very vividly because "that was one time that I had thought I had gone too far, and that all hell was going to break out. Fortunately, however, I was able to get everyone out of the bar and back to the Friendship Centre without any major problems."

I also want to mention that after I got to know Dr. Adams as a colleague and friend, I found out he loved to play tennis. So, every once in a while, we would play a game against each other. It wasn't long before I realized that he took his tennis very seriously because, when on the court, he was all business. Now, I don't want to sound as if I think I'm a great player—I'm far from being one—but I have played for a while, and I have a few moves on the court. I'm sure that in his prime Howard must have been an excellent player, but at the time when I used to play tennis against him, he was in his early seventies. Thus, it's understandable that at his age he wasn't that fast on the court. So, at times during a game I would feed him the ball so that we could get a rally going.

One time, when I was feeding him the ball, we got into a good rally and I had to make a few good returns because he was trying desperately to put away the point. So, finally I smacked a passing shot down the line and won the point. Well, he was furious that I won the point, and he yelled, "I could kick your ass off for that, Ron!"

Well, he said this so seriously that I laughed so hard, and he had to chuckle himself. I wanted to mention this because what it revealed to me was that he was a very competitive person.

An interesting and somewhat comical footnote to Howard's tennis playing was that he used to chastise me for playing golf, calling me "bourgeois," yet he never saw himself as bourgeois for playing tennis.

What I remember most about Howard is how he made you feel. He made me feel that what I was doing was important and that I had something to contribute to society. Many times I saw him nurture the minds of students, particularly Aboriginal students, simply by taking the time to speak to them, or to tell them that their thoughts and questions were important. Maybe this was why so many of us enjoyed being around Dr. Adams. In fact, many of us waited in anticipation for his arrival in Saskatoon. When he came in either the spring or in the summer, we always welcomed him as we would welcome the nice weather.

I often wondered why we looked forward to seeing Howard each year. Some of us may have seen him as a link to the past because we would jokingly acknowledge that, since his great-grandfather was Maxime Lépine, who fought valiantly along side Dumont and Riel in 1885, he was a descendent of "royal Métis blood." There's no doubt that we admired him for what he had accomplished. However, I think that for some of us he was more than a successful academic who wrote books or a political activist who never sold out to the establishment. Some of us really identified with Howard. We saw him as one of us, someone from our community, a Métis person who told our story, and who stood for our beliefs and values. It was as if, when he was here, we could stand up and say to the world, "Maybe it is true that we don't have much, but what we do have is Howard Adams."

In everything he did, he made us feel proud to be Métis.

Howard Adams, the Métis Political Conscience

Murray Hamilton

Spirit of the 1960s: Conscientization

In 1966, when Howard Adams returned from California to Saskatchewan, my family was in the process of relocating to the city of Regina. Like Howard, I had been raised in a small, predominantly Métis community—he in St. Louis, and I in Lebret, which is situated in the Qu'Appelle Valley. Howard had just obtained a Ph.D. in the History of Education, and I was just entering high school.

The late 1960s and early '70s were heady times, even in Saskatchewan. The idealism and the general anti-establishment ideology of the civil rights movement had spilled over into Canada. Howard Adams, newly arrived from his studies at the University of California-Berkeley, and armed with his anti-colonial and liberation theory, was like a messianic prophet who had come to deliver the Métis from colonization. Caught up in the euphoria of those times, some Métis remarked that Howard Adams reminded them of Louis Riel. Like Riel, he was educated, and he was returning from the United States after a long absence from the Métis community. Some even remarked that there was a strong physical resemblance. It was a comparison that Howard did not discourage.

Two years before Howard's return in 1964, the Liberals under Ross Thatcher had come to power in Saskatchewan, after twenty years of democratic-socialist rule under the CCF. Howard Adams and Ross Thatcher would butt heads many times, and it is interesting to speculate how Howard's profile would have developed under the CCF. In the 1960s, the separatist movement in Québec, radical unionism and Red Power were considered real threats to the security of the Canadian state. We know now that the RCMP did indeed take a very active interest in Howard Adams' activities.

At the grassroots level, however, the major concerns still centered around unemployment and housing. Generally, just trying to get by was still a major preoccupation for many Métis. My introduction to Métis issues came from the activities of my uncle Ray Hamilton, who in the early Sixties began working for the Indian and Métis Department, which was created by Ross Thatcher's Liberals. The issues were not always political. When Ray organized some minor renovations to our grandparent's small house on Jackrabbit Street in Lebret, I thought to myself, "Wow! This Métis thing can really do something!" Ray was a contemporary of Howard's and served as Provincial Secretary for the Métis Society of Saskatchewan (MSS) from 1971 to 1974.

In 1969, Howard organized the Saskatchewan Native Action Committee (SNAC). Others involved included Harry Daniels, later to become president of the Native Council of Canada, and Rod Bishop, a long-time Métis activist from Green Lake. For a time, SNAC occupied a small office on the second floor of a building on the south side of 11th Avenue in Regina. The door was painted red, and on the same floor there was a drop-in centre frequented by radical students from the University of Regina. One of these individuals was Murray Dobbin, who was involved with *Prairie Fire*, a radical newspaper, which shared the same floor as the fledgling Apollo motorcycle club. It was in this environment that I gained a very rudimentary understanding of colonialism and imperialism, and I began to think about the Métis situation in a broader societal context.

In the summer of 1973, I became involved MSS Local #9.   During that summer, I worked as a concrete finisher, and later that fall when I was laid off, I was approached by a Métis acquaintance from Lebret, to take part in a program being offered by Local #9. The course was labelled "Community Awareness Program," and the curriculum was a blend of Métis history, life skills and oral and written communication skills. It was designed to develop political awareness among Métis youth. We were encouraged to become actively involved in the Métis movement, and it was during this period that I first heard Métis leaders such as Howard Adams, Rod Bishop and Jim Sinclair speak. Until then, my historical knowledge of Métis issues had been confined to oral accounts of Joe Larocque and Thomas Major, Métis leaders from Lebret. The only book I had read on the Métis was George Stanley's *Riel*, which, unbeknownst to me, Howard had burnt in protest in 1969 at Duck Lake, some four years earlier.

Up to this point, I did not know Howard on a personal basis. I had been introduced to him and had heard him speak at meetings. In retrospect, many Métis, when describing Howard, state that he used academic language, which no one could understand. Although I had difficulty following some of his ideas, what struck me most the first time that I heard him was not so much the language, but the conviction and passion with which he conveyed his message. What I loved most about him was his open defiance of the establishment. Among Halfbreeds, I had often observed a tendency not to rock the boat, nor to question authority. Howard Adams not only questioned authority, he was in open defiance of it, and he challenged the state to do something about it. I was in awe, and at the same he scared the hell out of me. As Howard would say, my mind was still in a colonized state.

I saw Howard twice after that, and then he would be forced into political exile.

Co-optation Issue

Throughout the winter of 1973, as my apprenticeship into the Métis political world continued to evolve, I became aware of the internal tension that was beginning to mount between two factions in the MSS' upper echelons. The growing dispute centered about the issue of accountability and whether or not the MSS should accept core funding from the government. Howard, long a disciple of Malcolm Norris, was adamant that accepting core funding would lead to the co-optation of the Métis movement.

To understand Howard's position, we have to go back in history. In 1968, Pierre

Trudeau had been elected Prime Minister, and he had promised a "Just Society." However, his policies were really a continuation of Lester B. Pearson's efforts to build the modern welfare state. *The Unemployment Insurance Act* was rewritten, the Canada-Québec Pension Plans came into existence, the Company of Young Canadians was created, the Federal Department of Regional Economic Expansion was founded and Opportunities for Youth was established in 1971 to reduce youth unemployment. A number of programs were created with the dual purpose of achieving community development objectives and implementing employment creation strategies. This period also saw a dramatic increase in the amount of funding provided to all Aboriginal organizations, including the MSS. We know now that Trudeau's efforts to build the "Just Society" did not significantly alter the distribution of wealth among Canadians, particularly Aboriginal people, so what was the intent of these massive federal expenditures? Social theorists argue that welfare and job-creation expenditures increase in times of civil disorder and decrease during periods of social harmony. Howard knew that we were being co-opted and bought off through core funding and programs.

As early as 1966, Malcolm Norris had balked at the amalgamation of the Métis Association of Saskatchewan, representing the northern Métis locals, with the MSS, representing the south, because the latter, led by Joe Amyotte, had accepted two thousand dollars. By 1974, the largesse of government funding had become hundreds of thousands of dollars.

As a disciple of Malcolm Norris, Howard stated the following about the question of core funding in a 1976 interview conducted by Murray Dobbin:

> Let me make this really clear, that there was a number one priority, or number one thought, in Malcolm's mind about organizations, and about governments, and other kind[s] of institutions, and politics, and so on. It was, number one was, *that you never accept any money from the government!* And, you know, that was a prayer, and that was a declaration, and that was everything, a proclamation, and that was the rule. Malcolm firmly believed that there was no way that you would ever accept money from the government! ... And he repeated that, and repeated it, and he just drilled that into your head! ... I never realized that he was speaking with such truism, and such a prophecy, on everything[1].

Jim Sinclair became the MSS President in 1971. By 1973, the MSS Executive had become fractured, and there was considerable animosity between the Sinclair and Adams' factions. Disagreements over decentralization and accusations of fiscal mismanagement led Howard to file a report with the government in March 1973. In Howard's own words:

> Internal trouble started at the first council meeting in August, 1973. The major

---

[1] Typescript, personal copy.

argument took place between the two groups over decentralization. A motion was passed that programs of the Métis Society, it's [sic] programs, staff and governments grants, would be decentralized, autonomous authority would now be placed in Regional and Local Métis boards[2].

And it was Howard's opinion that "Jim Sinclair fought bitterly against this new plan of decentralization as it would seriously reduce his power and control over the finances".[3] In December 1973, Howard tabled a report on misspending with the MSS board itself, and also submitted a memo to Hugh Faulkner, then secretary of state.

The whole matter came to a head when the two sides clashed at a meeting on July 2, 1974 at the Union Centre in Prince Albert. The meeting immediately bogged down over whether or not to proceed with an Annual Assembly. In the words of one observer, a "real Halfbreed meeting broke out," complete with intimidations, accusations, fisticuffs and finally a physical assault on Howard by two female members of the Sinclair faction. Two days after the meeting, Howard sent a nine-page memo to provincial and federal authorities, outlining his concerns about the meeting and the general state of affairs within the MSS. The response from both levels of government was that they did not want to become involved in the Métis' internal affairs.

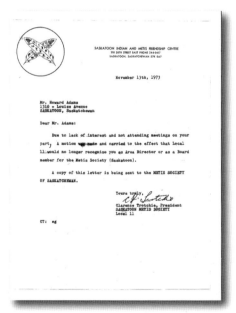

Local 11 of the Métis Society of Saskatchewan deposes Howard Adams as area director, November 13, 1973. Document Courtesy— Library and Archives Canada.

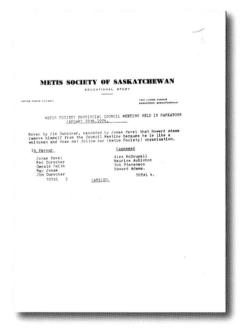

The Métis Society of Saskatchewan Provincial Council expels Howard Adams, January 29, 1974. Document Courtesy—Library and Archives Canada.

---

[2] Adams, Howard, "The Métis People and Their Problems," 9 pp. Report to Federal and Provincial Government Officials, July 5th 1974, p. 5. Library and Archives Canada, Howard Adams Fonds, Métis Society of Saskatchewan Correspondence and Related Material 1974, 4-4, Box 4.
[3] Ibid.

Why Did Howard Leave Saskatchewan in 1974?

In a recent discussion with my uncle, Ray Hamilton, he expressed the notion that throughout this period many people generally assumed that Howard was going to return to California. Others believe that Howard was forced into political exile. I think it was a little of both. He had been threatened, harassed, humiliated and finally physically assaulted. Moreover, I believe that he knew that the Métis struggle was entering a new phase, one of which he did not want to be a part, and, like Malcolm Norris, he foresaw the effects of government-sponsored political organizations upon the Métis. I believe that at this point, Howard made a conscious decision to return to academia and continue his work, refining and teaching decolonization theory to Aboriginal students.

Why he left when he did has always intrigued me, and when I got to know him on a more personal basis later, in the mid-80s, I often queried him about his departure in 1974. It was not a topic he liked to discuss, and, regretfully, on occasion I chastised him about leaving. When his second book, *A Tortured People*, came out in 1995, Howard autographed a copy for me and wrote, "to my good friend Murray, but cruel on my conscience." I am convinced, now, that Howard knew in 1974 what lay ahead, and simply did not want to be a part of it.

From 1976 until 1981, I served as a MSS regional director in the Prince Albert area. During this period, I met Howard's uncle Mederic McDougall. Mederic was an incredible man. He became a close friend, confidante and advisor. Medric was strongly committed to the Métis struggle and often talked about Howard and his beliefs. It was easy to see why Mederic had been such an influence on Howard. During my tenure as Regional Director, I began to realize that I knew very little about Métis history, and I began to read everything on which I could get my hands on. Howard's *Prison of Grass* had a major influence on my thinking, and I began to question the whole Métis political agenda. In 1981, disgusted with this agenda and my role in it, I decided to pursue university studies.

A year later, 1982, the Canadian constitution was repatriated, and for the first time the Métis were constitutionally recognized as one of Canada's Aboriginal peoples. Ironically, a process that Howard would have regarded as mere political intrigue by the colonizers, set in motion a chain of events that would help bring him back into the Métis fold. In 1976, the MSS changed its name to the Association of Métis and Non-Status Indians of Saskatchewan. The party line was that this had been done to accommodate a small minority of Non-Status Indians within the group. However, being present at the time, I know that the name change took place for the most part to shield the then-president, Jim Sinclair, from growing criticism. To his credit, Sinclair always declared himself to be an Indian. However, many Métis had always found it unacceptable that the MSS President was, in fact, a self-identified Indian. With the constitutional recognition of the Métis in 1982, there began an internal movement within Saskatchewan to return to a Métis-only organization with a Métis-specific agenda. A long and acrimonious debate ensued, culminating in 1988, when the Métis-only faction narrowly won a court-ordered referendum on the matter.

During this period, Howard had started teaching courses during the summer months at the University of Saskatchewan. Howard was invited to be a guest speaker at the 1988 Gabriel Dumont Institute (GDI) Annual Cultural Conference. I know that this was a big moment for Howard. He had been gone from the Métis political scene since 1974, and many of his old political foes had been vanquished, notably his old nemesis, Jim Sinclair. As one of the leaders of the Métis-specific faction, I knew that we were using Howard in a way, but he knew it as well. Howard was still one of the most well-known Métis, and he had not lost any of his fiery oratorical skills. At the time, I think, Howard held out some hope that things would change, but within a year he knew that all that had happened was that the "old guard" had been replaced by the "young Turks," and that the movement was as co-opted as ever.

In February 1989, I began work with the GDI at the University of Saskatchewan, and for the next ten years, every summer, I had the opportunity to meet and work with Howard. It is only now that I realize how lucky I was, and some days I am deeply ashamed that I did not take that opportunity more seriously. We got along, but we did not always agree, and we spent hours discussing colonization, political theory and Métis conscientization. It was not all academic banter. In many ways, Howard was just a Halfbreed with a great sense of humour, and sometimes over many pints of beer we would laugh for hours recalling stories from the old days.

Howard could also be very melancholy. His office was just down the hall from mine, and many days after he finished teaching his classes he would retreat there and work on his papers and course work. He would sometimes get very frustrated with himself, and I recall one day, when he walked into my office, plunked down a paper he was working on, and in exasperation exclaimed, "Will there ever be a clear thought?"

Holy Cow! Métis Cows!

Howard, even at this stage in his life, was generous with his time and quite willing to "raise a little hell." In 1996, I received a phone call from our old friend Rod Bishop, who was involved in a dispute with the Province of Saskatchewan over Métis land around Green Lake. As always, Bishop was succinct and to the point, and he instructed me, "Hamilton, you get that Adams up here! Never mind all that bullshit theory, we've got things to do up here!"

Upon our arrival in Green Lake, we found out that our objective was to move some cows from the Silver Lake Farm across the highway to a Métis-controlled community pasture, signifying that it was the Métis, and not the provincial government, who were in control of the farm's operations. With the support of approximately one hundred fellow Métis from Green Lake and elsewhere, the removal of the cattle began. The press had been called, and three or four different camera crews showed up, much to Howard's delight—he was still a draw!

At the entrance to the community pasture, he gave his press release. In his classic pose, with his left hand on his hip and his right hand extended skyward, and his eyes partially closed, he made the grand statement: "Those are Métis cows!" Later at Rod Bishop's house, over tea we jovially asked Howard, "When you said those were Métis cows, did you mean they belonged to the Métis, or they were actually Métis or hybrid cows?" Well, we laughed for hours, and when the television report aired, we laughed all the more, especially Howard.

Howard's Position and Legacy

Howard was a complex person, and just when you thought you had him figured out—well, you didn't. Many of his contemporaries perceived him as a hypocrite since his political activities took place in the Métis world, while he chose to live in middle-class suburbia. However, such thinking was reflective of the times when the Métis credo was "you can get ahead, but don' get ahead of me!" In his writings, Howard often stated that he was a Marxist. He certainly was left-of-centre, and a Métis nationalist but like most individuals he was a blend of ideologies and beliefs.

I have heard many people say that Howard was ahead of his time. In retrospect, it was Howard that was in sync with his leftist contemporaries, and it was Métis political thinking that had not caught up. Howard expressed what some might label Marxist tendencies, believing that the Métis struggle, and broader society in general, should be in a state of constant change, evolution and, preferably, revolution. Howard taught us that revolution means more than a historical event; it means a change of consciousness. He reveled in acts of civil disobedience, and his often impassioned and inflammatory oratories were custom-made for the press. Howard had a flair for the dramatic, and sometimes his statements to the press were completely without basis. Howard was the Métis Che Guevera, always looking for the next fight, but certainly bored, if not incompetent, with administrative matters.

HOWARD ADAMS: OTAPAWY! is sure to spark criticism and controversy. Howard's legacy will have far-reaching impact. The Métis have had many great political theorists, some formally schooled and some not, but Howard charted a new course. He was the first to apply colonization theory and the political method of conscientization to the Métis situation. In analyzing and deconstructing state policies, Howard foresaw the dangers of co-optation, dangers that have become a reality. Howard also opened the doors to academia and the intellectual world for the Métis, and for that we owe him a good deal.

Howard was fully cognizant that the co-optation process was not restricted to the political organizations. He often spoke about how the colonial policies and structures of the academic world had not allowed the full development of Métis conscientization, and how the Métis were left with a tenuous hold of White western education. On many occasions, Howard chided himself for attempting to effect change from within the confines of mainstream universities, which he considered to be conservative entities operating assimilationist policies. Concurrently, I think Howard was happiest when teaching Métis students about Métis history. Howard incessantly stated that it was a must for Métis students to develop a Métis consciousness, which could only be achieved through a re-examination of ourselves and our history. Only through political awareness could we become a self-sufficient political, social and economic force.

Those of us who have consciously or otherwise become co-opted and serve as "house niggers" (a term used by Black Liberation theorists for those who sit with the "masters") in Aboriginal, provincial and federal institutions, or in the even more conservative settings of a university, understand and applaud Howard Adams, but in most instances we lack his conviction and passion for the task at hand.

Howard Adams at UC Davis and DQU[1]

Roxanne Dundar Ortiz

Dear…,

How wonderful that you are doing this project. Of course, I would be honoured to have a small piece included. I have just finished a third book in a series of three historical/literary works of memoir (the inspiration for these was Howard's *Prison of Grass*), this one covering the period 1975-1992. I wrote of Howard's influence on me (I have pasted the two paragraphs below). Unfortunately, I don't have any of Howard's letters to me from British Columbia when he moved back. We wrote regularly. I can understand why he didn't write about Davis. It was hell for him.

…

Because DQ faculty members were mostly drawn from Native American Studies professors at nearby UC Davis, I was able to connect with a larger circle of colleagues. Among these was UC Davis professor Howard Adams (now deceased), a militant Métis leader from Saskatchewan, Canada. Howard was also a Marxist theorist and a specialist on colonization who influenced my own thinking profoundly and permanently. He introduced me to the development and colonization studies of André Gunder Frank, James Crockroft, Samir Amin, Pierre Jalé, Pablo Gonzales Casanova, and many others

---

[1] D-Q U (Deganawidah-Quetzlcoatl University) is the name of an Indian-Chicano Community College in the California Central Valley near Davis, California, founded in 1971 by Jack D. Forbes, David Risling and other Indian and Chicano teachers and students from nearby University of California at Davis. What started out as the occupation of an (partially) abandoned US Army communications site by Native activists from Alcatraz Island and northern California, today has developed into one of many tribally-controlled Community Colleges in the United States. Howard Adams supported D-Q U and taught there for a time as a volunteer. See Jack D. Forbes and Howard Adams. *DQU: A Model of Grassroots Community Development* (Davis, CA: U C Davis, Tecumseh Center, 1976); also Hartmut Lutz, author and editor, *D-Q University: Native American Self-Determination in Higher Education* (Davis, CA: U.C Davis, Dept of Applied Behavioral Sciences, 1980.)

published by the Monthly Review Press. Howard's brilliant book, *Prison of Grass*, was an unusual and effective combination of his own life history as a Métis growing up in severe poverty and social deprivation along with a parallel scholarly history of the birth of the Métis (a new nation of a bilingual/bicultural mixture of Cree Indian and French) and their resistance movements, beginning with the uprising led by Louis Riel. Howard's was the first study to apply colonization and development theory-previously focused on Asia, Africa, and Latin America—to a Native American situation.

One of Howard's colleagues at Davis, Jack Forbes, who was the primary architect of both DQ and UC Davis' Native American Studies Department, introduced the term "Native American" for "American Indians," though he preferred simply to use "American" to refer to Indigenous Americans and force all others to hyphenate. Jack also created a Native American centred theory of colonization that included Chicanos as Indigenous Americans. In these definitions, Jack and Howard agreed. Their differences, however, were vast, and their personalities and egos also clashed. Howard was a Marxist who viewed the reservation land base and resources, along with democratically-elected native governments, as essential to a necessary nation-building process. Jack had a utopian view of a pan-Indian America with no boundaries. My own view developed as an amalgam of the two.

Jack Forbes and Howard Adams established the terms of a theoretical debate that also would consume the American Indian Movement, and soon the international project of Indigenous peoples. The pervasive theme of Cold War anti-communism tinged the debate, particularly in Latin America, with many Indigenous leaders condemning Marxism as a "white man's theory." I had experienced similar anti-communism in the women's liberation movement a few years earlier, enunciated under the slogan that Marx was "a man." I did not budge from my own positive regard for Marxian theory as a framework for understanding anything and everything, and I too would be red-baited, just as I had been in the women's liberation movement.[2]

Howard Adams: Radical Métis (Inter-)Nationalist

Hartmut Lutz

Today, I remember and miss him as a very dear friend, a great intellectual, an internationally-known scholar and a seriously engaged political activist. He was a committed researcher and a passionate teacher. He loved talking to and instructing others, especially the young, but likewise enjoyed listening and learning for himself. Throughout his life, he remained curious, ever eager to learn more, but never compromised his radical

---

[2] Excerpt from Roxanne Dunbar-Ortiz's forthcoming book, *State Sponsored Terrorism: A Memoir of the US Contra War in Nicaragua* (South End Press, Spring 2005). By permission of the author.

Howard Adams speaking at Indian Culture Days, University of California-Davis, April 26, 1980. Photograph Courtesy—Hartmut Lutz.

rock-bottom conviction that, yes, a better life should and would be possible for all—a life in self-determination, a life without class exploitation, a life without racial hatred, and a life without gender or sexual oppression.

When, in the fall of 1979, I entered Howard Adams' office at Native American Studies Tecumseh Center at the University of California-Davis for the first time, it felt a bit like "coming home" because on his bookshelves sat mutual acquaintances and friends. There were not only many of the then standard books read and taught in Native American Studies—Dee Brown, Vine Deloria, Jr., Jack D. Forbes, Black Elk, Rupert Costo, Maria Campbell and Harold Cardinal—but also many books by other thinkers that I had sitting on my own shelves at home, like Karl Marx and Friedrich Engels, Malcolm X, Frantz Fanon, Albert Memmi, Herbert Marcuse, Frederick Douglass, Paolo Freire or Paul Sweezy. Some of the latter I had not seen in a long time, and I had given up hope of finding them anywhere in Native American Studies in the USA. But here they were, and Howard had read them. It is amazing how much of a bond, internationally, that we can establish through reading and learning, without ever being aware of intellectual kin and political comrades on the other side of the world. Such "kinship ties" are particularly pertinent, and can be uplifting intellectually, especially emotionally, for people who are marginalized at home because of their political persuasions or their ethnic or gender identity constructions.

By the end of Howard's life, his *Prison of Grass* (1975) had become an international classic. This was brought home to me in August 2000 when I attended a conference on "American and Canadian Native Literatures" in Bombay (now Mumbai) that was organized by Dr. Coomi Vevaina from the University of Mumbai, who had brought together literary scholars from all over India. During the conference, Howard's study of Fourth World colonialism, *Prison of Grass*, was referred to repeatedly. In a non-western society like India, which in the past had suffered from the same colonial rulers as Native North America, Howard's analysis of colonial oppression and the struggle for liberation seemed to be appreciated in a most profound way. Here, his radical Métis nationalist writings could be received for what they are, unhampered by a cold war anti-communist mindset that often distorts intellectual perception in western societies.

The internationalist dimension of Howard's political activism and theoretical writings remained counterbalanced by and grounded in his origins in the Métis community of St. Louis, Saskatchewan. Although he led the White middle-class life of a university professor—a life of which he often spoke self-critically, ironically and with a certain amount of contempt—Howard's heart remained with his place and people. In our first recorded conversation, on April 10, 1980 in Davis, California, he referred to this origin in his opening sentence: "I was born in Saskatchewan, Canada."

I never saw Howard in a more happy and relaxed state than when he was interacting with Aboriginal students in Saskatchewan and Vancouver. Even though his years of "passing" and his university education had put considerable distance between himself and his St. Louis neighbours and kin, in his nocturnal hours of suffering from depression and insomnia, when he took refuge at his desk and wrote the scattered memoirs and fragments of fiction that he referred to as his "hate pieces," his mental wanderings took him back to St. Louis. Occasionally he managed to cope with his feelings of anger and existential frustration by converting negative energy into something encouragingly beautiful, like, for example, his autobiographical short story "The Colonized Halfbreed." It articulates "Howie's" anger against those who exploit the Métis peasants, but it ends with a scene that expresses in most romantic terms the love he felt for his Saskatchewan homeland:

> There were some beautiful times in our Halfbreed world. You had to be born in it, grow up in it, and live in it in the most profound way. Every evening, all summer, I had a very special and lonely chore: hunt the milk cows, herd them home and milk them. It was always a beautiful long evening of roaming and riding with my favourite friends, Pinto the Pony and Dusty the dog. We roamed through the woods, valley and hills sharing nature with the wild animals and birds of the evening. The woods were filled with the chatty creatures. …This chore was special because it was in the timeless quiet evening when the sun faded in the wide western sky … All summer long, every evening, I hunted the cows on the open range. I'd ride miles and miles and never meet a soul. Those hours were to be the most beautiful and precious of my life. It was the solitude, the aloneness with the naked and virgin environment I loved so much. I almost hated to herd the cows home.[1]

Even while passing as a White Berkeley student, at the moment of his "political awakening," a moment, perhaps, of Howard's most profound existential crisis, when after Malcolm X's speech he had to decide "whether to be part of the problem, or part of the solution," his thoughts took him back to St. Louis, to seek advice from his revered uncle Mederic McDougall:

> I've had kind of…sort of, let's say, lucky breaks, crises, moments when things touched me that turned me around. I would say, Malcolm X's speech turned me around. … I wanted to walk away by myself, and I did, and I didn't go to class that afternoon. I can always remember I walked away and I went into the

---

[1] Howard Adams, "The Colonized Halfbreed," in *Four Feathers: Poems and Stories by Canadian Native Authors,* ed. Hartmut Lutz (Osnabrück: VC Verlagscooperative, 1992),p. 42.

campus where I was, but in an area that was a little isolated, and it's this beautiful … afternoon. I just sat there and thought about it the entire afternoon. And I thought about it in terms of my own situation… And then what I did was, I wrote to my uncle back home in St. Louis who I knew, knew all the history of our family. And I wanted to know exactly a lot of things about my ancestors. And that was the first time that I found out that my great-grandfather had been one of the real leaders, the commanders, in the last Indian war in 1885… [T]hen, I also became much more revolutionary, you know, then I started thinking politically, very politically… Malcolm X was the one that really impressed me… to a political awakening.[2]

It seems typical of Howard that at this moment of existential revelation and crisis, he walked away from other people to be alone with nature, to work things out in his own heart and mind. The experience of having to work out things in solitude may even explain Howard's affinity with existentialism:

You know one thing that really got me involved, and I think it is part of the alienation, is existentialism! That really seemed to speak to me. And it goes, partly I guess, with the loneliness and everything that I was experiencing in my life. Loneliness, because I was away from my people, my own community.[3]

Howard and I had many wonderful conversations. Often, we completely forgot about time and prompted each other to more and more thinking and questioning. Sometimes, we laughed in the delight of discovering that the other was another soul who felt and thought in corresponding ways, who had read and learned similar ideas and had, from a very different walk of life on a different continent, come to comparable conclusions. We did not always agree, but that only added to the challenge of our discussions.

Twice after such conversations, on the next day Howard said to me-and he also wrote in books he gave me—"Hartmut, you are really the best friend I have." I was almost shocked by the loneliness entailed in that statement, and I have always felt humbled by this admission, always grateful for him saying that, but never quite feeling I could possibly deserve it. Dedicating this year of my life to helping edit and publish his autobiographical manuscripts seems the least that I can do to try to live up to his esteem.

Working on his scattered autobiographical and fictional writings revealed yet another aspect of his complex personality: Howard, the man who suffered immense

---

[2] Howard Adams, "'Allende Was By All Means on the Right Track': An Interview with Howard Adams," unpublished. Davis, CA, UC-Davis, Tecumseh Center, April 10, 1980, © Hartmut Lutz. Parts of this interview were later published in German in *Achte Deines Bruders Traum: Gespräche mit nordamerikanischen Indianer(inn)en,* 2nd ed., ed. Hartmut Lutz (Osnabrück: Druck- und Verlagscooperative, 1997), pp.48-56.
[3] Howard Adams, "Howard Adams", *Contemporary Challenges: Conversations With Canadian Native Authors,* ed. Hartmut Lutz (Saskatoon: Fifth House, 1991), p. 152.

psychological anguish, who paid a staggering emotional price for his "passing," and Howard, the "romantic" and "womanizer" who, at least in his fiction, took advantage of his good looks and charisma. The latter is an aspect I never saw in him before. Ruth, my wife, is not the only woman who stresses that she always felt comfortable and respected in Howard's presence, and that she experienced none of the male chauvinism from him that she observed in other charismatic leader figures.

But even in Howard's texts dealing with the romances of Tony the womanizer, Howard's fictional alter ego, there remains Thea, a strong female character, a steadfast, supportive and very attractive woman whom Tony learns to love and respect in a most profound and mature way.

Whoever met Howard's wife, Margaret, knows that Thea's character is modeled after her, and whoever observed Marge and Howard interacting, or who listened to Howard speak about his wife, comes to understand that it was Marge, the longshoreman's daughter, whose solidarity and love supported him throughout his life. Marge, Howard once said, kept him straight. So, whatever is said in praise of Howard's achievements must also be said in acknowledgement of Marge's support. The two were a team, and Howard was the first to insist on that. Their political solidarity with all oppressed peoples, and their radical rejection of exploitative hierarchies, consciously included gender relations. That was another aspect of Howard's personality, which made relating to him so comfortable for many people in the world.

Remembering Howard Adams

Geary Hobson

I met Howard Adams face to face in 1996 at the "Returning the Gift" gathering in Penticton, British Columbia. When I introduced myself to him, telling him that I had read and was an admirer of *Prison of Grass*, I was rewarded with that wonderful smile of his, and a friendliness that still moves me deeply even now as I think of it eight years later.

But in another sense, I had met him twenty years before, when I first read *Prison of Grass*. I think this is always the way it is with writers and works that we particularly admire: we "meet" them endlessly each time we enter their world through the agency of their words. Not only that, but I think we are also continually "meeting" them each time we recall an idea of theirs, a particularly and uniquely crafted image, a certain noteworthy episode, a striking situation and certainly memorable portraits of human character that we have gleaned from their works and can associate with no one else but themselves. Such provocations of memory rekindle our catalogue of associations with regard to that writer and his or her works.

So, by the time the gathering at Penticton came along, I had, in effect, "met" Howard many times before. *Prison of Grass* had a profound effect on me when I read it in 1976. I had been writing and publishing for a few years by then, but even though I would most often take an admittedly subjective stance in my non-fiction work with regard for the necessity of advocating strongly on behalf of Native people and our history, I think that I still had many professional reservations about how and to what extent I ought to employ the personal example within the context of discussing Indian issues—that is, of referencing a private experience to illustrate a particular universal idea. My reading of Scott Momaday, Malcolm X, Eldridge Cleaver, Vine Deloria and others of the late 60s provided excellent models for me in employing the passionate tone, the "Speaking from within the culture" stance, but it was *Prison of Grass* that liberated me even further in my thinking about this with regard to writing of Native peoples within a historical context. Especially crucial for me was the shock of recognition that I experienced in encountering several of Howard's personal examples in the text, which he utilizes to more effectively lay bare aspects of colonialist bullying that is all too often accompanied by verbal and psychological violence as it unmasks itself in all its varieties of cultural oppression. In *Prison of Grass*, as every reader of it knows, Howard frequently makes reference to particular personal experiences to showcase White-Canadian racism as he knew it as a boy in Saskatchewan in the 30s. I not only recognized in my reading of it that I could do that, too—the reporting of personal atrocity to make more vivid my points of argument—but that Howard and I had quite a great deal in common.

There is, for example, a passage in *Prison of Grass* where Howard tells about the time when, as a teenager in rural Saskatchewan, he was once harassed by a couple of Mounties who seemed to have nothing better to do that evening than to abuse a somewhat White-looking boy for being Métis by making incredibly racist remarks about Native women from the community from which Howard came. Reading this passage brought not one shock of recognition, but two. Not only, I realized, could I, too, use such personal examples in my non-fiction, but there was also the more personal and immediate recognition of the fact that Howard and I were more alike than I had first imagined. I am also a *métis* (with the small m, since my people are not an official category in the American South, unlike Métis in Canada)—or, as I would say when I was growing up in lower Mississippi Valley area, a "Chicot" (although the term is rarely used by anyone, Chicot or otherwise, anymore)—and, I suppose, by all accounts more White- than Native-looking. Like Howard, I, too, was once the unwilling witness and respondent to the attitudes of certain White yokels toward Native women. In fact, for several months now, I've been reliving that long-ago event in my early manhood, as well as revisiting Howard's narration of the Mountie episode, in a short story that I have just finished. In my attempts to recall the dialogue part of the event, as well as the physical violence that accompanied it, I have found myself meeting Howard on an almost daily basis. Therefore, Hartmut's invitation to contribute this brief note about Howard and his influence has been pleasantly serendipitous.

My tormentors were not Mounties, but rather fellow Marines. They were, nonetheless, as I see them in my mind's eyes so many years later, versions of racist hoodlums likely cut from the same piece of rotten cheese as Howard's Saskatchewan Mounties. Like Howard's "good ole boys," my tormentors were also bent on teaching me a lesson. They did "teach" me one, but I warrant to say it was not the one that they thought they were imparting, and I like to think that maybe after all these years I am now getting the last laugh.

I told Howard about this event in my early life, and how I saw it as a common thread linking us. He agreed and we discussed the close parallels between the two events. I also told him of how I think that I got a slight bit of insight into his particular area of rural Saskatchewan in a driving trip that I made across there in 1991. I stopped at a service station where one is expected to pay before pumping. Not all that overtly conscious that I perhaps looked anything out of the ordinary, and not greatly "Indian-looking," I had the experience of having the clerk deliberately ignore me as I stood before him to pre-pay for my gasoline while he waited on four different—and White—customers before he finally graced me with his attention. This is a common occurrence in the Prairie Provinces, Howard told me. This and similar incidents have happened to me here in the United States, but that was the first time for it to happen to me in Canada.

Each time that I think of these incidents, and others similar to them, that Native people still face in the "enlightened" nations of the United States and Canada, it is as if I am meeting Howard again and again. Although many fine writers in the Native American literary community—and to hell with any consideration for that stupid artificial governmental barrier between Native peoples both north and south of the 49th parallel—have written most effectively about these and similar matters, and particularly on issues with which all Native peoples are still contending, no one has done it quite like Howard has. I remember these events in both my and Howard's life, and in the continuing growth of Native literature and sovereignty. Remembering is meeting.

Howard Adams—A Personal Remembrance

Wolgang Klooss

Métis Elders Walter Fiddler (left) and Mederic McDougall (right) at the Fish Creek Battle Site, September 1987. Photograph Courtesy—Hartmut Lutz.

Howard and I met only twice, both times in Vancouver—first at the old home they shared with his mother-in-law, later in the new home that Marge and he had built. Our first encounter took place just prior to a journey through Manitoba and Saskatchewan in the autumn of 1987. When I saw

Howard again in October 1998, he had only three more years to live.

While our brief encounters probably left no traces in Dr. Adams' memory,[1] he has remained a presence in my life. His thoughts had accompanied me academically since the late 1970s, when I first read *Prison of Grass: Canada from a Native Point of View* (1975), and thus became exposed to some of Howard's ideas. It was through this work that Howard entered my thinking—a book to which I have frequently returned in my teaching during the past twenty-five years, and to which I have repeatedly referred in my own research on the Canadian West and the Métis people.

In this way, Howard has always been more of an intellectual and spiritual presence for me than a personal acquaintance or even a close friend. It is largely through his writings that a feeling of kinship emerged, something of which he can hardly have been aware. Professor Adams, the restless mind, political activist, Métis historian, writer and critic has shaped my reading of the history of Western Canada considerably. When I finally met him in 1987, my research on the representation of the Métis in English-Canadian writing had already been completed and was about to be published.[2] I remember very fondly that Howard was pleased to hear that students and academics outside the Métis community and even outside Canada were interested in the history of his people, and that scholars like himself or writers like Maria Campbell and Beatrice Culleton had an audience abroad.

The Mederic McDougall Memorial Gate at the St. Louis Cemetery (donated by Marge and Howard Adams), September 1990. Foreground right: Wolfgang Klooss. Photograph Courtesy—Hartmut Lutz.

---

[1] This assumption is too modest. Howard remembered Wolfgang and his research quite well and asked about him during later visits (Hartmut Lutz — HL).

[2] Wolfgang Klooss' monumental book, *Geschichte und Mythos in der Literatur Kanadas: Die englischsprachige Métis- und Riel-Rezeption* (Heidelberg: Winter, 1989) (trans: *History and Myth in Canadian Literature: The Anglophone Reception of Métis and Riel*) is still the most comprehensive study of the portrayal of Métis people and Louis Riel in Canadian literature, and not just in English-language literature. (HL).

When Hartmut and I set out for Saskatchewan to visit the sites of the Northwest Rebellion, Howard had not only shared with us his views on Native life on the Prairies, on Louis Riel and Gabriel Dumont, and on Batoche and Duck Lake, but he had also gave us the names and addresses of relatives, friends and acquaintances who were ready to welcome us. In this way, we visited St. Louis, on the South Saskatchewan River, close to where Howard had been born, with its Catholic convent where he received his high school education and which he so despised. Here we met Howard's uncle Mederic McDougall, who had been prepared for our visit by Howard, and who generously offered to act as our local guide. He put us in touch with Walter Fiddler, an elder from near Batoche, and ninety-three year old Madame Pilon, with whom the four of us visited in Wakaw. She had personally experienced the aftermath of Batoche and still seemed so traumatized and shy to speak that her daughter and Mederic voiced her bitter memories in English.

Our encounter with Madame Pilon brought home to us all too clearly how much hardship Canada's Indigenous peoples have undergone, whereas Mederic McDougall's friendly presence, his humour and engaging talks brought some relief to the confounded minds of two travelling companions. At the same time, for me Mederic's latest activity seemed an embodiment of the irony of history. After he had shown us his work at the St. Louis cemetery,[3] where at the age of eighty-four he had straightened-out, cleaned and single-handedly restored the gravestones, concrete slabs and markers, incurring a hernia in the process, he led us to the Duck Lake cemetery, where we were introduced to two Métis workers, one of them a direct descendant of Gabriel Dumont. This individual had been to Germany with the Canadian Army, and now, together with the other labourer, tried to reset the weathered graves in parallel lines. The emerging pattern represented a grid system *en miniature*, i.e. the same kind of imposed metric system that had brought unrest, violence and warfare to the Western Plains. Mederic observed the activities of the two workmen with great pleasure, and insisted on absolute straightness of the different rows. Ever since, I have remembered him as "Mederic the Metric." Upon my second meeting with Howard in 1998, I mentioned this episode. Howard burst out in good-humoured laughter: "My uncle—the Pope-admiring socialist."

Throughout our travel, Howard had been with us. He gave us directions, established contacts and prepared us for a journey through the country of his birth, his home, a part of Canada so beautiful in autumn, so vast and spacious that we repeatedly asked ourselves why its Native peoples were expelled or had to live on road allowances. Imperial history, of course, had long provided us with its disturbing answers.

The journey to Métis country, with Howard as our spiritual guide, has stayed on my mind ever since. Upon my last encounter with Howard, he gave me his personal copy of Murray Dobbin's *The One-and-A-Half Men: The Story of Jim Brady and Malcolm Norris, Metis Patriots of the Twentieth Century* (1981) as a gift, something for which I felt very

---

[3] After Mederic McDougall's death in 1989, to commemorate his uncle's commitment to the Métis' cause and to acknowledge the work he did for the St. Louis graveyard, Howard and Marge Adams donated money and commissioned the "Mederic McDougall Memorial Gate" to be erected at the entrance of the metrically-straightened graveyard (HL).

proud and remain grateful.

Epiphany in Saskatchewan:
Or Burning the Queen's Portrait at Prince Albert

Konrad Gross

In the [Latin] Christian calendar, Epiphany, which is celebrated on January 6 or the twelfth night after Christmas, commemorates the manifestation of Christ to the Three Magi, who for that special purpose had travelled an immensely long distance by following a star in the sky. Nineteen hundred odd years later, James Joyce divested the term of its religious meaning, but he would not in the least have dreamt that one day his understanding of epiphany would assume particular significance at Prince Albert in the Canadian Prairie Province of Saskatchewan. *The Oxford Companion to English Literature* (1988 edition) states that epiphany is a sudden revelation of the "whatness of a thing" and the moment in which "the soul of the commonest object seems to us radiant." Some people never experience such a revelatory moment in their whole life, however hard they may struggle for it. For others, such a precious moment can occur out of the blue and quite unexpectedly. This was the case when the fiery radiance of one of the commonest objects under a prairie sky, a Canadian one-dollar bill, gave rise to a moment of a truly epiphanous nature, witnessed by three latter-day Magi, Howard Adams, Hartmut Lutz and myself. I should not leap ahead with my story, but start right from the beginning.

In September 1989, some seventy years after Joyce's ground-breaking definition, Hartmut and I toured the Métis country, going to the various sites of the 1885 Métis resistance, among them Batoche and Duck Lake, before we reached Howard's birthplace, St. Louis on the South Saskatchewan River. We checked into the St. Louis Hotel and then entered the adjacent drinking establishment, better known as Harry's Watering Hole, where we spent a long evening in the company of a group of Métis youngsters who challenged us to games of pool and helped us to empty pitcher-after-pitcher of beer. Naturally, my memory has retained only selected moments of that evening, none of which turned out to be an epiphany despite all the beer that was consumed. However, what I remember vividly were proposals by one of the young drinkers to meet us again the next morning for the "real story" of Howard Adams, an offer that Hartmut and I politely turned down. The next day, I met Howard for the first time: a man whose book *Prison of Grass* had been an eye-opener for me.

Howard was so different, not the angry political activist who I had expected, but an extremely kind and highly considerate person who showed us around Prince Albert, drove with us to the confluence of the South and North Saskatchewan Rivers

Howard Adams burning the Queen, Prince Albert, SK, September 1989. Photograph Courtesy—Hartmut Lutz.

and solved, in a highly admirable and friendly manner, a tricky situation in a bar frequented chiefly by Natives and Métis. During that day, we talked endlessly on serious and less serious topics. Howard was a mine of information for one of my research fields, the fur trade in Canada. He did not forget his promise to send me the copy of a M.A. thesis that one of his students had written on the subject. And it was also fun to talk with Howard. Among our less serious topics of the day was a remark by Elder Walter Fiddler that "Howard has money to burn!"

Two days later, on September 23, that remark led to an epiphany that transformed Howard from one of the Bible's wise men into a trickster figure who, together with Hartmut and me as accomplices, committed a subversive political act. When a match was struck to light a Canadian dollar bill held by Howard, we were not concerned with the "whatness" of this common object, but the fiery radiation of the portrait of the gracious Queen Elizabeth II, which, under Howard's triumphant smile and before Hartmut's camera eye, was soon reduced to ashes.

Three years later, in the summer term of 1992, I used this event to introduce Howard to my students, who then addressed my Canadian Studies class and held my students spellbound with his version of Métis history. In the evening, I took Howard and his wife Marge to the celebrations of the famous *Kieler Woche*, where I was finally able to return some of the hospitality that he had meted out to me during those fateful days of crime without punishment at Prince Albert, Saskatchewan.

Dimensions in Canadian History: Working with Howard Adams

Rose Klinkenberg

My first introduction to Howard was in 1989, when he asked me to help him edit some material that he was writing for another book on Canadian history. I was cautious, knowing that editing work that is close to someone's heart is a tricky business at the best of times. But Howard could write. More than that, it was delightful to talk to him. His charm and enjoyment of discussion asserted itself within minutes, and through this not only was I hooked, but we became good friends.

We were soon immersed in regular discussions about the Seigneurial system, the fur trade, the French and Indian Wars, the settlement of Québec, Eurocentrism and Indian slavery. As an immigrant from Scotland, my own knowledge of Canadian history was limited to that provided by the Canadian school system. But Howard saw a different history. Events and actions for him had different interpretations, and some happenings in Canadian history were, he felt, of more importance than that which standard history texts allowed.

Howard deplored the accepted Eurocentric view of Canadian history. Instead, he wanted to explore questions such as: What were the French and Indian Wars all about? Who was given land to settle? What really made the fur trade successful? How frequent were French-Indian marriages? What influence did First Nations people have on the development of Québec and Canada?

One of the most interesting aspects for Howard, one that was scarcely covered in the history texts, was the topic of Indian slavery. Just how common was Indian slavery? Who were the slave traders?

"Oh," said Howard in that deep long voice of his, "slavery was a bigger thing than mainstream historians like to say. In most texts, they give it a paragraph, a slight mention. And they talk mostly about African slaves.[1] Well, there is more to it than that."

From there we delved into the slavery picture. He had Marcel Trudel's work on slavery,

---

[1] Even today, while slavery in Canada is acknowledged, there is still a tendency to focus exclusively on black slavery. This is apparent in the following excerpt from an Internet reference article. While Indian slavery is mentioned, and while the numbers of Indian slaves in Canada was greater than those of Africans, it is mentioned almost as an afterthought: Slavery in Canada began in the 1600s. Most slaves were used as domestic house servants, although some performed agricultural labor. The first recorded slave purchase occurred in New France in the region known today as Quebec; the year was 1628. The purchase was of a young boy from Madagascar, who was given the name Olivier Le Jeune. By the early 1700s, Africans began arriving in greater numbers to New France, mainly as slaves of the French aristocracy. When the British took over in 1759, there were more than 1,000 slaves living in Quebec. Of course the British aristocracy had African slaves also. Just after the American Revolution in 1783, British Loyalists brought over 2,000 African slaves to British Canada. Approximately 1,200 of the African slaves were taken to Nova Scotia, 300 to Quebec (Lower Canada) and 500 to Ontario (Upper Canada). A few others were taken to Prince Edward Island, Cape Breton Island, and Newfoundland. Historian Marcel Trudel has recorded 4092 slaves throughout Canadian history, of which 2692 were Indians, owned mostly by the French, and 1400 Blacks owned mostly by the British, together owned by approximately 1400 masters. The region of Montreal dominated with 2077 slaves, compared to 1059 for Quebec City overall and 114 for Trois-Rivières. Several marriages took place between French colonists and slaves: 31 unions with Indian slaves and 8 with Black slaves. In 1793, under the leadership of Lieutenant Governor John Graves Simcoe, a bill had been passed by the Legislature of Upper Canada making it illegal to bring a person into the colony to be enslaved. Slavery formally ended in the two Canadas in 1834 after the British Parliament passed an act abolishing the institution throughout the Empire. (http://www.nationmaster.com/encyclopedia/Slavery-in-Canada, accessed April 23, 2004)

translated from the French into English. He also pulled together primary documents on Indian slavery. He had details on the number of Indian slaves, who owned them, where they came from, the advertisements posted in New France putting a slave up for sale and the number of slaves owned by Marguerite d'Youville, Canada's first saint.

"Quite often," Howard said, "Indian slaves were recorded as 'Pawnee', [sic — *panis*] a word that was often used as a generic designation, with the slaves themselves coming from several First Nations. They were brought great distances along the fur trade routes by La Vérendrye." La Vérendrye, he pointed out, was the brother of Marguerite d'Youville.

When Oka occurred, Howard's determination to write about the topic of Eurocentrism grew. He shifted focus to work on this subject, culminating in his book, *A Tortured People*. He wanted to show that history had been coloured in a way that entrenched racism towards Aboriginal people in many ways, and he included the slavery issue in this as something that he felt had been played down, yet deserved more prominence.

His passion for First Nations and Métis people was strong. He told stories of his own life growing up in Saskatchewan, of poverty and of racism. He told me about Louis Riel and Maxime Lépine, his great-grandfather, who was part of Riel's provisional government. He told me about his own struggles with the Hudson's Bay Company during the 1960s, and what he perceived as unfair treatment of First Nations and Métis people. He was angry about both past and present injustice. It was an anger that burned very deeply and very strongly, and that surfaced in his writings. This anger at injustice drove him in his research.

But no matter how serious his work, or how deep his anger, it was always delightful to talk to Howard. Our discussions were never-ending and always enlightening. There was always so much to talk about, and we would routinely wander off-topic and down all sorts of paths. But most of all, the Howard I knew had a great sense of humour. One of the last things he said to me was at a dinner, when he recounted his favourite scene of checking into a hotel. "Every time I check in to a hotel," he said," and they ask me if I have a reservation, I never know what to say."

Remembering Howard

Anette Brauer

Every morning at work, I pass by a picture on the office wall that brings a smile to my face. On it, a man is holding a burning dollar bill, his eyes beaming with joy. Howard.

My first contact with him was a virtual one. In 1991, during my first stay in Canada, I bought a National Film Board video called "The Other Side of the Ledger." About twenty minutes into the film, in a sequence taped at a meeting between representatives of the Hudson's Bay Company (HBC) and Canadian First Nations people, Howard fearlessly exposes the HBC's mechanisms of exploitation of Aboriginal people in Canada's north.

A year later, my colleagues and I organized an international conference entitled, "Peoples in Contact: Remembering the Past-Sharing the Future." There was no doubt in my mind that Howard Adams had to be our guest from Canada.[1] As a Métis activist and acclaimed political author, he knew what it was like to be a member of a marginalized group in Canada. I was convinced that he would be very outspoken on what it would take to improve the relations between peoples of different political, social and ethnic backgrounds.

The Native American Studies (NAS) workshop where Howard was expected to speak united students, German Indianthusiasts[2] and almost all GDR[3] scholars who had worked in that field, three in all. For us, who during the time of socialism had hardly ever had the chance to meet Aboriginal people from North America, it was an honour to meet Howard Adams. At the same time, however, we were not sure whether our views in NAS would survive the scrutiny of somebody who had been living in those situations that we could only study in an abstract, theoretical way. What's more, would our perspectives on and suggestions for solutions of issues like racial discrimination, colonization and exploitation be acceptable?

In retrospect, I find it rather unfair to have turned Howard into a test of our ideas. Less than two years earlier, East and West Germany had been reunited, and my friends and colleagues, were still struggling to come to terms with capitalism, a society that propagated the virtues of democracy and a free market over the sins of centralized socialism. Every day, our long-held views were questioned, and it was only logical to look for directions from people who had dealt with capitalism all their lives.

Howard listened to our contributions attentively, then he got up and spoke. He positioned himself against racial discrimination and racism, ideas that we all shared. But, probably to the surprise of some workshop participants, he continued by clearly focusing on the roots of it all—the economic interests of the ruling class and the power

---

[1] The papers presented at our conference were later published in Annette Brauer et al (eds). *Peoples in Contact: Remembering the Past—Sharing the Future* (Frankfurt am Main: Peter Lang, 1994).

[2] "Indianthusiasts" (also "Hobbyists") are people interested in reconstructing and reliving Indian life of the past in their free time.

[3] German Democratic Republic, the so-called East Germany that existed from 1949 until 1990.

structure in capitalist society. Western society, according to Howard, was in a crisis, and to believe in the goodness of capitalism was wasted energy. This political and economic system was inherently inhumane and had to be changed from the core.

His firm Marxist views were visible again later that evening, when Howard and his wife Marge visited my family and me in my typical 1950s GDR flat, with its tile ovens and walls barely held together by the wallpaper because at the time of construction sand was available and cement was not. For those few hours, both had a chance to experience very real remnants of socialism. I had studied the works of Marx and Engels, and based on some of their ideas the GDR government had provided medical services and education to all free of charge. I had given birth to two children while completing first my teacher's degree and then my postgraduate studies. The social system had offered free daycare facilities for my children, and already during my studies I had been guaranteed a teacher's job.

Howard took in my stories almost anxiously. As I answered his many questions about everyday life under socialism, I felt respected and assured that it was important to remember the past, good and bad. To be sure, Howard was not concerned with pure nostalgia. Rather, by sharing what had been, we were thinking of the future. There had to be an alternative to capitalism. The question was of what that alternative could be.

So, after twelve years of living under capitalism, as I walk by the picture of Howard symbolically burning that dollar note, this question is still with me. The ideas that Howard and I shared in 1992 are less popular then ever, at least here in Germany. That fact, however, does not mean that they are wrong. Maybe, if all our hearts were filled with Howard's great enthusiasm for the struggle against oppression, the world would be better off today.

Entering the classroom, I remember Howard.

The "Doctor" is In

Rhonda Carriere

We met Dr. Adams some time in early 1994. My sister Carmen had uncovered our Métis heritage and confirmed what we had long suspected when she reconnected with cousins on a recent trip to Winnipeg. Our grandparents moved west in the 1950s and thought it best to start over as "French" Canadians, thus hiding any reference to their Métis past in the small towns surrounding Winnipeg. Both had come from large, well-known Métis families, the Carrieres and Hamelins. Moving to Burnaby, British Columbia afforded them and their two sons a clean slate in the prosperous West.

Not unfamiliar with Métis history—both my sister and I had university educations—we were nevertheless unprepared to meet a piece of living Métis history in the person of Dr. Howard Adams. We had been invited to one of the first meetings of the Vancouver Métis Association through Ken Fisher and his co-op radio program, "Métis Matters." It was a small affair, held in the East Vancouver house of one of the early members on a warm spring evening. We walked into a smoke-filled room of half a dozen people, both of us in our twenties and by far the youngest of those present, to sit down and listen while Dr. Adams held court. Talk of revolution, takeover, and protest filled the room, lead by one dapper man with a huge smile and a sparkle in his eye. He seemed glad to have two "beautiful young ladies" join the meeting.

These ideas, clashing against our middle-class upbringing, could have caused us to leave the room and never come back again, but there was something so charming and captivating in this leader of the small group, and we returned to attend future meetings. We wondered about the obvious deference and respect given to this older gentleman whom everyone always called "Doctor." On the outside, he was a small man, even grandfatherly, but a torrent of energy came from within that bubbled up and oozed out his every pore. He was very charismatic, and before long we, too, called him "Doctor," affording him the respect that he was due.

A love of education and activism was in his blood. He was a strong grassroots organizer, and it was very exciting to work with him to build the Vancouver Métis Association. He gave us copies of his books, which we devoured in our hunger to learn more about the Métis people. We were often welcomed into Howard's home, where the two of us worked closely with him on projects to improve Métis education in the Vancouver area and in the province of British Columbia. Those times spent with him were always about so much more, as he taught us both volumes about what it means to be a Métis, more than we could get from any history book.

Carmen taught high school, and invited Dr. Adams to talk about the Métis in one of her Grade Ten Social Studies classes. Though he sometimes scared people with his approach, cleverly crafted to expose the undercurrent of hidden racism in the strata of White society, he got people talking and thinking about how things were and are for both Métis and Aboriginal people in this country. He always baited people with a twinkle in his eye.

We celebrated with Dr. Adams when he was recognized with an *Aboriginal Achievement Award* in 1999. We looked on with delight as Howard tried to recruit Joshua, Carmen's three-month old son in beaded moccasins and baby-sized Métis sash, to be a fighter for justice.

In my job with the Native Ministries Program of the Vancouver School of Theology, I have occasion to meet many interesting Aboriginal people, including educators, medicine people, traditional and Christian spiritualists and activists from Canada and the USA. One of my fondest memories of Dr. Adams was an evening of lively conversation and debate about the Métis role in history, especially as it related to resistance, with the people who had gathered for the Native Ministries summer program. I had invited

Dr. Adams to dinner as I had been challenged, or rather baited, by others to defend the Métis against claims that they were traitors to their Aboriginal brothers and sisters by their intermingling with Whites. Outraged by this idea, I called on Dr. Adams for his wealth of knowledge and ready debating skills, and was not disappointed. Howard was a marvel, completely in his element, bringing a new level of understanding and respect for the Métis to those with whom he spoke. I knew Howard as a friend, but I know that a larger than life reputation followed him around. After the evening, others who knew of him seemed quite impressed that I had hosted this little dinner.

We are both grateful to have known him and terribly regret that we can no longer go by his house to have tea and learn from him. We owe much of our Métis education to him. The lessons will continue, as his words and fighting spirit will not die. He was, and will remain, an inspiration to all who had the pleasure to know him.

"That's Howard Adams!"

Dan Kruk

When invited to submit a short paper for this book, celebrating some aspect of Howard's life and work, it was suggested that I consider writing something along the lines of an academic-style paper or a personal memoir, or even a political statement in tribute to a man who issued his fair share of them. However, when it came to writing something about a person I admired not only as an activist and scholar, but also as a friend and comrade, I found that I couldn't confine myself to one style of writing. For me, when discussing Howard Adams, there is no avoiding reference to his academic and political contributions, nor can I avoid relating how much he meant to me in a personal sense. What follows, then, is a combination of the three suggested themes, since when discussing Howard Adams there is no escaping the academic, political and personal.

In the first years of my repatriation to the Métis Nation (I was adopted by a non-Aboriginal couple in 1968), I devoured vast reams of popular and academic literature concerning Métis people. I read many of the standard texts: Maria Campbell's *Halfbreed*; Beatrice Culleton's *In Search of April Raintree*; Murray Dobbin's *One and Half Men*; Marcel Giraud's *The Métis in the Canadian West*; and Antoine Lussier and Bruce Sealy's *The Métis: Canada's Forgotten People,* to name a few. It was a frenzied rush to understand my "new" identity, to understand where I came from and, more importantly, to understand the socio-political and economic processes that led to the breakdown of the Métis Nation and, by extension, that of my own biological family. Although most of the texts that I read were of use, I craved something more than personal and historical descriptions of being Métis in Canada. What was missing was a rigorous class-based analysis articulated by an *authentic* Aboriginal voice that would explain what happened to my nation and my birth family. I needed something that would validate and go beyond what I already saw through my Marxist lens.

My search for Métis/Aboriginal-specific writings that located the source of oppression in the economic and political system, as opposed to well-meaning descriptions of the domination of Aboriginal people as some sort of expression of western culture, seemed to be futile. Eventually, in a small second-hand bookstore, I found a book written by Howard Adams. It was *Prison of Grass*.

For avid readers and writers, there are times when the experience of reading a book becomes a life-altering experience. In terms of reading *Prison of Grass*, there is no other way to describe the experience in any other words. Here was a man who wasn't afraid to name the oppression of Aboriginal people for what it was: a tool and function of the political and capitalist system. Howard's dramatic tone and succinct analysis throughout the book captured my imagination.

In a step-by-step process, Howard dismantled conventional notions of Aboriginal life and oppression in Canada. Moreover, he effectively used his own personal experiences as an Aboriginal person in the workforce and in the education system against the backdrop of colonialism to connect the personal with the political. In short, his deconstruction of the economic and political processes that contributed to the oppression of Métis people, and the effects that it had on the individual, personalized what I believed to be the origins of dysfunction in my birth mother's family: the economic marginalization, overrepresentation in the justice system, the addictions and the physical and sexual abuse were a part of the broader colonial experience. I had found what I was looking for.

Despite the value of Howard's critique of colonialism and what it has meant for the Métis Nation and for Métis people as individuals, perhaps his greatest contribution is his analysis concerning government-funded Aboriginal representative organizations and the elites who inhabit leadership and bureaucratic positions within such organizations. He identified a number of conditions that still demand attention today:

> The real function of these collaborator leaders from the government's point of view is to prevent any mass radical movement from developing and to check social action that would embarrass or threaten the government. Budget programs occupy almost all of their time, so they seldom become involved in any social action that might affect their finances. … Thus it is [that government-funded Aboriginal political organizations are] inclined to attract persons who are opportunists, drifters, hucksters, uncommitted and non-political workers.[1]

While it is true that these conditions exist in virtually all aspects of society throughout the world, they are especially acute in our communities. However, I'm not prepared to

---

[1] Howard Adams, *Prison of Grass* (Saskatoon, SK: Fifth House Publishers, 1989) p., 159.

charge every Aboriginal politician and bureaucrat as guilty of the above offences. There are decent individuals within our institutions trying to make a difference despite the cronyism and nepotism. But, in reality, these conditions do exist and are a part of the terrain in Aboriginal self-government. What Howard contributed was a sophisticated yet accessible articulation of the challenges that many Métis people intuitively knew but had not yet expressed in a more concrete fashion. It was, in the tradition of Malcolm Norris and Jim Brady, a way for Métis people to engage in critical analysis and debate about the internal oppression that they faced in their own communities and institutions.

When I first met Howard in 1997, we were at a meeting of Métis people in Vancouver, British Columbia. We were in a small meeting room where maybe a dozen people were sitting around a table and perhaps another dozen or so more were standing up close by, discussing a report that Howard had just completed concerning the socio-economic status of Métis people in Vancouver. I was sitting mid-table with Howard on my left, at the head. Up until that time, I had not met any other progressives in Métis politics, but that evening I did. The language and analysis that accompanied the descriptions of his findings was unmistakable. Soon, after asking Howard some questions about the report and, more importantly, allying myself with him on a few points of debate with others, we identified one another as potential comrades. However, at this point, I still hadn't been introduced to Howard. I leaned over to the person sitting next to me on my right and whispered, "Who's the old guy?" I can still remember the look I got. "You don't know who he is?" he whispered back. "No," I shook my head. The fellow looked genuinely surprised and replied, "That's Howard Adams."

Within days of meeting Howard, I was on the phone with him, grilling him about his politics and experiences. More importantly, I was testing my own politics and analysis against a person who was highly developed and a fantastic teacher. He was gracious and generous with his time. When sharing his stories there wasn't the slightest hint of arrogance or conceit, and, in light of his minor celebrity, he was extremely down to earth, still engaged in the struggle. It was clear from Howard's intensity and sincerity that there was no use celebrating personal and collective past glories as there was still work to be done.

Eventually he and I became friends, and, in turn, my own political development took another step. From Howard, I learned about the true meaning of commitment to one's ideals despite the fact that they may be unpopular with others. His example taught me that forwarding an agenda of progressive politics and all that it entailed would be difficult, and that it would open oneself up to ferocious criticism from those who where threatened by such an agenda. In spite of all the attacks and attempts to isolate him, he never abandoned what he believed in and rejected expediency in exchange for a place within established leadership circles. The job of raising the consciousness of Métis people and improving their conditions was too important to trade off for personal benefit. It just wasn't Howard's way.

The friendship that I had with Howard Adams was an honour and privilege. It was a friendship and a student-teacher relationship that has affected me profoundly. Whenever I'm engaged in activist politics, I always view my involvement through the scrim of a precise question: What would Howard do? The question isn't a disrespectful and glib play on the Christian-inspired bumper sticker, "What would Jesus do?," and, moreover, it should be understood that the question isn't an orthodoxy rooted in some activist fundamentalism. Instead, the question serves as a personal touchstone that guides aspects of my own engagement in social justice activities. It is nothing more than a deep respect for what Howard Adams embodied: a love of the Métis Nation and commitment to improving the lives of all people through the rearranging of the economic and political order.

Finally, I want to thank Howard's partner, Marge Adams, for sharing him with all of us in the Métis Nation. Marge's contributions to the Métis struggle must be noted, as many of her talents were put to good use behind the scenes. Her work in strategic planning, organizing meetings, rallies and establishing the *New Breed* newspaper were an integral part of the struggle. Marge gave much to our movement, and more so as it was her partner who was often on the front lines and away from home at meetings and organizing trips throughout the Métis Homeland.

Marge, I know Howard expressed regret about the time that he spent away from you during those years, and he was grateful for your support. Both you and Howard made our situation better than it was before. From those of us then and now, thank you.

Howard's Last Dream

Rene Inkster

Howard's book *Prison of Grass* was an assigned reading for a First Nations course that I took in 1989. Although I did not know then that I was a Halfbreed, I was deeply moved by his passionate descriptions of the effects caused by colonialism of Aboriginal people. Nine years later, after having discovered my heritage, and knowing that Howard lived in nearby Vancouver, I telephoned him.

He was in his 70s, and I knew from people with whom he worked closely that he was not always able to contribute to conversations as he once had. So, I was pleased to hear warmth, interest and charm when he answered the phone. My first impression of his kind and sensitive side grew during the entire time I knew him. He listened to the tale of my heritage discovery and my desire to learn more about Métis culture. I explained that I had grown up in and around Native Canadian issues and had been involved in Aboriginal adult basic education for the past eight years. He summarily began quizzing my understanding of Métis matters. And so my second impression of the man was that his mind was sharp as a tack.

After our initial chat in 1998, it became my privilege to visit Howard and his wife Marge many times during the next few years. Our conversations were never dull. Indeed, I found myself stimulated by the range of topics in which we engaged. Soon I began to do some consulting work for Howard. Sometimes, I noticed that he would stop talking or repeat himself, but it was easy for him to regain his train of thought when I reworded or emphasized a point that he had forgotten. His momentary loss of memory did not affect our conversations.

In my journal entry for January 25, 2000, there is a note that Howard talked of his desires to have Métis culture explored regularly in Vancouver high school classrooms. He knew that I was advocating for education about Métis in Fraser Valley primary and elementary schools. He knew, too, that I was working on a community partnership literacy project to write the first book describing British Columbia's Métis, which had recently been accepted for funding.

Adamant about wanting to produce at least one secondary level Social Studies program about the Métis, Howard desired to know more about proposal writing. Finally, he desired that we produce a proposal for the Vancouver school district. At the time, it was clear that Howard's ambitions were not focused on primary or elementary education as mine were. He told me to find someone else to create curricula at those levels. He wanted to form an education committee consisting of several Métis educators whom we knew, as well as ourselves. And, he added, he wanted the committee to establish contact with presidents of colleges and universities, and with federal and provincial governments. He was galvanized to achieve three goals: to have Social Studies programs about Métis taught in Vancouver high schools; to create a curriculum complete with the materials and aids needed for School District 39; and to have at least one program about the Métis available province-wide and listed in the Ministry of Education's curriculum guide. Unfortunately, as noble as Howard's goals were, I could not help him, as my time was already committed to the literacy project.

For me, Howard was a consummate educator, and a complex and humble yet proud man. Several times in our late January conversation, I encouraged him to think about his contributions to Canada's changed attitude towards Aboriginal people, and to submit to an archive all his papers that documented his contributions to this change. I said that it would be one way of getting information about Métis issues into the hands of academic researchers. He laughed my suggestions off, saying something evasive. But several days later, he hired me to put his papers in order.

Howard's work habits could be seen in the older papers that he gave me to read. His work was neat and his spelling and sentence structure were of decent quality. But it surprised me that he had only a half a banker's file box of folders the first time I saw them. As his interest in preserving his achievements grew in the ensuing weeks and months, he found more folders and papers. During the next few months, as we put Howard's papers in order and ran down those that were missing, he never forgot that one of the goals for preparing his papers was to have Métis information readily available for high school students' access. He knew his work in twentieth–century issues and matters had influenced or affected the way that Aboriginal people were treated in Canada and the United States. As the months passed, I realized that Howard's memory was seeping away, for longer periods each time we met, leaving him staring into the lovely garden that he and Marge tenderly groomed. Yet our discourses over wonderful meals together with Marge remained vibrant and flowing. If he was aware of the blank spaces, he never spoke of them to me. However, he did occasionally comment that some days he did not get much done on his memoirs, another project on which he had begun working. He once said that he needed stimulation to stay focused and productive.

By now, I had also read more recent papers, written in the early 1990s. I could see that some of them contained a lot of spelling and sentence structure errors. He allowed me to clarify what he wanted to say in these essays. He said that he would send them to his typist, but the retyped essays were only a little more clearly understood than his first version. Another couple of important essays disappeared altogether. Although he tried several times, Howard was not able to recall what happened to them. I now feared speaking to my friend about rewriting any more of his essays.

I did not see Howard the final few months of 2000, but in the spring of 2001, after finishing the other project, I visited him to resume working on his papers, which had been stored in a cardboard box in his office. In the previous fall, we had made a "gentlemen's agreement" that he would not disturb the papers that I had carefully prepared into thematic and chronological files. I was alarmed to see that he had pulled out papers for which people had asked him, as well as files that he needed for writing his memoirs. Although he had photocopied some, he had given others to certain people, expecting to have them returned. These papers were never recovered. Still more alarming was that as we worked at that first meeting in 2001, he removed papers from folders at points in our conversation and tossed them into the nearby wastebasket, saying that he did not need them anymore. Several times, I gently reminded him of what the papers meant to his collection. I pulled them out and held on to them because he threw them back into the wastebasket when I did not.

I worried for my friend. I could see that he was easily confused. I worried for the completion of his dream of having documents available for student research, and I decided to visit more frequently. The next few times, he blustered a little when I retrieved papers out of the wastebasket. Gently associating some activity that he had done with the papers seemed to sooth him. He let me rescue and re-file these important papers back into the box. Furthermore, he no longer took items from the box. He seemed to appreciate that everything in the box was key to the success of his dream.

I think that our relationship also changed at this point. He seemed willing to accept that his memory was failing, and so we worked more closely, more harmoniously. He matter-of-factly engaged in discussion about some papers that he had written since 1996. The essence of what he wanted to say was in them, but the sentence structure was confusing, spelling mistakes were rampant, and his edits were discombobulated. I thought some were important essays that filled out perspectives not covered in his other works. I offered what I thought he was saying in these essays. He agreed with some parts, and what I had misinterpreted he quickly corrected. In this way, he reconstructed what he had intended to say. He allowed me to type and read the essays back to him for his approval.

During the summer of 2001, Howard and Marge vacationed in California. During that six-week period, I now had a full box of Howard's original papers, books and materials. I then compared all the original papers in every folder that I had created for the archives against the master set that I had made when I first got the papers in 2000. I then made a photocopy of every original that Howard gave me to give me access to information in the papers. In that way, I could sort, group and file my copies and leave the originals with Howard, as I did not want to be liable if any went missing. It was this set of original papers filed into a fonds style collection of folders from which Howard had been "pilfering" during the months that I had worked elsewhere.

While Howard vacationed, I used the copies to re-assemble the originals stored in the box. Original papers and whole folders had been disappearing from the fonds for several months, and so those no longer in Howard's folders had to be copied from my working model and entered into his original collection.

Although Howard at first thought that I had lost the papers, he recanted when I told him that I was able to produce copies of the original papers in his care from my master. He was very concerned that he had lost papers and searched for them for several weeks. He found some and was so anxious to get them to me that he threw them in a manila envelope and mailed them ordinary post instead of letting me pick them up at the house. Fortunately, the tattered and torn envelope arrived shortly after his phone call. Months before, he would not have done such a thing. Realizing them as irreplaceable, he would have waited for me to pick them up.

I think that Howard's concern was always to have as many of his papers as possible preserved and delivered to Library and Archives Canada, so that secondary and post-secondary students and scholars could access them and thereby learn first-hand about actions that he took to reduce the colonialism that Métis and First Nations people faced daily.[1] He was so self-disciplined that he unconsciously exercised this mental goal during these last few months of his life. He also seemed to want completion of this

---

[1] Initially, Howard had wanted to donate his materials to the Native Studies Department at the University of Saskatchewan in Saskatoon, but when Library and Archives Canada showed keener interest, he changed his mind. Presently, Library and Archives Canada are in the process of creating an Internet finding aid for the Howard Adams Fond, and they are putting a complete copy of the entire collection on microfilm to be given to the University of Saskatchewan. (Personal information to the editors by Dr. Art Grenke, Archivist at the Social and Cultural Archives, Canadian Archives Branch of the Library and Archives Canada, Ottawa, April 23, 2004.)

fonds preparation because he felt that it was important for the Métis to be recognized by all Canadians as having made tremendous contributions to the social, economic and cultural identity of the country.

In mid-2001, as work on his papers was ending, he knew that he was struggling to keep his memory. He knew that he repeated himself as he talked, and that he had been doing these things for some months. He may have known that he was becoming less able to communicate, because he was much more willing to accept responsibility for tasks that he failed to accomplish, such as going to the University of British Columbia archival libraries to replace items that had gone missing from the box. He said that he felt guilty that he was not working on his memoirs. But he was happy. He knew that his papers were going to be accessed for a more realistic societal Canadian picture than he had known as a Halfbreed youth and young adult.

Howard was likely aware that he would not create the curriculum that he desired to put into Vancouver schools. He may have put in place some of the desire to provide an educational program about the Métis into preparation of his papers for Library and Archives Canada because, in his contract to send his papers there, he stipulated that any Canadian high school that wanted a copy of his fonds should be allowed to purchase one.

He said that once the fonds were finished, he was happy knowing that Canadian and international students could access his works at a national site, and that the Royal Canadian Mounted Police and Canadian Security Intelligence Service sites could also be accessed in order to provide a more comprehensive picture of his Aboriginal rights activities to those students.

Howard passed away shortly after making this statement that part of his dream fulfilled.

Conscientization: From Karl May to Howard Adams

Sylvia Walsh

Sometimes the most obvious things escape our attention. So it was for me, when reflecting on Howard Adams, the person, teacher and dialectical historian. Yes, I knew Howard as a fellow teacher and colleague from the Institute of Indigenous Government (IIG) in Vancouver, where, in 1999, he taught "The Transformation of Indigenous Society," a course that reflected Howard's *weltanschauung* about how the social formation of capitalism determines the particular character in which "self-designated 'superior' cultures assumed the right to penetrate and dominate 'inferior cultures'" (Harry Magdoff, 1973). Thus, he engaged our students in a profound dialogue about imperial history, racism and the politics of colonization. Our students loved Howard, the kind and gentle man, the angry, impatient historian and fighter, the passionate teacher and educational transformer.

Howard also played an important part in my own personal history and journey toward concientization about colonization, oppression and racism. As a child, growing up in post-war Berlin, I, like many other German kids from eight to eighty years of age, read and loved Karl May's road books about North American "Indians." Although these stories painted a somewhat romanticized portrait of Aboriginal life and culture in North America, they also dealt with issues of justice and injustice, values, good and bad attitudes and behaviours and, most of all, friendship between two people from very different cultural backgrounds.

The events were gripping and exciting, and Winnetou, the noble Apache Chief, became my hero. He was good-looking, a great leader, brave, wise and kind, and he knew how to make a clear distinction between real friends and traitors. I fell in love with Winnetou and the Aboriginal culture that Karl May described in these books. The effect was that when John Wayne's Westerns were played in the movie theatres, we all cheered for the Indians and booed the cowboys. Such was my early exposure to North American culture and values.

Years later, after immigrating to Canada and then spending time at the University of Arizona, where my husband Don studied, I finally met some real life Apaches and Navajos. Of all the possible coincidences, I got a small part in a John Wayne movie called *El Dorado*. There I met Nino Cochise, who was the technical advisor for some of the scenes, and Eddy Little Sky, an actor in the film. I finally found my Winnetou, and I tried to convince him to contact film studios in Germany, who were filming a series on Winnetou. (A French actor in West Germany and a Yugoslav actor in East Germany later played the part.)

Upon moving to Canada, and studying for five years at the University of Regina, I was finally exposed to real Aboriginal issues. During the time of Jean Chrétien's "White Paper," some of us "radicals" protested the racist intent of this paper. Some of my teachers, among them Professor Stan Rands, who had been an advocate of human and Aboriginal rights, held meetings and stay-overs at his home with some Aboriginal peoples on their way to Ottawa.

In 1975, I was introduced to Howard Adams' book, *Prison of Grass*. Howard opened my eyes wide. Here was a real-life book about real-life Aboriginal people and real-life issues that mattered. The whole puzzle suddenly fell into place. It was not that I did not know anything about colonization and the oppression of Aboriginal peoples in North America. After all, I did my M.A. at the University of Regina, which, at the time, was considered the "Red Campus" in Canada. The insight that I gained from reading Howard's book was that I had not recognized the painful effect of colonization on the mindset of Aboriginal peoples.

At this time, I was offered a sessional teaching appointment in Psychology, and I used Howard's book to demonstrate how institutional racism had permeated Canadian society and reinforced racist attitudes and behaviours. Howard's powerful description of his own experience in *Prison of Grass*, both in chapter one, "The Basis of Racism," and chapter fifteen, "Decolonization and Nationalism," offered analyses that went much deeper than just learning about "Indians." It provoked racist images and deep-seated feelings of "blaming the victims." It was difficult for white middle-class students to recognize that their political silence played a part in keeping racism alive.

In 1977, I was invited to participate in program development at the Saskatchewan Indian Federated College (SIFC), now called the First Nations University of Canada. Finally, I had the opportunity to interact with Aboriginal scholars, teachers, students and Elders, both at the college and throughout Saskatchewan. I learned first-hand what Howard had described in *Prison of Grass*. I encountered the colonized mindset of students, political leaders and educators. Transforming the colonized mindsets of students became my obsession. The books that were most influential in this task were Frantz Fanon's *The Wretched of the Earth*, Paulo Freire's *The Pedagogy of the Oppressed*, Howard's *Prison of Grass*. A good shot of Critical Theory as helped.

Conscientization, according to Freire, involves the process of historical reflection, becoming aware of the nature of one's limiting situation and recognizing the possibilities of transforming that situation through praxis. For Aboriginal peoples, that process involves knowing the true history of colonization, the effects of colonization on the mindset of people and identifying that true decolonization can only be achieved through self-determination and action by Aboriginal peoples themselves.

After several years of program development, teaching and developing curriculum for SIFC, I decided to complete a Ph.D. in Higher Education at Arizona State University. Armoured with a conscientizised perspective, I again encountered racist attitudes by the majority of mainstream educators that were reflected in their sense of superiority toward both Aboriginal and Chicano students. Of course, there are some pearls to be found, even in the desert of Barry Goldwater country.

Dr. Raymond Padilla, who followed in Paulo Freire's footsteps, and who was engaged in excellent dialectical research that supported Native American and Chicano students in their studies and research became my mentor. I also connected with the "Indian Leadership Program," a graduate program that provided some direction for Aboriginal students and provided a place of belonging to those few Native American students, alienated in a campus numbering 45,000 students. Most of the courses reflected mainstream curriculum, but provided value-added cultural elements. All in all, the program at that time lacked the historical and political reflection to move students forward to self-determination and true leadership.

In 1994, wearing my badge of academic acceptance from what Howard would have called the "Ivory Tower Elitist Club," I came to Vancouver to start another chapter on my learning curve. A friend, who knew of my work in Saskatchewan, approached me about the possibility of getting involved in the establishment of an Aboriginal college in Vancouver. I was hired by the Union of British Columbia Indian Chiefs, whose principles about Aboriginal title and self-determination for Indian nations sent shock waves though the establishment. It was a great opportunity to develop an Indigenous-controlled institute, mandated to establish programs for the study of Indigenous government. For the first two years, I was the Director of Planning and Development at the institute, and in the following years a group of like-minded faculty developed and taught an exciting post-secondary program that was second to none in North America. Its mission was to provide our students with the knowledge, skills-training and research opportunities that were intended to maximize their leadership opportunities in areas of political, economic, social and cultural service. The goal of the program was to empower Indigenous peoples to exercise effectively their right of self-determination in their territories in ways that fully reflect Indigenous philosophy, values and experience throughout the world.

In 1999, Dr. Howard Adams, who had just received the *National Aboriginal Achievement Award*, joined our ranks. It was a dream come true for our students, who had read Howard's work in two of my courses: "The Nature of Racism" and "Decolonization and Self-determination." The senior faculty were extremely honoured to have a scholar like Howard at the institute. He consequently developed a course on the "Transformation of Indigenous Society." Also in 1999, Howard had just revised his book, *A Tortured People: The Politics of Colonization.*

At that time, all was not well at the Institute, and the reactionary politics of a new authoritarian administration undermined our efforts to move ahead toward a four-year degree program in Indigenous Government Studies (IGS). The administration's aim was to change the Institute's political direction, turning the IGS program into a watered-down mainstream program with an emphasis on administration and social work. Our students protested because they understood what internal colonization is all about. They were being silenced and not allowed to voice their concerns and objections to the Board of Governors, who were misled by the administration, even though most members were Aboriginal individuals.

In December 1999, the majority of our students held a walkout and carried signs like "Decolonize the IGS." The students had assumed conscient?ed leadership, and the progressive faculty joined them, among them our friend Howard Adams. Once again, it was back to the barricades, opposing unilateral decision-making, authoritarianism and injustice, and, once again, Howard proved that he walked the talk. At one of our education council meetings, while presenting our grievances to the administration after being publicly called the "Gang of Four" (Theo Collins, Alejandro Palacios, Lix Lopez and myself), he listened attentively to the administration's arguments for proposing this new mainstream direction and the opportunist voices of colonized staff, and concluded, "Well, I am with the Gang of Four!"

Afterword

Hartmut Lutz

Counted altogether, the tangle of Howard Adams' manuscripts (**AB**, **TB**, **MISC**), from which the autobiographical materials were culled, comprised 571 pages. Despite such an apparent wealth of material, his autobiographical texts leave many gaps in the story of his life, and thus raise questions that may remain unanswered forever.

What should we make of his Mountie years? Why did he not explain anything about the training that he received at Rockcliffe? There is also the issue of suffering from depression. How much of Almighty's spiritual and psychological agony is based on Howard Adams' own experiences with depression? Or take Tony's amorous adventures and his never-ending supply of women. How much of Tony, the womanizer, is actually based on the life of Howard Adams, and why did Howard create such a character? There are also the time gaps in both the autobiographical parts and in Tony's story. Why didn't Howard write anything about his career as a professor in Native American Studies at the University of California-Davis and his retirement years in Vancouver and Saskatchewan, a span of 26 years? There is also the question of identifying his contemporaries. Why do we learn so little about the people with whom he interacted in the 1960s and '70s in Saskatchewan? Why did he give so very few names of people to whom he was close, and none of his opponents? Protection of privacy is easily understood, but why did he not write at all about his fourteen years as a professor of Native American Studies with the Tecumseh Center, University of California-Davis, or his brief involvement with Deganawidah-Quetzalcoatl University, a grassroots Indian-Chicano community college near Davis? Was it just the "hell" for him that Roxanne Dunbar-Ortiz speaks of in her contribution to this book?

When I first met Howard in Davis, California in 1979, we immediately connected on a political level, sharing many convictions. At the same time, I was (and remain) a great admirer of Jack D. Forbes. I also had great respect for the late Barbara Hutchinson. The then-department head, David Risling, became something like a mentor and cherished father figure for me. They were Howard's colleagues at the Tecumseh Center. To my disappointment, and my lasting emotional discomfort, relations between the latter three on one side and Howard on the other were obviously strained, which is putting it euphemistically. But throughout the year that my family and I lived in Davis, Howard never let a negative comment pass his lips about his colleagues, who were all members of Native-American nations.

Our editing deliberately avoided any attempt to fill in any gaps beyond the scope of what Howard had indicated in the texts that he left. Some of the silences will best be known to Marge, who shared them, or maybe to a few of his contemporaries. If the academic and political interest in Howard Adams' life and work continues among Aboriginal and non-Aboriginal people, later biographers may decide to research some of these questions and fill in some of the gaps. Thanks to Howard Adams' own initiative, and thanks to the efforts of Rene Inkster and the commitment of Margaret Adams, there are four full boxes of materials for research in the Howard Adams Fonds at Library and Archives Canada in Ottawa, where Dr. Art Grenke has carefully prepared them for access. There are also books, articles and reviews that Howard Adams published throughout his career.

Strands in a Sash: The Lives of Howard, Tony and Almighty

While we were not able or willing to fill in gaps in Howard's life narratives, it is a different thing to treat as literature the autobiographical textual strands that constitute Part I of this book. They form a literary text somewhere between historiography, autobiography, memoir and prose fiction, and they should be read as such. To better understand Howard's political vision, his texts also need to be read within the context of other autobiographical and political writings that he knew or used as models for the Métis' anti-colonial struggle. In the following, therefore, I shall attempt to follow both approaches, reading the texts first as autobiography and fiction, and then position Howard's life-writing in relation to its historical and political contexts.

In our joint "Preface," we conceptualized the three interwoven narrative life-strands as a sash. The warps are constituted by the lives of Tony, Almighty and Howard, as narrated in Howard Adams' autobiographical manuscripts. They reflect the life struggles of three Aboriginal male characters—two of them fictional, one "real"—who lived some time between 1921 and 2001 in Saskatchewan and British Columbia, with forays into California and other parts of the world. Howard Adams, the author, wrote the texts at different times in his life. Even when put together, the length of time spanned by this narrative warp is shorter than the duration of Howard's life. The three strands may be read consecutively or separately. That is how we read them, after having disentangled them from the pile of "WRITINGS, <u>ALL TYPES</u>." But such a reading often becomes boring and repetitive. Instead, we decided to stretch the warp between the poles of Howard's life, and then interweave and fill them with the multicoloured weft yarns spun by Howard himself, so that they would form one joint narrative account, albeit tinged in the different colours of the separate narrative voices, and with different degrees of fictional license or factual accuracy. But all three are authentic in the sense that they were written by Howard Adams, and not one of these texts would have been written had Howard Adams not intended them to be read at the time.

Autobiography: First Person Howard as the Non-fictional Protagonist

Howard Adams' non-fictional autobiographical texts, told in the first person narrate a first cycle in Howard's life. It begins with his departure for the RCMP Depot in Regina, but then immediately leaps back to relate chronologically to his birth, childhood and youth at his home in the Métis "ghetto" of St. Louis, Saskatchewan. Thus, the very opening of the narrative triggers the same suspense-evoking questions, which are also employed in the classic opening passages of such famous life-histories as Daniel Defoe's *Robinson Crusoe* or Maria Campbell's *Halfbreed*. In both, the reader learns from the beginning that the protagonist left home, but is not told why. The question poses itself as to when the protagonist left, and more importantly, what drove her or him away. Readers are inclined to read on and to learn why.

Howard Adams' autobiographical narrative goes on to relate how the young ghetto-dwelling ignoramus "makes it" as a Mountie, receives an education in the outside world (the **AB** fragment ends with his years as an University of British Columbia undergraduate), and how he later returns almost triumphantly to his Saskatchewan home as Dr. Howard Adams, the first Métis Ph.D. in Canada. He unites and leads his people on the path towards self-determination, convincing them with the truth of his political analyses and the spellbinding power of his skills as an Aboriginal orator. After that, the concluding pieces in Howard's autobiography are little more than mere frames for the texts of Howard's famous speeches, which are recreated verbatim. The **MISC** autobiographical narratives also end abruptly, and the autobiography proper remains silent until one episode, very late in Howard's life, when, after having watched the movie *Out of Africa*, he remembers his struggle. The autobiographical narratives make no mention by name of Howard's conflict with the James Sinclair faction of the Métis Society of Saskatchewan, nor is anything said about why Howard left Canada, about what happened in his academic life after he had left the University of Saskatchewan in Saskatoon for the University of California in Davis in 1975 or what he experienced between his return to Canada in 1987 and his death in 2001. Thus, by leaving out what may be called his "exile" and the beginning of the second cycle in Howard's life, his unfinished autobiographical texts recapture only the first and most celebratory part of what may be read as his success story.

At first glance, Howard's autobiography seems to follow the "classic" Franklinian autobiographical model, "from rags to riches"—but only almost. Benjamin Franklin's autobiography recaptures and celebrates his success as a self-made man, a bourgeois individual who pulls himself up by his bootstraps and becomes a rich capitalist entrepreneur, an inventor, a Quaker politician and a pragmatist philosopher, and has since served as a much-emulated role model for the (White middle-class) American

Dream. By contrast, Howard's success is not measured in terms of individual self-realization, neither by the degree of his personal power nor by his supposed nearness to salvation. Rather, it is measured in terms of the growing political awareness and increasingly radical activism of the Aboriginal "masses" (Howard's term) in Saskatchewan, whose teacher and spokesperson he chose to be, and to whose struggle he committed his career. In the life-project narrated in the unfinished autobiography, Howard's going out to "better" himself and to receive as comprehensive an education as possible does not follow the self-serving ultimate goal of achieving individual success by securing a seat among the ruling elite. Rather, his striving for higher education is understood as a means towards an ultimate social and political end, collective not individual, and which lies beyond his immediate self-interests.

The narrative relates how Howard Adams partly achieved this goal after going through a cycle that is reminiscent of the structure followed in the medieval European grail-quest epics, where the hero starts out in ignorance, is tossed in a sea of doubts, temptations and failures, but finally, through suffering, compassion and taking responsibility, achieves an enlightened state of fulfilment, redemption and even "bliss." In reality, of course, Howard Adams was no Perceval, and in the end, the Indian and Métis masses in Saskatchewan at that time could provide for him no blissful state of achievement. Quite the contrary, in hindsight some members of the Métis and Indian organizations with whom Howard interacted may well be accused of having chased him out. In his contribution for this volume, Murray Hamilton argues that Howard probably realized in 1974 that there was little left for him to contribute to the Métis struggle in terms of his own political insights, and that co-optation and infighting were to follow. I agree with Murray's explanation. Howard probably realized that it had become time for him to go. He was more of a radical activist, a critical analyst of policies, than a long term political administrator, and I believe that in the long run, academic pursuits and intellectual debates would have seemed more attractive to him than living the life of those he called the masses, for whom he spoke and whom he loved. As a result, his "exile" in California was probably an ambiguous state of existence, both a banishment from his people, whom he always missed, but also a liberation from the social restraints and petty jealousies that are characteristic of the famous "crab basket," a metaphor for any poor and powerless community in which an individual who climbs to the top and sticks out his head is pulled under by his own neighbours, colleagues or kin. The basket needs no lid. Internal dissension will keep the community occupied and docile. But besides escaping from the crab basket, leaving Saskatchewan was probably also his best option in terms of his personal health. There is support for such an explanation among the materials at Library and Archives Canada. Howard suffered from depression, and he and Marge hoped that the California sunlight would do him good.

After Howard left Saskatchewan in the winter of 1974/75, he and Marge had to start all over on a second cycle, again going through isolation, alienation, conflict and doubt, until reaching the relative serenity of their retirement years in Vancouver. Howard shared with young Aboriginal students and activists in British Columbia and Saskatchewan the rich reservoir of his knowledge and experiences, and his overwhelming and often romanticizing love for his people (while passionately hating the abject conditions of internal colonization under which they were forced to live). I have never seen Howard's eyes sparkle more than when he spoke to or about young people like Donna Heimbecker in Saskatchewan, or the Carriere sisters and Dan Kruk in British Columbia. Again, Howard's success and happiness in the second cycle of his life, as in his first, must also be measured in terms of his connectedness with his people, and by the quality of his contribution to their social advancement.

Fiction in the Third Person:
Tony as the Protagonist of an Unfinished Novel

Tony's Biography (**TB**) is best understood as the fragment of a larger novel that was either never finished or partially destroyed. This conclusion may be deduced from the fact that some pages of this text were arranged as paginated sequences. Some even had typed and numbered chapter headings, like "CHAPTER TEN," with the handwritten addition "Mountie in Gravelbourg," or the handwritten caption "Chapter 12: Wood Mountain & Sue," or a scribbled insertion "Chpt. 20—Search for Sue—Years L." But there were no chapters one to nine in the pile of original manuscripts, no concluding chapters after chapter twenty, nor a complete sequence from chapters ten to twenty. From the manuscripts, then, we can neither tell how the autobiographical Tony novel was meant to have started nor how it would have ended. Some of the headings seem to be the results of a much later attempt to edit or rearrange an already existing typescript, which also bears many scribbled corrections and insertions. I have concluded that, regrettably, Howard destroyed large parts in the process. So, the textual material that we found consisted of a series of extended fragments. We lay these parallel to the **AB** and **MISC** sequences and then integrated them as large strands, which they almost equal in length (**AB** has 96 pages; we used 138 pages of **MISC**, and our salvaged **TB** selection had 196 typed pages). The narration in the preserved parts of the manuscript starts at the moment when Tony Parker, the high school student, questions the accuracy of history textbooks and begins organizing his classmates to distrust Euro-Canadian historiography. It ends with Tony Bruce and some of his Métis comrades discussing revolutionary nationalism and cultural revival.

As a fictional but autobiographically inspired text, the Tony sequences explore additional models of learning and achieving personal progress, which at times ideologically contradict those in the autobiographical texts. More obviously than the first person narratives, the **TB** narrative follows the format of a *Bildungsroman*, i.e. an account of an individual's learning and maturing process. Compared to the autobiographical texts, Howard's fictional explorations concentrate on the psychological aspects of a young Métis individual. The incongruity between the two surnames Parker and Bruce can be guessed at, but not fully be resolved. Most likely, it was based on a change of mind that occurred during the writing, which would have been edited out if Howard had pursued this project any further. Nearer the conclusion of the narrative, especially after Tony's obsessive search for Sue, Tony grows psychologically more flat, and towards the end of the manuscript he, like Howard's autobiographical self, turns into little more than a mouthpiece for a political discourse on Métis liberation and revolutionary nationalism.

Creating a fictional character like Tony gives the author poetic license to explore extremes, both in the positive and negative. Accordingly, Tony is a very ambivalent figure. On the one hand, he seems like an idealized version of Howard, the brilliant orator, the fearless revolutionary activist and the superior intellectual. On the other hand, however, he is a very romantic but often inconsiderate, inconstant and immature womanizer, a self-serving macho man, a cunning and servile flatterer of his superiors and a vindictive opportunist. When compared to the autobiographical Howard, who also relates some amorous relationships, the fictional character Tony is far more involved in his affairs, and he seems to explore different forms of love and success. Carefully constructed parallelisms, as well as the deliberate use of contrasting opposites in the text, support the impression that the **TB** narrative is indeed a creative fiction, intended to be "Tony's novel." This is not obvious at first, because Tony's first love affair seems no different than that of the autobiographical narrator. Tony's infatuation with Sylvia, the commanding officer's daughter, so closely resembles Howard's romance with Edie that, apart from a few minor details in the plot, both experiences seem identical—a very romantic juvenile affair.

But, with both the Sue and Judy episodes, "Tony's novel" abandons the autobiographical fold. Tony's love for Sue, who does not appear as a character in the autobiographical narratives, starts out as a much more mature affair than the Sylvia/Edie romance, especially because there is no ethnic self-denial, and the two share a union-oriented socialist ethic. Sue's father and mother fully sanction their marriage plans. At first, Tony keeps up his passing, but neither Sue nor her family exhibit any racist reactions against Tony's Métis background. Ironically, it is Tony who articulates strong feelings of internalized racism when he "graciously" apologizes to his extended family for his intention to marry a White girl. (Unfortunately, the text says nothing about Sue's reaction to being taxed in such condescendingly ethnocentric terms.) For Sue, Tony is even willing to overcome the jealous resistance of his all-dominant mother. But then, perhaps due to his inability to put his resolution into practice and seriously hurt his mother and abandon the Métis values that she represents, Tony's behaviour becomes inconsistent and reckless. He jeopardizes his future with Sue when he leaves for British Columbia, and then takes a considerably long time before contacting her again and inviting her to the coast. Their romance in Vancouver is described as idyllic and harmonious, and the novel seems to be headed for a happy end, but their bliss is abruptly shattered when Sue is called back to Saskatchewan to see her mother in hospital. Their ways part forever. Much later in the "Tony novel," the memory of Sue comes to haunt the jilted Tony, and Sue's image assumes a larger than life presence, with such urgency that he cannot control his wanderings or his drinking, and Tony loses his grip on reality

By comparison, Tony's courtship and later marriage to Judy Knox, who also has no equivalent in the autobiography, seems almost callously rational and sexualized. He uses her for his own social upward mobility because Judy seems to guarantee access to a White upper middle-class world that Tony is seeking to enter for furthering his career. Besides, she is a willing partner in bed and a hard working student. Judy, on the other hand, uses Tony for the comfort of having a steady partner who is good looking, "manageable," and career-minded enough not to interfere with her own plans. Both rank their careers before their relationship. Judy's parents are opposed to the marriage for reasons of class, and Tony continues his passing because he anticipates their hatred of Aboriginal people. Both Judy's racism and Tony's own careerism lead him to conceal his Aboriginal origins and upbringing, emotionally the most essential part of his inner being. The shattering showdown comes when they are called to Saskatchewan to visit his mother in hospital, and Judy finds out that her dying mother in law is "Indian."

Within the structure of the "Tony novel," the Judy and Sue sequences are carefully orchestrated. Sue seems to stand for everything that allows Tony to keep his identity and cherish the things that he really values—family kinship within the Métis fold while also being welcome in a White family; staying in his home region in Saskatchewan; being able to participate in a socialist political project. Judy, however, stands for cultural alienation. She seems to represent a way of life that is an irreconcilable opposite to Tony's original values—denial of his Métis origin and having to pass as White, and life in an urban setting marked by capitalist competition and consumerism. There are two decisive turning points, both connected to situations that are thematically paralleled along questions of loyalty to origin and family: (1) Sue is called home to Saskatchewan to attend her mother in hospital, and Tony sees her for the last time; and (2) Judy finds out that Tony's hospitalized mother is Aboriginal, insists on being taken home to her parents in Vancouver and Tony sees her for the last time. In both cases we may conclude on a more abstract level that the text conveys the idea that loyalty to the mother, and to the cultural mores conveyed by her, cement the ideological boundaries of class and race, and impede trans-cultural marriage.

While neither Sue nor Judy appear in the autobiographical narratives, Sue seems to be more than a mere fiction. In the passage that describes Sue's departure for Regina, the text says that Tony "watched Sue go through the gate, and disappear down the ramp." However, a handwritten correction the next sentence reads: "I didn't realize it, but she had walked out of my life forever." (pg. 122) This handwritten slip of the pen or editorial correction was entered into the "Tony novel" manuscript at a later date. It marks a sudden perspective shift from the third person narrator Tony to that of the first person, thereby suggesting a far greater autobiographical factuality of the fictional Sue than her absence from all autobiographical texts seems to indicate.

Viewed from the context of the entire text, the "Tony novel" explores and eventually refutes the possibility of passing as a Whiteman and securing entry to a successful career in mainstream society. Tony's experiences with the "rat race" expose the social callousness, racism and coldness of Judy's world as a psychologically harrowing environment that dehumanizes even those who seem to profit from it. For Tony, the price that he has to pay for entering the White middle class means the irreparable loss of Sue, a painful alienation from his kin and a denial of the most essential parts of his Métis ethics. The price is too high.

Fiction in the First Person: Almighty as an First Person Narrator

Even more so than the "Tony novel," the Almighty episode is a fragment. Since it was contained in the "WRITINGS, ALL TYPES" pile, the text appeared to us to be another one of Howard's Miscellaneous autobiographical pieces, and even the narrator's ethnic self-identification as "Indian" is congruous with other autobiographical passages, where "Redman" or "Indian" are used instead of "Halfbreed" or "Métis". However, both the narrator's girlfriend Marguerite and his psychoanalyst, the Doctor persistently use the name "Almighty," leading us to believe that Almighty is a fictional character created to explore other aspects of Howard Adams' life and character not covered in "Tony's novel" or in the autobiography proper. The character's name is symbolically framed after a historical character who stood up as an Indian against the White colonial oppressors, but who tragically perished in the process.

Almighty is hospitalized, and he is so much "out of it" that he does not recognize his beloved Marguerite. Instead, he picks imaginary bugs out of her hair, jumps up and down and shouts condemnations at the Whiteman. This protagonist seems to have reached a psychotic state that can be a severely pathological form of manic-depression, or bipolar disorder. Individuals suffering from this affliction undergo periods of deep depression, apathy and hopelessness, and then change into bouts of manic activity, euphoria and, sometimes, self-aggrandizing tendencies. We witness streaks of such arrogance in one of the autobiographical school episodes (e.g. at the sports meet, and also in Tony's arrogance after he has cheated at Social Studies and now claims his superior marks to be "the workings of a Halfbreed brain"). At the beginning of his experience, Almighty is obviously in a state of such severe depression that his behaviour has turned psychotic. This creates for Howard Adams, the author, the opportunity to demonstrate how the structures of racism, internal colonialism and cultural alienation combine to pathologize the oppressed, causing them to withdraw into regressive behaviour, which makes ruling them easier for the colonizer. The Almighty episode also fictionalizes the dangerous and often abrupt transition from the depressive to the manic stage, when Almighty, the convalescent, suddenly sees himself as an expert on psychoanalytical theory and starts lecturing with great enthusiasm not only Marguerite but even the doctor. At the same time, we hear the voice of Howard Adams, the political analyst, speaking through Almighty and using his protagonist for a case study in Frantz Fanon's theories about the psychological effects of colonial oppression. In the process, Almighty provides pertinent insights into the psyche of those whom Howard elsewhere called the compradors of the Indian Affairs department.

After having read the autobiographical account of Howard's days in grade school, the Almighty episode does not come as a surprise to the reader. In school, Howard tells us he constantly struggled against losing awareness of reality around him, and he developed painful strategies to avoid being sucked into an existential nothingness. The narrator seems to be slipping in and out of various states of mental awareness. Later, the narrator shifts between, on the one hand, being identical with the young school kid, and on the other, a much later period in Howard's life, from where he concludes, retrospectively, "But now, I'm spiteful. I'm filled with revenge, hostility and disgust, the psychopathology of colonialism." (pg. 33) The complex time shifts in the narrator's perspective make this almost a perfect example of the erratic voice of an "unreliable narrator," akin to Edgar Allan Poe's classic madman in "The Tell-Tale Heart." But we as readers are given enough reliable clues to understand that such states of delusions and hallucinations in the narrator's youth must have accompanied Howard all his life, if not as actual pathological states, certainly as haunting and unsettling memories. The experiences of being in an in-between state, between a functioning mental normality and an extreme sensual awareness beyond material reality, provided the author with a most profound personal understanding of what he calls the "psychopathology of colonialism."

Again, the author has created a fictional character who explores an extreme form of behaviour caused by the ills of a system that he was bent to expose and overcome. While Tony's suffering exposes the psychologically destructive effects of passing as White in a dehumanizing capitalist rat race, Almighty's agony lays open the dehumanization of the Indigene by the colonizer. But Almighty also exemplifies the ability of the colonized to identify, analyze and target for dismantling the ills of a system that needs to be overcome. If Tony represents the "Whiteman" alter ego, Almighty is an "Indian" counterpart. Howard Adams, the Métis writer, has created them both. He is neither of them, but he knows them both intimately.

Both the "Tony and Sue" and the "Marguerite and Almighty" episodes are clearly marked as fiction, but, again, the interface between fact and fiction is extremely porous. Again, there is a slippage of identity from Marguerite to Sue (and thus via Tony, even towards Howard), and there are the parallels between Almighty's behaviour and that of the autobiographical accounts in both the school episodes, as well as in the later *Out of Africa* reminiscence. These slippages speak of periods of immense psychological agony, marked by alienation, loneliness, anger and despair. Howard Adams' pain demands our empathy. His ability to create and act positively, even out of the depths of his suffering, deserves our admiration. Howard once told me that in his sleepless nights he would write what he called his "hate pieces." Some of them contain extremely beautiful passages. It would seem to me that in his depression Howard sought and found what James Bartleman, a fellow "Halfbreed" and fellow depressive (although from quite a different political spectrum) calls in his autobiography, *On Six Continents* (2004), "the therapeutic magic of the pen".

Taken together the autobiographical narrator, Tony and Almighty present an ambivalent and contradictory composite character who is essentially fictional in as much as every autobiographical "I" can never be a one-to-one equation of the author's own self. Together, they embody a selection of only those aspects of the author's identity that he chooses to share with the reader. The textual slippages between the autobiography, Tony and Almighty, or between Marguerite and Sue, are the stylistic expressions of how closely the three stories were connected in Howard's mind, long before we had the idea of weaving them together. It is at the interfaces between fiction and fact that the autobiographical self finds its most complex expression.

"Conscientization" through Writing

After having discussed some of Howard Adams' narrative strategies, which transcend the boundaries between autobiography and fiction, the following explores some of his political beliefs and the topics and themes that he chose to discuss in the story of his own life. His text is positioned not only within the larger context of political theory, but also within the literary context of autobiographical writings by other authors of colour in North America, especially African-American and Aboriginal authors.

Historiography: The Métis Struggle

Howard Adams was rooted in St. Louis, Saskatchewan. He stressed this fact in his books, articles and interviews. Writing about the Métis way of life in his autobiography, he made a list of Métis activities, which reads almost like a poem, an elegy to the communal sharing. Similarly, when Howard relates his memories of roaming the wide landscape, his style tends to become more elaborate than his normal prose. Such shifts in register, style and even genre may be read as indications of greater emotional involvement. When dealing with memories of his mother or growing up in the Halfbreed world on the north bank of the South Saskatchewan River (not, in fact, on the St. Louis side), Howard's writing also grows more sentimental than the analytical mind of a social theorist or historiographer. At the same time, and sometimes in a sentence immediately following an "elegiac" passage, he stresses emphatically how he hated the poverty of Métis subsistence. Obviously, his cherished emotional ties with his land and people were at odds with his political awareness of social injustice in the "ghetto." This tension between nostalgia for the irredeemable past of his childhood and youth, and his outrage at the coarse harshness of the destitution in which he grew up, remained irreconcilable and unresolved throughout his life.

It is hard to define Howard's political position. Certainly, he was a materialist. He had little patience with Christian or Aboriginal belief systems, and this is where he and I had controversial discussions—not about Christian churches or the missionary onslaught, but about Aboriginal traditionalism, which he was inclined to dismiss as ossifying, conservative and superstitious. He saw Aboriginal religious ceremonies not as of value in themselves but, if admissible at all, only as temporary expressions of Indigenous cultural autonomy, a means to the end of fostering revolutionary nationalism. Beyond that, he regarded cultural nationalism as reactionary and backwards, prone to become co-opted by the rulers, serving to retard rather than stimulate action for social change. In this, he obviously adhered to Marx's notion of religion as a political pacifier and "opiate of the masses."

In my perception, Howard's Marxism oscillated between the repetition of official party positions and the anti-authoritarian refutation of all dogmatism. He believed in revolution, and he wanted to believe in the political success of applied socialism, sometimes, I think, turning a blind eye to the repression and lies told in its name by authoritarian governments trying to make socialist state economies compete successfully within a world overwhelmingly dominated by capitalist structures. Like most socialist idealists, he was shocked by the collapse of socialism in Eastern Europe, and in his last years he became increasingly concerned with the capitalist rampage called globalization. His later trips to Cuba may have been undertaken as an antidote.

Howard's political practice, as described in his autobiographical writings, seems more pragmatic and more grassroots-oriented than in his published books and articles. He obviously enjoyed the limelight and his role as a great speaker and leader of

"Der Leader": Caricature by Fred Kelly, no date.
Photograph Courtesy—Library and Archives Canada.

293

the masses. An undated caricature by F. Kelly (possibly a student) in the Howard Adams Fonds portrays him in a fantasy uniform, a character somewhere between a Russian general, Benito Mussolini, Adolph Hitler and Fidel Castro. But he was also a committed grassroots activist who travelled to Métis communities and had long consciousness-raising discussions with members of "the masses." True to the political optimism of the 60s, he seems to have been steadfastly committed to revolutionary action "from the bottom up," which meant educating and agitating the proletariat, or, as Sylvia Melchior-Walsh describes it so well in her contribution, "conscientization."

"Tony's novel" describes the protagonist's activities as conscious guerrilla tactics like those laid down in Mao's *Little Red Book*, where the revolutionary is expected to move among his people like a fish in water—and Tony does: "Most of the settlements had heard about Tony Bruce, so he was welcomed in each town or ghetto reserve." Even the name shift from Tony Parker to Tony Bruce seems consistent with the development of Tony's political career. The surname Parker echoes the last name of Quanah Parker (c. 1845-1911), the famous Comanche chief, also a Halfbreed, who fought an unsuccessful war against the Americans, but later advocated acquiescence and became a businessman (echoed by Tony, the careerist). By contrast, the last name Bruce may point to two directions. Bruce is a prominent surname in the St. Louis-Batoche region, and, according to Murray Hamilton, the name appears in connection with Métis resistance in the later half of the nineteenth century. An additional possibility is that Howard coined the name after the first Scottish king, Robert I, "the Bruce" (1274-1329), who fought a long harrowing war of attrition against the English, culminating in the Battle of Bannockburn (1314). What may have attracted Howard to the figure of Robert the Bruce is that the Scottish hero used guerrilla tactics and, according to nationalist mythology, had the support of the masses. Perhaps more so than Howard the narrator, who does not always shun manipulating the masses, Tony relied on conscientization and the convincing power of education to understand structures of oppression and develop strategies for deconstructing them. Howard oscillated between his consent to the ideological conformity of official socialist states and his commitment to revolutionary antiauthoritarian strategies from the grassroots. The inherent contradiction in this position seems best captured by Murray Hamilton, who, in a conversation, called Howard "closer to Che than to Fidel."

Howard was decisively influenced by Frantz Fanon, Albert Memmi, and even Paolo Freire, and their theories of anti-colonial liberation and the pedagogy of the oppressed. He also told me once that Sartre's existentialism fascinated him. It came as a surprise to me that in the Almighty episode the author shows considerable knowledge of psychoanalytical theory because I remember a discussion with Howard about Herbert Marcuse (whose works bring together the antiauthoritarian, liberating elements in both Marxist and Freudian theories), but at that time (the late 80s), I did not gain the impression that Howard had actually read Freud or that he took the "bourgeois" psychoanalytic approach seriously. Almighty, however, suggests differently.

Howard was a great orator, and his autobiographical manuscripts reflect that fact. His belief in the convincing power of the spoken word finds expression in his speeches at Batoche and Duck Lake. It also finds expression in his argumentative style, which, according to Walter J. Ong, is a typical oral strategy, and often relies more on amassing supportive evidence and repeating arguments and facts (which are then better remembered), than on the logical causality of the ideas presented or the empirical facts substantiating them. In hindsight, it seems consistent with the orator's intention that Howard cast his autobiography in a multi-generic fictional and factual format to evoke audience response both on an emotional and a rational level.

The Personal as the Political: African–American and Métis Autobiographical Writings

Historical incidents and social movements in the 1960s in the United States profoundly influenced Howard's political convictions and his activist strategies. As a graduate student at University of California-Berkeley, he experienced first-hand the beginnings of the student movement, and he was in the US when President John F. Kennedy was shot in Dallas on November 22, 1963, and fifteen months later when Malcolm X was assassinated in New York City on February 21, 1965. He witnessed how in those years Black people in the US and Africa were spearheading the momentum that swept through North America and other parts of the world in the wake of the civil rights and the decolonization struggles (the student movement and the African–American, Chicano, Native American and Asian–American movements), and the anti-colonial national liberation fronts throughout the world. These, and the growing worldwide protest against the Vietnam War, crystallized into a situation in which, just for a few years in the latter half of the 60s, it seemed as if the established order of things in the Western World, which had been politically ossified in years of cold war stagnation, could and would be changed towards a more humane, colourful, democratic, egalitarian and sharing society. I am convinced that Howard shared the revolutionary optimism of those times, which in hindsight looks almost naïve, since many strands within those grassroots movements soon lost their power for political action. To this day, the (second) women's movement, formed as a reaction to the chauvinist arrogance of male leaders in the student and African-American movements, seems to be the only group of (formerly?) marginalized people who have achieved lasting changes in society, at least regarding the politics of gender.

After the US withdrawal from Vietnam, the peace movement lost most of its impetus. Howard must have witnessed with regret how parts of the student movement drifted into an escapist hippie culture, others into New Age organizations, most into apathy, while many former activists got stuck in middle class positions during their "long march through the institutions." Howard would have also realized that conditions were not conducive towards revolutionary violence because small but influential segments of the more radicalized parts of the Black, American Indian, Chicano and student movements allowed themselves be provoked into, and finally become embroiled in, futilely violent actions, often set up by the state, which led to their criminalization or even to the liquidation of activists like the leadership of the Black Panther Party or some members of the American Indian Movement. Most ethnically-defined action groups and movements disintegrated in the 1970s into ideological factionalism or split up with the emergence of class differences among the poor, which led to co-optation of parts of their elite who managed to achieve positions in the career middle class, thereby often becoming the compradors to rule their own people. Howard later fought most vigorously against the latter group among the Native leadership in Canada, those whom he called the co-opted "comprador regime," who did the colonizer's dirty work of oppression by manipulating and corrupting the masses with a system of granting or withholding personal favours and funding.

While witnessing these liberation processes in the US in the 60s, Howard (and his fictional alter ego Tony) grew very excited. He wanted to apply to the situation of the Métis and Indians in Saskatchewan what he had learned from the student movement in California, and especially what he had seen from the African-American struggle. Like the more radical Black power advocates and the leaders of other visible minority groups in the 1960s and '70s in the US, Howard saw the oppressed racial groups in North America as internally colonized nations and as diasporic members of the Third World, and he saw his own Métis and Indian brothers and sisters as members of the Indigenous Fourth World. Their struggle for liberation was seen as part of the anti-colonial liberation struggle internationally. Next to Frantz Fanon in France and Algeria, and Walter Rodney in Britain and the Caribbean, Malcolm X had become the leading figure promoting Black revolutionary liberation in North America, as opposed to Dr. Martin Luther King's reformist policies. Howard was one of Malcolm X's ardent admirers, especially after he had listened to a speech by Malcolm X on the Berkeley campus. Elements of Malcolm X's work are also found in Howard's autobiographical writings, and I think he was at least as influenced by African-American autobiographies as by those of Native American or Canadian Aboriginal authors.

The Autobiography of Malcolm X, based on his interviews with author Alex Haley, appeared only weeks after the assassination. It generated increased interest in African-American autobiographical works and encouraged the re-publication of prominent slave narratives, such as *The Narrative of the Life of Frederick Douglass, An American Slave* (1845) and other classics, like Richard Wright's *Native Son* (1940) or *Black Boy* (1945). These were all books that Howard had on his shelves. Within a short period of time a whole range of contemporary Black autobiographies appeared in print and created a communal voice that could no longer be overheard by the general public. African-American authors (and, later, other minority authors) faced a dilemma of what has been termed the "dual audience" (Karrer/Lutz, 19)—that is, they had to write with two opposing groups of readers in mind. They could write for their own ethnic constituency of readers, who were fewer in numbers, economically poorer and often less literate than the dominant mainstream, or, often consciously doing so, they could write for the (White) literary mainstream, who in the past had either silenced or neglected them, or carried stereotypical expectations marked by a literary tradition that distorted and ridiculed racial minorities. So they had to write against both the silencing and the distortion of their voice. Gradually, African Americans and other minority authors gained control of their own publishing by creating their own small presses or appearing in university presses that were independent of the large publishing conglomerates.

Much has been written about autobiographical writing by African Americans and other ethnic minority authors. Among these, a 1978 article by German scholar Klaus Ensslen provides some general insights, which seem pertinent in the context of Malcolm X's—and, by extension, also Howard Adams'—autobiography. Ensslen developed a model of three different types of Black autobiographies, with protagonists ranging from the politically unconscious upholders of the status quo, through "Franklinian" Black role models, to the politicized radicals who want to overcome the existing (dis)order of things. The first category treats episodes in the individual's life as a string of coincidental, haphazard and non-reflected occurrences, seemingly unconnected to the social structure of the surrounding society. The second category follows, more or less consciously, the bourgeois individualist tradition, to highlight a role model (e.g. of a professional in sports or politics) whose career is propagated as paradigmatic for private and collective aspirations. The third type of autobiography is marked by a radical political conscientization of the perspective on individual experience, thus presenting and reflecting the experiences of the autobiographical first person as mirrors for larger societal structures. Malcolm X's autobiography belongs to that last category. I would say that Howard's books, *Prison of Grass* (1975) and *A Tortured People* (1999), as well as his autobiographical texts in Part I of this book, all belong to that category of highly-politicized autobiographical writings by minority authors. The books show that the personal is indeed the political, and attention is often deflected from the narrative first person towards the group as a whole, and towards the larger political context. In some cases, this is also true for autobiographically inspired or oriented books by other Aboriginal authors that came out in the 1970s (Maria Campbell, Harold Cardinal, Minnie Aodla Freeman, Elizabeth Goudie, Alma Green, Lee Maracle, Mike Mountain Horse, Wilfred Pelletier, Peter Pitseolak, Duke Redbird, Chief John Snow, John Tetso, Anthony Apakark Thrasher and Jane Willis).

Often, early autobiographical publications were based on collaboration with non-Aboriginal editors, writers or friends. Sandra Carolan-Brozy's unsurpassed study of collaborative Métis autobiographies, *"How to Tell a (life)Story": Die Spannungsfelder Autorschaft-Autorität...* (1999), explores in great detail what is at stake when Aboriginal authors collaborate with non-Native authors or editors to tell the stories of their lives.

What happens to their voices, and what happens to the voices of the collaborators, which must be somewhere, but are generally not expressed? The editorial constellation of Part I of this book, however, does not fit into any of Carolan-Brozy's nor any other critic's categories (nor does Part II fit into the autobiographic genre proper). Like many postmodern texts, Part I is a multi-generic, poly-vocal text without closure, and yet it was not written to become a literary exercise in postmodernist life-writing. While Howard was struggling with his autobiography, I once told him that I wished that I had the time and means to come over to Canada and help him with his project. He said that he liked the idea. But there was no chance for such a more conventional collaboration. In hindsight, that seems just as well because what we have now is the posthumous selecting and editing of Howard's own words by a small but multicultural editorial collective. Sadly, we had no chance to present the manuscript to Howard for final approval, so any mistakes in the weaving of this sash are our own.

Many early autobiographical texts express the contradictions with which the Aboriginal individuals saw themselves faced, and the conflicts arising from being simultaneously alienated from their own people and their simultaneous feelings of being attracted to them. Often, the protagonists seem to be spun centrifugally outward into an unwelcoming mainstream world, while a centripetal force (i.e. their longing to return, to be reconnected and be healed) simultaneously pulls them back. Some protagonists manage to go back and appreciate their home culture, place of birth and kinship ties in a more profound way later in their lives, whereas others continue their existence in the mainstream world, often paying a high price in terms of psychological and physical suffering. Howard's autobiographical writings reflect these processes. What distinguishes them from most others is the high degree of political reflection and abstraction with which he explicates his individual experiences as the necessary results of internal colonialism. For him, a return to St. Louis was mentally and economically impossible, and although he felt drawn to his beloved Elder, Uncle Mederic, this did not entail a permanent physical return, but rather the determination to fight as a political activist, to overcome the structures that created the "ghetto," and as a teacher to help others understand those same structures in the hope of overcoming them. Howard paid a high price for his inability to return.

In his 1991 article on Maria Campbell's *Halfbreed* and Beatrice Culleton's *In Search of April Raintree*, Wolfgang Klooss states that: "the promotion of historical consciousness and the search for (ethnic) identity have become prime issues in contemporary Canadian Métis literature." (Klooss, 207) He explores *Halfbreed* for the ambivalence of love and hate that the narrator/author Maria has for her people, and he states that her feelings develop along the following formula: "original love—fear—shame—self-hatred" (213). After remembering the stories and teachings of her Cheechum, she begins a journey of healing that results in what Howard would have described as a process of conscientization, and that follows the following formula: "historical consciousness-acceptance of ethnicity—political engagement—decolonisation" (214). By comparison, Klooss describes the formula that Culleton's April Raintree follows, and which led her to pass as White, as: "social prejudices—adoption of alienated value structures-racial shame—ethnic self-denial" (218). In both cases, the adoption of the values and ideals of the dominant White culture and ruling class led to a painful denial of Aboriginal identity that results in "passing."

"If ... visible distinction coincides with class ... passing becomes one variant of the mainstream theme of upward mobility, of the American Dream" (Karrer/Lutz, 40). While passing seems to be an option for individuals whose visibility does not fix them into the mould of the colonized and allows them to transgress the class distinctions demarcated by visibility, their self-hate and ethnic self-denial exact a price of them that would eventually destroy their ability to function as successful members of a White middle-class world, be it through substance abuse or clinical depression. Howard's Tony, and even Howard himself for a time in his life, succumbed to the possibility of "passing," and as in the formula identified by Klooss for Maria Campbell's autobiography, gaining historical consciousness enabled him to overcome self-hatred and self-denial. After having listened to Malcolm X, he contacted his uncle Mederic McDougall, the St. Louis oral historian, and embarked on a conscientization process that led him towards political actions. Unlike the protagonists Maria and April, however, he did not have to face what Dieter Herms called the "triple oppression" of race, class and gender. In concluding his article, Wolfgang Klooss quotes Maria Campbell's introduction to *In Search of April Raintree*, and identifies the type of autobiographical model that the book does (not) follow:

> "[*In Search of April Raintree* is] the kind of writing that will begin the healing of our people and help a dominant society understand and feel the lives of a people it almost destroyed." ... *Halfbreed* and *In Search of April Raintree* belong not exactly to the kind of success story known since Benjamin Franklin's *Autobiography* (1867). Instead they are works of protest similar to the *Autobiography of Malcolm X* (1964). Protest, however, is at least a first step towards recognition and acceptance. (Klooss, 221)

All three autobiographical texts—Maria Campbell's autobiography, Beatrice Culleton's novel and Howard Adams' interwoven life histories—describe similar processes of overcoming alienation and self-denial with various degrees of psychological, social and political depth. All three authors used writing about their lives as an instrument of conscientization and healing, and all three seem to say that a White mainstream career cannot serve as a role model because it leads into an emotional cul-de-sac.

It is interesting, in this context, to compare Howard's writings to the books of another Aboriginal man who left his home to pursue a career, who lived a White upper middle-class life, and who much later in his life, after having been traumatized, came to realize the staggering emotional price that he paid for his successful career. James Bartleman, Lieutenant Governor of Ontario, had an Anishnabe mother and a White father, grew up in poverty in Muskoka and became a successful Canadian diplomat, but fell into a deep and harrowing depression after having been robbed and almost killed in a hotel room in South Africa. Writing down the story of his life in two books, *Out of Muskoka* (2002) and *On Six Continents: Life in the Canadian Foreign Service* (2004), Bartleman discovered, like Maria Campbell, Beatrice Culleton and Howard Adams, "the therapeutic magic of the pen" (*On Six Continents*, 243). While James Bartleman's autobiographical writings would clearly fall into Ensslen's second category, constructing a role model for aspiring young (Aboriginal) people that follows the vested interests of the Canadian state, Howard's autobiographical texts fall with equal clarity into the third category (i.e. the radical politicization), which questions and deconstructs the very same bourgeois role model that Bartleman extols. Howard repeatedly expressed his intention to overcome capitalism and dismantle the state whose interests Bartleman propagated with Canadian nationalist pride and personal conviction. And yet, despite the vast differences between the two careers and the political stances of their protagonists, they both reflect the high price that they have to pay for leaving their home cultures and for "passing," deliberately or unintentionally, in the dominant world. At one stage, Bartleman, the exemplary social climber, writes:

> Like half-breeds everywhere, I thought that I would always be an Aboriginal without a home, condemned to share Indian grievances against white society and to understand white attitudes to Indians (*Out of Muskoka*, 134).

These words could also serve to explain the quintessential Halfbreed dilemma that Howard himself and his autobiographical character, Tony Bruce, experience: to be able to see each world, the Aboriginal and the White, with the eyes of the other, and at the same time to be seen oneself alternatively and ambivalently as belonging or not belonging to the one world or the other—a schizoid dilemma. This double ambivalence of loyalty provides no permanent or comfortable location of identity, because the very ground that the individual stands on is forever prone to shifting, and any balance may seem precarious and only temporary. The middle ground seems never secure or stable, and I believe that the slippages that we see in Howard's autobiographical texts are an expression of this dilemma. It took Chicana author Gloria Anzaldúa's 1987 book, *Borderlands/La Frontera: The New Mestiza*, to radically deconstruct and reconstruct the perception of Mestiza- or Métis-ness, not as deficient state but rather as an asset, understanding the Halfbreed's ability to access different cultures and world views not as a restricting capacity, but as an enlightening and liberating one—a conscientization that we all need.

While politically developing an internationalist perspective bent on decolonization, the class struggle, and the deconstruction of capitalism, which he identified as the root cause of all social evils, Howard Adams remained at the same time a Halfbreed with strong emotional ties to his birthplace, family and stories, and with a sterling knowledge of Métis history. This was the strength of Howard Adams' enlightened and politicized ethnic identity.

Works Cited:

Bartleman, James. *Out of Muskoka*. Manotick, Ontario: James Bartleman and Penumbra Press, 2002.

_____. *On Six Continents: A Life in Canada's Foreign Service 1966-2002*. Toronto: McClelland and Stewart, 2004.

Campbell, Maria. *Halfbreed*. Halifax: Formac Publishing, 1973.

Cardinal, Harold. *The Unjust Society: The Tragedy of Canada's Indians*. Edmonton: Hurtig, 1969.

_____. *The Rebirth of Canada's Indians*. Edmonton: Hurtig, 1977.

Carolan-Brozy, Sandra. *'How To Tell a (Life) Story': Die Spannungsfelder Autorschaft-Autorität und Schriftlichkeit-Mündlichkeit in zeitgenössischen Auto-Biographien kanadischer Indianer*. Frankfurt am Main: Peter Lang, 2001.

Ensslen, Klaus. "Schwarze Autobiographie in den USA seit 1960." In *Gulliver: deutsch-englische Jahrbücher*, Bd. 3. Berlin: Argument Verlag, 1978, pp. 96-116.

Freeman, Minnie Aodla. *Life Among the Qallunaat*. Edmonton: Hurtig, 1978.

Goudie, Elizabeth. *Woman of Labrador*. ed. David Zimmerley. Toronto: Peter Martin Associates, 1973.

Herms, Dieter. "La Chicana: Dreifache Diskriminierung als Drittweltfrau." In *Gulliver: deutsch-englische Jahrbücher*, Bd. 10: "Frauenstudien,". Berlin: Argument Verlag, 1981, pp. 79-93.

Karrer, Wolfgang, and Hartmut Lutz. "Minority Literatures in North America: From Cultural Nationalism to Liminality." In *Minority Literatures in North America:*

Contemporary Perspectives, eds. W. Karrer and H. Lutz. Frankfurt am Main: Peter Lang, 1991, pp. 11-64.

Klooss, Wolfgang. "Fictional and Non-Fictional Autobiographies by Métis Women" In *Minority Literatures in North America: Contemporary Perspectives*, eds. W. Karrer and H. Lutz. Frankfurt am Main: Peter Lang, 1991, pp. 205-225.

Maracle, Lee. *Bobbi Lee: Indian Rebel*. Toronto: Women's Press, 1990.

Mountain Horse, Mike. *My People the Bloods*. Calgary: Glenbow Alberta Institute and Blood Tribal Council, 1979.

Ong, Walter J. *Orality and Literacy: The Technologizing of the Word*. London, New York: Methuen, 1982.

Pelletier, Wilfred and Poole, Ted. *No Foreign Land: The Biography of a North American Indian*. Toronto: McClelland and Stewart, 1973.

Pitseolak, Peter. *Pitseolak: Pictures out of My Life*. ed. Dorothy Eber. Toronto: Oxford University Press, 1978.

_____. *People from Our Side: A Life Story*. Edmonton: Hurtig, 1975.

Redbird, Duke. *We are Métis: A Métis View of the Development of a Native Canadian People*. Willowdale, Ontario: Ontario Metis and Non-status Indian Association, 1980.

Snow, Chief John. *These Mountain Are Our Sacred Places: The Story of the Stoney Indians*. Toronto and Sarasota: Samuel Stevens, 1977.

Tetso, John. *Trapping Is My Life*. Toronto: Peter Martin Associates, 1970.

Thrasher, Anthony Apakark. *Thrasher: Skid Row Eskimo*. Toronto: Griffin House, 1976.

Willis, Jane. Geniesh: *An Indian Girlhood*. Toronto: New Press, 1973.

A Bibliography of Howard Adams' Publications

Rene Inkster and Hartmut Lutz

The most comprehensive annotated list of Howard Adams' publications, speeches, and interviews, as well as articles about him and reviews of his works are housed in the Library and Archives Canada in Ottawa, in the "Howard Adams Fond," Box 2, File 13. Rene Inkster, who was working with and for Howard Adams until 2001, compiled that list. It comprises 32 pages. The following bibliography is partially based on Inkster's compilation, but lists only published works.

Monographs

The Education of Canadians: 1800-1867. Montréal: Harvest House, 1968.

Prison of Grass: Canada From the Native Point of View. Toronto: New Press, 1975.

Prison of Grass: Canada From a Native Point of View. Rev. Ed. Saskatoon, SK: Fifth House Publishers, 1989.

A Tortured People: The Politics of Colonization. Penticton, BC: Theytus Books, 1995.

Tortured People. The Politics of Colonization. Revised Edition. Penticton, BC: Theytus Books, 1999.

Co-authored with Jack D. Forbes:
DQU: A Model of Grassroots Community Development. Davis, CA: University of California-Davis, Tecumseh Center, 1976.

Articles

"Some Useful Suggestions for Student Teachers." In *Pedantics 1957.* The Yearbook of the Ontario College of Education, published annually by the literary committee of the college. Toronto: Pyramid Printers, 1957. [Howard Adams Fonds, Box 2, file 25 at Ottawa, Library and Archives Canada]

"The real Egerton Ryerson," *Monday Morning: Canada's Magazine for Professional Teachers* 2.2 (October 1967): 32-33.

"The Indian-Metis Liberation," *The Podium* 1.4 (March 1968): 13-14.

"The Roots of Separatism," *History of Education Quarterly* 8.1 (Spring 1968): 35-42.

"The Haves and Have Nots." In *I Am an Indian,* ed. Kent Gooderham, 159-160. Toronto: Dent and Sons, 1969.

"The Cree as Colonial People," *Journal of Western Canadian Anthropology* 1.1 (1969): 120-124.

"Education or Brainwashing," *Horizons: The Marxist Quarterly* 28 (Winter 1969): 14-18.

"The Revolutionary Movement of the Indians and Metis," *Our Generation* 7.2 (1970): 91-95.

"Part I: Confrontations—Dr. Howard Adams, President, The Metis Association of Saskatchewan (panel contribution)." In *Canadian Confrontations: Hinterland Against Metropolis.* Proceedings of the Eleventh Annual Meeting of the Western Association of Sociology and Anthropology, Banff, Alberta, Dec 28-30, 1969, ed. Arthur K. Davis, 12-18. Edmonton: University of Alberta Printing Service, 1970.

"Alienation and the Races: Howard Adams, Professor of Sociology, University of Saskatchewan: Panel contribution." In *Alienation and Violence in the North-American Community.* Proceedings of the 13th Annual Canadian-American Seminar—1971, ed. J. Alex Murray, 92-97. Windsor, ON: University of Windsor Press, 1972.

"The Need for a Revolutionary Struggle," *New Breed Magazine* (Jan 1972), 6.

"Unexpected Results from Metis Survey," *New Breed Magazine* (Feb 1972), 10.

"The Unique Metis," *Perception: A Canadian Journal of Social Comment* 1.2 (Nov/Dec 1977): 48-50.

"Red Powerlessness: Bureaucratic Authoritarianism on Indian Reservations," *Cornell Journal of Social Relations* 18.1 (1984): 28-40.

"The Metis." In *Racial Oppression in Canada*, ed. Peter Li and B. Singh Bolaria, 61-79. Toronto: Garamond, 1985.

"Yesterday: The Key to a Better Tomorrow," *New Breed Magazine*. Commemorative Issue, 1885-1985. 16:7 (1985): 4-6.

"Causes of the 1985 Struggle," In *Riel to Reform: A History of Protest in Western Canada,* ed. George Melnyk, 75-85. Saskatoon, SK: Fifth House Publishers, 1992. [Excerpt from *Prison of Grass*].

"Thoughts on the Constitution and Aboriginal Self-Government," *Native Studies Review* 8.2 (1992): 99-108.

"The Colonized Halfbreed / Das kolonisierte Halbblut," In *Four Feathers: Poems and Stories by Canadian Native Authors/Vier Federn: Gedichte und Geschichten kanadischer Indianer/innen und Métis*. O.B.E.M.A. [Osnabrück Blilingual Editions of Minority Authors]. No. 7, ed. and trans. Hartmut Lutz and students, 28-45. Osnabrück: Druck-und Verlagscooperative, 1992; 2nd. ed. 1993.

"Mixed Bloods," In *Peoples in Contact: Remembering the Past—Sharing the Future*, eds. A. Brauer, C. Römer, S. Markmann and H. Lutz, 29-39. Frankfurt am Main: Peter Lang, 1994.

Book Reviews

"Heather Robertson, *Reservations Are For Indians* (1970)" *Canadian Dimension* 7. 3 (1970): 43-44.

"Christine Daniels and Ron Christiansen. *The White Man's Laws*" *Queen's Quarterly* 83.3 (Autumn 1976): 511-2.

"Chief John Snow. *These Mountains are Our Sacred Places*" *New Mexico Historical Review* 55.4 (1980): 351-2.

"Howard Adams comments on Eric Waddell's review of *Prison of Grass: Canada from a Native Point of View* (*Reviews in Anthropology* 6.1: 71-84)" *Reviews in Anthropology* 6.1 (Winter 1979): 130-133.

"Daniel H. Page. *History of the North American People*" *Queen's Quarterly: A Canadian Review* 91.2 (Summer 1984): 456-457.

"Ward Churchill. *Marxism and Native Americans*" *American Indian Culture and Research Journal* 8.4 (1986): 58-62.

"S. Jonas, E. McCaughan and E. Sutherland Martinez, ed. and trans. *Guatemala: Tyranny on Trial*" *American Indian Culture and Research Journal* 9.3 (1987): 91-94.

"J.R. Miller. *Sweet Promises: A Reader on Indian/White Relations in Canada*" *American Indian Culture and Research Journal* 16.2 (1992): 256-260.

"Georges E. Sioui. *For an American Indian Autohistory*" *Native Studies Review* 8.2 (1992): 143-146.

List of Contributors:

Margaret (Baxter) Adams was born in 1932 and raised in Vancouver, British Columbia. She graduated from the University of British Columbia with two masters degrees—one in Sociology, the other in Library Science. For several years, she taught at the elementary and high school levels, and completed her career as an adult educator for the Vancouver School Board. Currently, she is enjoying a busy retirement in Vancouver, volunteering her time to animal welfare causes and various political activities.

Ron Bourgeault is originally from North Battleford, Saskatchewan. He was active with Howard Adams in Métis politics and the Saskatchewan Waffle (the former radical wing of the New Democratic Party) during the 1970s. Presently, he teaches in the Department of Sociology, University of Regina, Regina, Saskatchewan.

Anette Brauer grew up and received her schooling and higher education in Greifswald (north-eastern Germany) during the time of Socialism. She earned her Ph.D. in the field of Native American Studies in 1990 at Greifswald University, and has since taught classes there on a variety of subjects in North American Studies.

Maria Campbell grew up in a Métis community in north-central Saskatchewan in the 1940s and 1950s. Her autobiography, *Halfbreed*, has been translated into many languages and is the most important book authored by a Métis person in Canada. An untiring cultural and political activist for Métis rights, she has concentrated her work on oral tradition, literature and film, especially by and for women and children. Among her books are *Achimoona* (1985), *The Book of Jessica* (with Linda Griffith, 1989) and *Stories of the Road Allowance People* (1995). Winner of the 2004 Canada Council for the Arts' *Molson Lifetime Achievement Award,* she lectures in the Department of Native Studies, University of Saskatchewan, Saskatoon, Saskatchewan.

Rhonda Carriere is the Associate Director of the Native Ministries Program of the Vancouver School of Theology at the University of British Columbia. She resides in Ladner, British Columbia with her daughter Sophie.

Roxanne Dunbar-Ortiz is a historian, writer and activist in the field of international Indigenous issues. Among her publications are *The Great Sioux Nation* (1975), *Roots of Resistance: Land Tenure in New Mexico 1680-1980* (1980), *Indians of the Americas: Human Rights and Self-Determination* (1984), and *Caught in the Crossfire: Miskito Indians in Sandinista Nicaragua* (1988). She is author of three recent works of political memoir.

Konrad Gross was born in 1940 in Mecklenburg, in eastern Germany, and spent his youth in Bavaria and Hesse without becoming a genuine Bavarian or Hessian. Instead, he became a Canadianist due to a superb post-doctoral year (1972/73) at the University of British Columbia. He has been teaching at the University of Kiel (in northern Germany) since 1978, where he is still an ardent prophet of Canadian Studies.

Murray Hamilton is a Métis and considers Lebret, Saskatchewan his cultural home. He spent his formative years in Lebret and believes its history and people shaped his identity and worldview. He has spent most of his life advocating issues of concern to the Métis, particularly education initiatives. He is the Program Coordinator for the Gabriel Dumont Institute's Saskatchewan Urban Native Teacher Education Program at the University of Saskatchewan, Saskatoon, Saskatchewan.

Donna Heimbecker is a Métis woman of Cree and German decent. She is a graduate of the Gabriel Dumont Institute's Saskatchewan Urban Native Teacher Education Program at the University of Saskatchewan and has worked as a classroom teacher, project manager, cultural awareness facilitator, Aboriginal employment development consultant and community developer. She is the founder and general manager of the Saskatchewan Native Theatre Company, and has worked collaboratively with cultural/arts leaders in developing innovative Aboriginal cultural/arts programs that make a positive impact on the lives of individuals, communities and the arts industry. She believes that the arts are a powerful means of developing healthy, strong and vibrant individuals and communities.

Geary Hobson is a professor of English at the University of Oklahoma, specializing in Native American literature. He is the author of *The Last of the Ofos* (2000), a novel, and the editor of *The Remembered Earth: An Anthology of Contemporary Native American Literature* (1979), as well as other works. In 2003, he received the *Lifetime Achievement Award* from the Native Writers' Circle of the Americas.

Rene Inkster was born in Regina in 1941, across from the RCMP barracks, but spent most of her childhood in Alberta. She has always been active in social and educational matters, following in her Métis auntie Harriet Inkster's footsteps, to establish goodwill and better friendships that will benefit everybody involved. Now living in the Lower Fraser Valley, British Columbia, she enjoys her children's families, and visiting her siblings and their families in Edmonton.

William Johnson enjoyed a long post-Howard career, first as a lecturer in Sociology at the University of Toronto, then as a reporter and columnist at the *Globe and Mail* and other publications. He is author of several books on Québec and federal politics, contributes a weekly commentary on the Canadian Public Affairs Channel (CPAC) and wrote a book on the Conservative Party of Canada leader Stephen Harper through McClelland & Stewart in 2005. A member of the Parliamentary Press Gallery in Ottawa, he received the *Order of Canada* and lives in Gatineau, Québec with his wife, Carol Bream.

Eugene Kaellis (BS, MS, DDS, PhD) is a former associate professor of Oral Biology at the University of Saskatchewan, which is where he met Howard. Since then, he has been a journalist and author.

Rhoda Kaellis (Associate of Arts, Fashion Institute of Technology & Design, New York City and Associate of Arts, Applied Communications, Victoria, British Columbia). She is a published author, journalist, sculptor and political activist. She met Howard and Marge in 1967 in Saskatoon, Saskatchewan.

Rose Klinkenberg is a Glasgow-born ecologist and writer, and friend of Howard Adams. She worked with Howard for several years assisting him with his writing and research and currently resides in British Columbia.

Wolfgang Klooss, a former President of the Association for Canadian Studies in German-Speaking Countries, is Chair of English and Director of the Centre for Canadian Studies at the University of Trier (Germany). His postdoctoral "Habilitation"-thesis, *Geschichte und Mythos in der Literatur Kanadas: Die englischsprachige Métis und Riel-Rezeption* (1989) is still the most comprehensive study on the presentation of the Métis and Louis Riel in Canadian literature.

Dan Kruk, who lives in Vancouver with his partner and daughter, is a former commercial fisher and logger. In the latter part of the 1990s, he also worked as an organizer for the United Fishermen and Allied Workers Union-Canadian Auto Workers. In September 2003, he resumed full-time studies at the University of British Columbia and works part-time as a deckhand on a tugboat. He misses Howard terribly.

Ron Laliberte is Métis and was born in 1949 at Prince Albert, Saskatchewan. He is the second oldest of Alveda and Max Laliberte's eight children. Ron describes his early life in Prince Albert as consisting of poverty and numerous moves to different homes that resulted in the family residing in all areas of the city. He moved to Saskatoon in the early 1970s to work in construction while simultaneously finishing his grade twelve education. He attended the University of Saskatchewan in the 80s and finished his M.A. in Sociology in 1994. A tenured faculty member of the Department of Native Studies, he is currently completing his Ph.D. in the Department of Sociology at the University of Calgary, studying Aboriginal labour in southern Alberta's sugar beet industry.

Hartmut Lutz was born in 1945 in Rendsburg, Schleswig-Holstein (northern Germany), where he also grew up. Educated in West Germany, England, Sweden and the US, he has taught in Europe and on Turtle Island, and is now chairing North American Studies at the University of Greifswald. He and his wife Ruth Lutz-Preiskorn live with their cats and trees in Bömitz, a tiny Pommeranian village near the Baltic Sea and the Polish border.

James Pitsula was born in Manitoba, but was raised and educated in Saskatchewan (except for graduate studies at York University, Toronto). He has been teaching at the University of Regina's Department of History since 1978. His interests include Aboriginal, political, social and educational history.

Sylvia Melchior-Walsh was born and raised in Berlin, Germany. After immigrating to Canada, she lived in Toronto during the 1960s, where she met her husband Don, a football player with the Saskatchewan Roughriders and student at the University of Arizona. Together, they travelled a long and winding road with their children, Lutz and Lorraine. In Regina, Saskatchewan, Sylvia earned both her B.A. and M.A., and in Arizona she earned a Ph.D. in Higher and Adult Education. Presently the Director of the Canadian Centre for Indigenous Leadership and Development in Vancouver, British Columbia, Sylvia has worked with First Nations students for a quarter of a century, both at the Saskatchewan Indian Federated College in Regina and at the Institute of Indigenous Government in Vancouver. With both feet on the ground and her positive Berlin spirit, she envisions the day when all First Nations people will finally assume their Aboriginal rights as self-determining nations. The realization of this vision would be worth the trip.

Craig Oliver, the Ottawa bureau chief for CTV News, is one of Canada's foremost political journalists. He has received numerous awards for his lifelong commitment to independent news reporting. In his outstanding career, he initially specialized in news from the Prairies, where he witnessed the Métis struggle in Saskatchewan. In the 1960s and '70s he covered Howard Adams' activism with a sympathetic yet critically independent eye.

Rose Richardson (formerly Bishop) was among the first people to introduce Howard Adams to residents of northern Saskatchewan. She encouraged him to work not only on political and environmental concerns, but also social and cultural matters-and with humour! She and her husband, Ric Richardson, operate Keewatin Junction Station (the former Meadow Lake CPR railway station), a café and meeting place, where they share Métis food, arts and traditional medicines with visitors from all over the world.